Houghton Mifflin Harcourt

Texas GO Math!

Volume 1

Printed in the U.S.A.

ISBN 978-0-544-06177-4
10 11 0928 22 21 20 19
4500743247 B C D E F G

Cover Image Credits: (The Alamo) ©Michael DeFreitas/Getty Images; (refinery) ©Lynn Johnson/Getty Images; (landscape) ©David Hensley/Getty Images; (turtle) ©Kristina Vackova/ Shutterstock.

Dear Students and Families,

Welcome to **Texas Go Math!**, Grade 4! In this exciting mathematics program, there are hands-on activities to do and real-world problems to solve. Best of all, you will write your ideas and answers right in your book. In **Texas Go Math!**, writing and drawing on the pages helps you think deeply about what you are learning, and you will really understand math!

By the way, all of the pages in your **Texas Go Math!** book are made using recycled paper. We wanted you to know that you can Go Green with **Texas Go Math!**

Sincerely,

The Authors

Made in the United States
Printed on 100% recycled paper

Texas GO Math!

Authors

Juli K. Dixon, Ph.D.
Professor, Mathematics Education
University of Central Florida
Orlando, Florida

Edward B. Burger, Ph.D.
President
Southwestern University
Georgetown, Texas

Matthew R. Larson, Ph.D.
K-12 Curriculum Specialist for Mathematics
Lincoln Public Schools
Lincoln, Nebraska

Martha E. Sandoval-Martinez
Math Instructor
El Camino College
Torrance, California

Consultant

Valerie Johse
Math Consultant
Texas Council for Economic Education
Houston, Texas

Volume 1

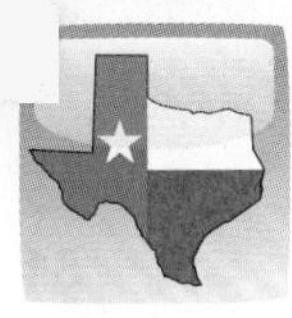

Unit 1 • Number and Operations: Place Value, Fraction Concepts, and Operations

Module 1 Whole Number Place Value

Module 2 Decimal Place Value

Look for these:

H.O.T. Problems Higher Order Thinking
Multi-Step Problems

Homework and Practice

Homework and TEKS Practice in every lesson.

GO DIGITAL Resources

DIGITAL RESOURCES
Go online for the Interactive Student Edition with Math on the Spot Videos. Use *i*Tools, the Multimedia eGlossary, and more.

Module 3 Fraction Concepts

Module 4 Compare Fractions

Module 5 Add and Subtract Fractions

Look for these:

H.O.T. Problems
Higher Order Thinking
Multi-Step Problems

GO DIGITAL Resources

DIGITAL RESOURCES
Go online for the Interactive Student Edition with Math on the Spot Videos. Use *i*Tools, the Multimedia *e*Glossary, and more.

Volume 1

Unit 2 • Number and Operations: Whole Number and Decimal Operations

Module 6 Add and Subtract Whole Numbers and Decimals

Module 7 Multiply by 1-Digit Numbers

Look for these:

H.O.T. Problems
Higher Order Thinking
Multi-Step Problems

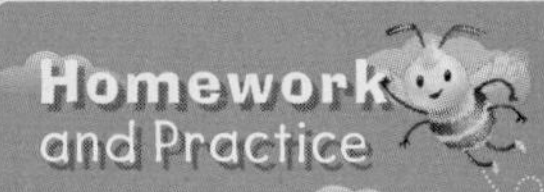

Homework and TEKS Practice in every lesson.

Look for these:

H.O.T. Problems
Higher Order Thinking
Multi-Step Problems

Module 8 Multiply 2-Digit Numbers

Module 9 Division Strategies

Module 10 Divide by 1-Digit Numbers

GO DIGITAL Resources

DIGITAL RESOURCES
Go online for the Interactive Student Edition with Math on the Spot Videos. Use *i*Tools, the Multimedia *e*Glossary, and more.

Volume 2

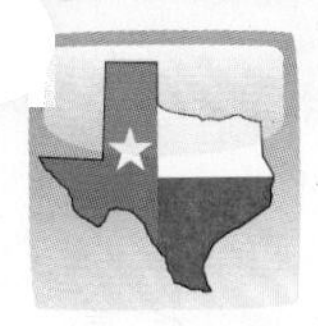

Unit 3 • Algebraic Reasoning

Module 11 Algebra: Multi-Step Problems

Module 12 Number Patterns, Perimeter, and Area

Look for these:

H.O.T. Problems
Higher Order Thinking
Multi-Step Problems

Homework and TEKS Practice in every lesson.

Volume 2

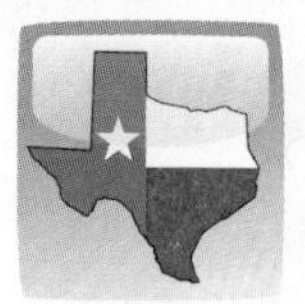

Unit 4 • Geometry and Measurement

Module 13 Geometry Concepts

Module 14 Measure Angles

Look for these:

H.O.T. Problems
Higher Order Thinking
Multi-Step Problems

GO DIGITAL Resources

DIGITAL RESOURCES
Go online for the Interactive Student Edition with Math on the Spot Videos. Use *i*Tools, the Multimedia *e*Glossary, and more.

Module 15 Customary and Metric Measures

Module 16 Time and Money

Volume 2

Unit 5 • Data Analysis

Module 17 Represent and Interpret Data

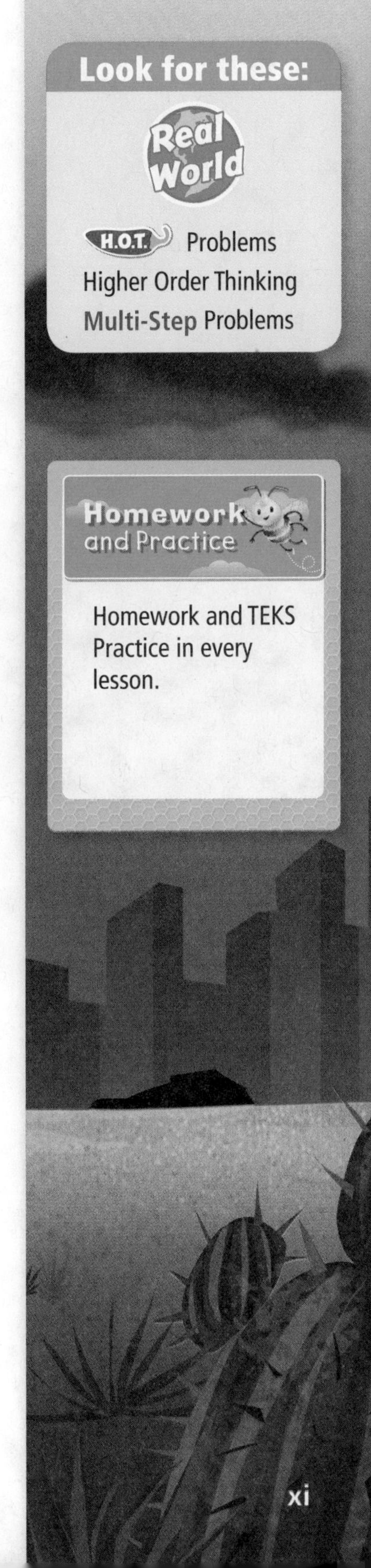

Look for these:

H.O.T. Problems
Higher Order Thinking
Multi-Step Problems

Volume 2

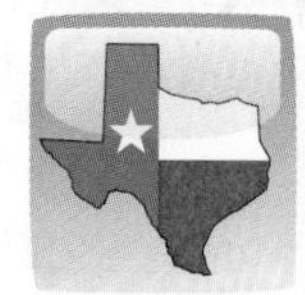

Unit 6 • Personal Financial Literacy

Module 18 Financial Literacy

GO DIGITAL Resources

DIGITAL RESOURCES
Go online for the Interactive Student Edition with Math on the Spot Videos. Use *i*Tools, the Multimedia *e*Glossary, and more.

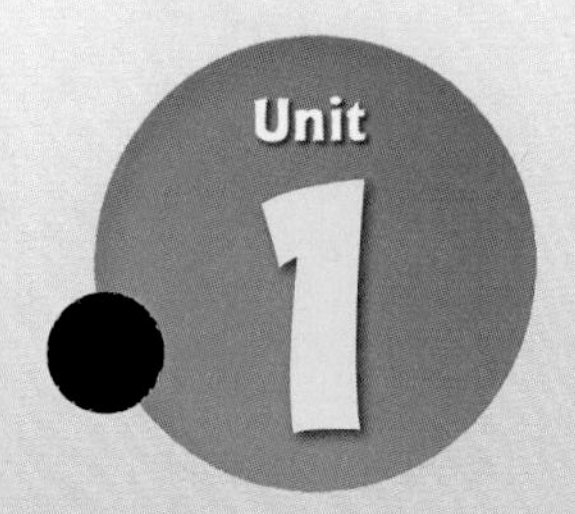

Number and Operations: Place Value, Fraction Concepts, and Operations

Show What You Know 

Check your understanding of important skills.

Name ______________________________

▶ Read and Write Numbers Within 1,000

Write the number in different ways.

1. standard form: ________
   word form: ________
   expanded form: ________

2. standard form: ________
   word form: ________
   expanded form: ________

▶ Fractions of a Whole

Write a fraction that names the shaded part.

3. 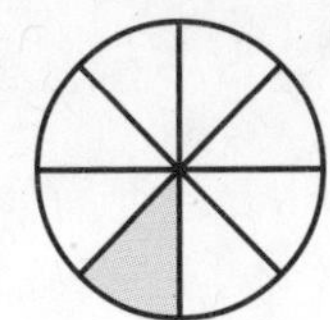 ____

4. 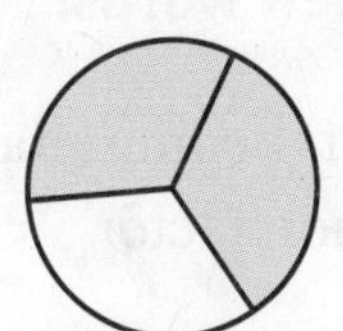 ____

5. 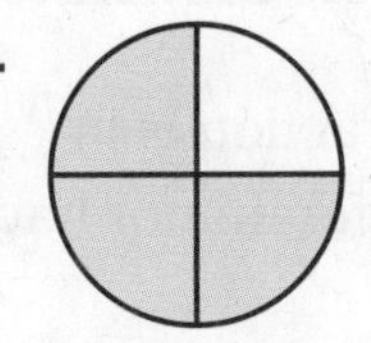 ____

6. 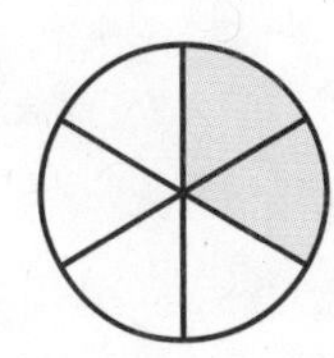 ____

7. 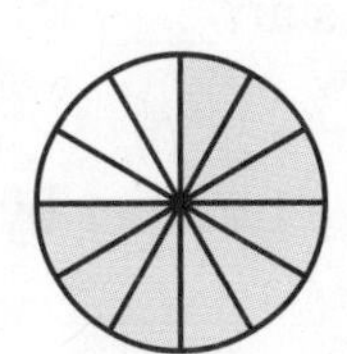 ____

8. 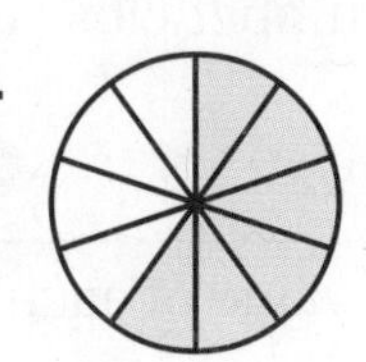 ____

▶ Fractions on a Number Line

Complete the number line. Draw a point to show the fraction.

9. $\frac{4}{5}$

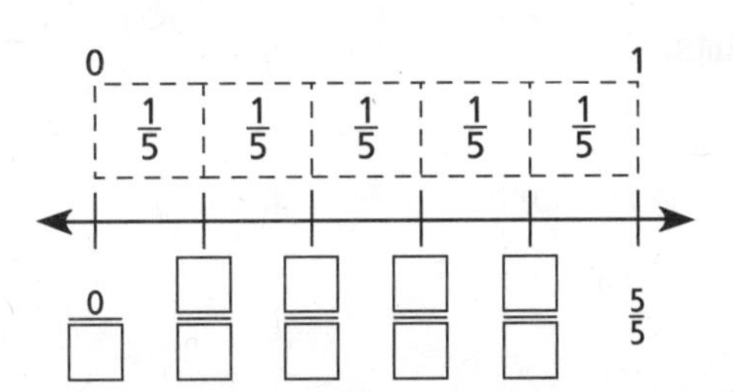

10. $\frac{3}{8}$

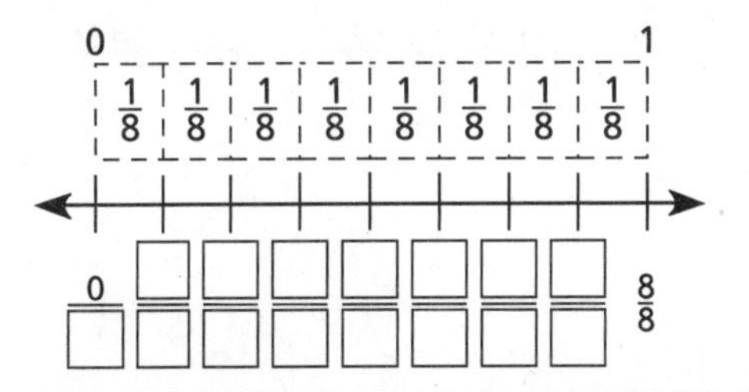

GO DIGITAL Assessment Options: Soar to Success Math

Vocabulary Builder

▶ Visualize It

Complete the flow map by using the words with a ✓.

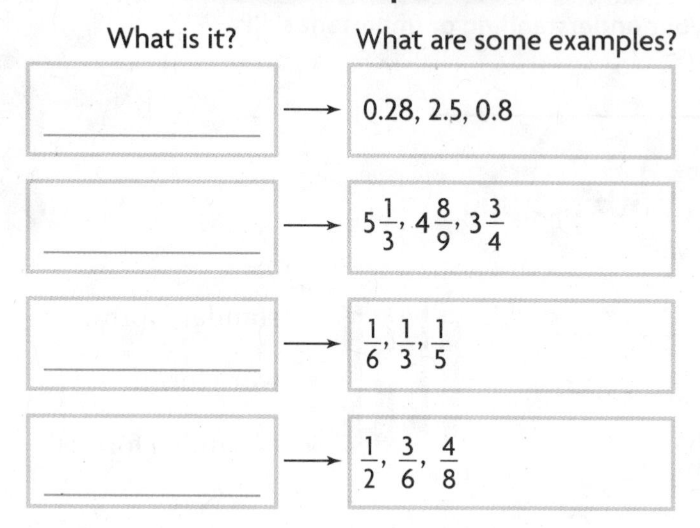

Preview Words

- benchmark
- ✓ decimal
- decimal point
- ✓ equivalent fractions
- estimate
- expanded form
- hundredth
- ✓ mixed number
- ✓ period
- round
- simplest form
- standard form
- tenth
- ✓ unit fraction

▶ Understand Vocabulary

Complete the sentences by using preview words.

1. A fraction is in ________________ if the numerator and denominator have only 1 as a common factor.

2. A number close to an exact amount is an ________________.

3. ________________ is a way to write a number by showing the value of each digit.

4. A ________________ is a known size or amount that helps you understand a different size or amount.

5. A ________________ is one of ten equal parts.

6. A ________________ is one of one hundred equal parts.

• Interactive Student Edition
• Multimedia eGlossary

Name ________________________

Vocabulary

Look at the number in the place-value chart. Use this number to complete the word web.

Billions				Millions				Thousands				Ones		
hundreds	tens	ones		hundreds	tens	ones		hundreds	tens	ones		hundreds	tens	ones
		8	,	8	2	7	,	6	1	0	,	7	3	1

Expanded Form
shows the value of each digit in the number
1. Finish writing the expanded form of the number.
8,000,000,000 + ________

Ways to Write a Number

Word Form
uses words to write a number
2. Finish writing the word form of the number.
eight billion ________

Standard Form
the simplest way to write a number using digits
3. Write the standard form of the number. ________

1. ________________
____
____
____
____
____

2. ________________________________
____

3. ________________________________

Writing How can you write the number 7,536,301,398 in word form?

____

____

Reading Look for this book in your library. *Digging for Bird Dinosaurs: An Expedition to Madagascar*, by Nic Bishop.

Get Ready Game

Fraction Action!

Object of the Game Compare fractions and be the first player to get 8 points.

Materials

- fraction strips (2 sets)
- Fraction Cards

Set Up

Place the 1 whole fraction strip in front of the players; it will remain there for the game. Shuffle the fraction cards, and place them face down in a stack.

Number of Players 2

How to Play

1. Player 1 draws a card from the stack. He or she makes the fraction with the fraction strips and places them under the 1 whole strip.
2. Player 2 draws a card from the stack. He or she makes the fraction with the fraction strips and places them under Player 1's strips.
3. Players decide whose fraction is greater. The player with the greater fraction gets one point. If the two fractions are equivalent, both players get one point.
4. The first player to earn 8 points is the winner.

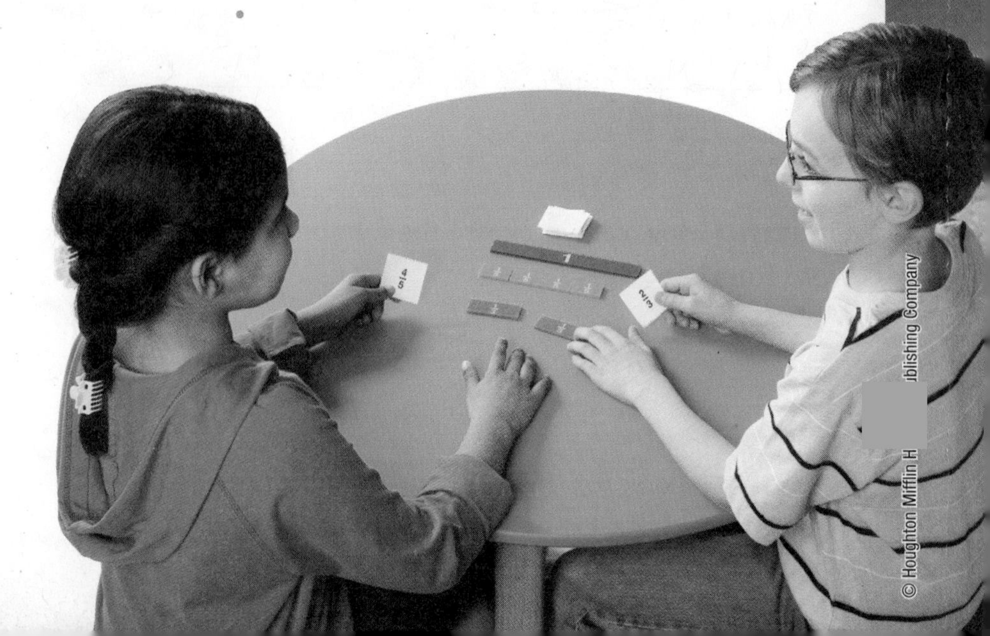

Name ___________________________________

TEKS Number and Operations—4.2.A

MATHEMATICAL PROCESSES
4.1.D, 4.1.F, 4.1.G

1.1 Place Value and Patterns

Essential Question

How can you describe the relationship between two place-value positions?

Investigate

Hands On

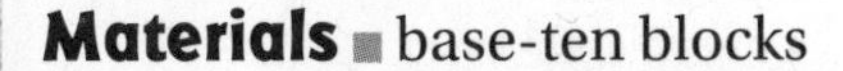

Materials ■ base-ten blocks

You can use base-ten blocks to understand the relationships among place-value positions. Use a large cube for 1,000, a flat for 100, a long for 10, and a small cube for 1.

Number	1,000	100	10	1
Model				
Description	large cube	flat	long	small cube

Complete the comparisons below to describe the relationship from one place-value position to the next place-value position.

A.
- Look at the long and compare it to the small cube.

  The long is ______ times as much as the small cube.
- Look at the flat and compare it to the long.

  The flat is ______ times as much as the long.
- Look at the large cube and compare it to the flat.

  The large cube is ______ times as much as the flat.

B.
- Look at the flat and compare it to the large cube.

  The flat is ______ of the large cube.
- Look at the long and compare it to the flat.

  The long is ______ of the flat.
- Look at the small cube and compare it to the long.

  The small cube is ______ of the long.

Math Talk

Mathematical Processes

How many times as much is the flat compared to the small cube? the large cube to the small cube? **Explain.**

Make Connections

You can use your understanding of place-value patterns and a place-value chart to write numbers that are 10 times as much as or $\frac{1}{10}$ of any given number.

Hundred Thousands	Ten Thousands	One Thousands	Hundreds	Tens	Ones
			3	0	0
		?	300	?	

10 times as much as — $\frac{1}{10}$ of

__________ is 10 times as much as 300.

__________ is $\frac{1}{10}$ of 300.

Use the steps below to complete the table.

STEP 1 Write the given number in a place-value chart.

STEP 2 Use the place-value chart to write a number that is 10 times as much as the given number.

STEP 3 Use the place-value chart to write a number that is $\frac{1}{10}$ of the given number.

Number	10 times as much as	$\frac{1}{10}$ of
10		
70		
9,000		

Share and Show

Complete the sentence.

1. 500 is 10 times as much as __________.

2. 20,000 is $\frac{1}{10}$ of __________.

Use place-value patterns to complete the table.

Number	10 times as much as	$\frac{1}{10}$ of
3. 50		
4. 3,000		

Number	10 times as much as	$\frac{1}{10}$ of
5. 400		
6. 90		

H.O.T. **Complete the sentence with 100 or 1,000.**

7. 200 is __________ times as much as 2.

8. 700,000 is __________ times as much as 700.

9. 4,000 is __________ times as much as 4.

10. 600 is __________ times as much as 6.

Name ___________________________

Problem Solving Real World

H.O.T. Multi-Step **Sense or Nonsense?**

11. Mark and Robyn used base-ten blocks to show that 300 is 100 times as much as 3. Whose model makes sense? Whose model is nonsense? **Explain** your reasoning.

Mark's Work

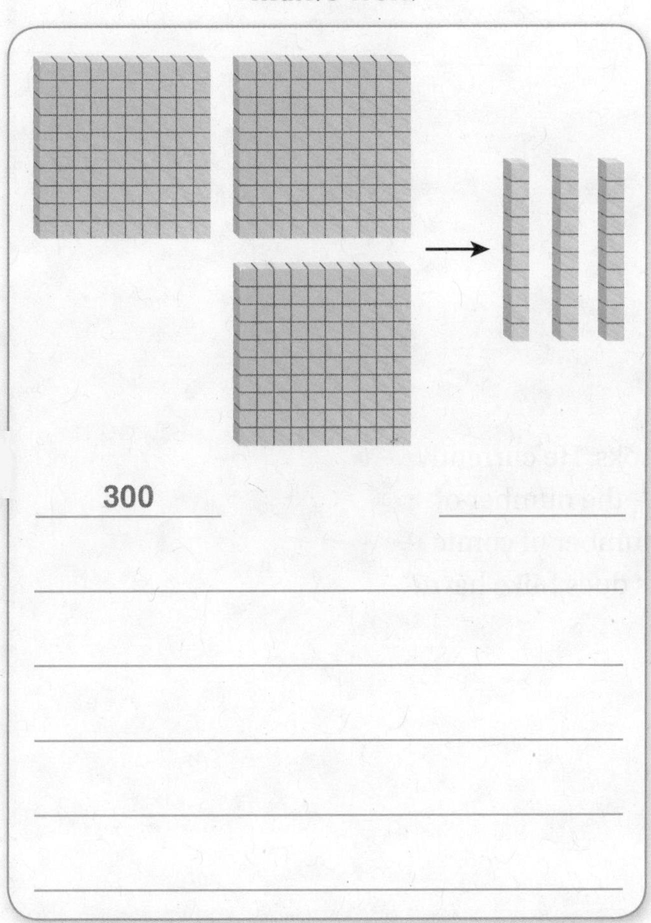

Robyn's Work

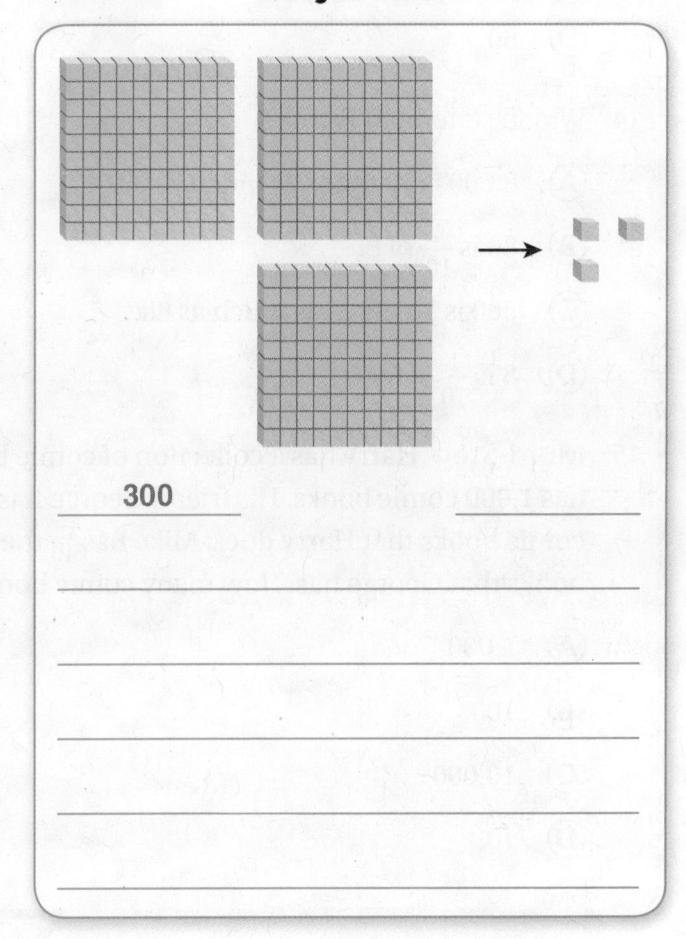

12. H.O.T. **Explain** how you would help Mark understand why he should have used small cubes instead of longs.

Daily Assessment Task

Fill in the bubble completely to show your answer.

13. Melinda has 500 pennies in a jar. Brenda has 10 times as many pennies as Melinda does. How many pennies does Brenda have?

Ⓐ 50,000

Ⓑ 5

Ⓒ 5,000

Ⓓ 50

14. Which statement is true?

Ⓐ 8,000 is 10 times as much as 80.

Ⓑ 80 is $\frac{1}{10}$ of 8.

Ⓒ 800 is 10 times as much as 80.

Ⓓ 8 is $\frac{1}{10}$ of 800.

15. **Multi-Step** Harry has a collection of comic books. He currently has 1,000 comic books. His friend George has $\frac{1}{10}$ the number of comic books that Harry does. Mike has $\frac{1}{10}$ the number of comic books that George has. How many comic books does Mike have?

Ⓐ 1,000

Ⓑ 100

Ⓒ 10,000

Ⓓ 10

TEXAS Test Prep

16. Sam has 1,300 dimes. Anna has $\frac{1}{10}$ the number of dimes that Sam does. How many dimes does Anna have?

Ⓐ 13,000

Ⓑ 13

Ⓒ 130

Ⓓ 3

Homework and Practice

TEKS Number and Operations—4.2.A
MATHEMATICAL PROCESSES 4.1.D, 4.1.F, 4.1.G

Name ______________________

1.1 Place Value and Patterns

1. Emma and Jamie used base-ten blocks to show that 40 is one-tenth of 400. Whose model makes sense? Whose model is nonsense? **Explain** your reasoning.

Emma's Work

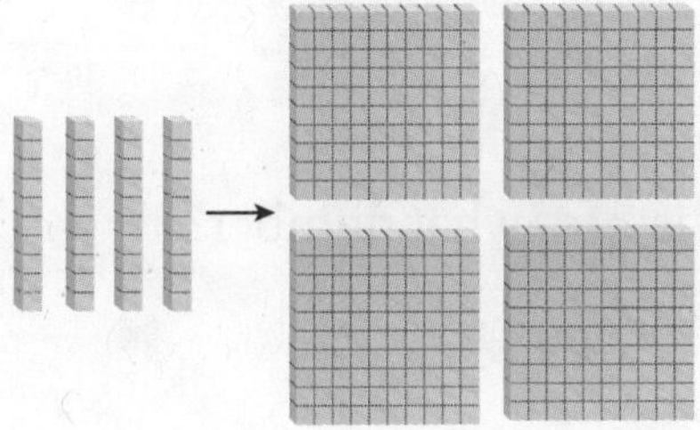

Jamie's Work

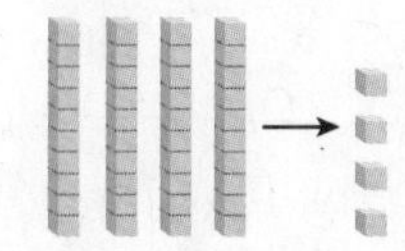

400 ______ 400 ______

Problem Solving Real World

2. Lisa had 3 dollars. She went to the bank and exchanged the 3 dollars for 30 dimes.

Describe the relationship between the value of a dollar and the value of a dime.

Lesson Check

TEXAS Test Prep

Fill in the bubble completely to show your answer.

3. Which statement is true?

Ⓐ 500 is 10 times as much as 50.

Ⓑ 500 is $\frac{1}{10}$ as much as 50.

Ⓒ 50,000 is 1,000 times as much as 5.

Ⓓ 5 is $\frac{1}{10}$ as much as 500.

4. 7,000 is ten times as much as what number?

Ⓐ 70

Ⓑ 7

Ⓒ 70,000

Ⓓ 700

5. Which statement is true?

Ⓐ 90 is $\frac{1}{10}$ of 100.

Ⓑ 900 is 100 times as much as 9.

Ⓒ 9,000 is 1,000 times as much as 90.

Ⓓ 9 is $\frac{1}{10}$ of 900.

6. 720 is $\frac{1}{10}$ of what number?

Ⓐ 7,200

Ⓑ 72

Ⓒ 7

Ⓓ 72,000

7. **Multi-Step** The owner of Pattie's Party Shop ordered 4 cartons of balloons. How many balloons did she order?

1 carton = 10 boxes

1 box = 10 packages

1 package = 10 balloons

Ⓐ 40

Ⓑ 400

Ⓒ 40,000

Ⓓ 4,000

8. **Multi-Step** Greg bought 2 boxes of balloons. He used half of them to decorate his yard. He used 40 to decorate his porch. He used the rest inside his house. How many balloons did he use inside?

Ⓐ 6

Ⓑ 6,000

Ⓒ 60

Ⓓ 600

Name ______________________________

1.2 Read and Write Numbers

Essential Question How can you read and write numbers through billions?

Unlock the Problem

The International Space Station uses 262,400 solar cells to convert sunlight to electricity.

Write 262,400 in standard form, word form, and expanded form.

Use a place-value chart.

Each group of three digits separated by a comma is called a **period**. Each period has hundreds, tens, and ones. The greatest place-value position in the billions period is hundred billions.

Write 262,400 in the place-value chart below.

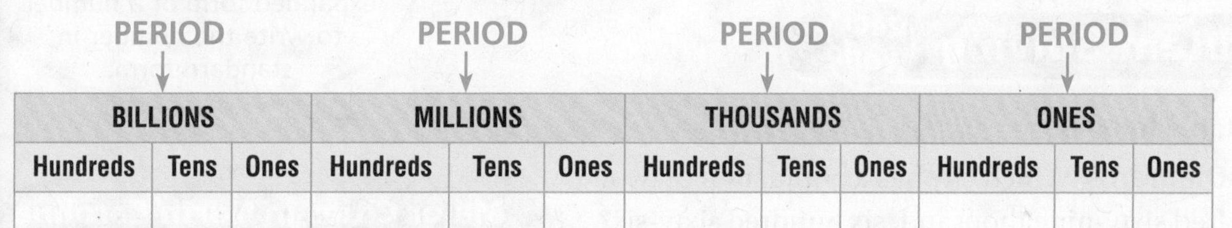

PERIOD ↓ BILLIONS			PERIOD ↓ MILLIONS			PERIOD ↓ THOUSANDS			PERIOD ↓ ONES		
Hundreds	Tens	Ones	Hundreds	Tens	Ones	Hundreds	Tens	Ones	Hundreds	Tens	Ones

The number 262,400 has two periods, thousands and ones.

Standard Form: 262,400

Word Form: two hundred sixty-two thousand, four hundred

Expanded Form: 200,000 + 60,000 + 2,000 + 400

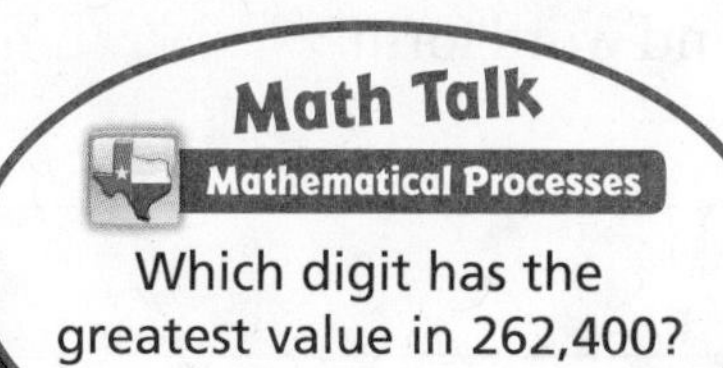

Try This! Use place value to read and write numbers.

Standard Form: 475,856,144

Word Form: four hundred seventy-five ____________,

eight hundred fifty-six ____________, one hundred forty-four

Expanded Form: ____________ + 70,000,000 + 5,000,000 +

____________ + ____________ + 6,000 + ____________ + 40 + 4

Share and Show

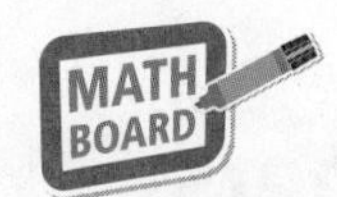

1. How can you use place value and period names to read and write 12,324,904 in word form?

Read and write the number in two other forms.

2. four hundred eight thousand, seventeen

3. 65,058

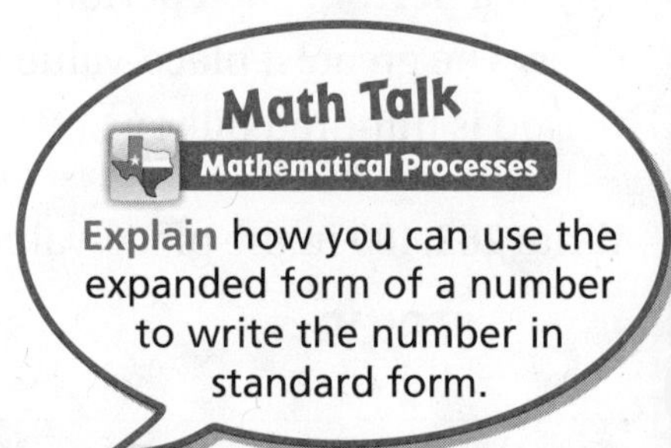

Problem Solving

Use the table for 4–5.

4. **Use Diagrams** Which city has a population of two hundred sixty-nine thousand, six hundred sixty-six?

5. Write the population of Raleigh in expanded form and word form.

Major Cities in North Carolina

City	Population*
Durham	228,330
Greensboro	269,666
Raleigh	403,892

*U.S. Census Bureau 2010 Estimated Population

6. H.O.T. **Multi-Step What's the Error?** Sophia said that the expanded form for 605,970 is 600,000 + 50,000 + 900 + 70. **Describe** Sophia's error and give the correct answer.

Name ______________________

Unlock the Problem (Real World)

7. H.O.T. Mark tossed six balls while playing a number game. Three balls landed in one section, and three balls landed in another section. His score is greater than one hundred thousand. What could his score be?

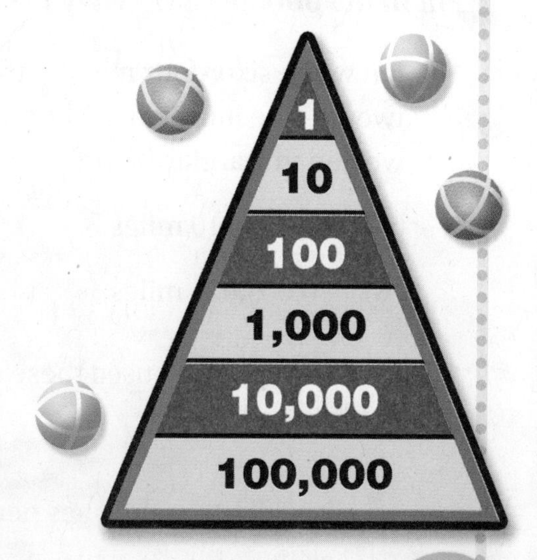

a. What do you know? ______________________

____

____

b. How can you use what you know about place value to find what Mark's score could be? ______________________

____

____

____

____

____

____

c. Draw a diagram to show one way to solve the problem.

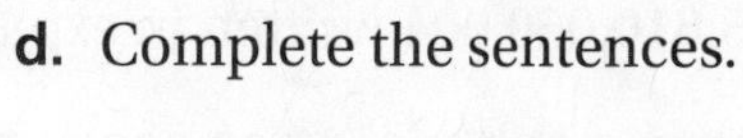

d. Complete the sentences.

Three balls could have landed in the ______________________ section.

Three balls could have landed in the ______________________ section.

Mark's score could be ______________________

______________________.

8. There are 2,750 sheep on a farm. Write the number of sheep in word form and expanded form.

____

9. What is twenty-seven million, four hundred eight thousand, nine hundred forty-five written in standard form?

____

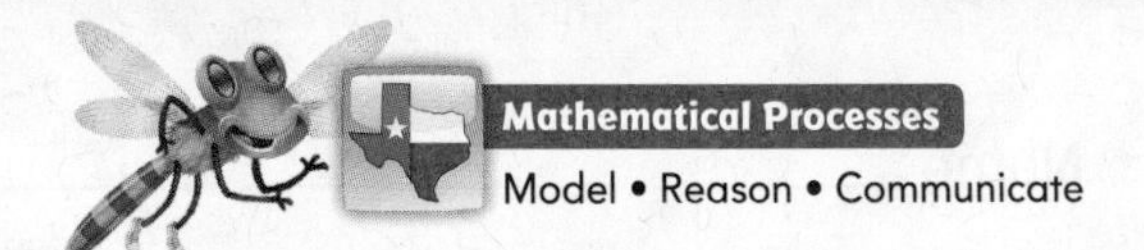

Daily Assessment Task

Fill in the bubble completely to show your answer.

10. Jen wrote sixty-four million, three hundred five thousand, twenty-one miles on the board. Which is this number written in standard form?

Ⓐ 64,350,210 miles

Ⓑ 30,605,021 miles

Ⓒ 64,021,305 miles

Ⓓ 64,305,021 miles

11. **Multi-Step** Mark used these clues to describe a number to his friend.

- The digits in the ones period are 682.
- The word form of the thousands period is seven hundred thirty thousand.
- The digits in the hundred millions and one millions places are the same.

Which number could Mark have described?

Ⓐ 682,730,151

Ⓑ 151,703,682

Ⓒ 730,151,682

Ⓓ 151,730,682

12. Which shows 5,610,050,004 written in expanded form?

Ⓐ 50,000,000 + 6,000,000 + 100,000 + 50,000 + 4

Ⓑ 600,000,000 + 20,000,000 + 4,000,000 + 5,000 + 400 + 5

Ⓒ 5,000,000,000 + 600,000,000 + 10,000,000 + 50,000 + 4

Ⓓ 5,000,000 + 600,000 + 10,000 + 5,000 + 0 + 4

TEXAS Test Prep

13. The new football stadium was filled to capacity with 105,840 fans. What is the value of the digit 5 in 105,840?

Ⓐ 500

Ⓑ 5,000

Ⓒ 50,000

Ⓓ 500,000

Homework and Practice

TEKS Number and Operations—4.2.B
MATHEMATICAL PROCESSES 4.1.D, 4.1.G

Name ______________________

1.2 Read and Write Numbers

Use the table for 1–4.

1. Write the population of Lubbock in word form.

____

____

____

Population of Texas Cities	
City	**Population***
Lubbock	233,740
Henderson	13,812
Dallas	1,223,229
Arlington	373,698

*U.S. Census Bureau 2011 Estimated Population

2. What is the expanded form for the population of Arlington?

____

____

____

____

Problem Solving Real World

3. All four cities have the same digit in one place. What is the place? Write the value of the digit.

____

____

____

____

____

4. Which city has a population that is about 100 times the population of Henderson? Write the population in word form.

____

____

____

____

____

Lesson Check

★ TEXAS Test Prep

Fill in the bubble completely to show your answer.

5. Which shows three hundred five million, two hundred eighty thousand, four hundred ninety-six written in standard form?

Ⓐ 300,528,496

Ⓑ 350,208,469

Ⓒ 305,028,496

Ⓓ 305,280,496

6. During the week of the county fair, 15,609 entry tickets were sold. Which shows 15,609 written in expanded form?

Ⓐ 10,000 + 5,000 + 600 + 9

Ⓑ 10,000 + 5,000 + 600 + 90

Ⓒ 1,000 + 500 + 60 + 9

Ⓓ 1,000 + 600 + 9

7. There were 94,172 people at a football game. Which digit is in the thousands place in this number?

Ⓐ 9

Ⓑ 1

Ⓒ 4

Ⓓ 7

8. Richard got 5,263,148 hits when he did an Internet search. What is the value of the digit 6 in this number?

Ⓐ 60,000

Ⓑ 600,000

Ⓒ 6,000

Ⓓ 6,000,000

9. Multi-Step Mason tossed 6 balls onto this number board. Two landed on 10,000. Two others landed on 100,000. One ball landed on 1. One ball landed on 100. What is Mason's score?

Ⓐ 220,101

Ⓑ 22,101

Ⓒ 2,121

Ⓓ 210,201

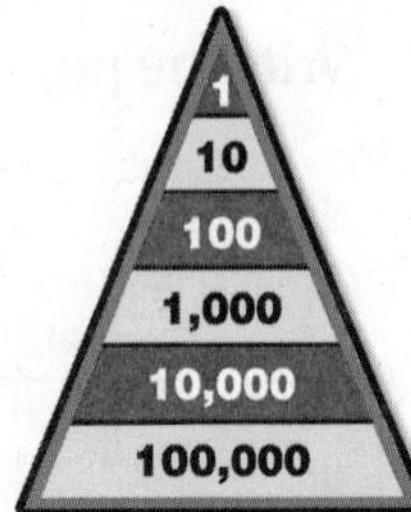

10. Multi-Step Katy tossed 7 balls onto this number board. Her score was 130,210. Which correctly lists the sections where the balls landed?

Ⓐ 100,000 (1) 10,000 (3) 100 (2) 1 (1)

Ⓑ 100,000 (1) 10,000 (3) 100 (2) 10 (1)

Ⓒ 10,000 (1) 1,000 (3) 100 (2) 10 (1)

Ⓓ 10,000 (1) 1,000 (3) 100 (2) 1 (1)

Name ______________________________

1.3 Compare and Order Numbers

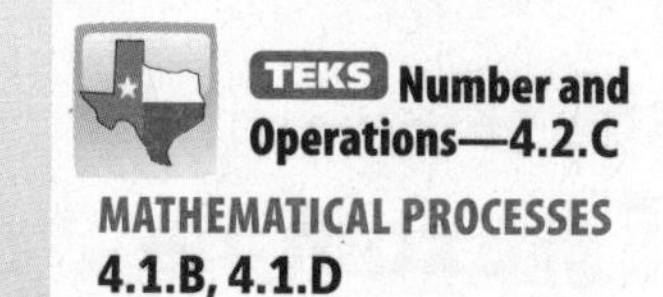

TEKS Number and Operations—4.2.C
MATHEMATICAL PROCESSES
4.1.B, 4.1.D

Essential Question How can you compare and order numbers?

Unlock the Problem

Grand Canyon National Park in Arizona had 651,028 visitors in June and 665,188 visitors in July. In which month did the park have more visitors?

- How many visitors were there in June?
  ____
- How many visitors were there in July?
  ____

Example 1 Use a place-value chart.

You can use a place-value chart to line up the digits by place value. Line up the ones with the ones, the tens with the tens, and so on. Compare 651,028 and 665,188.

Write 651,028 and 665,188 in the place-value chart below.

THOUSANDS			ONES		
Hundreds	Tens	Ones	Hundreds	Tens	Ones

Start at the left. Compare the digits in each place-value position until the digits differ.

STEP 1 Compare the hundred thousands.

651,028

665,188

6 hundred thousands ◯ 6 hundred thousands

↑ Write <, >, or =.

The digits in the hundred thousands place are the same.

STEP 2 Compare the ten thousands.

651,028

665,188

5 ten thousands ◯ 6 ten thousands

↑ Write <, >, or =.

5 ten thousands is less than 6 ten thousands so, $651{,}028 < 665{,}188$.

Since $651{,}028 < 665{,}188$, there were more visitors in July than in June.

Example 2 Use a number line to order 10,408; 10,433; and 10,416 from least to greatest.

Locate and label each point on the number line. The first one is done for you.

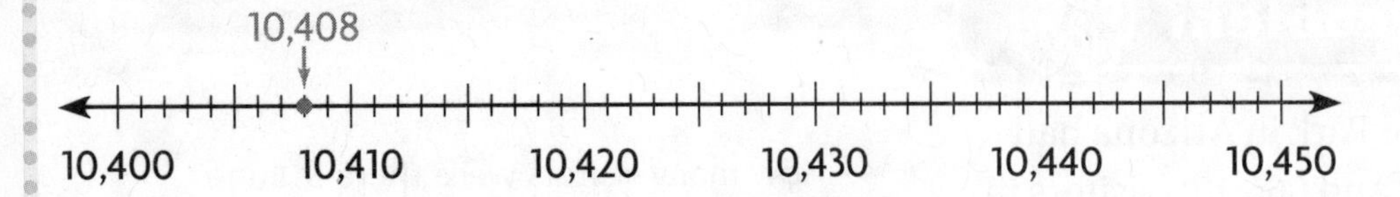

Think: Numbers to the left are closer to 0.

So, the numbers from least to greatest are 10,408; 10,416; and 10,433.
10,408 < 10,416 < 10,433

Share and Show

1. Compare 145,158,190 and 145,185,170.
Write <, >, or =. Use the place-value chart to help.

MILLIONS			THOUSANDS			ONES		
Hundreds	Tens	Ones	Hundreds	Tens	Ones	Hundreds	Tens	Ones
1	4	5,	1	5	8,	1	9	0
1	4	5,	1	8	5,	1	7	0

145,158,190 ◯ 145,185,170

Compare. Write <, >, or =.

2. 7,458,562,333 ◯ 7,457,541,753

✓ 3. 56,991 ◯ 52,880

4. 708,651,515 ◯ 629,672,484

5. 1,430,620 ◯ 986,435

Order from greatest to least.

✓ 6. 20,650; 21,150; 20,890

____

Math Talk
Mathematical Processes
Explain how you ordered the numbers from greatest to least in Exercise 6.

Name ______________________

Problem Solving Real World

H.O.T. Algebra Write all of the digits that can replace each ■.

7. $567 < 5■5 < 582$ ______________

8. $3{,}408 < 3{,}■30 < 3{,}540$ ______________

Use the pictograph for 9–11.

9. In which month shown did the Grand Canyon National Park have about 7,500 tent campers?

____

10. Which months had more than 10,000 tent campers?

____

1. **What if** during the month of October, the park had 22,500 tent campers? How many symbols would be placed on the pictograph for October?

____

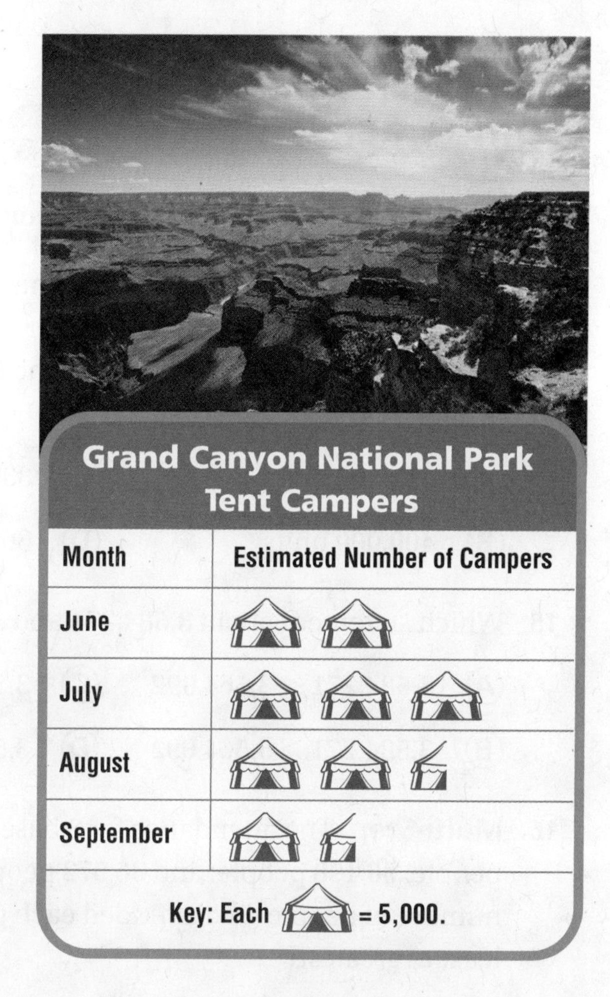

Grand Canyon National Park Tent Campers	
Month	Estimated Number of Campers
June	
July	
August	
September	

Key: Each = 5,000.

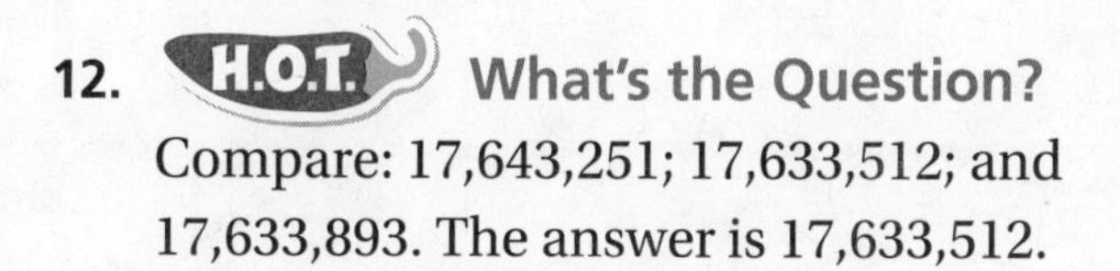

12. H.O.T. **What's the Question?**
Compare: 17,643,251; 17,633,512; and 17,633,893. The answer is 17,633,512.

____

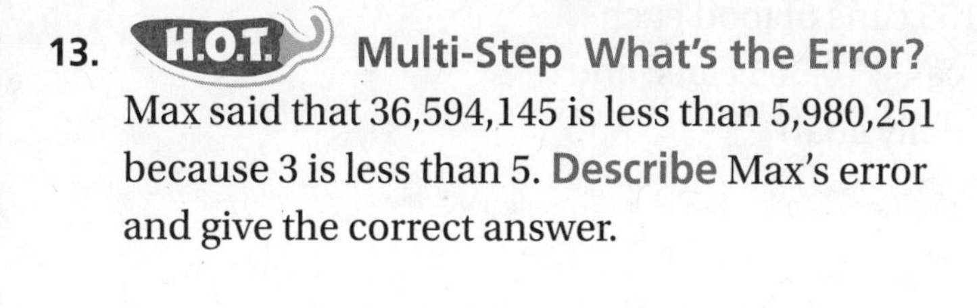

13. H.O.T. **Multi-Step What's the Error?**
Max said that 36,594,145 is less than 5,980,251 because 3 is less than 5. **Describe** Max's error and give the correct answer.

____

____

____

____

Write Math ▸ Show Your Work

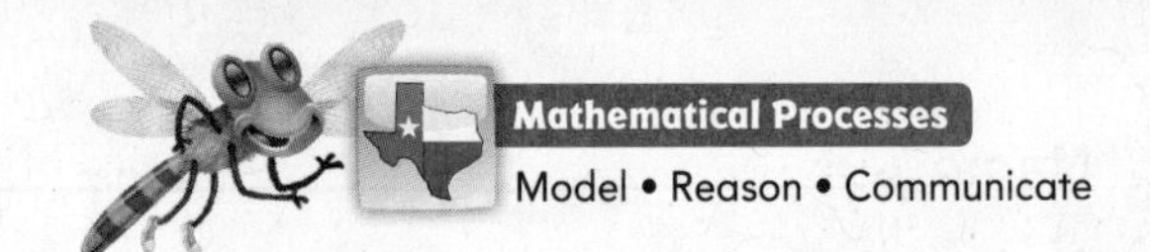

Daily Assessment Task

Fill in the bubble completely to show your answer.

14. The hotter a pepper, the higher the number of units it is rated. The Scotch bonnet pepper isn't as hot as a Fatali pepper. Which could be the rating of the Scotch bonnet pepper?

Ⓐ 325,500 units Ⓒ 330,000 units

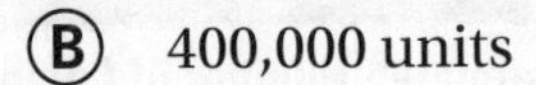

Ⓑ 400,000 units Ⓓ 300,000 units

Scotch bonnet

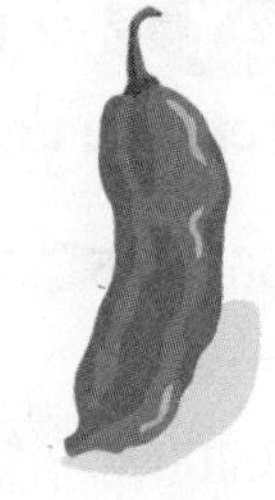

Fatali: 325,000 units

15. Which statement about 3,584,271 and 3,564,092 is true?

Ⓐ 3,584,271 < 3,564,092 Ⓒ 3,584,271 = 3,564,092

Ⓑ 3,584,271 > 3,564,092 Ⓓ 3,564,092 > 3,584,271

16. Multi-Step The attendance for 3 baseball games was 38,454 people; 38,198 people; and 36,572 people. Which shows the number of people who attended each game written in order from least to greatest?

Ⓐ 36,572 < 38,198 < 38,454

Ⓑ 38,454 < 38,198 < 36,572

Ⓒ 36,572 < 38,454 < 38,198

Ⓓ 38,454 < 36,572 < 38,198

TEXAS Test Prep

17. Zachary's school set a goal of collecting 12,155 cans of food each day. In the first 3 days they collected 12,250 cans; 10,505 cans; and 12,434 cans. Which total was less than their daily goal?

Ⓐ 12,434

Ⓑ 12,250

Ⓒ 12,155

Ⓓ 10,505

Homework and Practice

TEKS Number and Operations—4.2.C
MATHEMATICAL PROCESSES 4.1.B, 4.1.D

Name ____________________

1.3 Compare and Order Numbers

Compare. Write <, >, or =.

1. $6,462 ◯ $6,471

2. 453,536 ◯ 451,626

Order from greatest to least.

3. 87,262; 78,529; 78,811

____

4. 125,162; 212,225; 128,361

____

Write all of the digits that can replace each ■.

5. 735 < 7■4 < 761

____

6. 2,307 < 2■55 < 2,739

____

Problem Solving

Use the pictograph for 7–8.

7. During which months did more than 10,000 people attend the circus?

____

____

____

8. List the months in order from greatest attendance to least attendance.

____

____

____

____

Circus Attendance

Month	Number of People
May	
June	
July	
August	

Key: Each (tent) = 5,000.

Lesson Check

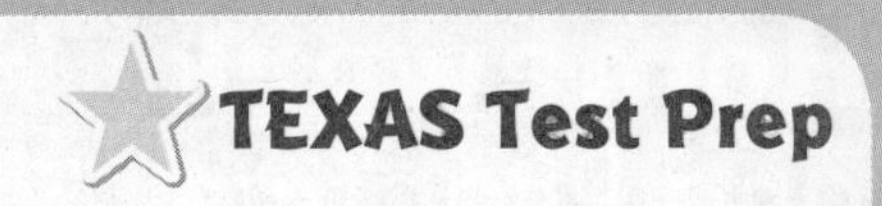

Fill in the bubble completely to show your answer.

9. Leah's car has 156,261 miles on the odometer. Casey's car has 165,002 miles on the odometer. Which statement correctly compares the two mileages?

Ⓐ $156{,}261 < 165{,}002$

Ⓑ $165{,}002 = 156{,}261$

Ⓒ $156{,}261 > 165{,}002$

Ⓓ $165{,}002 < 156{,}261$

10. Which number is greater than 53,614,293?

Ⓐ 35,828,781

Ⓑ 53,641,192

Ⓒ 53,416,998

Ⓓ 50,967,299

11. Which number makes this statement true?

$42{,}607 >$ __________ $> 40{,}352$

Ⓐ 40,255

Ⓑ 38,976

Ⓒ 42,875

Ⓓ 42,410

12. Which digits can replace the ■ to make a true statement?

$6{,}456 < 6{,}$■$12 < 6{,}788$

Ⓐ 5, 6

Ⓑ 4, 5, 6

Ⓒ 5, 6, 7

Ⓓ 4, 5, 6, 7

13. Multi-Step At Ted's Used Cars, the sales staff set a goal of $25,500 in sales each week. The sales for three weeks were $28,288; $25,369; and $25,876. Which total did not meet the goal?

Ⓐ $25,500

Ⓑ $28,288

Ⓒ $25,369

Ⓓ $25,876

14. Multi-Step Over three years a factory produced 3,516,235; 2,965,005 and 3,261,636 cans of soup. Which lists the numbers in order from least to greatest?

Ⓐ 2,965,005; 3,261,636; 3,516,235

Ⓑ 3,516,235; 3,261,636; 2,965,005

Ⓒ 2,965,005; 3,516,235; 3,261,636

Ⓓ 3,261,636; 2,965,005; 3,516,235

Name ______________________________

Round Numbers

TEKS Number and Operations—4.2.D
MATHEMATICAL PROCESSES
4.1.A, 4.1.B, 4.1.C

Essential Question How can you round numbers?

Unlock the Problem

During May 2008, the Mount Rushmore National Monument in South Dakota welcomed 138,202 visitors. A website reported that about 1 hundred thousand people visited the park during that month. Was the estimate reasonable?

- Underline what you are asked to find.
- Circle the information you will use.

An **estimate** tells you about how many or about how much. It is close to an exact amount. You can **round** a number to find an estimate.

One Way Use a number line.

To round a number to the nearest hundred thousand, find the hundred thousands it is between.

______________ < 138,202 < ______________

Use a number line to see which hundred thousand 138,202 is closest to.

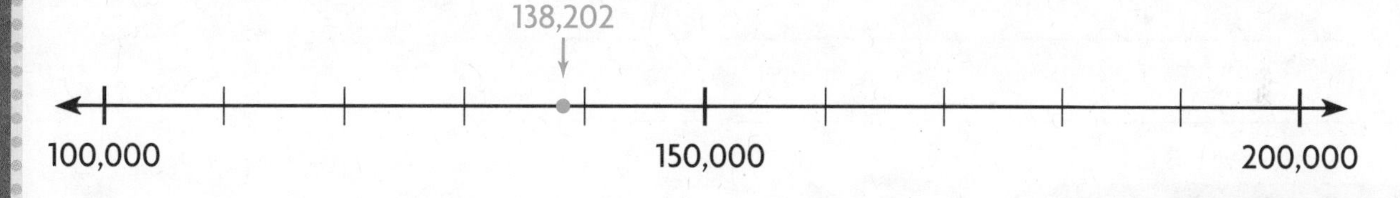

138,202 is closer to ______________ than ______________.

So, 1 hundred thousand is a reasonable estimate for 138,202.

Math Talk Mathematical Processes

Is 155,000 closer to 100,000 or 200,000? **Explain.**

1. What number is halfway between 100,000 and 200,000?

____

2. How does knowing where the halfway point is help you find which hundred thousand 138,202 is closest to? **Explain.**

____

____

Another Way Use place value.

Mount Rushmore is located 5,725 feet above sea level. About how high is Mount Rushmore above sea level, to the nearest thousand feet?

To round a number to the nearest thousand, find the thousands it is between.

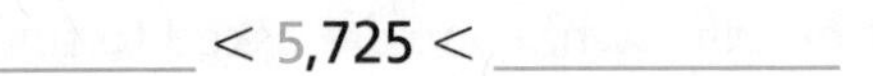

Look at the digit in the place-value position to the right.

5,725

Think: The digit in the hundreds place is 7.
So, 5,725 is closer to 6,000 than 5,000.

So, Mount Rushmore is about _____ feet above sea level.

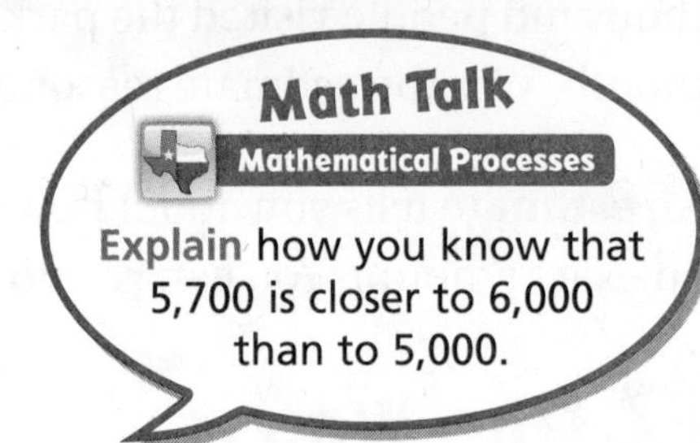

3. What is 250,000 rounded to the nearest hundred thousand? **Explain.**

_____

_____

_____

Share and Show

1. Suppose 255,113 people live in a city. Rounded to the nearest hundred thousand, about how many people live in the city? **Explain.**

_____ > 255,113 > _____

_____

Round to the place value of the underlined digit.

2. $93\underline{4},567$	✓3. $6\underline{4}1,267$	4. $1,\underline{2}34,890$	✓5. $3\underline{4}7,456$
_____	_____	_____	_____

Name ___________________________

Problem Solving Real World

Write Math ▸ Show Your Work

6. H.O.T. **Multi-Step Apply** The number 2,▇00 is missing a digit. The number rounded to the nearest thousand is 3,000. List all of the possibilities for the missing digit. **Explain** your answer.

____

____

____

____

____

7. H.O.T. **Multi-Step Evaluate Reasonableness** The 2008 population of Wyoming was counted as 532,668 people. What is a reasonable estimate of the 2008 population of Wyoming? **Explain.**

____

____

8. What is the greatest whole number that rounds to the number 277,300? What is the least whole number?

____

____

9. Sarah rounded the number 4,583,583 to 4,500,000 when her teacher asked her to round to the nearest hundred thousand. Jamal rounded the same number to 4,600,000 when asked to round to the nearest hundred thousand. Who is correct? **Explain** the error that was made.

____

____

____

0. What number is half way between 34,000 and 35,000?

____

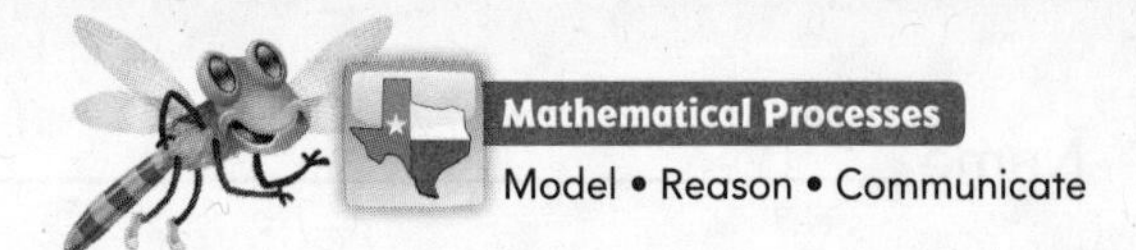

Daily Assessment Task

Fill in the bubble completely to show your answer.

11. The number of dogs at The Great North Dog Walk in 2011, rounded to the nearest thousand, is 23,000. Which could be the exact number of dogs?

Ⓐ 22,742

Ⓑ 23,500

Ⓒ 23,603

Ⓓ 22,455

12. A sports website had 2,684,735 visitors last year. Jerry rounded the number of visitors to the nearest hundred thousand for a newspaper article. Which number shows how he rounded 2,684,735?

Ⓐ 2,684,400

Ⓑ 2,680,000

Ⓒ 2,690,000

Ⓓ 2,700,000

13. **Multi-Step** Rachael rounded 16,473 to the nearest hundred. Then she rounded her answer to the nearest thousand. What is the final number?

Ⓐ 16,500

Ⓑ 17,000

Ⓒ 20,000

Ⓓ 16,000

TEXAS Test Prep

14. About 300,000 people attended a festival. Which number could be the exact number of people that attended the festival?

Ⓐ 389,001

Ⓑ 249,899

Ⓒ 252,348

Ⓓ 351,213

Homework and Practice

TEKS Number and Operations—4.2.D
MATHEMATICAL PROCESSES 4.1.A, 4.1.B, 4.1.C

Name ______________________________

1.4 Round Numbers

1. The number 5,▒00 is missing a digit. The number rounded to the nearest thousand is 5,000. List all of the possibilities for the missing digit. **Explain** your answer.

2. Andy and Elizabeth each rounded 2,639,456 to the nearest ten-thousand. Andy got 2,640,000. Elizabeth got 2,630,000. Who is correct? **Explain** the error that was made.

3. What is the greatest whole number that rounds to 67,400? What is the least whole number?

4. What number is half way between 170,000 and 180,000?

Problem Solving

5. A shopping channel shipped 467,023 packages last year. What is a reasonable estimate of the number of packages shipped? **Explain**.

6. A parking lot covers 32,420 square feet. What is its area to the nearest thousand feet? **Explain** how you round the number.

Lesson Check

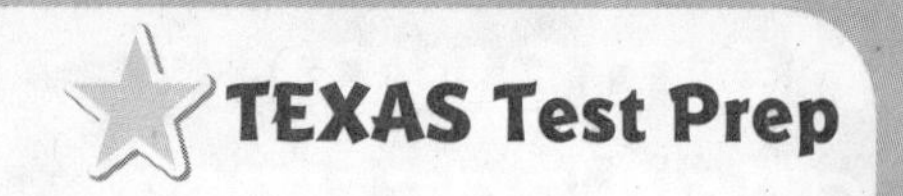

Fill in the bubble completely to show your answer.

7. The population of Forestville is 83,277. What is the population rounded to the nearest thousand?

Ⓐ 83,000

Ⓑ 80,000

Ⓒ 84,000

Ⓓ 90,000

8. To the nearest hundred thousand, there were 700,000 visitors to an amusement park last year. Which could be the exact number of visitors?

Ⓐ 784,312

Ⓑ 756,107

Ⓒ 685,280

Ⓓ 641,888

9. What is the greatest whole number that rounds to 54,300?

Ⓐ 53,399

Ⓑ 54,349

Ⓒ 53,999

Ⓓ 54,299

10. The number 15,■56 rounded to the nearest thousand is 15,000. Which numbers could be the missing digit?

Ⓐ 1, 2, 3, 4, 5

Ⓑ 1, 2, 3, 4, 5, 6

Ⓒ 0, 1, 2, 3, 4, 5

Ⓓ 0, 1, 2, 3, 4

11. Multi-Step A male elephant weighs 6,708 pounds. A female elephant weighs 5,823 pounds. To the nearest hundred, what is the total weight of the two elephants?

Ⓐ 7,000 pounds

Ⓑ 12,500 pounds

Ⓒ 6,000 pounds

Ⓓ 13,000 pounds

12. Multi-Step To the nearest hundred, a factory produced 3,600 jars of applesauce on Thursday and 4,200 jars of applesauce on Friday. To the nearest thousand, how many jars of applesauce did they produce on the two days?

Ⓐ 7,800

Ⓑ 7,000

Ⓒ 8,400

Ⓓ 8,000

Name ____________________

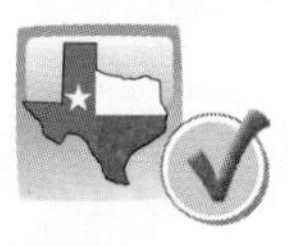

Module 1 Assessment

Vocabulary

Vocabulary
expanded form
period
round
standard form

Choose the best term from the box.

1. The ______________ of 1,723,850 is 1,000,000 + 700,000 + 20,000 + 3,000 + 800 + 50. (p. 11)
2. You can __________ to find *about* how much or how many. (p. 23)
3. In 192,860 the digits 1, 9, and 2 are in the same __________. (p. 11)

Concepts and Skills

Complete the sentence. TEKS 4.2.A

4. 7 is $\frac{1}{10}$ of __________
5. 800 is 10 times as much as __________

Write the number in two other forms. TEKS 4.2.B

6. 293,805

____

____

____

7. 20,000,000 + 6,000,000 + 300,000 + 5,000 + 20 + 6

____

____

____

Compare. Write <, >, or =. TEKS 4.2.C

8. 457,380 ◯ 458,590
9. 390,040 ◯ 9,040
10. 11,809 ◯ 11,980

Order from least to greatest. TEKS 4.2.C

11. 801,652; 801,114; 84,318

____

12. 6,551,111; 6,540,164; 6,547,894

____

Round to the place of the underlined digit. TEKS 4.2.D

13. <u>1</u>40,250 __________
14. 10,<u>4</u>50 __________
15. 12<u>6</u>,234 __________

Fill the bubble in completely to show your answer.

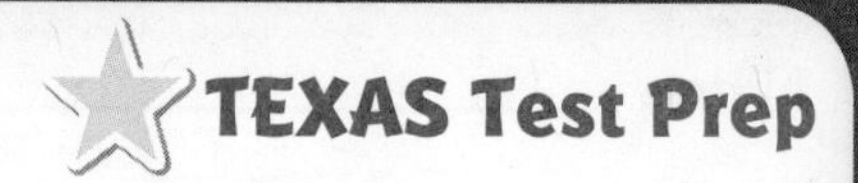

16. Matt did research on heights of volcanoes. He found that Lassen Peak is 10,457 feet, Mt. Rainier is 14,410 feet, Mt. Shasta is 14,161 feet, and Mt. St. Helens is 8,364 feet. Which height is the greatest? TEKS 4.2.C

Ⓐ 8,364

Ⓑ 14,410

Ⓒ 10,457

Ⓓ 14,161

17. Which number, rounded to the nearest ten-thousand, is 60,000? TEKS 4.2.D

Ⓐ 26,912

Ⓑ 53,024

Ⓒ 261,395

Ⓓ 62,093

18. Gail wrote the number seven million, six hundred forty-eight thousand, three hundred ninety-seven on the board. Which shows how Gail would write this number in standard and expanded form? TEKS 4.2.B

Ⓐ 768,397; 700,000 + 60,000 + 8,000 + 300 + 977

Ⓑ 70,648,397; 70,000,000 + 600,000 + 40,000 + 8,000 + 300 + 90 + 7

Ⓒ 7,648,397; 7,000,000 + 400,000 + 60,000 + 8,000 + 300 + 97

Ⓓ 7,648,397; 7,000,000 + 600,000 + 40,000 + 8,000 + 300 + 90 + 7

19. Company A sold 6,028,468 cans of corn during the last three months. What is the value of the digit 4 in the number 6,028,468? TEKS 4.2.B

Record your answer and fill in the bubbles on the grid. Be sure to use the correct place value.

			.		
⓪	⓪	⓪		⓪	⓪
①	①	①		①	①
②	②	②		②	②
③	③	③		③	③
④	④	④		④	④
⑤	⑤	⑤		⑤	⑤
⑥	⑥	⑥		⑥	⑥
⑦	⑦	⑦		⑦	⑦
⑧	⑧	⑧		⑧	⑧
⑨	⑨	⑨		⑨	⑨

Name ____________________________________

2.2 Explore Decimal Place Value

TEKS Number and Operations—4.2.B

MATHEMATICAL PROCESSES 4.1.D, 4.1.E, 4.1.F

Essential Question How can you find the value of a digit using its place-value position?

Unlock the Problem (Real World)

Connect Decimals, like whole numbers, can be written in standard form, word form, and expanded form.

How can you write the value of each digit in 5.76 using decimal expander strips?

Activity Explore expanded form.

Materials ■ decimal expander strips

STEP 1 Place the decimal expander strip in front of you, with the largest rectangle on the left-hand side.

STEP 2 Fold along the first two dashed lines as shown, keeping the largest rectangle toward the back.

STEP 3 Continue folding along the dashed lines. Then turn the paper around so that the largest rectangle is on the right-hand side.

STEP 4 Write 5, 7, 6, placing one digit in each section, as shown. Insert a decimal point before the 7.

5 .7 6

STEP 5 Unfold the decimal expander, and use numbers and symbols to write 5 + 0.7 + 0.06.

5 + 0.7 + 0.06

STEP 6 Use the second strip of paper to make another decimal expander for 5.76. This time, write the word that names the value of each digit. The strip should read 5 ones 7 tenths 6 hundredths.

5 ones 7 tenths 6 hundredths

- What are some other ways you can expand the decimal 5.76 by using both decimal expanders?

____

Math Talk Mathematical Processes

Explain how you can write 3.5 as 35 tenths.

Example Use a place-value chart.

▲ A shortfin mako shark may grow 20,000 teeth during its lifetime!

Shortfin mako shark teeth range in length from 0.64 centimeter to 5.08 centimeters. Eli found a Shortfin mako shark tooth measuring 2.54 centimeters on the beach.

You can use a place-value chart to help you understand decimal place value.

Write the decimal above in the place-value chart.

Ones	.	Tenths	Hundredths

What is the value of the digit 4 in 2.54?

The value of the digit 4 is ______ hundredths,

or __________.

Math Talk

Mathematical Processes

In the whole number 277, the value of each digit is 10 times as great as the place-value position to its right. **Explain** why, in the decimal 2.77, the value of the digit 7 in the tenths place is 10 times as great as the value of the digit 7 in the hundredths place.

Share and Show

1. What is the place-value position of the digit 8 in 0.98? ______________

Ones	.	Tenths	Hundredths
0	.	9	8

Write the value of the underlined digit.

2. 2.<u>1</u> ______________

3. 0.0<u>9</u> ______________

4. 6.5<u>4</u> ______________

✓5. 0.<u>3</u> ______________

Write the number in two other forms.

6. $3.0 + 0.9 + 0.02$ ______________

✓7. seventeen hundredths ______________

Name ________________________________

Problem Solving Real World

Practice: Copy and Solve **Write the number in two other forms.**

8. 8.26

9. one and two tenths

10. $10 + 6 + 0.7 + 0.02$

11. 95.31

12. **Explain** how you write the number 7.04 in expanded form.

____

____

____

____

Use the chart for 13–14.

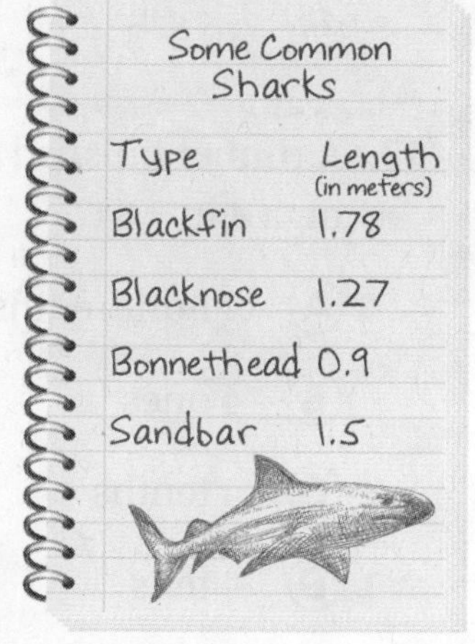

3. A marine researcher recorded the lengths of some sharks he observed offshore. The length of which shark has the digit 7 in the tenths place?

____

14. H.O.T. **Multi-Step What's the Error?** Randy said that the blacknose shark is one and twenty-seven tenths meters in length. **Describe** Randy's error and write the decimal in word form.

____

____

____

15. H.O.T. **What's the Question?** The answer is 275 hundredths.

____

____

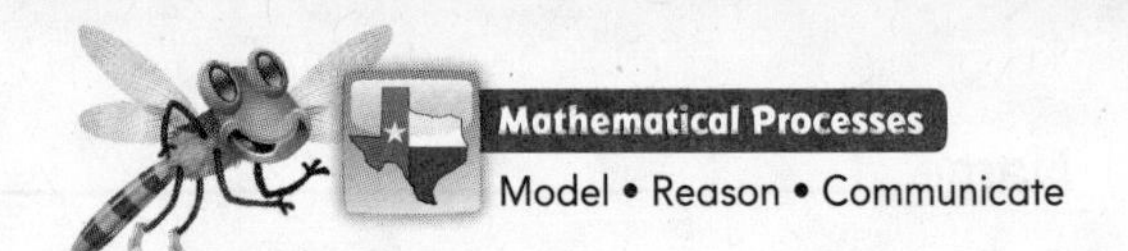

Daily Assessment Task

Fill in the bubble completely to show your answer.

16. An adult kangaroo jumps 7.6 meters in a single leap. What is 7.6 written in word form?

Ⓐ seven and one sixth

Ⓑ seven and six tenths

Ⓒ seven and six hundredths

Ⓓ seventy-six hundredths

17. During a blizzard, a city received 13.6 inches of snow. What is 13.6 written in expanded form?

Ⓐ $10 + 0.3 + 0.06$

Ⓑ $10 + 3 + 0.06$

Ⓒ $10 + 3 + 0.6$

Ⓓ $10 + 3 + 6$

18. A runner finished a race in 9.84 seconds. What is the value of the digit 4 in 9.84?

Ⓐ 4 hundredths

Ⓑ 4 ones

Ⓒ 4 tenths

Ⓓ 4 tens

TEXAS Test Prep

19. The average annual precipitation in Philadelphia, Pennsylvania, is 42.05 inches. What is the value of the digit 5 in 42.05?

Ⓐ five tens

Ⓑ five ones

Ⓒ five tenths

Ⓓ five hundredths

Name ______________________

2.2 Explore Decimal Place Value

Write the number in two other forms.

1. 6.7

____

2. one and twelve hundredths

____

3. $80 + 7 + 0.9 + 0.03$

____

____

4. 53.02

____

____

Write the value of the underlined digit.

5. 3.<u>6</u> ____________

6. 0.0<u>4</u> ____________

7. 9.<u>0</u>5 ____________

8. 2.8<u>1</u> ____________

Problem Solving

Use the chart for 9–10.

9. Jordan recorded the distances he walked this week. On which day did he walk two and twenty-five hundredths kilometers?

____

10. Leah said Jordan walked 3 and 5 tenths kilometers on Wednesday. What error did she make?

____

____

____

Distances Walked

Day	Distance (in kilometers)
Monday	2.7
Wednesday	3.05
Friday	2.25
Sunday	0.8

Lesson Check

TEXAS Test Prep

Fill in the bubble completely to show your answer.

11. What is 8.07 written in word form?

Ⓐ eight and seven tenths

Ⓑ eighty-seven tenths

Ⓒ eight and seven hundredths

Ⓓ eighty-seven hundredths

12. What is the value of the underlined digit in 37.0<u>8</u>?

Ⓐ 8 tenths

Ⓑ 8 ones

Ⓒ 8 tens

Ⓓ 8 hundredths

13. What is the expanded form for 70.26?

Ⓐ 7 + 2 + 0.6

Ⓑ 70 + 2 + 0.6

Ⓒ 7 + 0.2 + 0.06

Ⓓ 70 + 0.2 + 0.06

14. What is thirty-seven and nine tenths written in expanded form?

Ⓐ 30 + 7 + 0.9

Ⓑ 3 + 0.7 + 0.09

Ⓒ 30 + 7 + 0.09

Ⓓ 37 + 0.9

15. What is the place value of 9 in 42.96?

Ⓐ tenths

Ⓑ ones

Ⓒ tens

Ⓓ hundredths

16. Matthias walked around the track for 9.28 minutes. What is the value of the digit 2 in 9.28?

Ⓐ 2 ones

Ⓑ 2 tenths

Ⓒ 2 hundreds

Ⓓ 2 hundredths

17. **Multi-Step** During a rainstorm, Dallas received 1.25 inches of rain and Arlington received 3.25 inches. Which statement is true about 1.25 and 3.25?

Ⓐ The value of 2 is 2 tenths.

Ⓑ The value of 1 is 1 hundred.

Ⓒ The value of 5 is 5 tenths.

Ⓓ The value of 2 is 2 tens.

18. **Multi-Step** What is the value of the digit to the right of the underlined digit in 76.<u>5</u>6?

Ⓐ 6 hundreds

Ⓑ 5 tenths

Ⓒ 6 hundredths

Ⓓ 6 ones

Name ______________________

TEKS **Number and Operations—4.2.G, 4.2.H**
Also 4.2.E
MATHEMATICAL PROCESSES
4.1.E, 4.1.F

2.3 Relate Tenths and Decimals

Essential Question How can you record tenths as fractions and decimals?

Unlock the Problem

Ty is reading a book about metamorphic rocks. He has read $\frac{7}{10}$ of the book. What decimal describes the part of the book Ty has read?

A **decimal** is a number with one or more digits to the right of the **decimal point**. You can write tenths and hundredths as fractions or decimals.

Math Talk — Mathematical Processes

Explain how the size of one whole is related to the size of one tenth.

One Way Use a model and a place-value chart.

Fraction

Shade $\frac{7}{10}$ of the model.

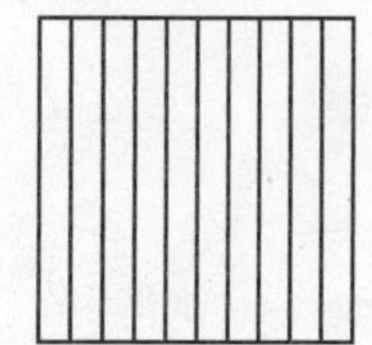

Think: The model is divided into 10 equal parts. Each part represents one **tenth**.

Write: ______________

Read: seven tenths

Decimal

$\frac{7}{10}$ is 7 tenths.

Ones	.	Tenths	Hundredths
	.		

↑ decimal point

Write: ______________

Read: ______________

Another Way Use a number line.

Label the number line with decimals that are equivalent to the fractions. Locate the point $\frac{7}{10}$.

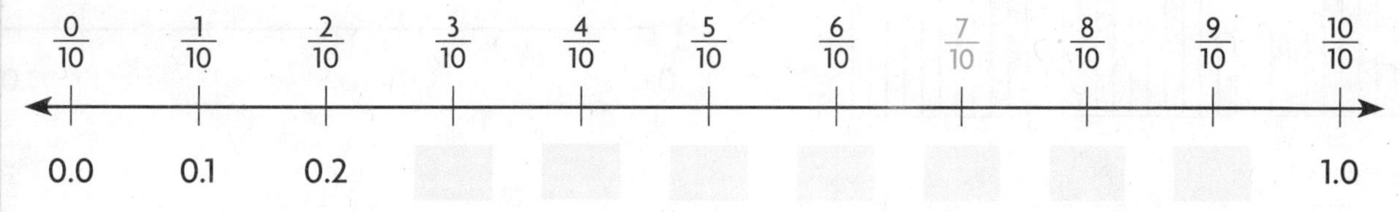

__________ names the same amount as $\frac{7}{10}$.

So, Ty read 0.7 of the book.

- How can you write 0.1 as a fraction? **Explain.**

____

Tara rode her bicycle $1\frac{6}{10}$ miles. What decimal describes how far she rode her bicycle?

You have already written a fraction as a decimal. You can also write a mixed number as a decimal.

Another Way Use a number line.

Label the number line with equivalent mixed numbers and decimals. Locate the point $1\frac{6}{10}$.

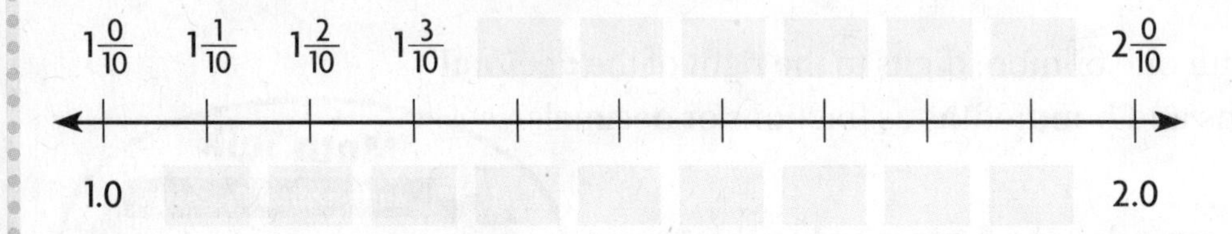

_____ names the same amount as $1\frac{6}{10}$.

So, Tara rode her bicycle _____ miles.

Share and Show

1. Write five tenths as a fraction and as a decimal.

   Fraction: _____ Decimal: _____

Ones	.	Tenths	Hundredths
	.		

Write the fraction or mixed number and the decimal shown by the model.

2.

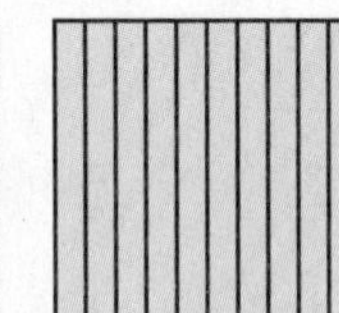
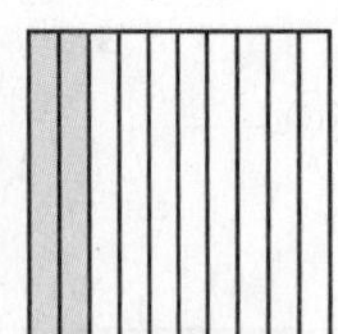

_____ _____

3.

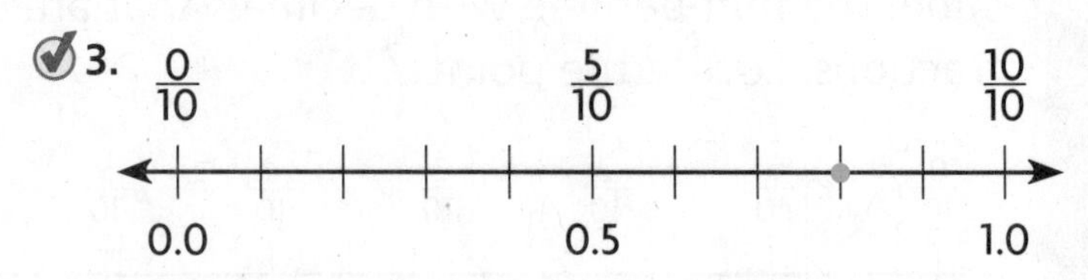

_____ _____

Math Talk
Mathematical Processes
How can you write $1\frac{3}{10}$ as a decimal? **Explain.**

Name ______________________________

Problem Solving Real World

Use the table for 4–7.

Ramon's Rock Collection	
Name	**Type**
Basalt	Igneous
Rhyolite	Igneous
Granite	Igneous
Peridotite	Igneous
Scoria	Igneous
Shale	Sedimentary
Limestone	Sedimentary
Sandstone	Sedimentary
Mica	Metamorphic
Slate	Metamorphic

4. What part of the rocks listed in the table are igneous? Write your answer as a decimal.

____

5. Sedimentary rocks make up what part of Ramon's collection? Write your answer as a fraction and in word form.

____

6. H.O.T. **Representations** What part of the rocks listed in the table are metamorphic? Write your answer as a fraction and as a decimal.

____

7. H.O.T. **Multi-Step What's the Error?** Niki wrote the following sentence in her report: "Metamorphic rocks make up 2.0 of Ramon's rock collection." **Describe** her error and give the correct answer.

____

____

8. Which decimal is the same as $\frac{1}{10}$? $\frac{6}{10}$? $\frac{3}{10}$?

____

9. Josh wrote $\frac{3}{10}$ of his paper on Thursday night and $\frac{5}{10}$ of his paper on Friday night. How much of his paper did he complete on Friday night, written as a decimal?

____

Write Math ▶ **Show Your Work**

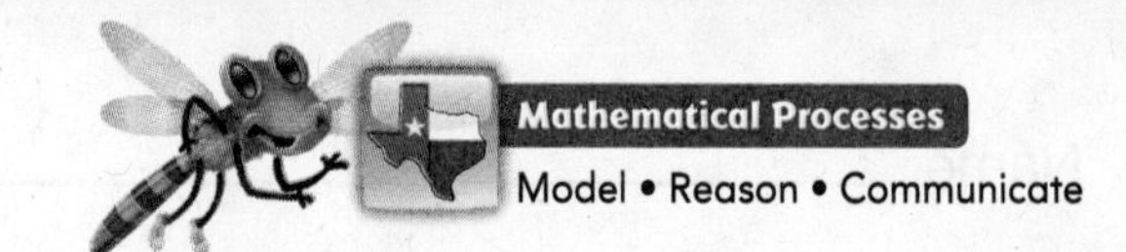

Daily Assessment Task

Fill in the bubble completely to show your answer.

10. Narwhal whales can weigh as much as $1\frac{8}{10}$ tons. What is $1\frac{8}{10}$ written as a decimal?

Ⓐ 8.10

Ⓑ 10.1

Ⓒ 1.10

Ⓓ 1.8

11. Multi-Step What fraction and decimal are shown by the point?

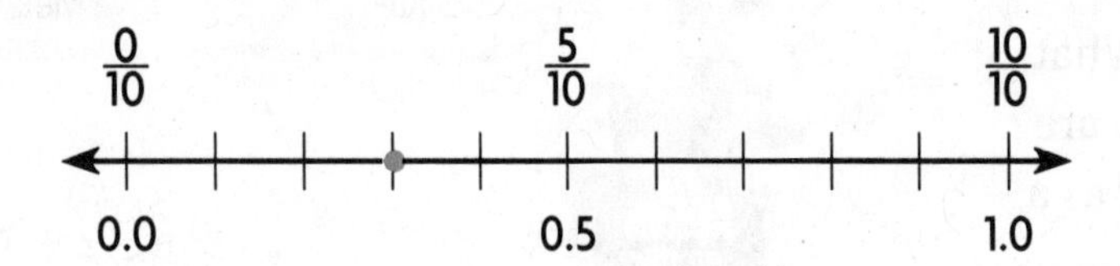

Ⓐ $\frac{3}{10}$ and 0.3

Ⓑ $\frac{3}{100}$ and 0.03

Ⓒ $\frac{8}{10}$ and 0.08

Ⓓ $\frac{2}{10}$ and 0.2

12. Which shows a way to write 0.7 as a fraction?

Ⓐ $\frac{7}{100}$

Ⓑ $\frac{2}{10}$

Ⓒ $\frac{7}{10}$

Ⓓ $1\frac{7}{10}$

TEXAS Test Prep

13. Rosa has a bookshelf where she stores her book collection. Four tenths of her books are mystery books. What is this amount written as a decimal?

Ⓐ 4.0

Ⓑ 0.4

Ⓒ 40.0

Ⓓ 0.04

Homework and Practice

TEKS Number and Operations—4.2.G, 4.2.H
Also 4.2.E
MATHEMATICAL PROCESSES 4.1.E, 4.1.F

Name ____________________

2.3 Relate Tenths and Decimals

Write the fraction or mixed number as a decimal.

1. $\frac{6}{10}$ __________

2. $\frac{1}{10}$ __________

3. $3\frac{9}{10}$ __________

Problem Solving Real World

Bradley has 10 coins in his pocket. Use the picture of the coins for 4–7.

4. What part of the coins are dimes? Write your answer as a decimal.

____

5. Quarters make up what part of the group of coins? Write your answer as a fraction and in word form.

____

6. What part of the coins shown are pennies? Write your answer as a fraction and as a decimal.

____

7. Amy said that nickels make up $\frac{1}{9}$ of Bradley's coins. What error did Amy make?

____

Lesson Check

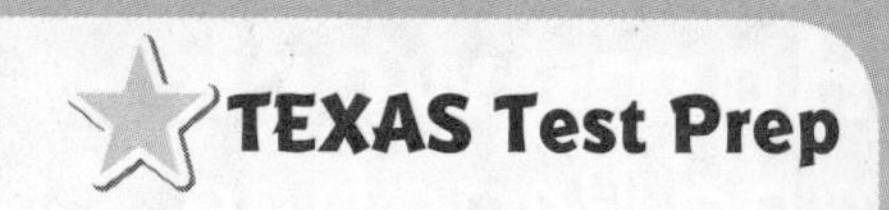

Fill in the bubble completely to show your answer.

8. Kristen rode her bicycle $2\frac{7}{10}$ kilometers to school. What is the decimal for $2\frac{7}{10}$?

Ⓐ 2.10

Ⓑ 27.1

Ⓒ 2.7

Ⓓ 7.210

9. Multi-Step A flat represents 1. Which names the mixed number and the decimal shown by the model?

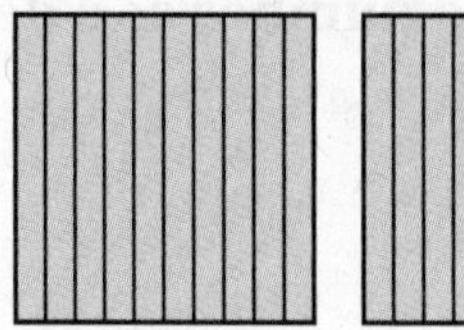 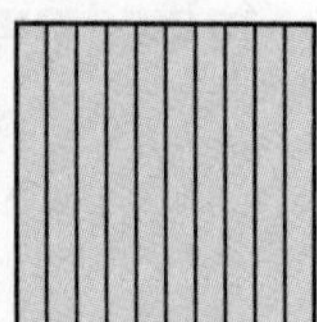 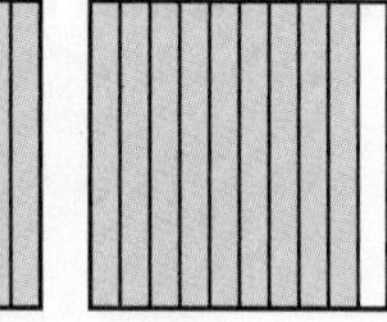

Ⓐ $2\frac{9}{10}$, 2.9

Ⓑ $2\frac{9}{100}$, 2.09

Ⓒ $\frac{29}{100}$, 0.29

Ⓓ $1\frac{9}{10}$, 1.9

10. Which shows eight tenths written as a fraction and as a decimal?

Ⓐ $\frac{8}{10}$, 0.08

Ⓑ $\frac{8}{100}$, 8

Ⓒ $\frac{8}{100}$, 0.8

Ⓓ $\frac{8}{10}$, 0.8

11. Multi-Step It is 1 kilometer from Owen's house to the park. The number line shows the distance he has walked. What is the decimal for the distance he has left to walk?

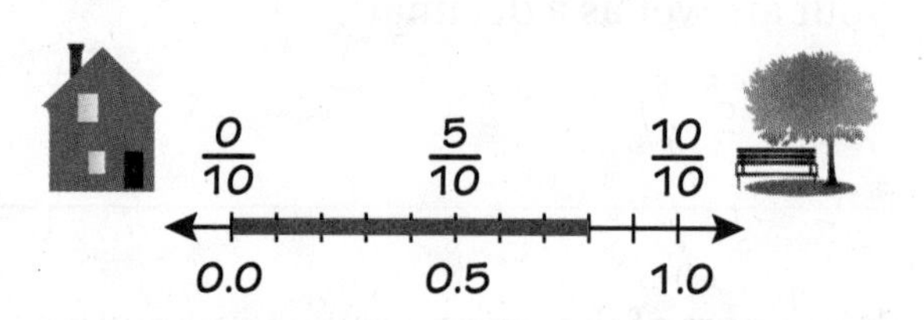

Ⓐ 0.8

Ⓑ 0.2

Ⓒ 2

Ⓓ 8

12. Which shows a way to write 0.9 as a fraction?

Ⓐ $\frac{9}{100}$

Ⓑ $\frac{90}{10}$

Ⓒ $\frac{9}{10}$

Ⓓ $1\frac{9}{10}$

Name ___

2.4 Relate Hundredths and Decimals

TEKS Number and Operations—4.2.G, 4.2.H
Also 4.2.E
MATHEMATICAL PROCESSES
4.1.D

Essential Question

How can you record hundredths as fractions and decimals?

Unlock the Problem (Real World)

In the 2008 Summer Olympic Games, the winning time in the men's 100-meter butterfly race was only $\frac{1}{100}$ second faster than the second-place time. What decimal represents this fraction of a second?

- Circle the numbers you need to use.

You can write hundredths as fractions or decimals.

One Way Use a model and a place-value chart.

Fraction

Shade $\frac{1}{100}$ of the model.

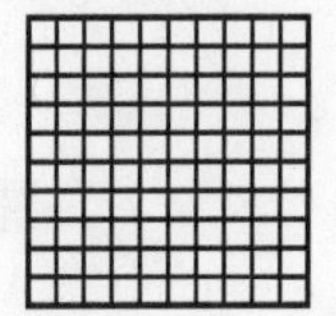

Think: The model is divided into 100 equal parts. Each part represents one **hundredth**.

Write: ___

Read: one hundredth

Decimal

Complete the place-value chart. $\frac{1}{100}$ is 1 hundredth.

Ones	.	Tenths	Hundredths
0	.	0	1

Write: ___

Read: one hundredth

Another Way Use a number line.

Label the number line with equivalent decimals. Locate the point $\frac{1}{100}$.

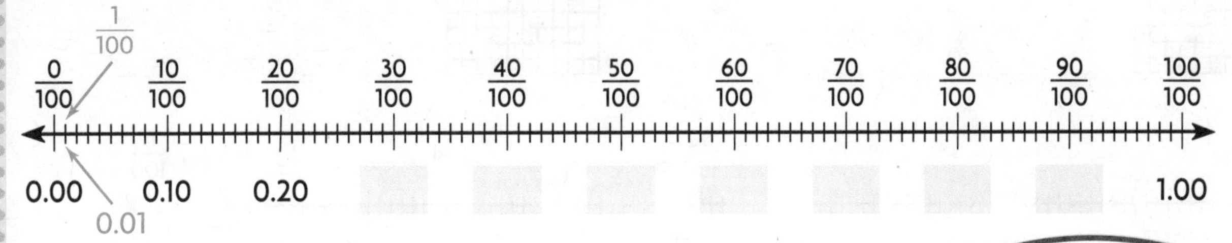

___ names the same amount as $\frac{1}{100}$.

So, the winning time was ___ second faster.

Math Talk
Mathematical Processes
Explain how the size of one tenth is related to the size of one hundredth.

Alicia won her 400-meter freestyle race by $4\frac{25}{100}$ seconds. How can you write this mixed number as a decimal?

Example Use a number line.

Label the number line with equivalent mixed numbers and decimals. Locate the point $4\frac{25}{100}$.

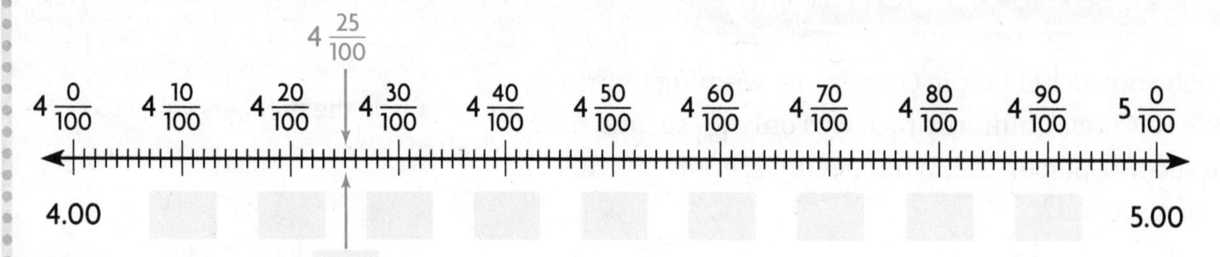

_______ names the same amount as $4\frac{25}{100}$.

So, Alicia won her race by _______ seconds.

Share and Show

MATH BOARD

1. Shade the model to show $\frac{31}{100}$.

Write the amount as a decimal. _______

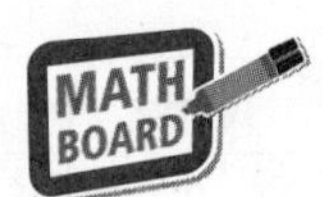

Ones	.	Tenths	Hundredths
	.		

Write the fraction or mixed number and the decimal shown by the model.

2. 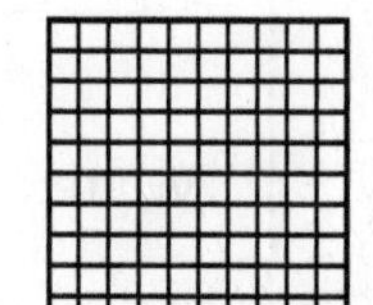 _______ _______

3.  _______ _______

4. 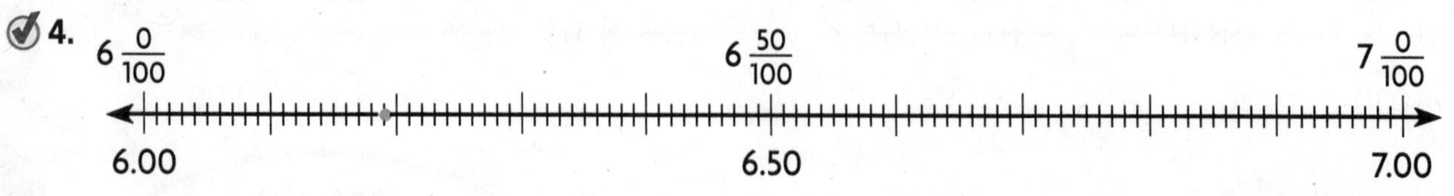

_______ _______

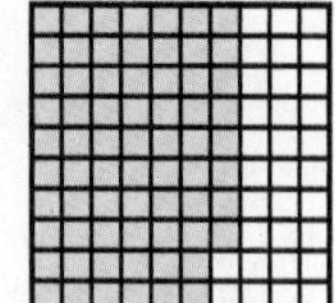

Math Talk
Mathematical Processes
Are 0.5 and 0.50 equivalent? Explain.

Name ______________________________

Problem Solving Real World

5. **H.O.T. Representations** Shade the grids to show three different ways to represent $\frac{16}{100}$ using models.

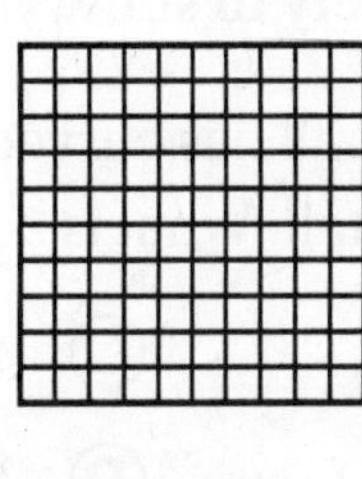

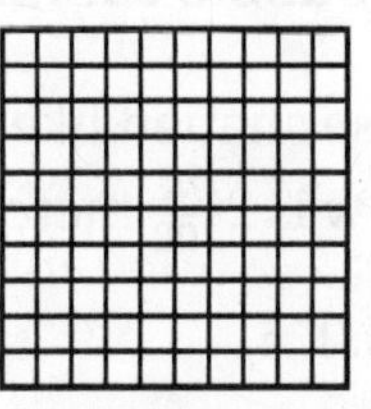

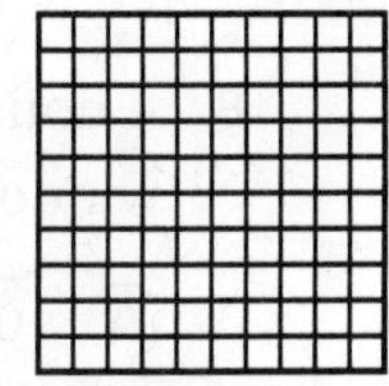

6. **Write Math** ▶ **Explain** how one whole, one tenth, and one hundredth are related.

____

____

Sense or Nonsense?

7. **H.O.T. Multi-Step** The Memorial Library is 0.3 mile from school. Whose statement makes sense? Whose statement is nonsense? **Explain** your reasoning.

Gabe said he was going to walk 3 tenths mile to the Memorial Library after school.

Tara said she was going to walk 3 miles to the Memorial Library after school.

____

____

____

____

____

____

____

____

____

____

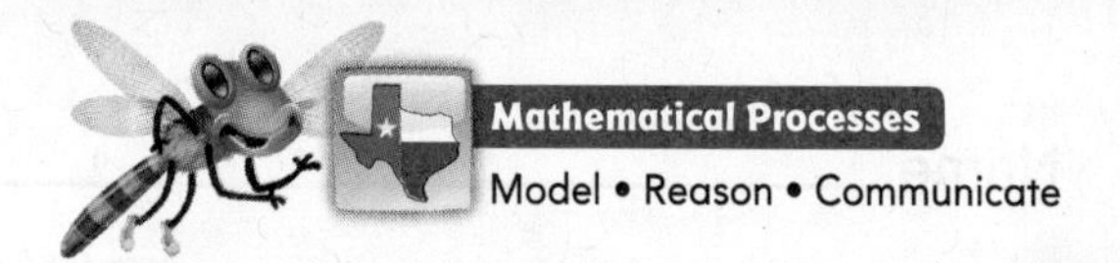

Daily Assessment Task

Fill in the bubble completely to show your answer.

8. A house shaped like a ball has curved windows. The largest window is $2\frac{75}{100}$ meters tall. What is $2\frac{75}{100}$ written as a decimal?

Ⓐ 0.275 Ⓒ 2.75

Ⓑ 2.175 Ⓓ 27.5

9. Barry made the model below to show the distance he and his sister hiked while on vacation. Which decimal does the model show?

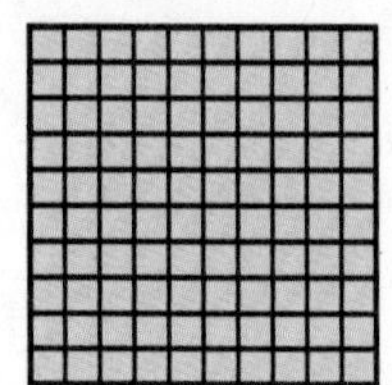 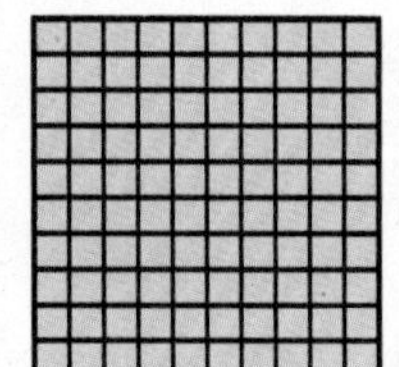 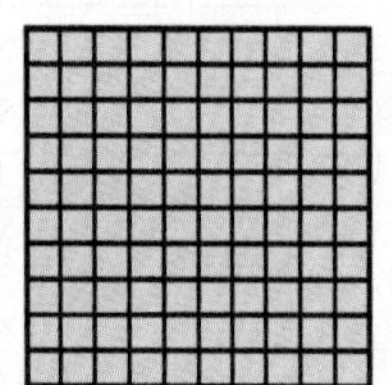 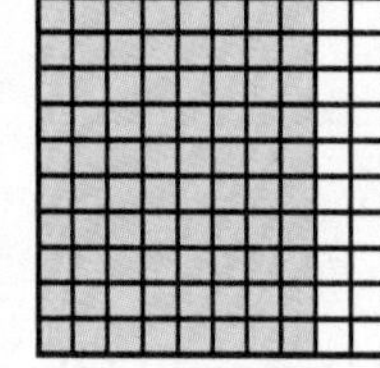

Ⓐ 4.80 Ⓒ 4.08

Ⓑ 3.80 Ⓓ 3.08

10. A quilt is made up of 100 equal squares. There is a star on 35 of the squares. Which decimal represents the part of the quilt with stars?

Ⓐ 35 Ⓒ 1.35

Ⓑ 3.5 Ⓓ 0.35

TEXAS Test Prep

11. Which is the fraction and decimal shown by the model?

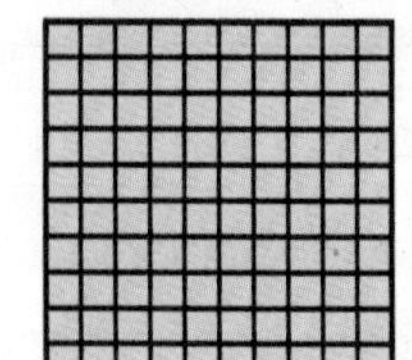 

Ⓐ $12\frac{9}{10}$; 12.9 Ⓒ $1\frac{09}{100}$; 1.09

Ⓑ $1\frac{29}{100}$; 1.29 Ⓓ $2\frac{90}{100}$; 2.90

Name ______________________

2.4 Relate Hundredths and Decimals

1. The fully shaded grid shows 1. **Explain** how these three models are related.

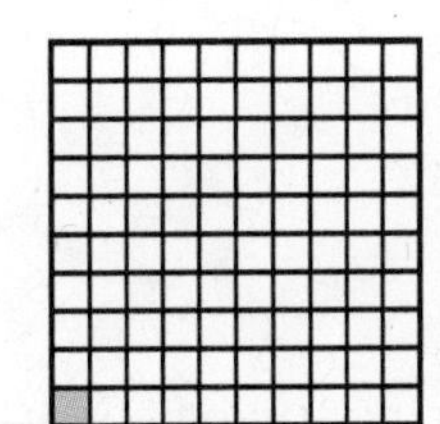
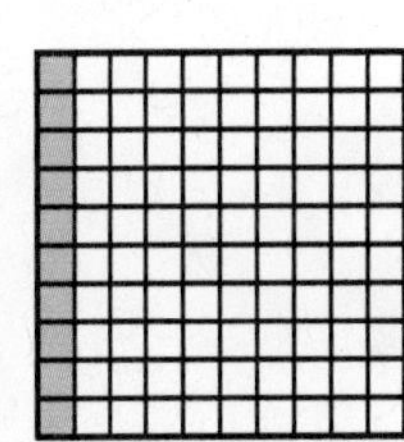
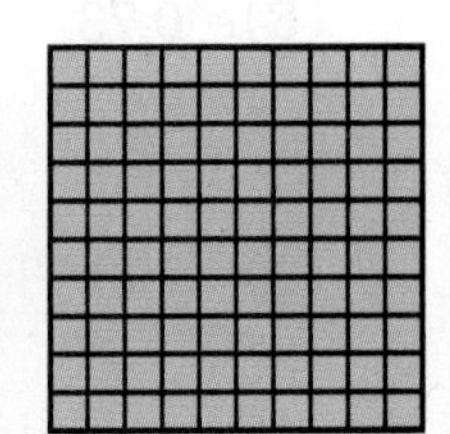

____

____

____

____

Problem Solving Real World

2. Emma and Charles saw this sign along the highway.

Emma said "It is seventy-five hundredths of a mile to Waterslide Park." Charles said, "It is seven and five-tenths miles to Waterslide Park."

Whose statement makes sense? Whose statement is nonsense? Explain your reasoning.

____

____

____

____

____

____

3. Jake said he has $\frac{8}{100}$ of a dollar in his pocket. Margie said that the decimal for $\frac{8}{100}$ is 0.8. What error did she make? What is the decimal form for $\frac{8}{100}$?

____

____

____

____

____

Lesson Check

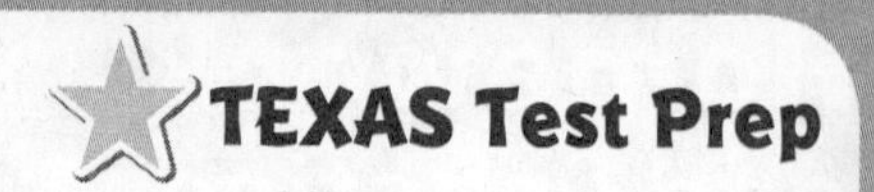

Fill in the bubble completely to show your answer.

4. What is the decimal for $\frac{73}{100}$?

Ⓐ 7.3

Ⓑ 0.73

Ⓒ 73

Ⓓ 100.73

5. A fully shaded grid shows 1. Which is the correct fraction or decimal for this model?

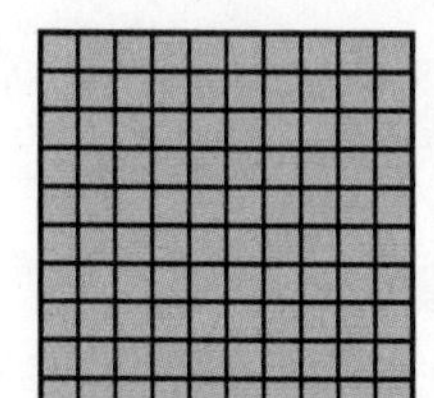 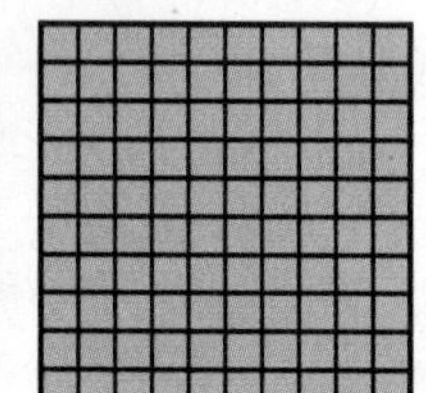 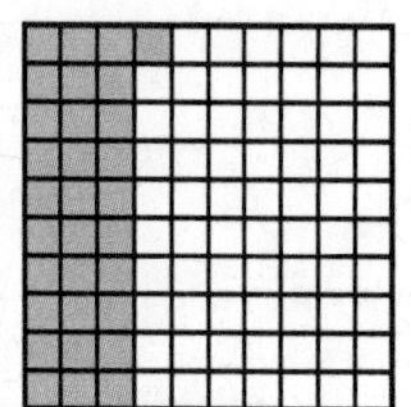

Ⓐ 231

Ⓑ 2.31

Ⓒ $2\frac{3}{100}$

Ⓓ $\frac{231}{10}$

6. Which fraction is marked with a dot on this number line?

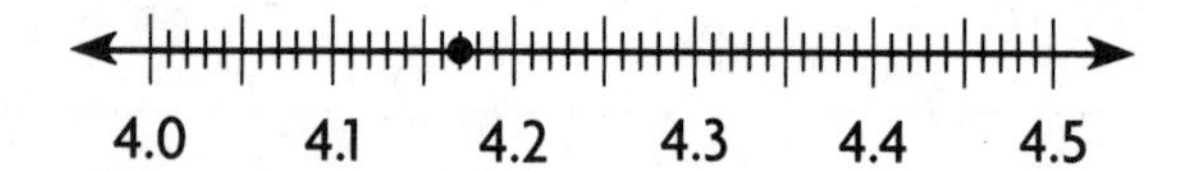

Ⓐ $4\frac{7}{10}$

Ⓑ $4\frac{7}{100}$

Ⓒ $4\frac{17}{100}$

Ⓓ $4\frac{17}{10}$

7. **Multi-Step** A dollar is 100 cents. A quarter is 25 cents. What fraction of a dollar is a quarter?

Ⓐ $\frac{4}{100}$

Ⓑ $\frac{100}{25}$

Ⓒ $\frac{25}{10}$

Ⓓ $\frac{25}{100}$

Name ____________________________

TEKS Number and Operations—4.2.E
Also 4.2.B
MATHEMATICAL PROCESSES
4.1.D, 4.1.E, 4.1.F

2.5 Relate Fractions, Decimals, and Money

Essential Question How can you relate fractions, decimals, and money?

Unlock the Problem Real World

Together, Julie and Sarah have $1.00 in quarters. They want to share the quarters equally. How many quarters should each girl get? How much money is this?

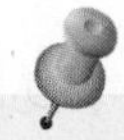

Remember
1 dollar = 100 cents
1 quarter = 25 cents
1 dime = 10 cents
1 penny = 1 cent

Use the model to relate money, fractions, and decimals.

4 quarters = 1 dollar = $1.00

$0.25 $0.25 $0.25 $0.25

1 quarter is $\frac{25}{100}$, or $\frac{1}{4}$ of a dollar.

2 quarters are $\frac{50}{100}$, $\frac{2}{4}$, or $\frac{1}{2}$ of a dollar.

$\frac{1}{2}$ of a dollar = $0.50, or 50 cents.

Circle the number of quarters each girl should get.

So, each girl should get 2 quarters, or $ __________.

Examples Use money to model decimals.

1 dollar

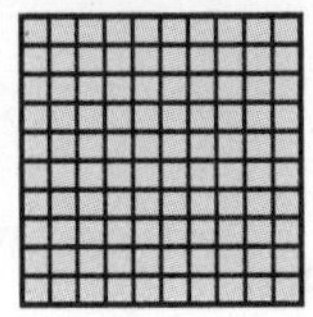

$1.00, or

__________ cents

10 dimes = 1 dollar

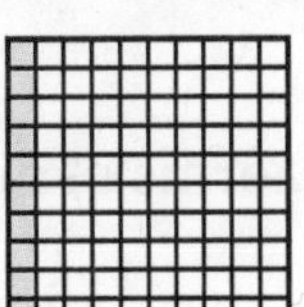

1 dime = $\frac{1}{10}$, or 0.10 of a dollar

$ __________, or 10 cents

100 pennies = 1 dollar

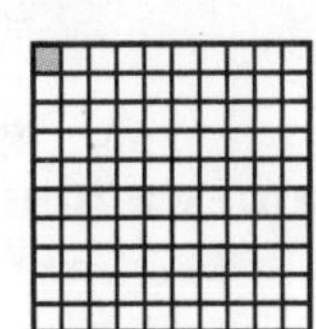

1 penny = $\frac{1}{100}$, or 0.01 of a dollar

$ __________, or 1 cent

Relate Money and Decimals Think of dollars as ones, dimes as tenths, and pennies as hundredths.

$1.56

Dollars	.	Dimes	Pennies
1	.	5	6

Think: $1.56 = 1 dollar and 56 pennies

There are 100 pennies in 1 dollar.
So, $1.56 = 156 pennies.

1.56 dollars

Ones	.	Tenths	Hundredths
1	.	5	6

Think: 1.56 = 1 one and 56 hundredths

There are 100 hundredths in 1 one.
So, 1.56 = 156 hundredths.

Share and Show

1. Write the amount of money as a decimal in terms of dollars.

5 pennies = $\frac{5}{100}$ of a dollar = ____________ of a dollar.

Write the total money amount. Then write the amount as a fraction or a mixed number and as a decimal in terms of dollars.

2.

______ ______ ______

3.

______ ______ ______

Write as a money amount and as a decimal in terms of dollars.

4. $\frac{92}{100}$ ______ ______

5. $\frac{7}{100}$ ______ ______

6. $\frac{16}{100}$ ______ ______

7. $\frac{53}{100}$ ______ ______

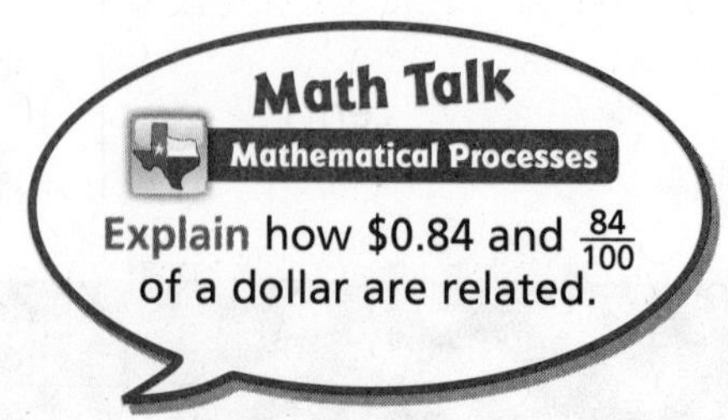

Name ________________________________

Problem Solving Real World

H.O.T. **Algebra** **Complete to tell the value of each digit.**

8. $1.05 = ______ dollar + ______ pennies, 1.05 = ______ one + ______ hundredths

9. $5.18 = ______ dollars + ______ dime + ______ pennies

5.18 = ______ ones + ______ tenth + ______ hundredths

10. Sam has 3 dollar bills, 2 quarters, 3 dimes, and 2 pennies in her pocket. When this amount of money is written in terms of dollars, what is the value of the digit in the tenths place? hundredths place?

____

Use the table for 11–12.

Pocket Change				
Name	**Quarters**	**Dimes**	**Nickels**	**Pennies**
Kim	1	3	2	3
Tony	0	6	1	6
Nick	2	4	0	2

11. **Use Diagrams** The table shows the coins three students have. Write Nick's total amount as a decimal and as a fraction in terms of dollars.

____

12. **H.O.T.** Kim spent $\frac{40}{100}$ of a dollar on a snack. Write as a money amount the amount she has left.

____

13. Jane has 2 dimes, 6 nickels, and 10 pennies in her pocket. What fraction of a dollar does Jane have in her pocket?

____

14. **H.O.T.** **Multi-Step** Travis has $\frac{50}{100}$ of a dollar. He has at least two different types of coins in his pocket. **Draw** two possible sets of coins that Travis could have.

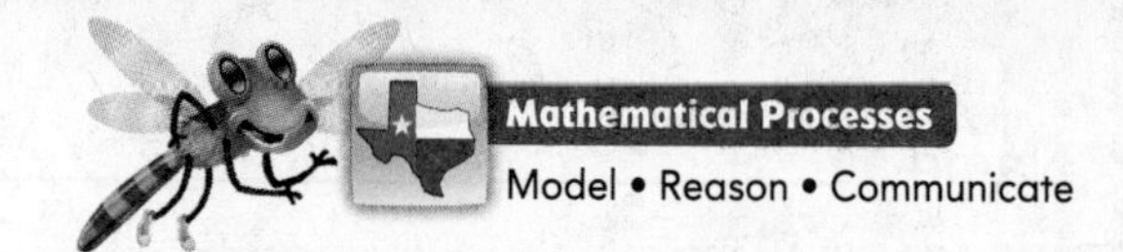

Daily Assessment Task

Fill in the bubble completely to show your answer.

15. The price written on a puzzle at a garage sale is $\frac{85}{100}$. What is this amount written as a decimal in terms of dollars?

Ⓐ 0.85　　Ⓒ 8.5

Ⓑ 8.05　　Ⓓ 85.00

16. The coins below show how much money Debbie gave her brother.

What is the amount written as a decimal in terms of dollars?

Ⓐ 0.70　　Ⓒ 0.72

Ⓑ 0.27　　Ⓓ 7.2

17. David has $0.68 left after buying lunch at school. Which shows the money amount written as a fraction in terms of dollars?

Ⓐ $\frac{68}{10}$　　Ⓒ $\frac{6}{100}$

Ⓑ $\frac{8}{10}$　　Ⓓ $\frac{68}{100}$

TEXAS Test Prep

18. Mia has two dollars and fifteen cents. What decimal names this money amount in terms of dollars?

Ⓐ 2.50　　Ⓒ 21.50

Ⓑ 2.15　　Ⓓ 0.15

TEKS Number and Operations—4.2.E
Also 4.2.B
MATHEMATICAL PROCESSES 4.1.D, 4.1.E, 4.1.F

Name ______________________

2.5 Relate Fractions, Decimals, and Money

Complete to tell the value of each digit.

1. $4.38 = _____ dollars + _____ dimes + _____ pennies

   $4.38 = _____ ones + _____ tenths + _____ hundredths

2. $2.05 = _____ dollars + _____ dimes + _____ pennies

   $2.05 = _____ ones + _____ tenths + _____ hundredths

Write as a money amount and as a decimal in terms of dollars.

3. $\frac{74}{100}$ _____ _____
4. $\frac{31}{100}$ _____ _____
5. $\frac{69}{100}$ _____ _____
6. $\frac{58}{100}$ _____ _____
7. $\frac{83}{100}$ _____ _____
8. $\frac{95}{100}$ _____ _____
9. $\frac{12}{100}$ _____ _____
10. $\frac{26}{100}$ _____ _____

Problem Solving

Use the table for 11–13.

	Quarters	Dimes	Nickels	Pennies
Mike	1	1	2	2
Jeannie	2	2	0	1
Alex	3	1	1	3

11. The table tells the coins three people have. Write Mike's total amount as a decimal and as a fraction in terms of a dollar.

    ____

12. Write Jeannie's total amount. Then write the amount as a fraction of a dollar and as a decimal in terms of dollars.

    ____

13. If Alex spends $\frac{63}{100}$ of a dollar, how much money will he have left?

    ____

Lesson Check

TEXAS Test Prep

Fill in the bubble completely to show your answer.

14. Which shows $0.87 written as a fraction in terms of dollars?

Ⓐ $8\frac{7}{10}$

Ⓑ $8\frac{7}{100}$

Ⓒ $\frac{87}{10}$

Ⓓ $\frac{87}{100}$

15. Write the total value of these coins as a decimal in terms of dollars.

Ⓐ 0.56

Ⓑ 0.056

Ⓒ 5.06

Ⓓ 56

16. Roxanna has $\frac{42}{100}$ of a dollar in change. Which shows the amount of change she has?

Ⓐ $4.20

Ⓑ $42

Ⓒ $0.42

Ⓓ $1.00

17. Jimmy has $\frac{30}{100}$ of a dollar. Which shows this amount in decimal form?

Ⓐ 0.33

Ⓑ 1.03

Ⓒ 1.3

Ⓓ 0.3

18. Multi-Step Jesse has 3 quarters and 4 dimes. If he spends $\frac{1}{2}$ of a dollar, how much money will he have left?

Ⓐ $0.65

Ⓑ $0.50

Ⓒ $0.55

Ⓓ $0.60

19. Multi-Step Jenny has 4 dollar bills, 2 quarters, 1 dime, and 3 pennies. When this amount of money is written as a decimal in terms of dollars, which digit is in tenths place?

Ⓐ 3

Ⓑ 6

Ⓒ 4

Ⓓ 5

Name ______________________________

2.6 Compare Decimals

TEKS Number and Operations—4.2.F

MATHEMATICAL PROCESSES 4.1.D, 4.1.F

Essential Question How can you compare decimals?

Unlock the Problem (Real World)

The city park covers 0.64 square mile. About 0.18 of the park is covered by water, and about 0.2 of the park is covered by paved walkways. Is more of the park covered by water or paved walkways?

- Cross out unnecessary information.
- Circle numbers you will use.
- What do you need to find?

____

____

One Way Use a model.

Shade 0.18. Shade 0.2.

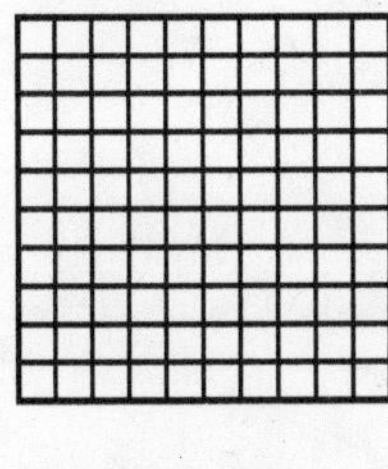
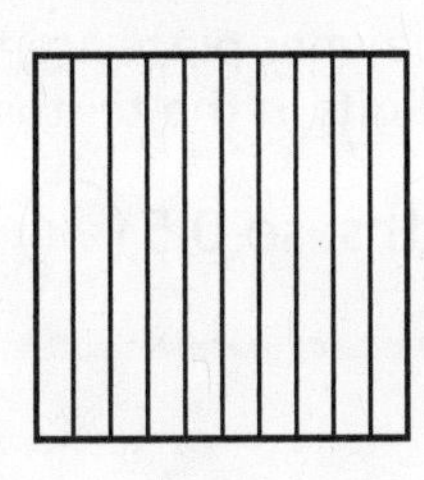

0.18 ◯ 0.2

Other Ways

A **Use a number line.**

Locate 0.18 and 0.2 on a number line.

Think: 2 tenths is equivalent to 20 hundredths.

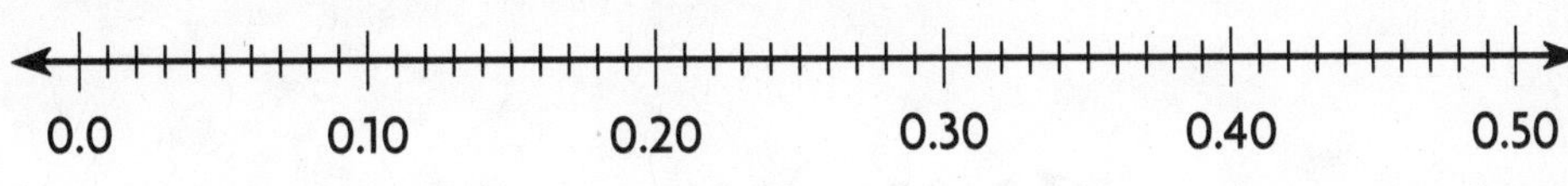

_____ is closer to 0, so 0.18 ◯ 0.2.

B **Compare equal-size parts.**

- 0.18 is _____ hundredths.
- 0.2 is 2 tenths, which is equivalent to _____ hundredths.

18 hundredths ◯ 20 hundredths, so 0.18 ◯ 0.2.

So, more of the park is covered by ______________.

Math Talk Mathematical Processes

How does the number of tenths in 0.18 compare to the number of tenths in 0.2? **Explain.**

Place Value You can compare numbers written as decimals by using place value. Comparing decimals is like comparing whole numbers. Always compare the digits in the greatest place-value position first.

Example Use place value.

Tim has 0.5 dollar and Sienna has 0.05 dollar. Who has more money?

MODEL

Tim

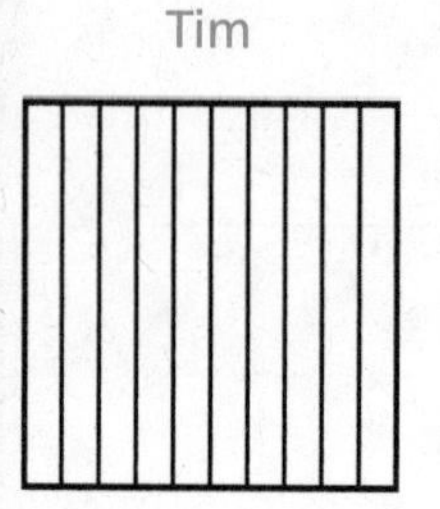

Sienna

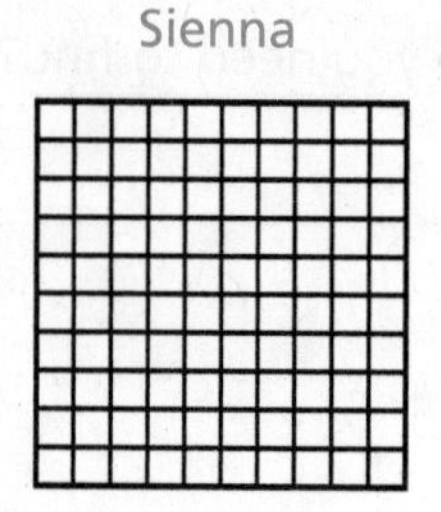

So, ______ has more money.

RECORD

Ones	.	Tenths	Hundredths	
	.			← Tim
	.			← Sienna

Think: The digits in the ones place are the same. Compare the digits in the tenths place.

5 tenths ◯ 0 tenths, so 0.5 ◯ 0.05.

Share and Show

1. Compare 0.39 and 0.42. Write <, >, or =. Shade the model to help.

0.39 ◯ 0.42

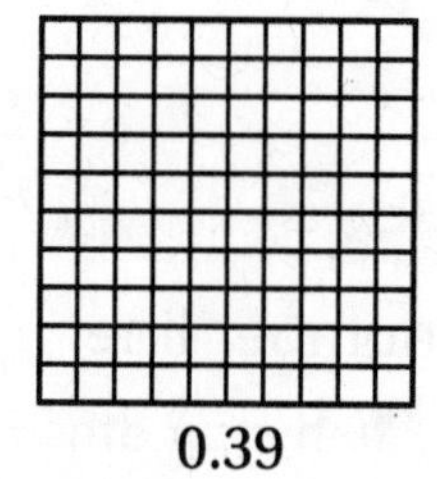

0.39

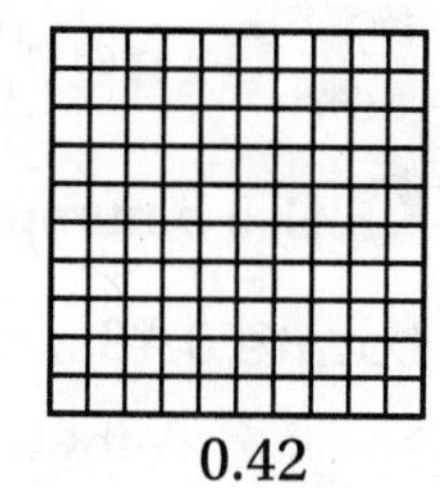

0.42

Compare. Write <, >, or =.

2. 4.5 ◯ 2.89

Ones	.	Tenths	Hundredths
	.		
	.		

3. 0.7 ◯ 0.54

Ones	.	Tenths	Hundredths
	.		
	.		

Math Talk

Mathematical Processes

Can you compare 0.39 and 0.42 by comparing only the tenths? **Explain.**

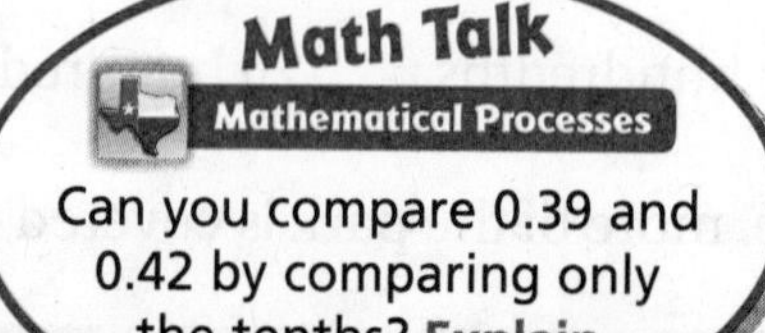

Name ______________________________

Unlock the Problem (Real World)

4. H.O.T. **Multi-Step** Ricardo and Brandon ran a 1500-meter race. Ricardo finished in 4.89 minutes. Brandon finished in 4.83 minutes. What was the time of the runner who finished first?

Ⓐ 15.00 minutes
Ⓑ 4.83 minutes
Ⓒ 4.89 minutes
Ⓓ Ricardo and Brandon tied for first.

a. What are you asked to find? ______________________________

____

b. What do you need to do to find the answer? ______________________________

____

c. Solve the problem.

d. Fill in the bubble for the correct answer choice above.

e. Look back. Does your answer make sense? Explain.

____

____

____

____

____

____

5. H.O.T. **Multi-Step** Jack had $14.53 in his pocket. Sam had $14.25 in his pocket. Jill had $14.40 in her pocket. Who had more money, Jack or Jill? Did Sam have more money than either Jack or Jill?

____

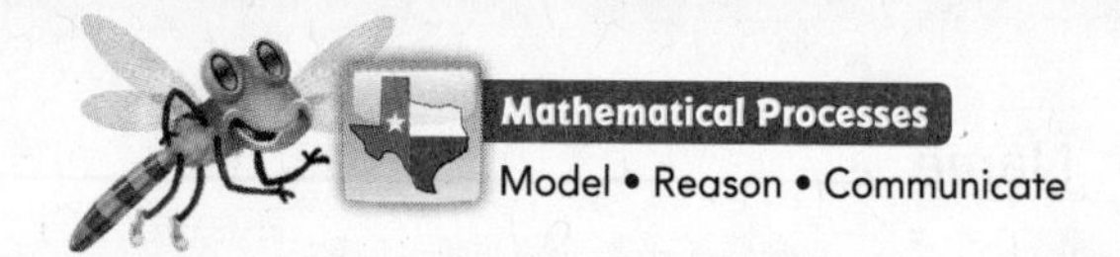

Daily Assessment Task

Fill in the bubble completely to show your answer.

6. **Multi-Step** The Venus flytrap closes in 0.3 second and the waterwheel plant closes in 0.2 second. Which decimal is less than 0.3 but greater than 0.2?

Ⓐ 0.01 Ⓒ 0.21

Ⓑ 0.32 Ⓓ 0.4

7. **Representations** Which model represents a number greater than 0.65?

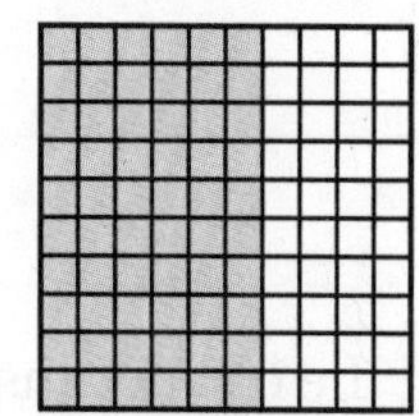

Ⓒ
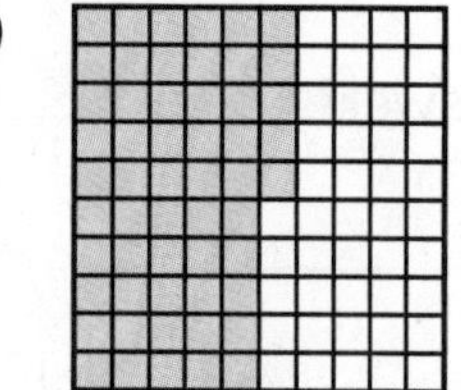

Ⓑ
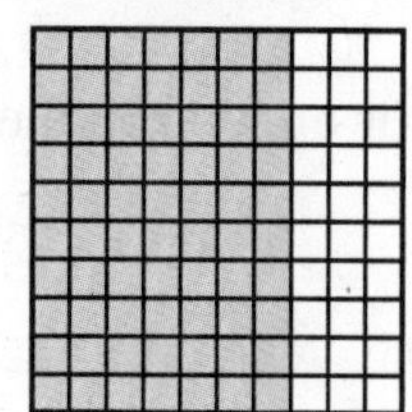

Ⓓ
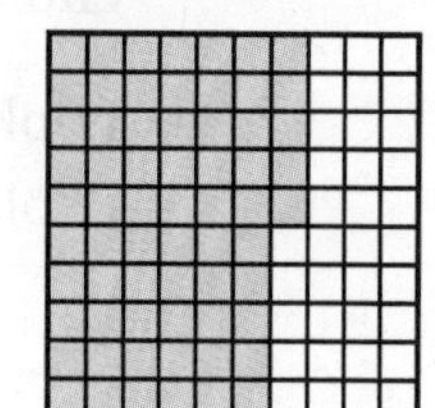

8. **Use Symbols** Compare 0.24 and 0.3. Which statement is true?

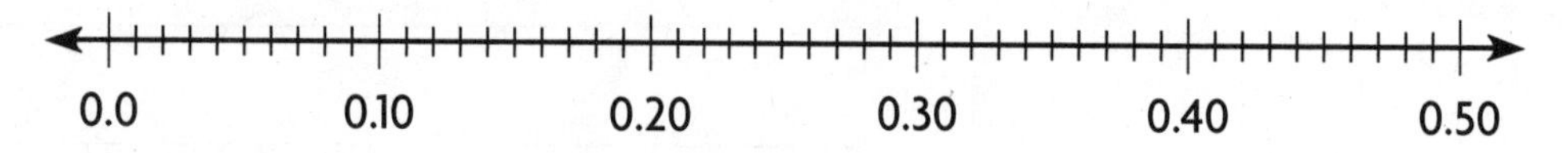

Ⓐ $0.24 > 0.3$ Ⓒ $0.3 < 0.24$

Ⓑ $0.24 = 0.3$ Ⓓ $0.24 < 0.3$

TEXAS Test Prep

9. Maria has $3.68 in her pocket. Dennis has less money in his pocket than Maria does. Which could be an amount that Dennis has in his pocket?

Ⓐ $3.60 Ⓒ $7.38

Ⓑ $3.78 Ⓓ $13.24

Name ______________________

2.6 Compare Decimals

Compare. Write <, >, or =. For 1–2, complete the table.

1. 0.26 ◯ 0.23

Ones	.	Tenths	Hundredths
	.		
	.		

2. 1.15 ◯ 1.3

Ones	.	Tenths	Hundredths
	.		
	.		

3. 0.9 ◯ 0.81

4. 1.06 ◯ 0.6

5. 0.25 ◯ 0.3

6. 2.61 ◯ 3.29

7. 0.38 ◯ 0.83

8. 1.9 ◯ 0.99

9. 1.11 ◯ 1.41

10. 0.8 ◯ 0.80

Problem Solving Real World

11. Neil and Anne each bought a book at a used book store. Neil paid $5.37 for his book. Anne paid $5.32 for her book. Who spent more money?

____

12. Lynn drove 14.06 miles to the store. Patrick drove 14.6 miles to the library. Who drove farther?

____

13. Barbara has $3.43 in her pocket. Kendra has $3.34 in her bank. Who has the greater amount of money?

____

14. Jordan and Shelly were raising money by walking around a track. Jordan raised $47.50 and Shelly raised $45.50. Who raised more money?

____

Lesson Check

TEXAS Test Prep

Fill in the bubble completely to show your answer.

15. Which model represents a number less than 0.27?

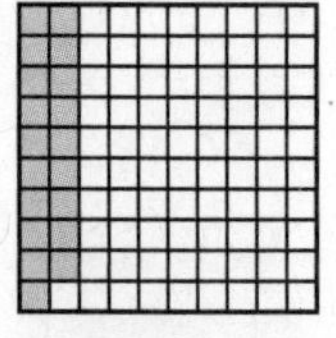

Ⓑ

Ⓒ

16. Compare 0.3 and 0.28. Which statement is true?

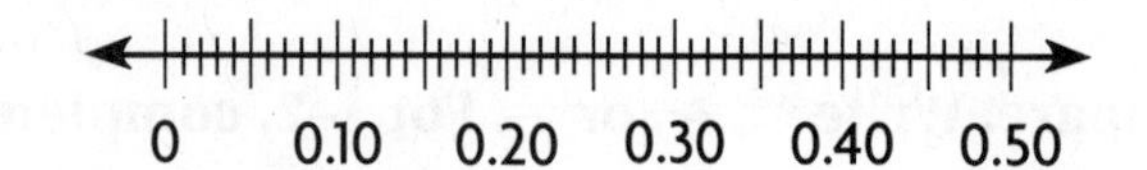

Ⓐ $0.3 > 0.28$

Ⓑ $0.28 = 0.3$

Ⓒ $0.28 > 0.3$

Ⓓ $0.3 < 0.28$

17. Jake's time for the 100 meter race was 11.46 seconds. Dan's time was faster. Which could be Dan's time?

Ⓐ 11.55 seconds

Ⓑ 11.73 seconds

Ⓒ 11.38 seconds

Ⓓ 11.49 seconds

18. Which of the following is less than 19.45?

Ⓐ 19.54

Ⓑ 19.44

Ⓒ 20.64

Ⓓ 20.53

19. **Multi-Step** Which of the following is more than \$4.72 and less than \$4.93?

Ⓐ \$4.81

Ⓑ \$3.99

Ⓒ \$4.68

Ⓓ \$3.89

20. **Multi-Step** Wayne has \$6.83. Christie has \$6.55. Kareem has \$6.79. Which statement is true?

Ⓐ Kareem has the least money.

Ⓑ Christie has more money than Kareem.

Ⓒ Wayne has less money than Christie.

Ⓓ Wayne has the most money.

Name ____________________

2.7 Order Decimals

TEKS Number and Operations—4.2.F
MATHEMATICAL PROCESSES 4.1.D, 4.1.F

Essential Question How can you order decimals?

Investigate

Materials ■ string ■ clothespins ■ marker ■ index cards

Order 1.2, 1.9, and 1.6 from least to greatest.

A. Use your marker to mark the location of benchmark decimals 1.0, 1.5, and 2.0 on your string.

B. Use clothespins and index cards to label the points you marked.

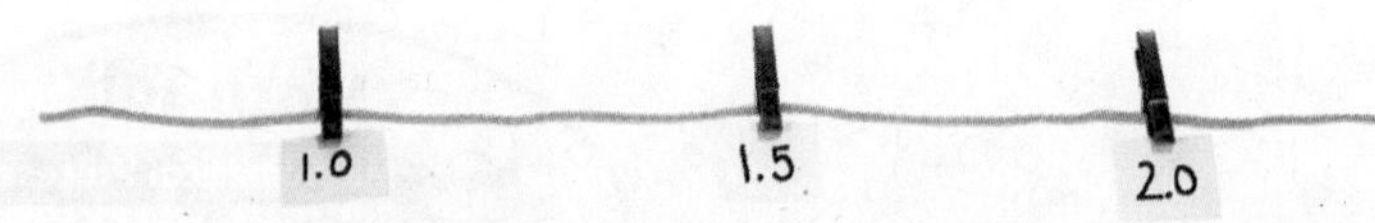

C. Now locate the points 1.2, 1.9, and 1.6 on your string by using clothespins and labeled index cards.

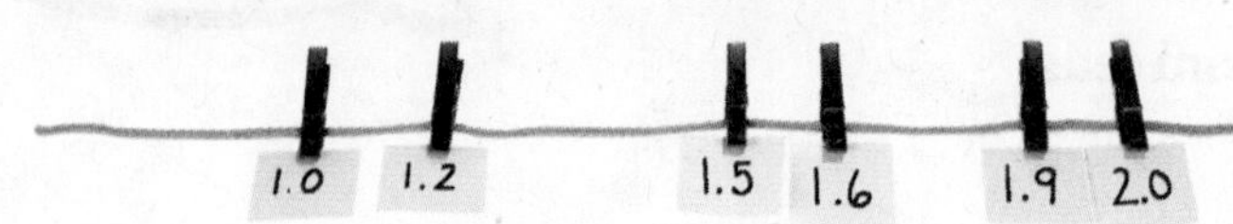

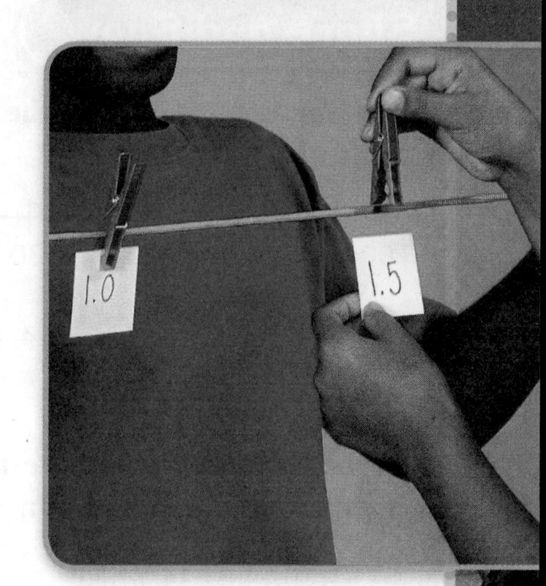

D. Draw a picture of the number line you modeled.

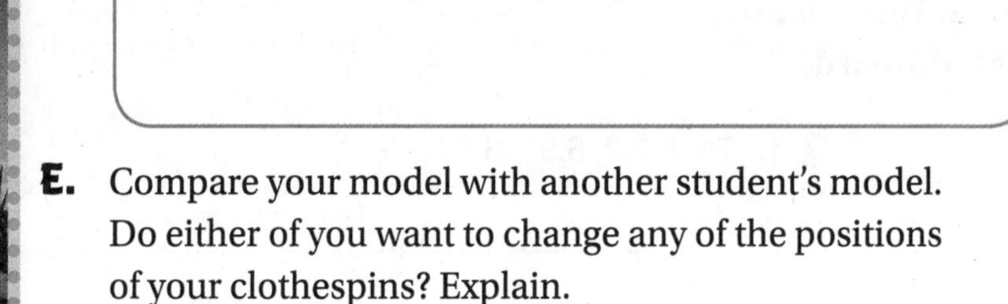

E. Compare your model with another student's model. Do either of you want to change any of the positions of your clothespins? Explain.

____

____

Make Connections

You can also use place value to order decimals.

Order $1.52, $0.87, and $1.56 from least to greatest.

STEP 1

Line up the decimal places.

Think: Compare the digits in the greatest place.

$1.52
↓ 0 < 1
$0.87
↓
$1.56

Since 0 < 1, ______ is the least.

STEP 2

Compare the tenths in the remaining decimals.

$1.52
↓ 5 = 5
$1.56

There is the same number of tenths.

STEP 3

Compare the hundredths in the remaining decimals.

$1.52
↓ 2 < 6
$1.56

Since 2 < 6, ______ is the greatest.

So, the order from least to greatest is

______, ______, ______.

Math Talk Mathematical Processes

How is ordering decimals similar to comparing decimals?

Share and Show

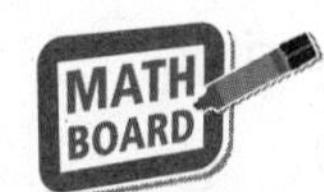

Use the number line to order the decimals from least to greatest.

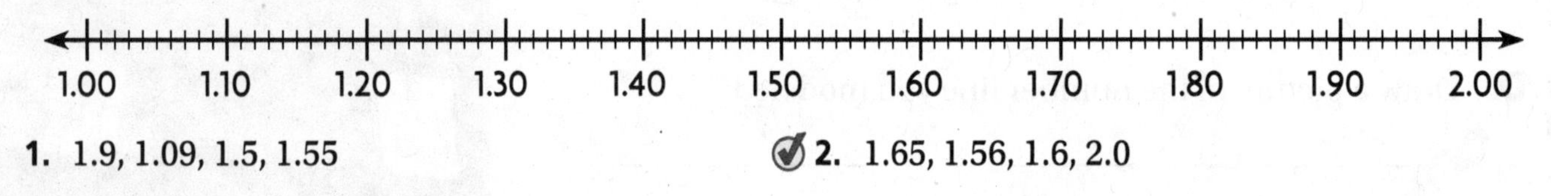

1. 1.9, 1.09, 1.5, 1.55

______

2. 1.65, 1.56, 1.6, 2.0

______

Order the decimals from greatest to least. You can use place value or a number line on your MathBoard.

3. $1.41, $0.14, $1.14, $1.40

______

4. 7.03, 7.3, 6.98, 6.89

______

Order the decimals from least to greatest. You can use place value or a number line on your MathBoard.

5. $1.35, $3.15, $1.53, $3.51

______

6. 6.25, 7.2, 6.93, 7.11

______

Name ______________________

Unlock the Problem

7. H.O.T. **Multi-Step** Martin's class drew a design using 10 by 10 grid paper. The table shows how much of each color was used in the design. Which color was the third-greatest part of the design?

Class Design

Color	Part of Design
Blue	0.28
Green	$\frac{2}{5}$
Purple	$\frac{1}{10}$
Orange	0.15
Yellow	0.07

a. What do you need to know?

____

____

b. Describe a strategy you could use to order the values in the table.

____

____

c. How might you use models to help you? ______________________

____

____

d. Show your work.

e. Complete the sentences.

The greatest part of the design was the color ____________.

The least part of the design was the color ____________.

The third-greatest part of the design was the color ____________.

8. H.O.T. **Use Symbols** Howard studied math for 0.75 hour. Carol studied math for 0.80 hour. Who studied math for the greater amount of time? **Explain.**

____

9. Mark has $3.23, Jen has $3.23, and Sally has $3.32. Who has the most money?

____

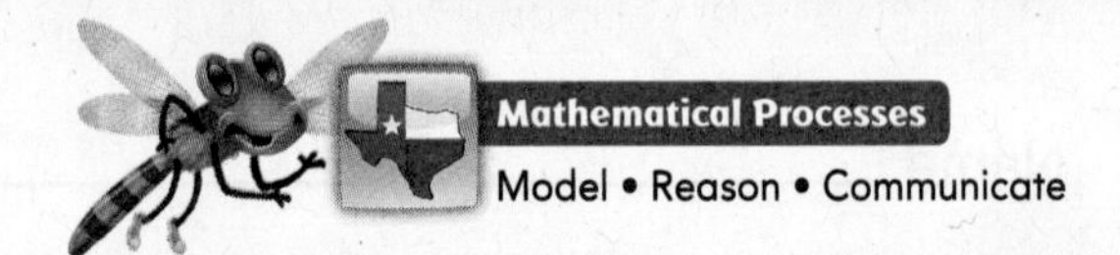

Daily Assessment Task

Fill in the bubble completely to show your answer.

10. Four cockroaches finished a race. Their winning times are 9.42 seconds, 8.3 seconds, 9.2 seconds, and 8.17 seconds. Which shows the winning times written in order from least to greatest?

Ⓐ 8.17 seconds, 8.3 seconds, 9.42 seconds, 9.2 seconds

Ⓑ 9.42 seconds, 9.2 seconds, 8.3 seconds, 8.17 seconds

Ⓒ 8.17 seconds, 8.3 seconds, 9.2 seconds, 9.42 seconds

Ⓓ 9.42 seconds, 8.3 seconds, 9.2 seconds, 8.17 seconds

11. Use place value to order 5.87, 6.14, 5.78, and 6.04. Which shows the decimals written in order from least to greatest?

Ⓐ 6.04, 6.14, 5.87, 5.78

Ⓑ 5.78, 5.87, 6.04, 6.14

Ⓒ 5.78, 5.87, 6.14, 6.04

Ⓓ 5.87, 6.04, 6.14, 5.78

12. **Representations** Use the number line to order the decimals.

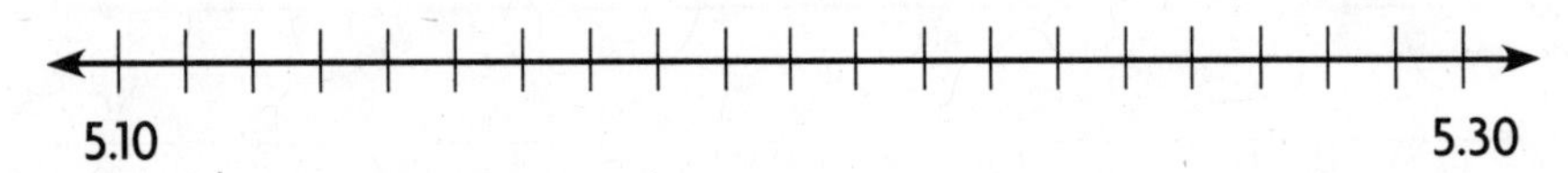

Which shows the decimals 5.16, 5.28, 5.11, and 5.21 written in order from greatest to least?

Ⓐ 5.11, 5.16, 5.21, 5.28

Ⓑ 5.16, 5.28, 5.11, 5.21

Ⓒ 5.21, 5.16, 5.11, 5.28

Ⓓ 5.28, 5.21, 5.16, 5.11

TEXAS Test Prep

13. Which of the following is less than 14.70?

Ⓐ 15.03

Ⓑ 14.09

Ⓒ 14.73

Ⓓ 14.7

Homework and Practice

TEKS Number and Operations—4.2.F
MATHEMATICAL PROCESSES 4.1.D, 4.1.F

Name ____________________

2.7 Order Decimals

Use the number line to order the decimals from least to greatest.

1. 1.11, 1.2, 1.01, 1.1

____

2. 1.32, 1.23, 1.3, 1.2

____

Order the decimals from greatest to least. You can use place value or a number line on your MathBoard.

3. \$2.15, \$1.89, \$1.09, \$1.90

____

4. 0.66, 0.06, 0.60, 0.96

____

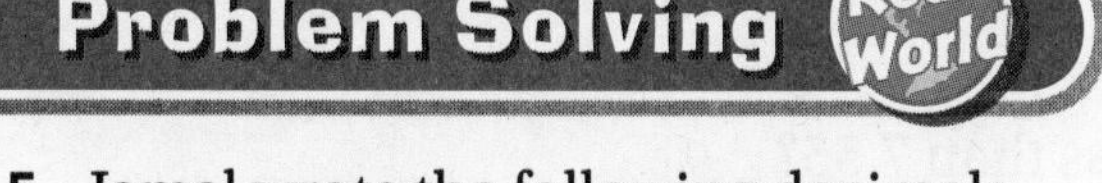

5. Jamal wrote the following decimals on the board.

4.24, 4.04, 4.18, 4.42

Order these decimals from least to greatest.

____

6. Anna paid \$13.32 for a teddy bear. Karl paid \$13.02 for a teddy bear. Cindy paid \$12.45 for her teddy bear and Mark paid \$14.50 for his teddy bear. Order the names from who spent the least to who spent the greatest for their teddy bear.

____

7. During recess, some students ran the 40-yard dash. Tim ran it in 5.64 seconds, Sarah in 5.46 seconds, Hannah in 5.60 seconds, and Jason in 5.49 seconds. Order the times from least to greatest.

____

8. Karen made four different hats. She used some blue ribbon for each hat. For one hat, she used 0.8 foot of ribbon. For another hat, she used 1.2 feet of ribbon. For the last two hats, she used 1.02 and 1.21 feet of ribbon. Order these amounts from greatest to least.

____

Lesson Check

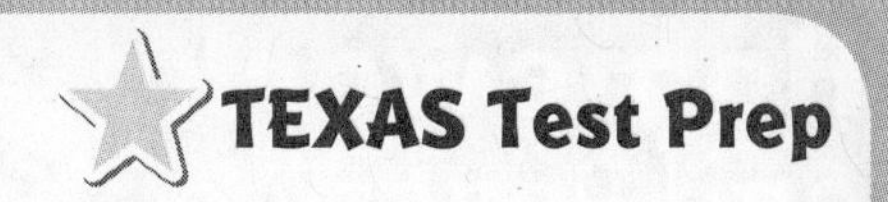

Fill in the bubble completely to show your answer.

9. Use the number line to order the decimals.

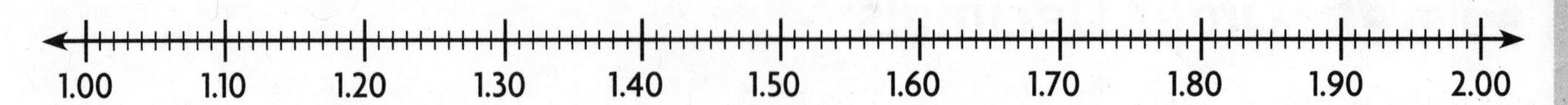

Which answer shows 1.31, 1.13, 1.3, and 1.1 in order from least to greatest?

Ⓐ 1.1, 1.3, 1.13, 1.31

Ⓑ 1.1, 1.13, 1.3, 1.31

Ⓒ 1.13, 1.1, 1.31, 1.3

Ⓓ 1.13, 1.31, 1.1, 1.3

10. Order these amounts of money from least to greatest.
$4.88, $5.19, $4.83, $5.02

Ⓐ $4.88, $4.83, $5.02, $5.19

Ⓑ $5.19, $5.02, $4.88, $4.83

Ⓒ $4.83, $4.88, $5.02, $5.19

Ⓓ $5.02, $5.19, $4.83, $4.88

11. Multi-Step Which number is greater than 7.23 and less than 7.55?

Ⓐ 7.59

Ⓑ 7.17

Ⓒ 7.6

Ⓓ 7.3

12. Multi-Step Cory, Margo, and Alyssa get the same allowance. Cory saved $\frac{2}{5}$ of his allowance. Margo saved 0.35 of hers. Alyssa saved 0.3 of hers. Which statement is true?

Ⓐ Cory saved the most.

Ⓑ Alyssa saved more than Margo.

Ⓒ Cory and Alyssa saved the same amount.

Ⓓ Margo saved more than Cory.

Name ______________________________

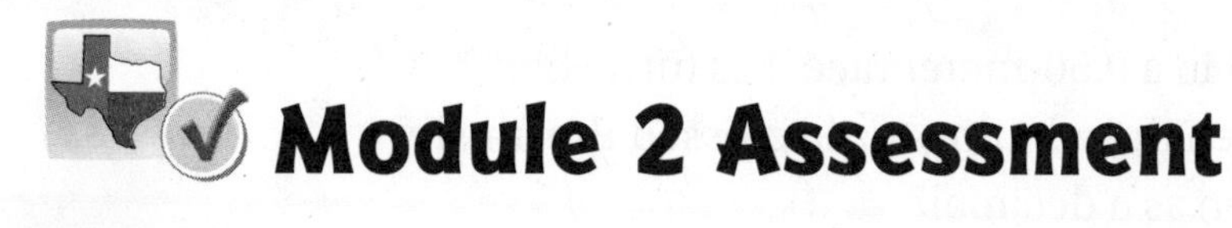

Module 2 Assessment

Vocabulary

Choose the best term from the box to complete the sentence.

Vocabulary
decimal
decimal point
hundred
hundredth

1. A symbol used to separate the ones and the tenths place is called a ________________. (p. 43)
2. The number 0.4 is written as a ____________. (p. 43)
3. A ____________ is one of one hundred equal parts of a whole. (p. 49)

Concepts and Skills

Complete the sentence. TEKS 4.2.A

4. 0.04 is $\frac{1}{10}$ of ____________
5. 0.6 is 10 times as much as ____________

Write the number in two other ways. TEKS 4.2.B

6. 2.0 + 0.5 + 0.04 ____________________
7. twelve hundredths ____________________

Write the fraction or mixed number and the decimal shown by the model. TEKS 4.2.E

8. 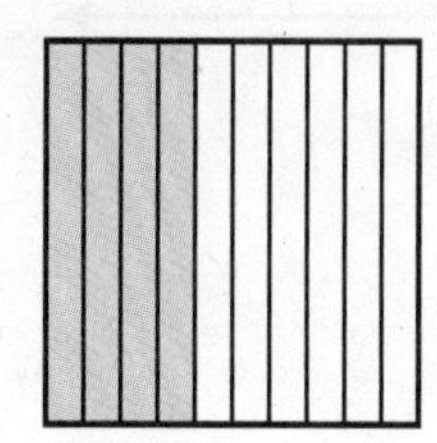

____________ ____________

9. 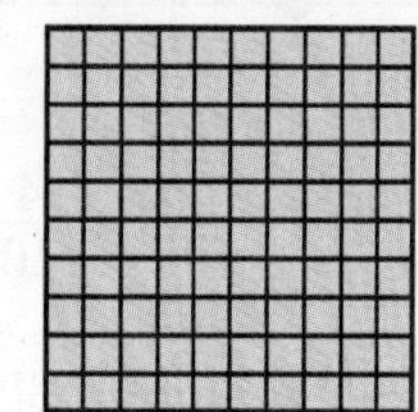

____________ ____________

Use the number line to order the decimals from least to greatest. TEKS 4.2.F

10. 1.18, 1.21, 1.05, 1.2 ____________________
11. 1.43, 1.34, 1.4, 1.3 ____________________

Fill in the bubble completely to show your answer.

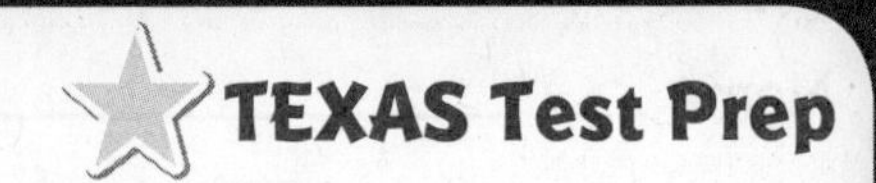

12. Ken's turtle competed in a 0.50-meter race. His turtle had traveled $\frac{49}{100}$ meter when the winning turtle crossed the finish line. What is $\frac{49}{100}$ written as a decimal? TEKS 4.2.G

Ⓐ 0.09 Ⓑ 0.49 Ⓒ 0.40 Ⓓ 4.90

13. Alex lives eight tenths mile from Sarah. What is eight tenths written as a decimal? TEKS 4.2.G

Ⓐ 8.0 Ⓑ 80.0 Ⓒ 0.8 Ⓓ 0.08

14. Which shows the decimals in order from greatest to least? You can use place value or a number line on your MathBoard. TEKS 4.2.F

Ⓐ 4.67, 4.56, 4.55, 4.6

Ⓑ 4.67, 4.6, 4.56, 4.55

Ⓒ 4.55, 4.6, 4.67, 4.56

Ⓓ 4.6, 4.55, 4.56, 4.67

15. Elaine found the following in her pocket. How much money was in Elaine's pocket? TEKS 4.2.E

Ⓐ \$1.45 Ⓑ \$1.30 Ⓒ \$1.40 Ⓓ \$1.04

16. Which fraction and decimal is shown by the point on the number line? TEKS 4.2.H

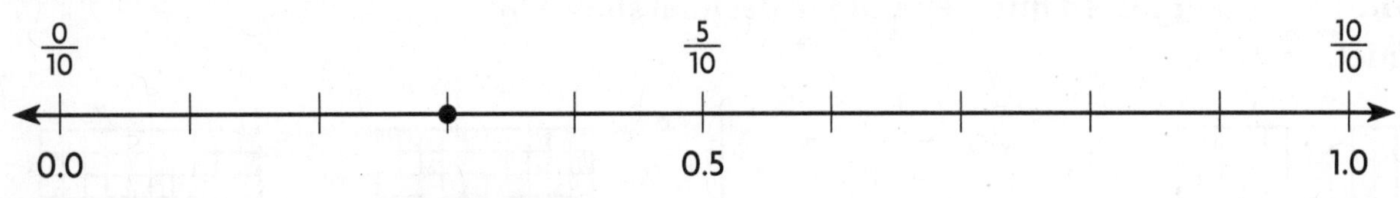

Ⓐ $\frac{1}{10}$; 0.1 Ⓑ $\frac{7}{10}$; 0.7 Ⓒ $\frac{4}{10}$; 0.4 Ⓓ $\frac{3}{10}$; 0.3

17. Which fraction and decimal is shown by the point on the number line? TEKS 4.2.H

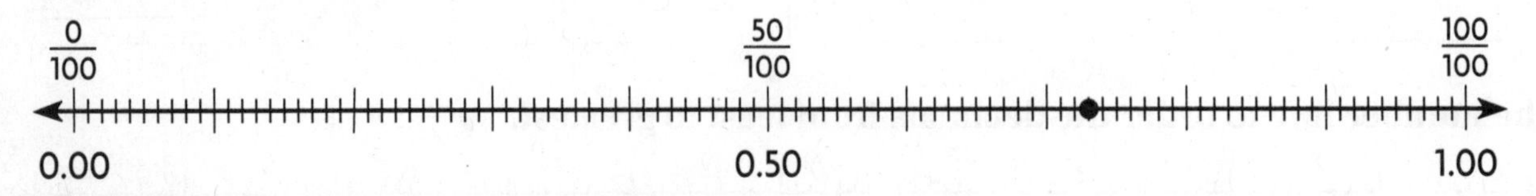

Ⓐ $\frac{57}{100}$; 0.57

Ⓑ $\frac{73}{100}$; 0.73

Ⓒ $\frac{86}{100}$; 0.86

Ⓓ $\frac{37}{100}$; 0.37

Name ______________________________

3.1 Equivalent Fractions

TEKS Number and Operations—4.3.C
MATHEMATICAL PROCESSES 4.1.A, 4.1.C, 4.1.D

Essential Question How can you use models to show equivalent fractions?

Investigate

Materials ■ color pencils

Joe cut a pan of brownies into third-size pieces. He kept $\frac{1}{3}$ and gave the rest away. Joe will not eat his part all at once. How can he cut his part into smaller, equal-size pieces?

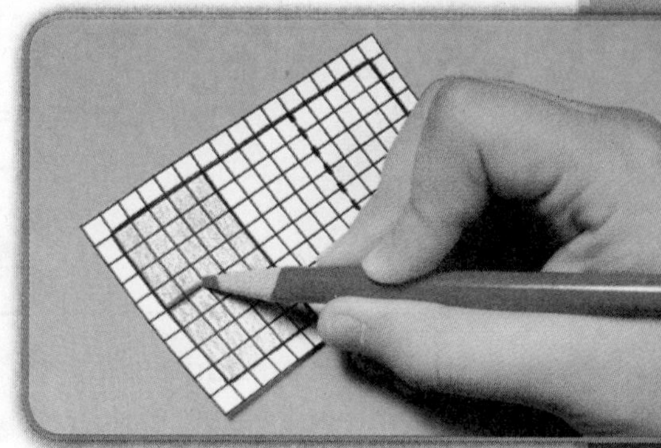

A. Draw on the model to show how Joe could cut his part of the brownies into 2 equal pieces.

You can rename these 2 equal pieces as a fraction of the original pan of brownies.

Suppose Joe had cut the original pan of brownies into equal pieces of this size.

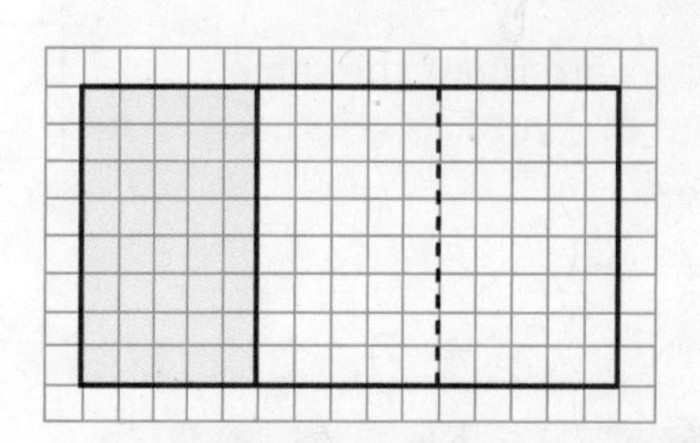

How many pieces would there be? ______

What fraction of the pan is 1 piece? ______

What fraction of the pan is 2 pieces? ______

You can rename $\frac{1}{3}$ as ______.

B. Now draw on the model to show how Joe could cut his part of the brownies into 4 equal pieces.

You can rename these 4 equal pieces as a fraction of the original pan of brownies.

Suppose Joe had cut the original pan of brownies into equal pieces of this size.

How many pieces would there be? ______

What fraction of the pan is 1 piece? ______

What fraction of the pan is 4 pieces? ______

You can rename $\frac{1}{3}$ as ______.

C. Fractions that name the same amount are **equivalent fractions**. Write the equivalent fractions.

$\frac{1}{3}$ = ―― = ――

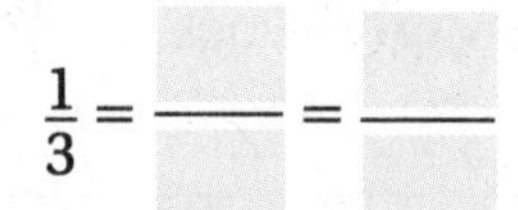

Make Connections

Savannah has $\frac{2}{4}$ yard of ribbon, and Lin has $\frac{3}{8}$ yard of ribbon. How can you determine whether Savannah and Lin have the same length of ribbon?

The equal sign (=) and not equal to sign (≠) show whether fractions are equivalent.

Tell whether $\frac{2}{4}$ and $\frac{3}{8}$ are equivalent. Write = or ≠.

STEP 1 Shade the amount of ribbon Savannah has.

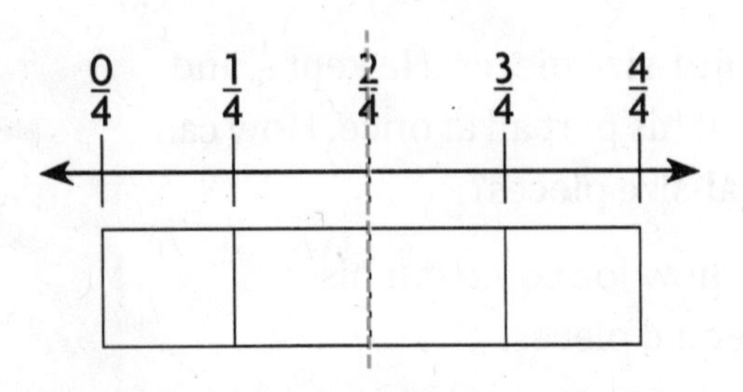

STEP 2 Shade the amount of ribbon Lin has.

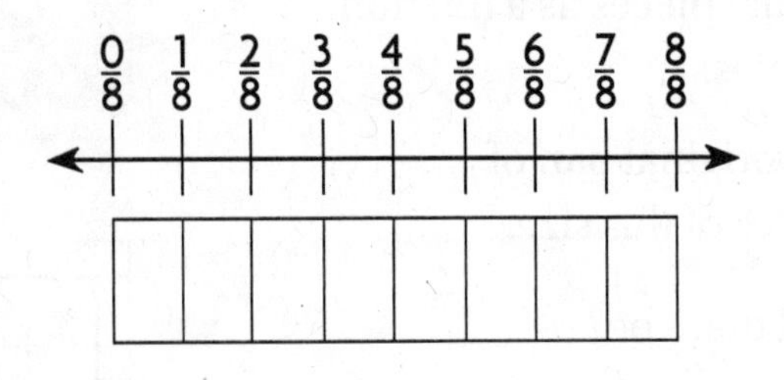

Math Talk

Mathematical Processes

How could you use a model to show that $\frac{4}{8} = \frac{1}{2}$?

Think: $\frac{2}{4}$ yard is not the same amount as $\frac{3}{8}$ yard.

So, $\frac{2}{4}$ ◯ $\frac{3}{8}$.

Share and Show

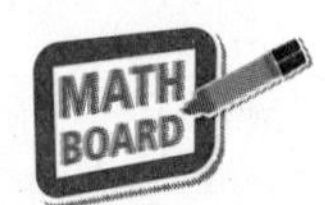

Use the model to write an equivalent fraction.

1\.

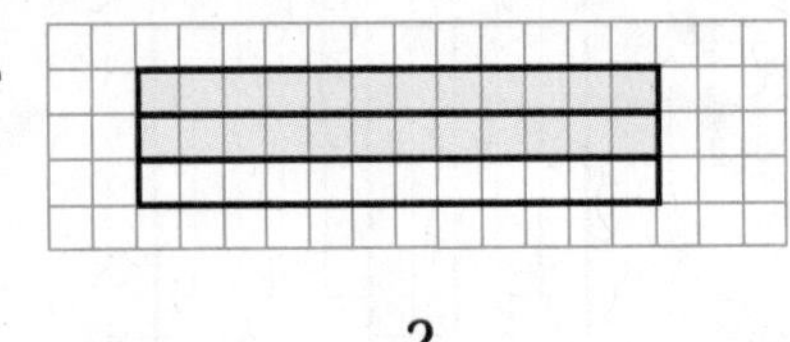

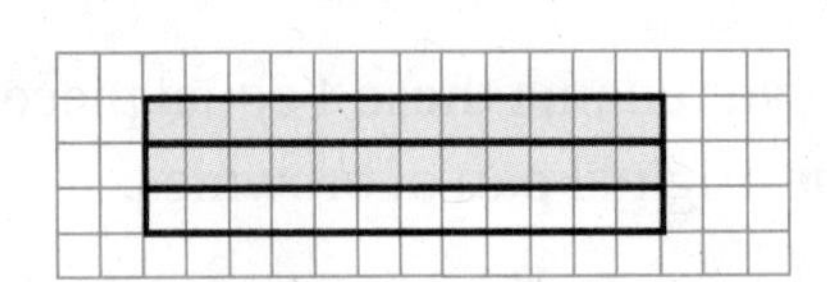

$\frac{2}{3}$ = ______

Tell whether the fractions are equivalent. Write = or ≠.

2\. $\frac{5}{8}$ ◯ $\frac{2}{4}$

3\. $\frac{5}{6}$ ◯ $\frac{10}{12}$

4\. $\frac{1}{2}$ ◯ $\frac{5}{10}$

5\. **H.O.T.** **Apply** Does $\frac{1}{3} = \frac{3}{9}$? Explain.

______

______

Name ________________________________

Problem Solving Real World

H.O.T. What's the Error?

6. **Reasoning** Ben brought two pizzas to a party. He says that since $\frac{1}{4}$ of each pizza is left, the same amount of each pizza is left. What is his error?

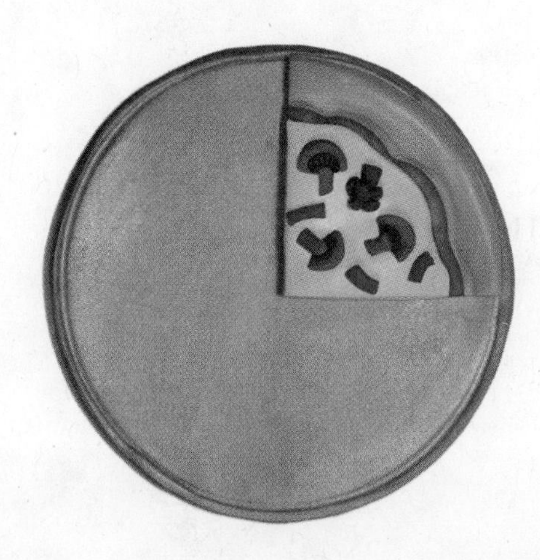

Describe Ben's error.

Draw models of 2 pizzas with a different number of equal pieces. Use shading to show $\frac{1}{4}$ of each pizza.

7. **H.O.T.** Tia had $\frac{3}{4}$ of her homework done. Maxwell had $\frac{7}{12}$ of his homework done. Had they done the same amount of homework? **Explain.**

____

____

8. **Multi-Step** Liu ran $\frac{2}{3}$ of a mile, Toby ran $\frac{3}{4}$ of a mile, and Raul ran $\frac{8}{12}$ of a mile. Who of the three ran the same distance?

____

____

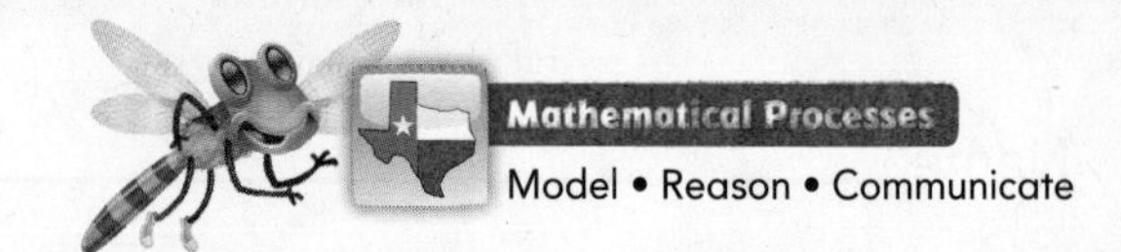

Daily Assessment Task

Fill in the bubble completely to show your answer.

9. Students in Beth's class made a sidewalk drawing on $\frac{1}{6}$ of a sidewalk. Jim's class made a drawing on an equivalent amount of another sidewalk. What fraction could be the amount of sidewalk Jim's class drew on?

Ⓐ $\frac{1}{12}$ Ⓒ $\frac{3}{4}$

Ⓑ $\frac{1}{3}$ Ⓓ $\frac{2}{12}$

10. **Use Diagrams** The dough recipe used $\frac{2}{5}$ cup of flour. Use the model. Which fraction is equivalent to $\frac{2}{5}$?

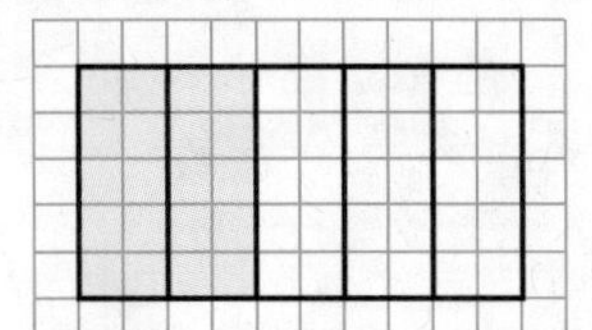
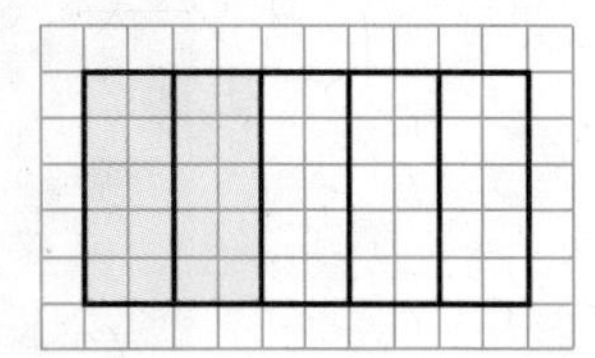

Ⓐ $\frac{2}{10}$ Ⓒ $\frac{2}{4}$

Ⓑ $\frac{4}{10}$ Ⓓ $\frac{4}{5}$

11. Jon ate $\frac{2}{8}$ of a veggie pizza. Laura ate an equivalent amount of a cheese pizza. Which fraction could be the amount of cheese pizza that Laura ate?

Ⓐ $\frac{1}{4}$ Ⓒ $\frac{1}{8}$

Ⓑ $\frac{2}{4}$ Ⓓ $\frac{2}{12}$

TEXAS Test Prep

12. Which fraction is equivalent to $\frac{3}{5}$?

Ⓐ $\frac{6}{8}$ Ⓒ $\frac{5}{10}$

Ⓑ $\frac{5}{3}$ Ⓓ $\frac{6}{10}$

Homework and Practice

TEKS Number and Operations—4.3.C
MATHEMATICAL PROCESSES 4.1.A, 4.1.C, 4.1.D

Name ______________________

3.1 Equivalent Fractions

Use the model to write an equivalent fraction.

1.

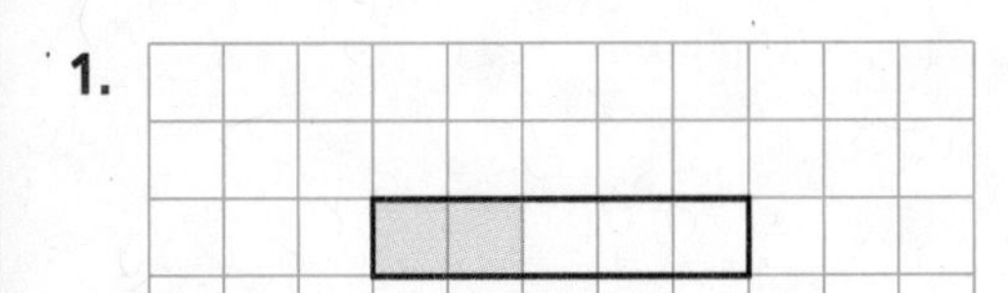

$\frac{2}{5}$ = ______

Tell whether the fractions are equivalent. Write = or ≠.

2. $\frac{3}{6}$ ◯ $\frac{1}{2}$

3. $\frac{2}{3}$ ◯ $\frac{4}{5}$

4. $\frac{1}{4}$ ◯ $\frac{4}{8}$

5. $\frac{2}{5}$ ◯ $\frac{4}{10}$

6. $\frac{1}{4}$ ◯ $\frac{1}{8}$

7. $\frac{1}{6}$ ◯ $\frac{2}{12}$

8. $\frac{2}{5}$ ◯ $\frac{6}{10}$

9. $\frac{4}{12}$ ◯ $\frac{1}{3}$

10. $\frac{1}{5}$ ◯ $\frac{2}{10}$

Problem Solving

11. Sam ate $\frac{1}{4}$ of a pizza. Claire ate $\frac{2}{8}$ of a pizza. Did they eat the same amount of pizza? **Explain.**

____

____

12. Lee spent $\frac{1}{3}$ of his day doing chores. Carrie spent $\frac{1}{6}$ of her day doing chores. Did Lee and Carrie spend the same amount of their day doing chores? **Explain.**

____

____

Lesson Check

TEXAS Test Prep

Fill in the bubble completely to show your answer.

13. Which fraction is equivalent to $\frac{6}{8}$?

Ⓐ $\frac{8}{6}$

Ⓑ $\frac{3}{4}$

Ⓒ $\frac{4}{6}$

Ⓓ $\frac{6}{14}$

14. Which fraction is equivalent to $\frac{2}{3}$?

Ⓐ $\frac{3}{5}$

Ⓑ $\frac{3}{2}$

Ⓒ $\frac{4}{5}$

Ⓓ $\frac{6}{9}$

15. Which fraction is equivalent to the shaded area shown?

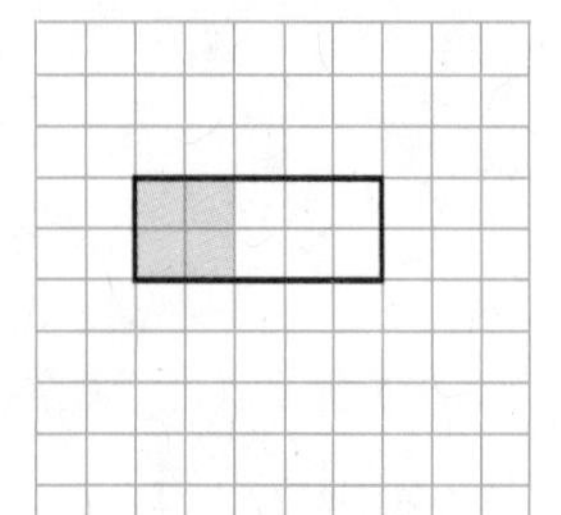

Ⓐ $\frac{5}{2}$

Ⓑ $\frac{5}{5}$

Ⓒ $\frac{2}{5}$

Ⓓ $\frac{10}{4}$

16. Which fraction is equivalent to the shaded area shown?

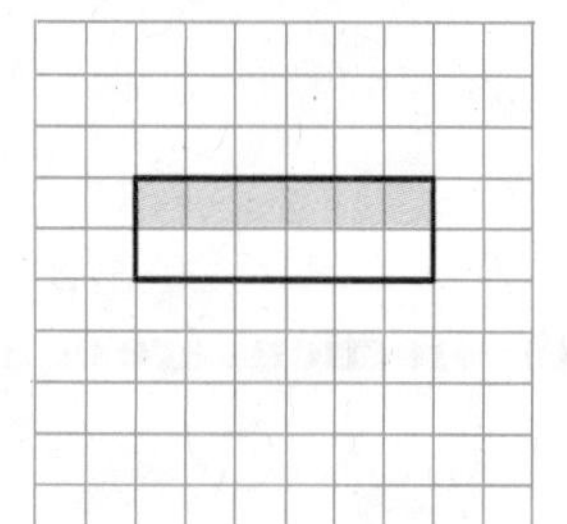

Ⓐ $\frac{6}{12}$

Ⓑ $\frac{6}{3}$

Ⓒ $\frac{1}{4}$

Ⓓ $\frac{12}{3}$

17. **Multi-Step** Maria made one dozen cookies. She gave six of the cookies to her teacher and three of the cookies to her friend. Which fraction is equivalent to the amount of cookies Maria gave away?

Ⓐ $\frac{3}{4}$

Ⓑ $\frac{3}{6}$

Ⓒ $\frac{3}{9}$

Ⓓ $\frac{3}{12}$

18. **Multi-Step** Pete, Joe, and Blake shared a large pizza. The pizza was cut into eight pieces. Pete ate two pieces, Joe ate two pieces, and Blake ate one piece. Which fraction is equivalent to the amount of pizza that was eaten by all the boys?

Ⓐ $\frac{8}{5}$

Ⓑ $\frac{1}{2}$

Ⓒ $\frac{8}{13}$

Ⓓ $\frac{5}{8}$

Name ______________________

3.2 Generate Equivalent Fractions

Essential Question How can you use multiplication to find equivalent fractions?

Unlock the Problem (Real World)

Hands On

Patty needs $\frac{3}{4}$ cup of dish soap to make homemade bubble solution. Her measuring cup is divided into eighths. What fraction of the measuring cup should Patty fill with dish soap?

- Is an eighth-size part of a measuring cup bigger or smaller than a fourth-size part?

____

Find how many eighths are in $\frac{3}{4}$.

STEP 1 Compare fourths and eighths.

Shade to model $\frac{1}{4}$.
Use fourth-size parts.

1 part

Shade to model $\frac{1}{4}$.
Use eighth-size parts.

2 parts

You need ______ eighth-size parts to make 1 fourth-size part.

STEP 2 Find how many eighths you need to make 3 fourths.

Shade to model $\frac{3}{4}$.
Use fourth-size parts.

3 parts

Shade to model $\frac{3}{4}$.
Use eighth-size parts.

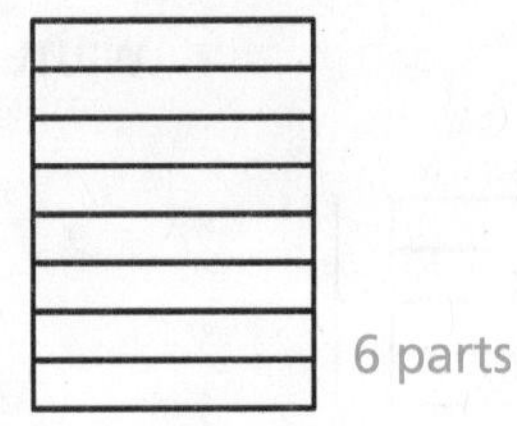

6 parts

You needed 2 eighth-size parts to make 1 fourth-size part.

So, you need ______ eighth-size parts to make 3 fourth-size parts.

So, Patty should fill $\frac{\square}{8}$ of the measuring cup with dish soap.

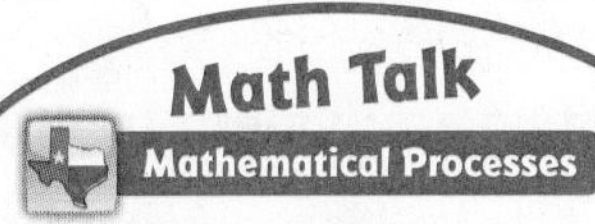

Math Talk Mathematical Processes

How did you know how many eighth-size parts you needed to make 1 fourth-size part? **Explain.**

1. **Explain** why 6 eighth-size parts is the same amount as 3 fourth-size parts.

____

Example Write two fractions that are equivalent to $\frac{1}{2}$.

MODEL	WRITE EQUIVALENT FRACTIONS	RELATE EQUIVALENT FRACTIONS
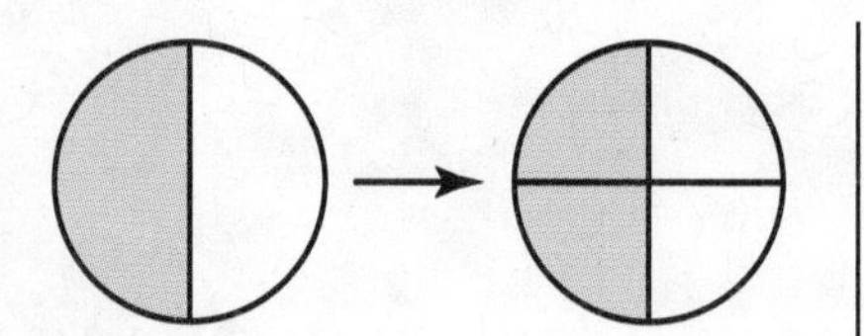	$\frac{1}{2} = \frac{\square}{4}$	$\frac{1 \times \square}{2 \times 2} = \frac{\square}{4}$
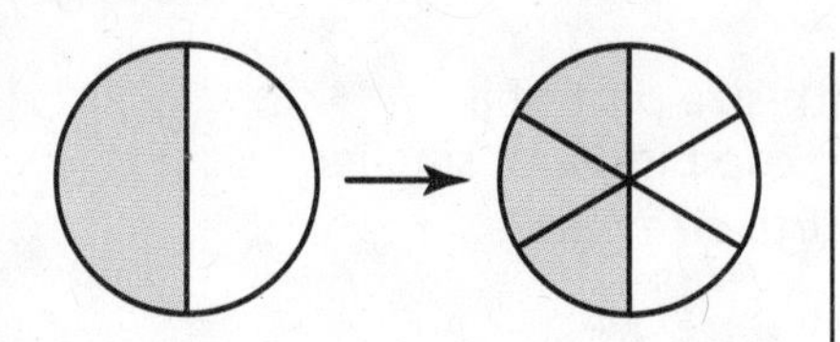	$\frac{1}{2} = \frac{\square}{6}$	$\frac{1 \times \square}{2 \times \square} = \frac{\square}{\square}$

So, $\frac{1}{2} = \frac{\square}{\square} = \frac{\square}{\square}$

Math Talk

Mathematical Processes

Explain how you can use multiplication to write a fraction that is equivalent to $\frac{3}{5}$.

2. Look at the model that shows $\frac{1}{2} = \frac{3}{6}$. How does the number of parts in the whole affect the number of parts that are shaded? **Explain.**

____

____

Share and Show

1. Write a fraction that is equivalent to $\frac{1}{3}$.

MODEL	WRITE EQUIVALENT FRACTIONS	RELATE EQUIVALENT FRACTIONS
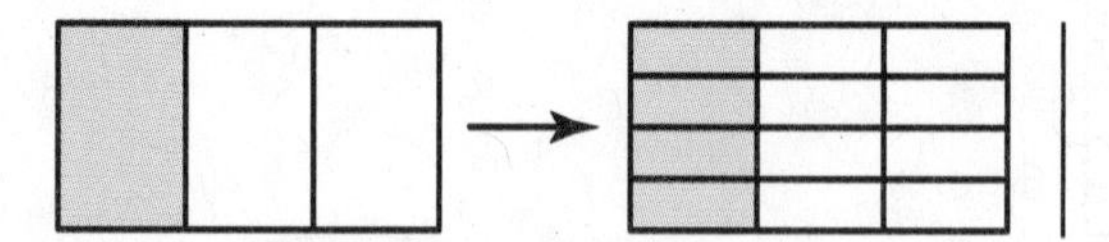	$\frac{1}{3} = \frac{4}{12}$	$\frac{1 \times \square}{3 \times \square} = \frac{\square}{\square}$

Write two equivalent fractions.

✓ 2. $\frac{4}{5} = \frac{4 \times \square}{5 \times \square} = \frac{\square}{\square}$

$\frac{4}{5} = \frac{4 \times \square}{5 \times \square} = \frac{\square}{\square}$

$\frac{4}{5} = \frac{\square}{\square} = \frac{\square}{\square}$

✓ 3. $\frac{2}{4} = \frac{2 \times \square}{4 \times \square} = \frac{\square}{\square}$

$\frac{2}{4} = \frac{2 \times \square}{4 \times \square} = \frac{\square}{\square}$

$\frac{2}{4} = \frac{\square}{\square} = \frac{\square}{\square}$

Name ______________________________

Problem Solving Real World

Use the recipe for 4–6.

Face Paint Recipe

$\frac{2}{8}$ cup cornstarch

1 tablespoon flour

$\frac{9}{12}$ cup light corn syrup

$\frac{1}{4}$ cup water

$\frac{1}{2}$ teaspoon food coloring

4. **Apply** How could you use a $\frac{1}{8}$-cup measuring cup to measure the cornstarch?

____

____

5. How could you use a $\frac{1}{8}$-cup measuring cup to measure the water?

____

____

6. **H.O.T.** Kim says the amount of flour in the recipe can be expressed as a fraction. Is she correct? **Explain.**

____

____

Write Math ▶ **Show Your Work**

7. **Write Math** ▶ **Explain** using words how you know a fraction is equivalent to another fraction.

____

____

____

____

8. **H.O.T.** **Multi-Step** Marcus needs $\frac{3}{4}$ cup of sugar. Marcus said he could not measure out the sugar using a $\frac{1}{6}$-cup measuring cup. Explain why not and suggest what size measuring cup will work.

____

____

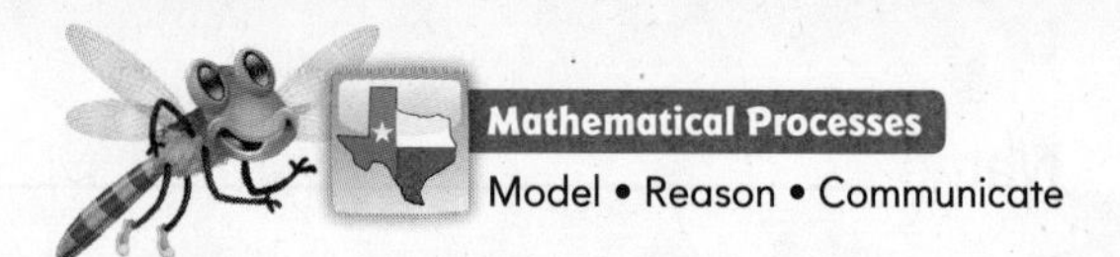

Daily Assessment Task

Fill in the bubble completely to show your answer.

9. Ten trees are growing in Cindy's yard. Of those, $\frac{3}{5}$ are pine trees. Which fraction is equivalent to $\frac{3}{5}$?

Ⓐ $\frac{10}{10}$
Ⓑ $\frac{5}{10}$
Ⓒ $\frac{6}{10}$
Ⓓ $\frac{1}{10}$

10. Clara read $\frac{2}{3}$ of a book. Which fraction is equivalent to what Clara read?

Ⓐ $\frac{5}{6}$
Ⓑ $\frac{4}{9}$
Ⓒ $\frac{6}{9}$
Ⓓ $\frac{2}{6}$

11. **Multi-Step** Ana uses equivalent amounts of seeds and corn to fill her bird feeder. Which could be the amount of seeds and corn that Ana uses?

Ⓐ $\frac{1}{4}$ cup seeds, $\frac{1}{8}$ cup corn
Ⓑ $\frac{1}{4}$ cup seeds, $\frac{2}{8}$ cup corn
Ⓒ $\frac{3}{4}$ cup seeds, $\frac{3}{8}$ cup corn
Ⓓ $\frac{3}{4}$ cup seeds, $\frac{7}{8}$ cup corn

TEXAS Test Prep

12. Raul needs a piece of rope $\frac{2}{3}$ yard long. Which fraction is equivalent to $\frac{2}{3}$?

Ⓐ $\frac{8}{15}$ yard
Ⓑ $\frac{6}{12}$ yard
Ⓒ $\frac{8}{12}$ yard
Ⓓ $\frac{4}{5}$ yard

Homework and Practice

TEKS Number and Operations—4.3.C
MATHEMATICAL PROCESSES 4.1.A, 4.1.C, 4.1.G

Name ______________________

3.2 Generate Equivalent Fractions

Write two equivalent fractions.

1. $\frac{3}{6} = \frac{\square \times \square}{\square \times \square} = \frac{\square}{\square}$

$\frac{3}{6} = \frac{\square}{\square} \times \frac{\square}{\square} = \frac{\square}{\square}$

$\frac{3}{6} = \frac{\square}{\square} = \frac{\square}{\square}$

2. $\frac{2}{5} = \frac{\square \times \square}{\square \times \square} = \frac{\square}{\square}$

$\frac{2}{5} = \frac{\square}{\square} \times \frac{\square}{\square} = \frac{\square}{\square}$

$\frac{2}{5} = \frac{\square}{\square} = \frac{\square}{\square}$

Problem Solving Real World

Use the recipe for 3–4.

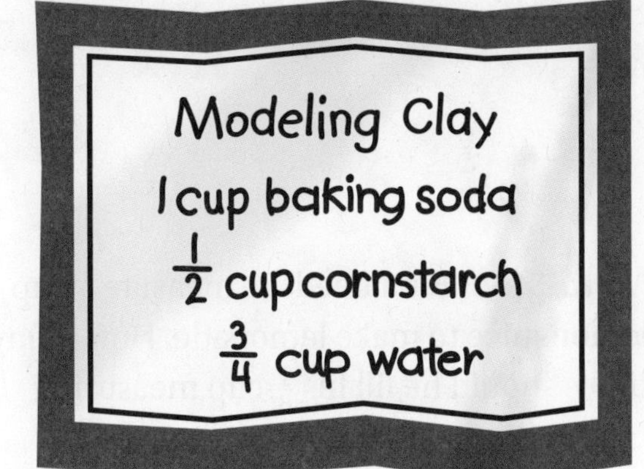

3. How could you use a $\frac{1}{4}$-cup measuring cup to measure the water?

____

____

4. How could you use a $\frac{1}{4}$-cup measuring cup to measure the cornstarch?

____

____

Lesson Check

TEXAS Test Prep

Fill in the bubble completely to show your answer.

5. Which two fractions are equivalent to $\frac{3}{10}$?

Ⓐ $\frac{6}{30}, \frac{9}{10}$

Ⓑ $\frac{1}{5}, \frac{3}{15}$

Ⓒ $\frac{6}{20}, \frac{9}{30}$

Ⓓ $\frac{12}{14}, \frac{6}{7}$

6. Sophie needs a piece of rope that is $\frac{3}{4}$ yard long. Which fraction is equivalent to $\frac{3}{4}$?

Ⓐ $\frac{9}{12}$

Ⓑ $\frac{4}{3}$

Ⓒ $\frac{4}{5}$

Ⓓ $\frac{6}{12}$

7. Theo needs to measure $\frac{3}{4}$ cup of water. He has a $\frac{1}{8}$-cup measuring cup. How many $\frac{1}{8}$ cups are in $\frac{3}{4}$ cup?

Ⓐ 4

Ⓑ 8

Ⓒ 6

Ⓓ 3

8. Sandra finished $\frac{1}{3}$ of her homework problems. Which fraction is equivalent to what Sandra finished?

Ⓐ $\frac{4}{6}$

Ⓑ $\frac{2}{6}$

Ⓒ $\frac{3}{8}$

Ⓓ $\frac{1}{6}$

9. **Multi-Step** Raul needs to measure $\frac{1}{4}$ cup lemon juice to make lemonade. How many times should he fill his $\frac{1}{8}$-cup measuring cup?

Ⓐ four times

Ⓑ three times

Ⓒ two times

Ⓓ eight times

10. **Multi-Step** Carrie needs $\frac{1}{3}$ cup of peanuts and $\frac{1}{3}$ cup of walnuts for her trail mix. Which fraction is equivalent to the total amount of nuts Carrie needs for her mix?

Ⓐ $\frac{2}{6}$

Ⓑ $\frac{3}{9}$

Ⓒ $\frac{3}{6}$

Ⓓ $\frac{6}{9}$

Name ______________________________

3.3 Simplest Form

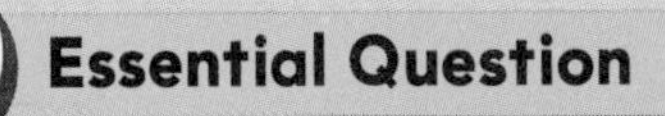

Essential Question How can you write a fraction as an equivalent fraction in simplest form?

Unlock the Problem — Real World

Vicki bought an ice cream cake cut into 6 equal pieces. Vicki, Margo, and Elena each took 2 pieces of the cake home. Vicki says she and each of her friends took $\frac{1}{3}$ of the cake home. Is Vicki correct?

- Into how many pieces was the cake cut?

  ____

- How many pieces did each girl take?

  ____

Activity

Materials ■ color pencils

STEP 1 Use a blue pencil to shade the pieces Vicki took home.

STEP 2 Use a red pencil to shade the pieces Margo took home.

STEP 3 Use a yellow pencil to shade the pieces Elena took home.

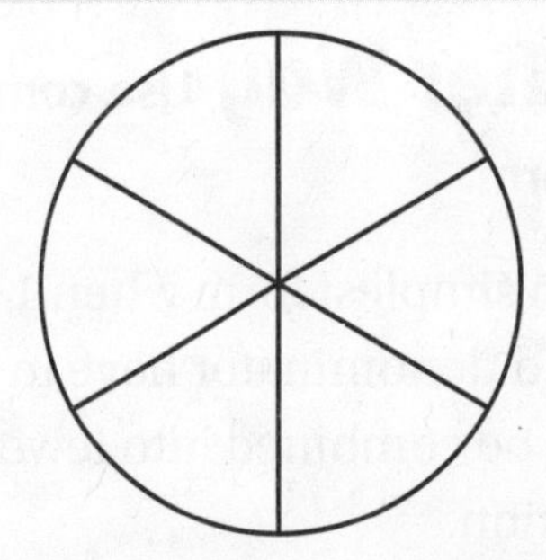

The cake is divided into _____ equal-size pieces. The 3 colors on the model show how to combine sixth-size pieces to make _____ equal third-size pieces.

So, Vicki is correct. Vicki, Margo, and Elena each took $\frac{\square}{\square}$ of the cake home.

Math Talk — Mathematical Processes

Compare the models for $\frac{2}{6}$ and $\frac{1}{3}$. **Explain** how the sizes of the parts are related.

- **What if** Vicki took 3 pieces of cake home and Elena took 3 pieces of cake home. How could you combine the pieces to write a fraction that represents the part each friend took home? **Explain**.

  ____

  ____

  ____

Simplest Form A fraction is in **simplest form** when you can represent it using as few equal parts of a whole as possible.

One Way Use models to write an equivalent fraction in simplest form.

MODEL	WRITE EQUIVALENT FRACTIONS	RELATE EQUIVALENT FRACTIONS
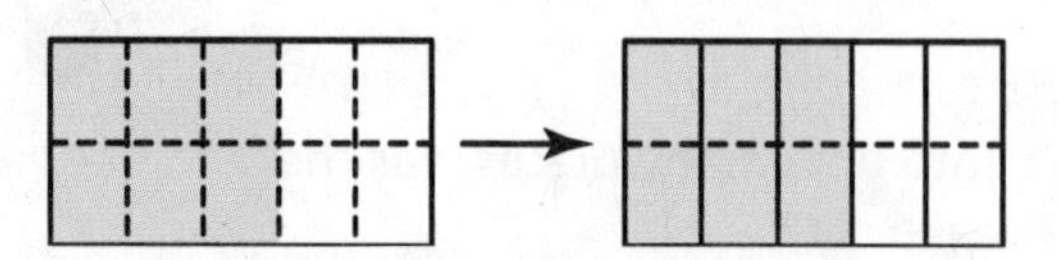	$\frac{6}{10} = \frac{\square}{5}$	$\frac{6 \div \square}{10 \div \square} = \frac{\square}{5}$

To simplify $\frac{6}{10}$, you can combine tenth-size parts into equal groups with 2 parts each.

So, $\frac{6}{10} = \frac{6 \div \square}{10 \div \square} = \frac{\square}{\square}$.

Another Way Use common factors to write $\frac{6}{10}$ in simplest form.

A fraction is in simplest form when 1 is the only factor that the numerator and denominator have in common. The parts of the whole cannot be combined into fewer equal-size parts to show the same fraction.

STEP 1 List the factors of the numerator and denominator. Circle common factors.

Factors of 6: _____, _____, _____, _____

Factors of 10: _____, _____, _____, _____

STEP 2 Divide the numerator and denominator by a common factor greater than 1.

$\frac{6}{10} = \frac{6 \div \square}{10 \div \square} = \frac{\square}{\square}$

So, $\frac{6}{10}$ written in simplest form is ______

Share and Show

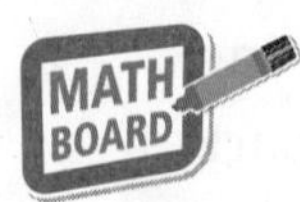

1. Write $\frac{8}{10}$ in simplest form.

$\frac{8}{10} = \frac{8 \div \square}{10 \div \square} = \frac{\square}{\square}$

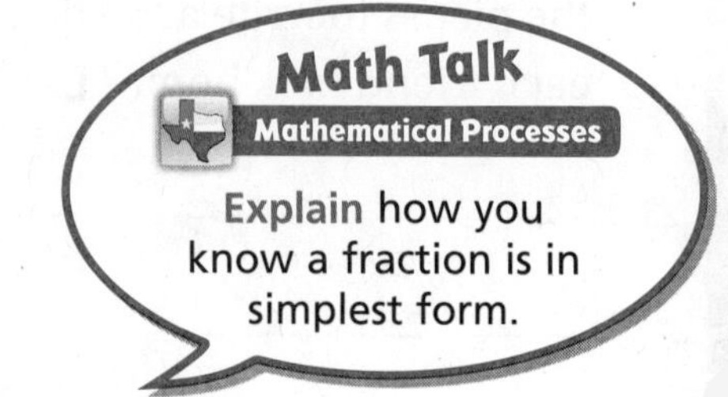

Write the fraction in simplest form.

2. $\frac{6}{12}$ ______
3. $\frac{2}{10}$ ______
4. $\frac{6}{8}$ ______
5. $\frac{4}{6}$ ______

Name ____________________

Problem Solving (Real World)

Use the map for 6–8.

6. **Use Diagrams** What fraction of the states in the Southwest region share a border with Mexico? Is this fraction in simplest form?

____

7. **H.O.T. What's the Question?** $\frac{1}{3}$ of the states in this region are on the Gulf of Mexico.

____

____

____

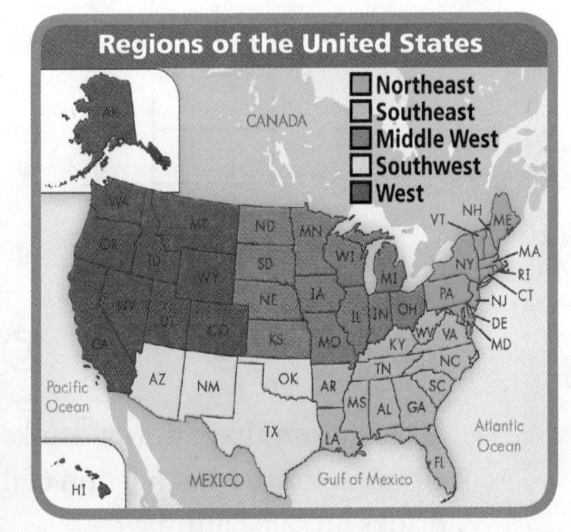

Write Math ▶ **Show Your Work**

8. **Multi-Step** What fraction of states are in the Southwest and Southeast regions combined? Write the fraction in simplest form.

____

9. **H.O.T. Sense or Nonsense?** Pete says that to write $\frac{4}{6}$ as $\frac{2}{3}$, you combine pieces, but to write $\frac{4}{6}$ as $\frac{8}{12}$, you break apart pieces. Does this make sense? **Explain.**

____

____

____

____

____

____

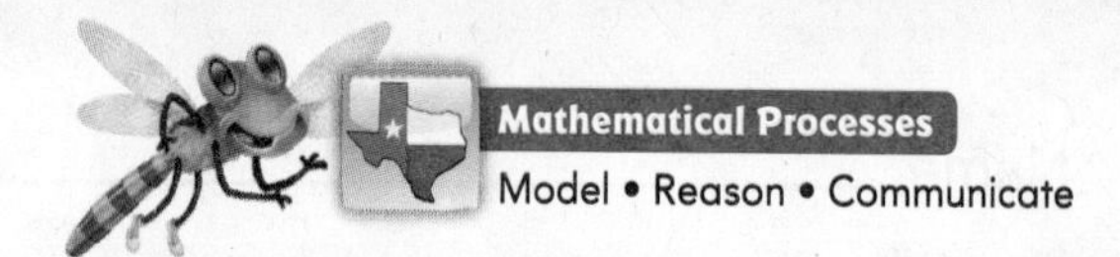

Daily Assessment Task

Fill in the bubble completely to show your answer.

10. **Use Diagrams** Emily's pet cat has lived with her for $\frac{8}{12}$ of the year. Use the models below. What is $\frac{8}{12}$ written in simplest form?

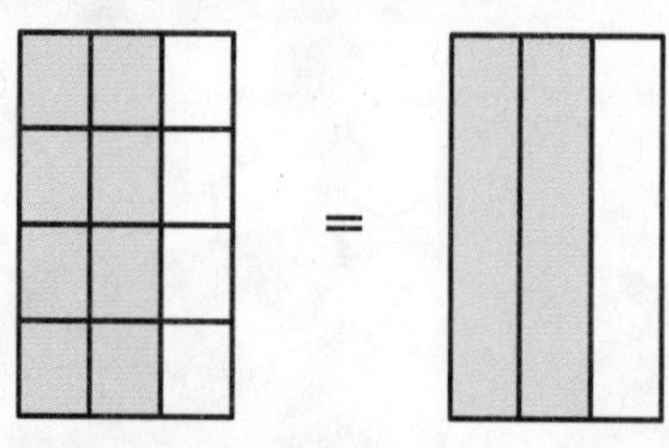

Ⓐ $\frac{2}{3}$ Ⓑ $\frac{1}{3}$ Ⓒ $\frac{2}{12}$ Ⓓ $\frac{4}{12}$

11. Six of 8 stores have power drinks on sale Saturday. In simplest form, what fraction of the stores has power drinks on sale Saturday?

Ⓐ $\frac{2}{4}$

Ⓒ $\frac{12}{18}$

Ⓑ $\frac{3}{4}$

Ⓓ $\frac{1}{2}$

12. **Multi-Step** There are 18 students in Jacob's homeroom. Six students bring their lunch to school. The rest eat lunch in the cafeteria. In simplest form, which shows the fraction of students that eat lunch in the cafeteria?

Ⓐ $\frac{1}{3}$

Ⓒ $\frac{6}{8}$

Ⓑ $\frac{12}{18}$

Ⓓ $\frac{2}{3}$

TEXAS Test Prep

13. Eight of 24 students bought lunch today. In simplest form, what fraction of the students bought lunch today?

Ⓐ $\frac{2}{3}$

Ⓑ $\frac{1}{3}$

Ⓒ $\frac{4}{12}$

Ⓓ $\frac{6}{9}$

TEKS Number and Operations—4.3.C
MATHEMATICAL PROCESSES 4.1.A, 4.1.B, 4.1.C, 4.1.D

Name ________________

3.3 Simplest Form

1. Write $\frac{4}{6}$ in simplest form.

$\frac{4}{6} = \frac{4}{6} \div \frac{\square}{\square} = \frac{\square}{\square}$

2. Write $\frac{2}{4}$ in simplest form.

$\frac{2}{4} = \frac{2}{4} \div \frac{\square}{\square} = \frac{\square}{\square}$

3. Write $\frac{3}{9}$ in simplest form.

$\frac{3}{9} = \frac{3}{9} \div \frac{\square}{\square} = \frac{\square}{\square}$

4. Write $\frac{12}{16}$ in simplest form.

$\frac{12}{16} = \frac{12}{16} \div \frac{\square}{\square} = \frac{\square}{\square}$

Write the fraction in simplest form.

5. $\frac{9}{12} =$ ______

6. $\frac{4}{8} =$ ______

7. $\frac{10}{12} =$ ______

8. $\frac{2}{12} =$ ______

9. $\frac{15}{20} =$ ______

10. $\frac{3}{9} =$ ______

Problem Solving

Use the map for 11 and 12.

11. What fraction of the states in the Middle West border states in the Southeast? Is this fraction in simplest form?

____

12. What fraction of all the states border the Gulf of Mexico? Write the fraction in simplest form.

____

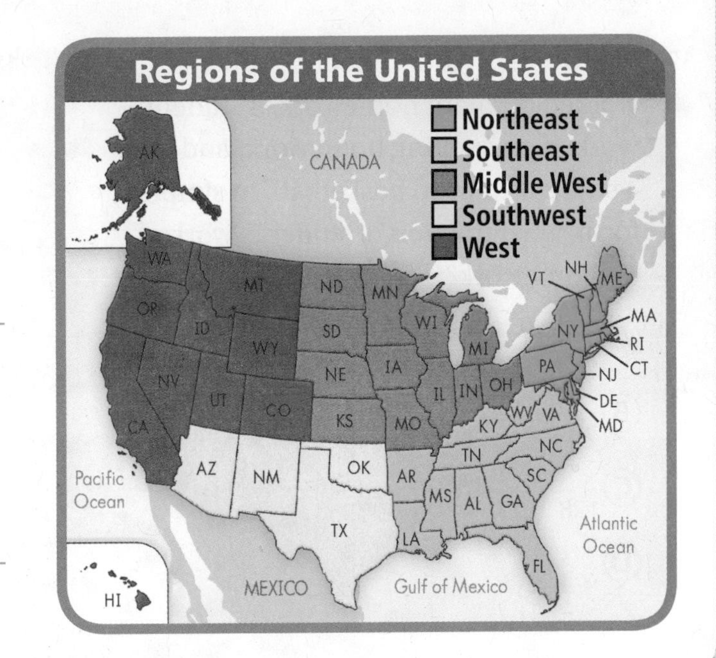

Lesson Check

TEXAS Test Prep

Fill in the bubble completely to show your answer.

13. What is the simplest form of $\frac{20}{100}$?

Ⓐ $\frac{2}{10}$

Ⓑ $\frac{4}{5}$

Ⓒ $\frac{10}{20}$

Ⓓ $\frac{1}{5}$

14. Twelve out of 14 players were on time for basketball practice. In simplest form, what fraction of the players was on time for practice?

Ⓐ $\frac{6}{14}$

Ⓑ $\frac{2}{7}$

Ⓒ $\frac{6}{7}$

Ⓓ $\frac{3}{14}$

15. What is the simplest form of $\frac{4}{24}$?

Ⓐ $\frac{1}{4}$

Ⓑ $\frac{1}{12}$

Ⓒ $\frac{2}{12}$

Ⓓ $\frac{1}{6}$

16. Fifteen out of 25 students in Ms. Taylor's class are girls. In simplest form, what fraction of the class is girls?

Ⓐ $\frac{3}{5}$

Ⓑ $\frac{2}{5}$

Ⓒ $\frac{10}{20}$

Ⓓ $\frac{3}{4}$

17. Multi-Step After school, 5 students worked on math homework, 3 students worked on spelling homework, and 4 students played basketball. In simplest form, what fraction of students worked on homework?

Ⓐ $\frac{2}{3}$

Ⓑ $\frac{3}{5}$

Ⓒ $\frac{4}{8}$

Ⓓ $\frac{1}{4}$

18. Multi-Step At the bake sale, Connie bought 4 chocolate chip cookies, Kevin bought 4 brownies, and Luis bought 6 sugar cookies. In simplest form, what fraction represents the number of cookies bought?

Ⓐ $\frac{2}{5}$

Ⓑ $\frac{5}{7}$

Ⓒ $\frac{2}{3}$

Ⓓ $\frac{6}{8}$

Name ________________________________

PROBLEM SOLVING
Find Equivalent Fractions

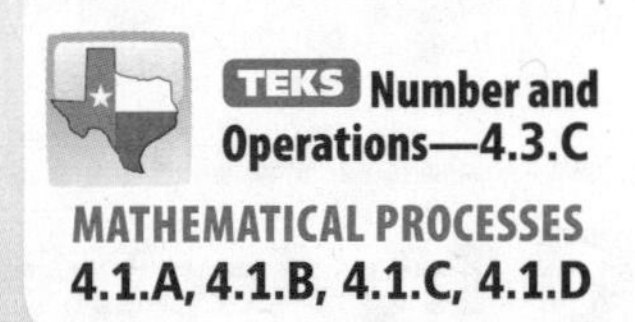

TEKS Number and Operations—4.3.C

MATHEMATICAL PROCESSES
4.1.A, 4.1.B, 4.1.C, 4.1.D

Essential Question How can you use the strategy *make a table* to solve problems using equivalent fractions?

Unlock the Problem

Anaya is planting a flower garden. The garden will have no more than 12 equal sections. $\frac{3}{4}$ of the garden will have daisies. What other fractions could represent the part of the garden that will have daisies?

Read		Plan
What do I need to find?	**What information am I given?**	**What is my plan or strategy?**
________ that could represent the part of the garden that will have daisies	______ of the garden will have daisies. The garden will not have more than ______ equal sections.	I can make a __________ to find __________ fractions to solve the problem.

Solve

I can make a table and draw models to find equivalent fractions.

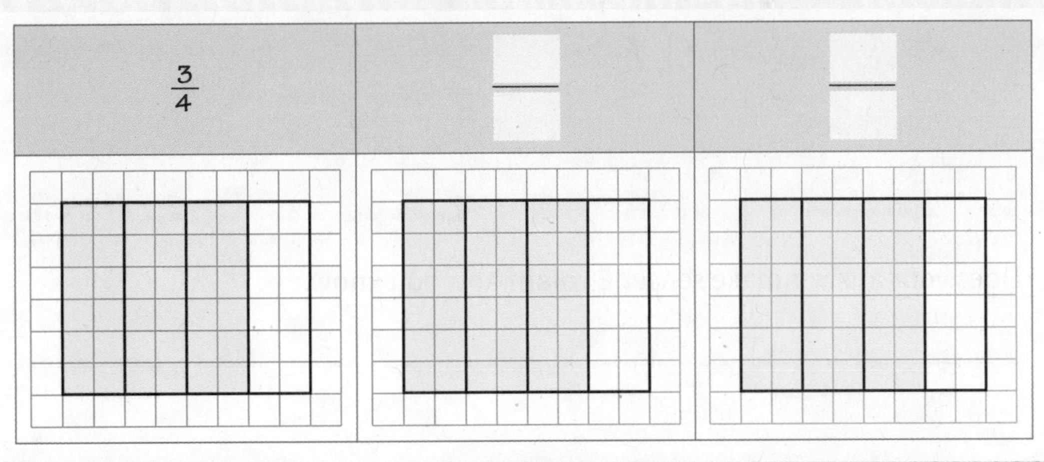

1. What other fractions could represent the part of the garden that will have daisies? **Explain.** ________________________________

____

Try Another Problem

Two friends are knitting scarves. Each scarf has 3 rectangles, and $\frac{2}{3}$ of the rectangles have stripes. If the friends are making 10 scarves, how many rectangles do they need? How many rectangles will have stripes?

Read		Plan
What do I need to find?	**What information am I given?**	**What is my plan or strategy?**

Solve

2. Does your answer make sense? **Explain** how you know.

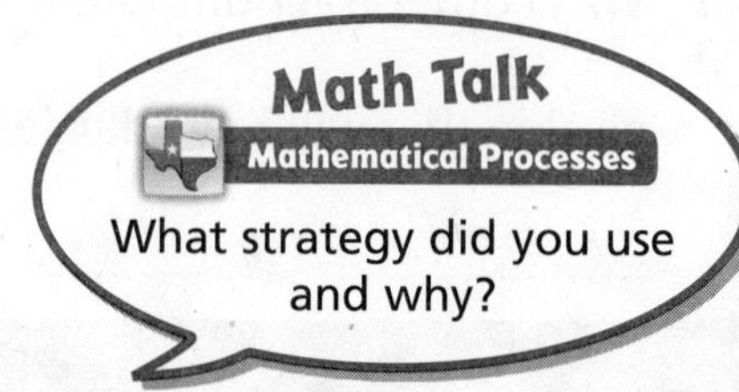

Name ______________________________

Share and Show

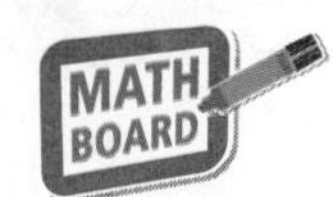

Tips

Unlock the Problem

- Use the Problem Solving Mathboard.
- Underline important facts.
- Choose a strategy you know.

1\. **H.O.T.** **Multi-Step** Keisha is helping plan a race route for a 10-kilometer charity run. The committee wants to set up the following things along the course.

> **Viewing areas:** At the end of each half of the course
> **Water stations:** At the end of each fifth of the course
> **Distance markers:** At the end of each tenth of the course

Which locations have more than one thing located there?

First, make a table to organize the information.

	Number of Locations	First Location	All the Locations
Viewing Areas	2	$\frac{1}{2}$	$\frac{1}{2}$
Water Stations	5	$\frac{1}{5}$	$\frac{1}{5}$
Distance Markers	10	$\frac{1}{10}$	$\frac{1}{10}$

Next, identify a relationship. Use equivalent fractions which have the same denominator. Circle the locations.

2\. **H.O.T.** **What if** distance markers will also be placed at the end of every fourth of the course? Will any of those markers be set up at the same location as another distance marker, a water station, or a viewing area? **Explain.**

____

____

Problem Solving

3\. **H.O.T.** **Multi-Step** A baker cut a pie in half. He cut each half into 3 equal pieces and each piece into 2 equal slices. He sold 6 slices. What fraction of the pie did the baker sell?

____

4\. **H.O.T.** **Reasoning** Andy cut a tuna sandwich and a chicken sandwich into a total of 15 same-size pieces. He cut the tuna sandwich into 9 more pieces than the chicken sandwich. Andy ate 8 pieces of the tuna sandwich. What fraction of the tuna sandwich did he eat?

____

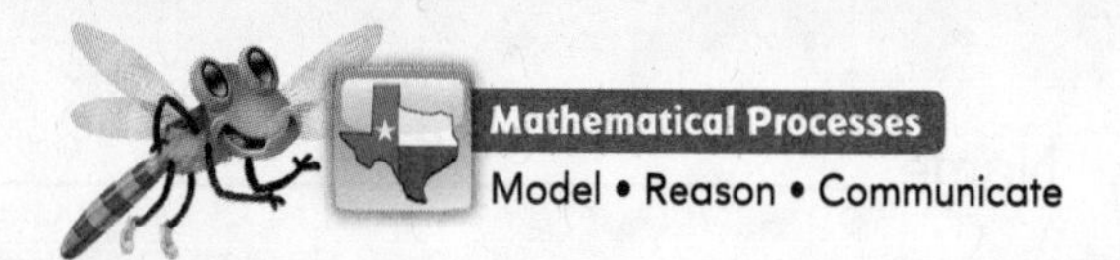

Daily Assessment Task

Fill in the bubble completely to show your answer.

5. **Apply** Of the 24 paper airplanes at a contest, $\frac{5}{6}$ of them are made from a single sheet of paper. What other fraction could represent the same amount of paper airplanes made from a single sheet of paper?

   Ⓐ $\frac{5}{12}$ Ⓒ $\frac{10}{12}$

   Ⓑ $\frac{2}{3}$ Ⓓ $\frac{8}{9}$

6. **Multi-Step** There are 18 puzzles in a crossword puzzle book. Christi finished 9 of the puzzles. Which fractions could describe the part of the crossword puzzle book that Christi finished?

   Ⓐ $\frac{6}{2}$ and $\frac{4}{5}$

   Ⓑ $\frac{3}{6}$ and $\frac{2}{3}$

   Ⓒ $\frac{6}{8}$ and $\frac{1}{2}$

   Ⓓ $\frac{1}{2}$ and $\frac{3}{6}$

7. **Multi-Step** David uses $\frac{2}{3}$ yard of cloth to make a bag. Which amounts are equivalent to $\frac{2}{3}$ yard?

   Ⓐ $\frac{8}{12}$ yard and $\frac{10}{12}$ yard

   Ⓑ $\frac{4}{6}$ yard and $\frac{8}{12}$ yard

   Ⓒ $\frac{4}{6}$ yard and $\frac{6}{12}$ yard

   Ⓓ $\frac{6}{9}$ yard and $\frac{6}{12}$ yard

TEXAS Test Prep

8. A comic-book store will trade 5 of its comic books for 6 of yours. How many of its comic books will the store trade for 36 of yours?

   Ⓐ 42

   Ⓑ 30

   Ⓒ 36

   Ⓓ 25

Name ____________________

3.4 Find Equivalent Fractions

1. Joanna is filling bags with candy. Each bag has 5 pieces of candy. Joanna wants $\frac{2}{5}$ of the candy in each bag to be chocolate bars. Solve using the table below.

Candy Bags	1									
Chocolate Bars	$\frac{2}{5}$									
Total Number of Bags										

2. If Joanna fills 10 bags of candy, how many pieces of candy will she need?

3. How many chocolate bars will she need for 10 bags of candy?

4. What other strategies could Joanna use to solve the problem?

Problem Solving Real World

5. Chandler is sewing a quilt. The quilt will have 18 equal squares. Of the squares, $\frac{1}{3}$ will be blue. What other fractions could represent the part of the quilt that will have blue squares? **Explain.**

6. On Chandler's quilt, $\frac{2}{3}$ of the squares will be red. What other fractions represent the part of the quilt that will be red? **Explain.**

Lesson Check

TEXAS Test Prep

Fill in the bubble completely to show your answer.

7. The table below shows equivalent fractions.

$\frac{4}{5}$	$\frac{8}{10}$	$\frac{12}{15}$	

Which fraction completes the table?

Ⓐ $\frac{12}{20}$

Ⓑ $\frac{14}{16}$

Ⓒ $\frac{16}{20}$

Ⓓ $\frac{24}{30}$

8. A grocery store will trade 1 of its fabric bags for 8 of your plastic bags. How many of the store's fabric bags will it trade for 32 of your bags?

Ⓐ 5

Ⓑ 3

Ⓒ 2

Ⓓ 4

9. Cara got 9 out of 10 test items correct. What is her score on the test out of 100?

Ⓐ 9

Ⓑ 90

Ⓒ 900

Ⓓ 19

10. Tracy buys $\frac{7}{8}$ yard of ribbon. What other fraction could represent this amount of ribbon?

Ⓐ $\frac{21}{32}$

Ⓑ $\frac{21}{24}$

Ⓒ $\frac{12}{16}$

Ⓓ $\frac{3}{4}$

11. Multi-Step Mrs. Lee cut a pizza in half. She cut each half into 2 equal pieces and then each piece into 3 equal slices. She served 8 slices. What fraction of the pizza did Mrs. Lee serve?

Ⓐ $\frac{2}{3}$

Ⓑ $\frac{3}{8}$

Ⓒ $\frac{1}{4}$

Ⓓ $\frac{1}{6}$

12. Multi-Step Kyle collected 7 smooth stones, 5 jagged stones, and 3 shells at the beach. Which fraction is equivalent to the fraction of his collection that is stones?

Ⓐ $\frac{5}{12}$

Ⓑ $\frac{4}{5}$

Ⓒ $\frac{5}{7}$

Ⓓ $\frac{7}{15}$

Name ______________________________

3.5 Write Fractions as Sums

Essential Question

How can you write a fraction as a sum of unit fractions with the same denominators?

Unlock the Problem

Emilio cut a sandwich into 8 equal pieces and ate 1 piece. He has $\frac{7}{8}$ of the sandwich left. Emilio put each remaining piece on a snack plate. How many snack plates did he use? What part of the sandwich did he put on each plate?

Each piece of the sandwich is $\frac{1}{8}$ of the whole. $\frac{1}{8}$ is called a **unit fraction** because it tells the part of the whole that 1 piece represents. A unit fraction always has a numerator of 1.

Example 1 Use fraction strips. Write $\frac{7}{8}$ as a sum of unit fractions.

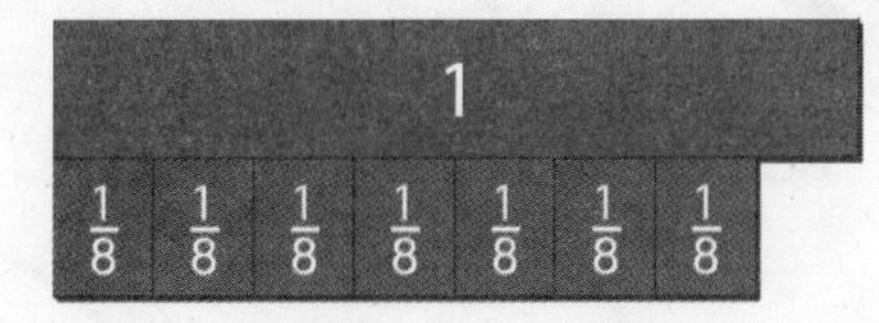

$\frac{7}{8}$ = _____ + _____ + _____ + _____ + _____ + _____ + _____

The number of addends represents the number of plates used.

The unit fractions represent the part of the sandwich on each plate.

So, Emilio used _____ plates. He put _____ of a sandwich on each plate.

- **What if** Emilio ate 3 pieces of the sandwich instead of 1 piece? How many snack plates would he need? What part of the sandwich would be on each plate? **Explain.**

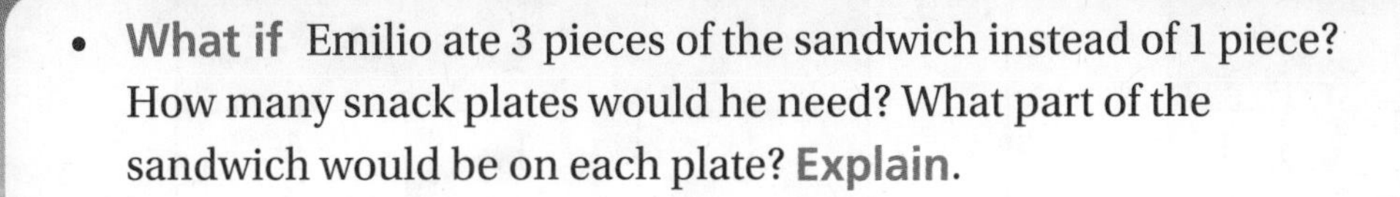

Example 2 Write a fraction as a sum.

Kevin and Olivia are going to share a whole pizza. The pizza is cut into 6 equal slices. They will put the slices on two separate dishes. What part of the whole pizza could be on each dish?

Shade the models to show how Kevin and Olivia could share the pizza. Write an equation.

Think: $\frac{6}{6}$ = 1 whole pizza.

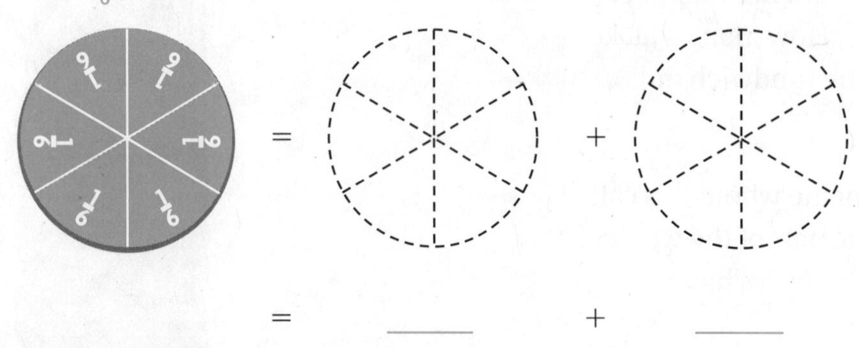

= ______ + ______

Share and Show

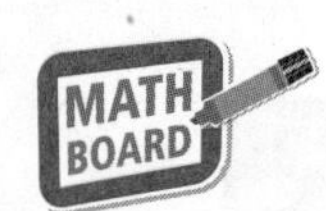

1. Write $\frac{3}{4}$ as a sum of unit fractions.

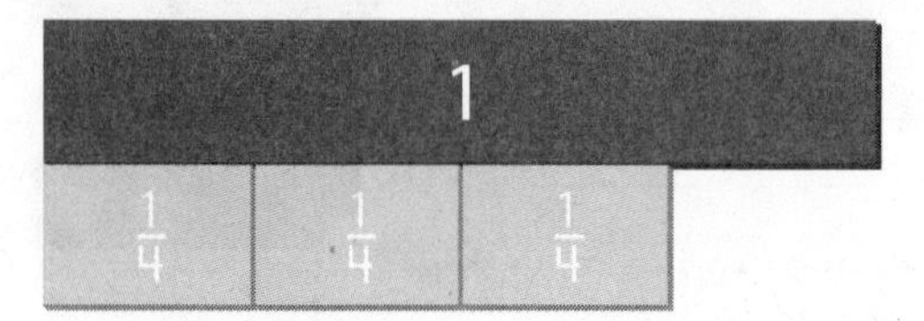

$\frac{3}{4}$ = ______ + ______ + ______

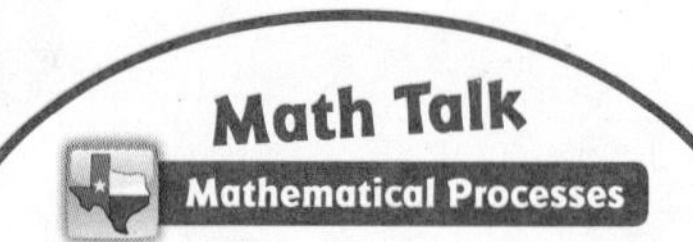

Explain how the numerator in $\frac{5}{6}$ is related to the number of addends in the sum of its unit fractions.

Write the fraction as a sum of unit fractions.

2.

1					
$\frac{1}{6}$	$\frac{1}{6}$	$\frac{1}{6}$	$\frac{1}{6}$	$\frac{1}{6}$	$\frac{1}{6}$

$\frac{5}{6}$ = ______________

3.

1		
$\frac{1}{3}$	$\frac{1}{3}$	$\frac{1}{3}$

$\frac{2}{3}$ = ______________

4. H.O.T. How many different ways can you write a fraction that has a numerator of 2 as a sum of fractions? **Explain.**

____

Name ______________________________

Problem Solving Real World

5. H.O.T. **Representations** Holly's garden is divided into 5 equal sections. She will fence the garden into 3 areas by grouping some equal sections together. What part of the garden could each fenced area be?

a. What information do you need to use?

____

____

b. How can writing an equation help you solve the problem?

____

____

c. How can drawing a model help you write an equation?

____

____

d. Show how you can solve the problem.

e. Complete the sentence.

The garden can be fenced into ______,

______, and ______ parts or ______, ______,

and ______ parts.

6. What is $\frac{7}{10}$ written as a sum of unit fractions?

____

7. H.O.T. **Multi-Step Apply** Kim read $\frac{3}{4}$ of her book over the weekend. What is $\frac{3}{4}$ written as a sum of unit fractions with a denominator of 12?

____

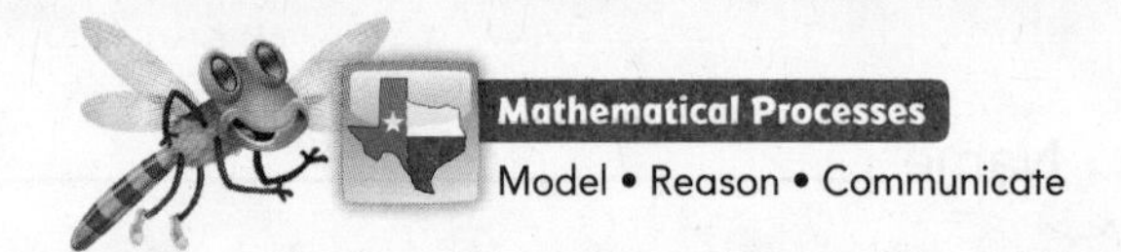

Daily Assessment Task

Fill in the bubble completely to show your answer.

8. Paula mixed strawberry yogurt and milk to make a smoothie. The smoothie fills $\frac{2}{3}$ cup. Which is $\frac{2}{3}$ written as the sum of unit fractions?

Ⓐ $\frac{2}{3} + \frac{2}{3}$

Ⓑ $\frac{1}{2} + \frac{1}{2}$

Ⓒ $\frac{1}{3} + \frac{2}{3}$

Ⓓ $\frac{1}{3} + \frac{1}{3}$

9. **Use Tools** Larry's dog, Rex, ate $\frac{3}{4}$ of a can of dog food. What is another way of writing $\frac{3}{4}$? Use fraction strips to answer the question.

Ⓐ $\frac{1}{4} + \frac{1}{4}$

Ⓑ $\frac{1}{4} + \frac{1}{4} + \frac{1}{4}$

Ⓒ $\frac{1}{4} + \frac{1}{4} + \frac{1}{4} + \frac{1}{4}$

Ⓓ $\frac{3}{4} + \frac{3}{4} + \frac{3}{4}$

10. Ben and his friends ate $\frac{6}{8}$ of a whole pizza. Written as a sum of unit fractions, which shows the amount of pizza Ben and his friends ate?

Ⓐ $\frac{1}{8} + \frac{1}{8} + \frac{1}{8} + \frac{1}{8} + \frac{1}{8} + \frac{1}{8}$

Ⓑ $\frac{1}{6} + \frac{1}{6} + \frac{1}{6} + \frac{1}{6} + \frac{1}{6} + \frac{1}{6}$

Ⓒ $\frac{1}{8} + \frac{1}{8} + \frac{1}{8} + \frac{1}{8} + \frac{1}{8} + \frac{1}{8} + \frac{1}{8} + \frac{1}{8}$

Ⓓ $\frac{1}{6} + \frac{1}{6} + \frac{1}{6} + \frac{1}{6} + \frac{1}{6} + \frac{1}{6} + \frac{1}{6} + \frac{1}{6}$

TEXAS Test Prep

11. Which is equivalent to $\frac{9}{12}$?

Ⓐ $\frac{5}{12} + \frac{3}{12}$

Ⓑ $\frac{3}{12} + \frac{2}{12} + \frac{1}{12} + \frac{1}{12}$

Ⓒ $\frac{5}{12} + \frac{2}{12} + \frac{2}{12}$

Ⓓ $\frac{4}{12} + \frac{4}{12} + \frac{1}{12} + \frac{1}{12}$

Homework and Practice

TEKS Number and Operations—4.3.A, 4.3.B
MATHEMATICAL PROCESSES 4.1.A, 4.1.B, 4.1.C, 4.1.E

Name ________________

3.5 Write Fractions as Sums

Write the fraction as a sum of unit fractions.

1.

1				
$\frac{1}{5}$	$\frac{1}{5}$	$\frac{1}{5}$	$\frac{1}{5}$	$\frac{1}{5}$

$\frac{2}{5}$ = ______

2.

1						
$\frac{1}{7}$	$\frac{1}{7}$	$\frac{1}{7}$	$\frac{1}{7}$	$\frac{1}{7}$	$\frac{1}{7}$	$\frac{1}{7}$

$\frac{6}{7}$ = ______

3. What is $\frac{4}{12}$ written as a sum of unit fractions?

______

4. What is $\frac{6}{8}$ written as a sum of unit fractions?

______

5. What is $\frac{8}{10}$ written as a sum of unit fractions?

______

6. What is $\frac{7}{9}$ written as a sum of unit fractions?

______

Problem Solving Real World

7. Hank cut a cake into 12 equal pieces and ate 2 pieces. He has $\frac{10}{12}$ of the cake left to serve on plates. What part of the cake did he put on each plate?

______

8. How many plates did Hank use to serve the cake?

______

Lesson Check

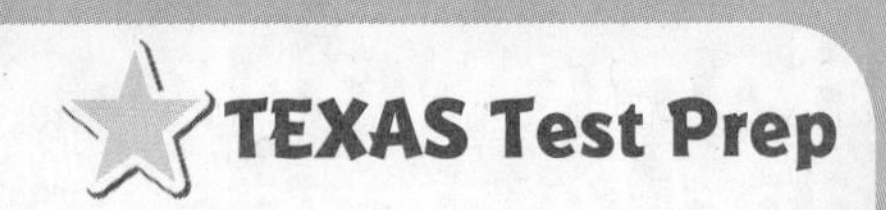

Fill in the bubble completely to show your answer.

9. What is $\frac{5}{6}$ written as a sum of unit fractions?

Ⓐ $\frac{3}{6}+\frac{1}{6}+\frac{1}{6}$

Ⓑ $\frac{1}{6}+\frac{1}{6}+\frac{1}{6}+\frac{2}{6}$

Ⓒ $\frac{6}{6}+\frac{1}{6}$

Ⓓ $\frac{1}{6}+\frac{1}{6}+\frac{1}{6}+\frac{1}{6}+\frac{1}{6}$

10. Which is equivalent to $\frac{8}{15}$?

Ⓐ $\frac{5}{15}+\frac{4}{15}$

Ⓑ $\frac{4}{15}+\frac{2}{15}+\frac{2}{15}$

Ⓒ $\frac{3}{15}+\frac{3}{15}+\frac{4}{15}$

Ⓓ $\frac{2}{15}+\frac{2}{15}+\frac{2}{15}+\frac{1}{15}$

11. Kay lives $\frac{5}{8}$ mile from her friend. Which is $\frac{5}{8}$ written as the sum of unit fractions?

Ⓐ $\frac{1}{8}+\frac{5}{8}$

Ⓑ $\frac{1}{8}+\frac{1}{8}+\frac{1}{8}+\frac{1}{8}+\frac{1}{8}$

Ⓒ $\frac{5}{8}+\frac{5}{8}$

Ⓓ $\frac{1}{8}+\frac{1}{8}+\frac{1}{8}+\frac{1}{8}$

12. Which is equivalent to $\frac{7}{12}$?

Ⓐ $\frac{1}{12}+\frac{1}{12}+\frac{1}{12}+\frac{1}{12}+\frac{1}{12}$

Ⓑ $\frac{7}{12}+\frac{1}{12}$

Ⓒ $\frac{5}{12}+\frac{3}{12}$

Ⓓ $\frac{1}{12}+\frac{1}{12}+\frac{1}{12}+\frac{1}{12}+\frac{1}{12}+\frac{1}{12}+\frac{1}{12}$

13. **Multi-Step** Leena walked $\frac{2}{3}$ of a mile. What is $\frac{2}{3}$ written as a sum of unit fractions with a denominator of 9?

Ⓐ $\frac{5}{9}+\frac{4}{9}$

Ⓑ $\frac{1}{9}+\frac{1}{9}+\frac{1}{9}+\frac{1}{9}+\frac{1}{9}+\frac{1}{9}$

Ⓒ $\frac{2}{9}+\frac{2}{9}+\frac{2}{9}$

Ⓓ $\frac{1}{9}+\frac{1}{9}+\frac{1}{9}$

14. **Multi-Step** William waters his plants on different days. He watered $\frac{1}{5}$ of the plants on Monday and $\frac{1}{5}$ of the plants on Tuesday. What fraction shows the part of the plants that William still needs to water this week?

Ⓐ $\frac{3}{5}$

Ⓑ $\frac{2}{5}$

Ⓒ $\frac{1}{5}$

Ⓓ $\frac{4}{5}$

Name ____________________

Rename Fractions and Mixed Numbers

TEKS Number and Operations—4.3.B
Also, 4.3.A

MATHEMATICAL PROCESSES
4.1.A, 4.1.B, 4.1.C, 4.1.F

Essential Question

How can you rename mixed numbers as fractions greater than 1 and rename fractions greater than 1 as mixed numbers?

Unlock the Problem

Real World

Hands On

Mr. Fox has $2\frac{3}{6}$ loaves of corn bread. Each loaf was cut into $\frac{1}{6}$-size pieces. If he has 14 people over for dinner, is there enough bread for each person to have 1 piece?

A **mixed number** is a number represented by a whole number and a fraction. You can write a mixed number as a fraction. To find how many $\frac{1}{6}$-size pieces are in $2\frac{3}{6}$, write $2\frac{3}{6}$ as a fraction.

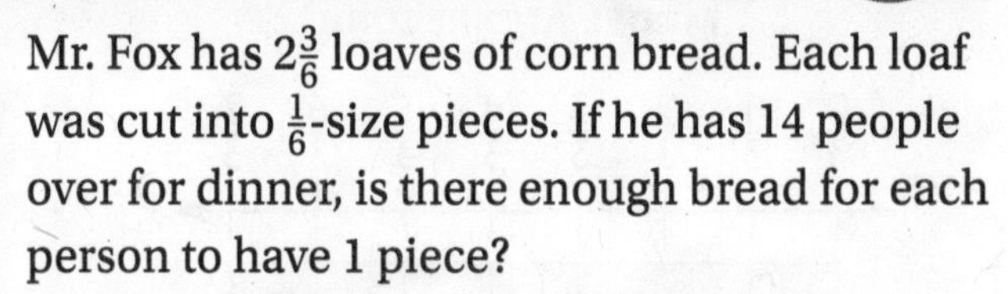

- What is the size of 1 piece of bread relative to the whole?

  ____

- How much bread does Mr. Fox need for 14 people?

  ____

Example Write a mixed number as a fraction.

THINK | MODEL AND RECORD

STEP 1 Model $2\frac{3}{6}$.

$2\frac{3}{6}$ = ______ + ______ + $\frac{\square}{\square}$

STEP 2 Find how many $\frac{1}{6}$-size pieces are in each whole. Model $2\frac{3}{6}$ using only $\frac{1}{6}$-size pieces.

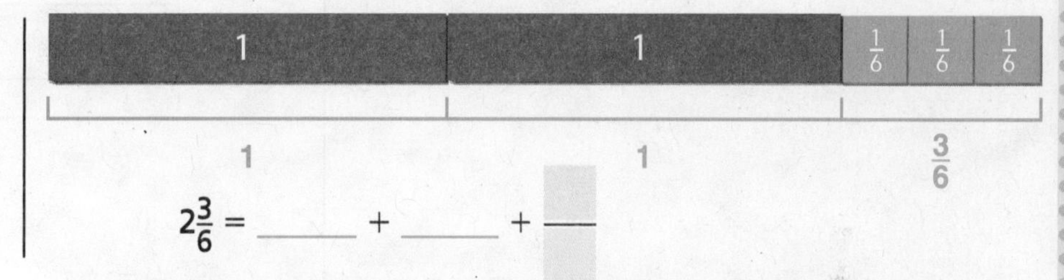

$2\frac{3}{6} = \frac{\square}{\square} + \frac{\square}{\square} + \frac{\square}{\square}$

STEP 3 Find the total number of $\frac{1}{6}$-size pieces in $2\frac{3}{6}$.

Think: Find $\frac{6}{6} + \frac{6}{6} + \frac{3}{6}$.

$2\frac{3}{6} = \frac{\square}{\square}$

There are ______ sixth-size pieces in $2\frac{3}{6}$.

So, there is enough bread for 14 people to each have 1 piece.

Example Write a fraction greater than 1 as a mixed number.

To weave a bracelet, Charlene needs 7 pieces of brown thread. Each piece of thread must be $\frac{1}{3}$ yard long. How much thread should she buy to weave the bracelet?

Write $\frac{7}{3}$ as a mixed number.

THINK	MODEL AND RECORD
STEP 1 Model $\frac{7}{3}$.	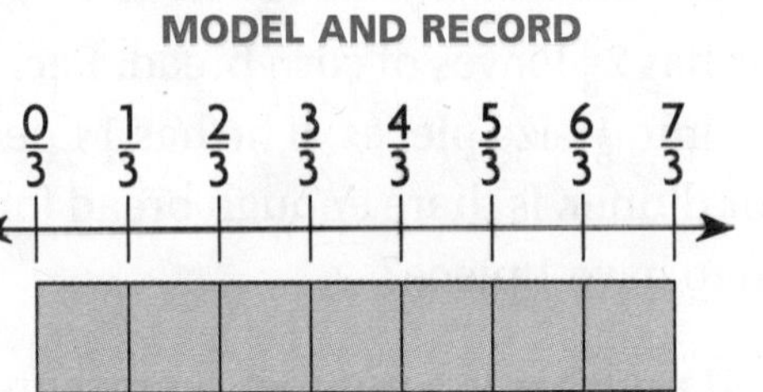 $\frac{7}{3}$ = ___ + ___ + ___ + ___ + ___ + ___ + ___
STEP 2 Find how many wholes are in $\frac{7}{3}$, and how many thirds are left over.	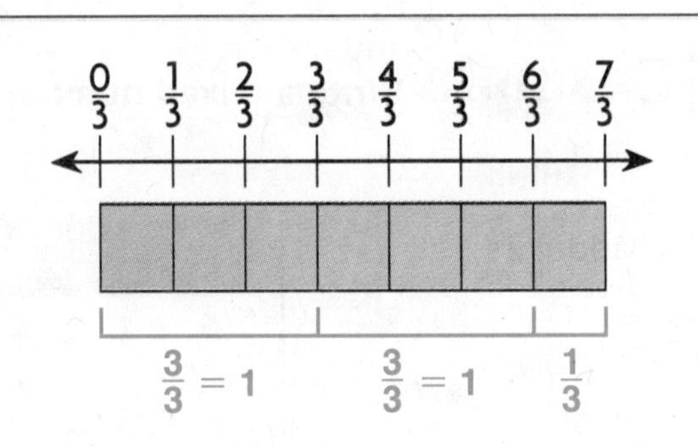 $\frac{7}{3}$ = ___ + ___ + ___
STEP 3 Write $\frac{7}{3}$ as a mixed number.	$\frac{7}{3}$ = ___ $\frac{\square}{\square}$

So, Charlene should buy ______ yards of thread.

Share and Show

Write the unknown numbers. Write mixed numbers above the number line and fractions greater than one below the number line.

1.

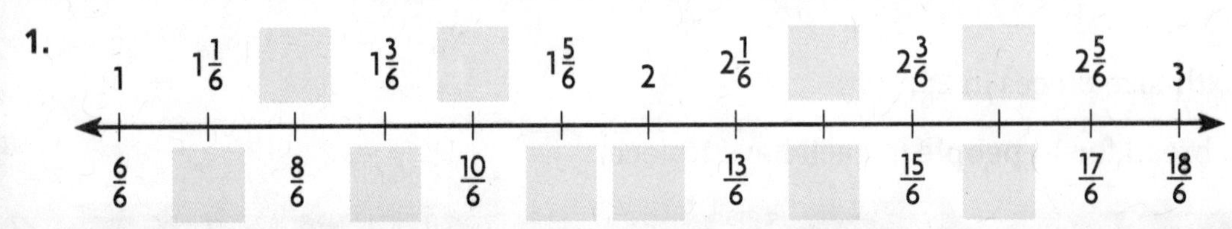

Name ______________________________

Write the mixed number as a fraction or the fraction as a mixed number.

2. $1\frac{1}{8}$ ______

3. $\frac{13}{10}$ ______

4. $1\frac{2}{3}$ ______

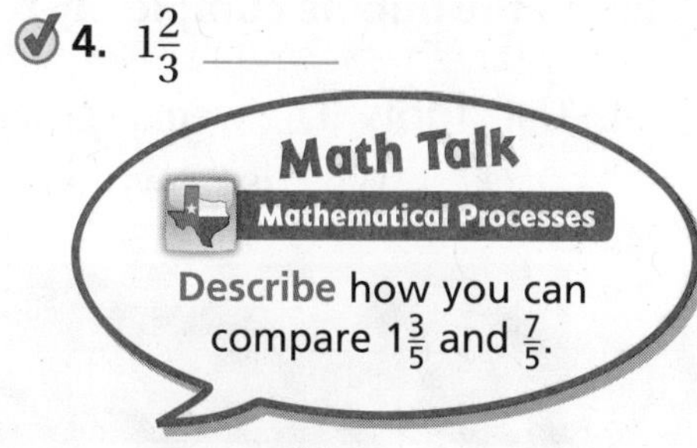

Algebra **Find the unknown numbers.**

5. $\frac{13}{7} = 1\frac{■}{7}$ ______

6. $■\frac{5}{6} = \frac{23}{6}$ ______

7. $\frac{57}{11} = ■\frac{■}{11}$ ______

Problem Solving Real World

Use the recipe to solve 8–10.

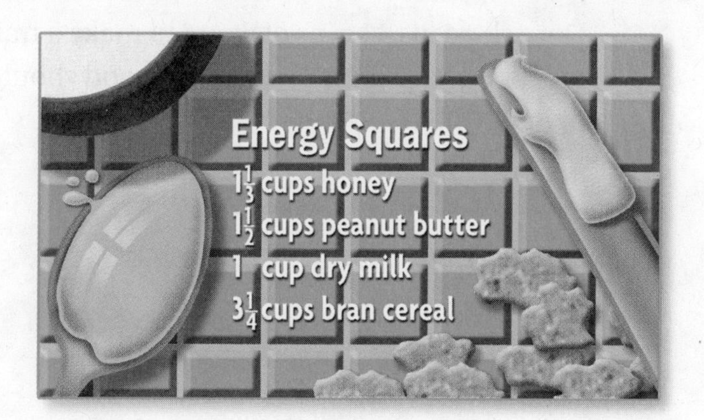

8. Cal is making energy squares. How many $\frac{1}{2}$ cups of peanut butter are used in the recipe?

____

9. What is the amount of bran cereal, written as a fraction greater than 1, that is used in the recipe?

____

10. H.O.T. **Apply** Suppose Cal wants to make 2 times as many energy squares as the recipe makes. How many cups of bran cereal should he use? Write your answer as a mixed number and as a fraction greater than 1 in simplest form.

____

11. Cal added $2\frac{3}{8}$ cups of raisins. Write this mixed number as a fraction greater than 1 in simplest form.

____

12. H.O.T. **Multi-Step** Jenn is preparing brown rice. She needs $1\frac{1}{2}$ cups of brown rice and 2 cups of water. Jenn has only a $\frac{1}{8}$-cup measuring cup. How many $\frac{1}{8}$ cups each of rice and water will Jenn use to prepare the rice?

____

13. **Multi-Step** Pen has $\frac{1}{2}$-cup and $\frac{1}{8}$-cup measuring cups. What are two ways he could measure out $1\frac{3}{4}$ cups of flour?

____

____

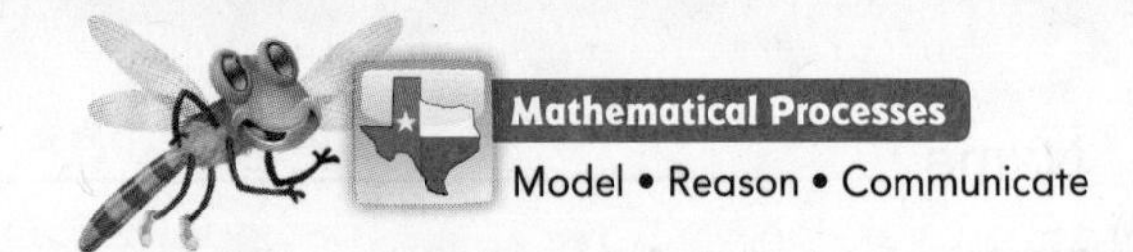

Daily Assessment Task

Fill in the bubble completely to show your answer.

14. Use Tools The weekly grocery list for a zoo includes $2\frac{3}{5}$ pounds of crickets. What is $2\frac{3}{5}$ written as a fraction?

1					1					$\frac{1}{5}$	$\frac{1}{5}$	$\frac{1}{5}$
$\frac{1}{5}$	$\frac{1}{5}$	$\frac{1}{5}$	$\frac{1}{5}$	$\frac{1}{5}$	$\frac{1}{5}$	$\frac{1}{5}$	$\frac{1}{5}$	$\frac{1}{5}$	$\frac{1}{5}$	$\frac{1}{5}$	$\frac{1}{5}$	$\frac{1}{5}$
$\frac{5}{5}$					$\frac{5}{5}$					$\frac{3}{5}$		

Ⓐ $\frac{10}{5}$

Ⓑ $\frac{3}{5}$

Ⓒ $\frac{13}{5}$

Ⓓ $\frac{1}{5}$

15. Derrick needs 4 strips of wood to make a frame. Each strip must be $\frac{1}{3}$ yard long. How much wood should Derrick buy to make the frame?

Ⓐ 1 yard

Ⓑ $1\frac{4}{3}$ yards

Ⓒ $\frac{1}{3}$ yard

Ⓓ $1\frac{1}{3}$ yards

16. A box of cereal contains $4\frac{3}{4}$ cups of cereal. Each serving is $\frac{1}{4}$ cup. How many servings of cereal are in the box?

Ⓐ 16

Ⓑ 19

Ⓒ 4

Ⓓ 3

TEXAS Test Prep

17. Which fraction greater than 1 can you write for $4\frac{5}{9}$?

Ⓐ $\frac{9}{9}$

Ⓑ $\frac{18}{9}$

Ⓒ $\frac{41}{9}$

Ⓓ $\frac{45}{9}$

TEKS Number and Operations—4.3.B *Also 4.3.A*
MATHEMATICAL PROCESSES 4.1.A, 4.1.B, 4.1.C, 4.1.F

Name ______________________

3.6 Rename Fractions and Mixed Numbers

Write the unknown numbers. Write mixed numbers above the number line and fractions greater than one below the number line.

1.

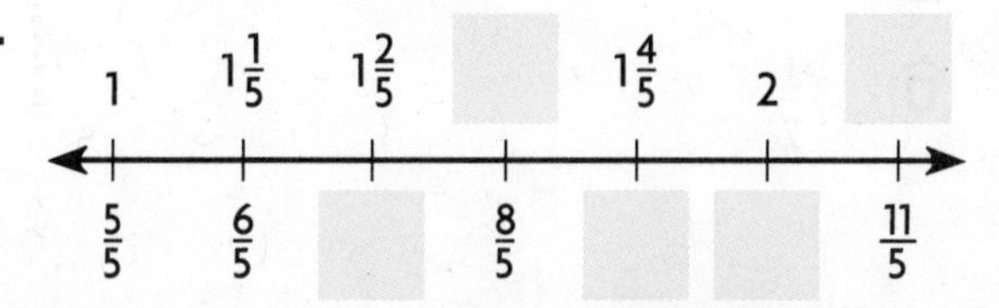

Write the mixed number as a fraction.

2. $2\frac{1}{4}$ ______

3. $3\frac{2}{3}$ ______

4. $4\frac{1}{6}$ ______

Write the fraction as a mixed number.

5. $\frac{7}{6}$ ______

6. $\frac{14}{2}$ ______

7. $\frac{8}{3}$ ______

Problem Solving

Use the recipe to solve 8–9.

8. Celia is making smoothies. How many $\frac{1}{4}$ cups of peaches are used in the recipe?

____

9. What is the amount of orange juice, written as a fraction greater than 1, that is used in the recipe?

____

Lesson Check

TEXAS Test Prep

Fill in the bubble completely to show your answer.

10. Calvin is making birdhouses to sell at the fair. So far he has finished $5\frac{1}{2}$ birdhouses. Which fraction greater than one represents this mixed number?

Ⓐ $\frac{10}{3}$

Ⓑ $\frac{6}{2}$

Ⓒ $\frac{5}{3}$

Ⓓ $\frac{11}{2}$

11. Which mixed number can you write for $\frac{24}{7}$?

Ⓐ $24\frac{1}{7}$

Ⓑ $4\frac{3}{7}$

Ⓒ $3\frac{3}{7}$

Ⓓ $3\frac{1}{7}$

12. Paolo uses $3\frac{1}{4}$ cups of oatmeal to make breakfast bars. What fraction greater than one represents this mixed number?

Ⓐ $\frac{13}{4}$

Ⓑ $\frac{12}{5}$

Ⓒ $\frac{4}{4}$

Ⓓ $\frac{31}{4}$

13. Which mixed number can you write for $\frac{13}{5}$?

Ⓐ $1\frac{3}{5}$

Ⓑ $13\frac{1}{5}$

Ⓒ $3\frac{2}{5}$

Ⓓ $2\frac{3}{5}$

14. **Multi-Step** Juanita is making bread. She needs $3\frac{1}{2}$ cups of flour. Juanita only has a $\frac{1}{4}$-cup measuring cup. How many $\frac{1}{4}$ cups of flour will Juanita use to prepare the bread?

Ⓐ 14

Ⓑ 7

Ⓒ 9

Ⓓ 12

15. **Multi-Step** Each day for 7 days, Mr. Cole used $\frac{1}{2}$ can of paint. Which mixed number represents how much paint Mr. Cole used after 7 days?

Ⓐ $7\frac{1}{2}$

Ⓑ $2\frac{1}{2}$

Ⓒ $3\frac{1}{2}$

Ⓓ $8\frac{1}{2}$

Name ________________________________

Module 3 Assessment

Vocabulary

Choose the best term from the box.

Vocabulary
unit fraction
equivalent fractions
factor

1. ____________________ name the same amount. (p. 75)

2. A ____________________ always has a numerator of 1. (p. 99)

Concepts and Skills

Write two equivalent fractions. TEKS 4.3.C

3. $\frac{2}{5}$ = _____ = _____

4. $\frac{1}{3}$ = _____ = _____

5. $\frac{3}{4}$ = _____ = _____

Tell whether the fractions are equivalent. Write = or ≠. TEKS 4.3.C

6. $\frac{2}{3}$ ◯ $\frac{4}{12}$

7. $\frac{5}{6}$ ◯ $\frac{10}{12}$

8. $\frac{1}{4}$ ◯ $\frac{4}{8}$

Write the fraction in simplest form. TEKS 4.3.C

9. $\frac{6}{8}$ ____________________

10. $\frac{25}{100}$ ____________________

11. $\frac{8}{10}$ ____________________

Write the fraction as a sum of unit fractions. TEKS 4.3.A, 4.3.B

12.

1				
$\frac{1}{5}$	$\frac{1}{5}$	$\frac{1}{5}$	$\frac{1}{5}$	$\frac{1}{5}$

$\frac{3}{5}$ = ____________________

13.

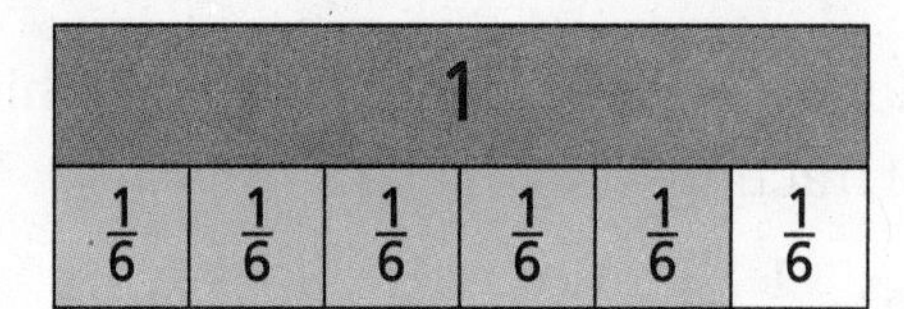

$\frac{5}{6}$ = ____________________

14.

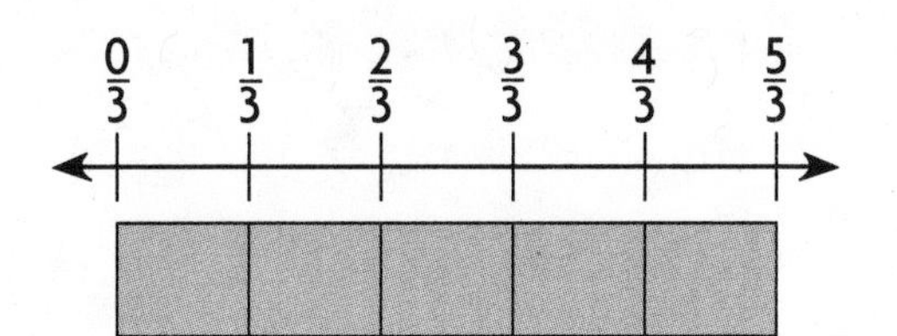

$\frac{5}{3}$ = ____________________

15.

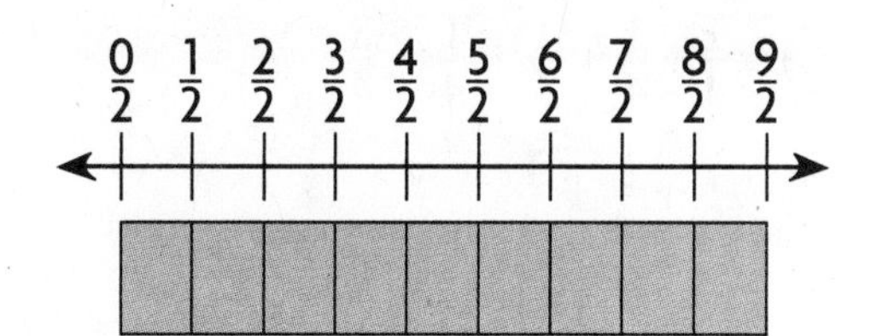

$\frac{9}{2}$ = ____________________

Fill in the bubble completely to show your answer.

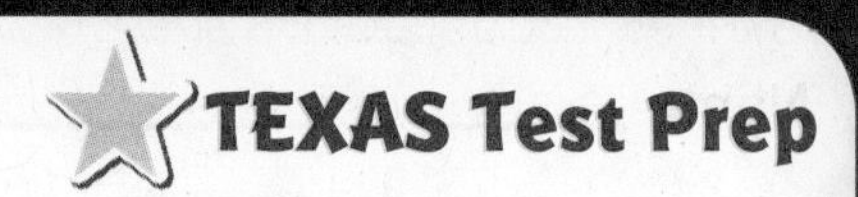

16. Sam needs $\frac{5}{6}$ cup mashed bananas and $\frac{3}{4}$ cup mashed strawberries for a recipe. Which shows a pair of fractions that are equivalent to $\frac{5}{6}$ and $\frac{3}{4}$? TEKS 4.3.C

Ⓐ $\frac{5}{12}$ and $\frac{3}{12}$

Ⓑ $\frac{10}{12}$ and $\frac{2}{12}$

Ⓒ $\frac{10}{12}$ and $\frac{9}{12}$

Ⓓ $\frac{2}{3}$ and $\frac{18}{24}$

17. Karen will divide her garden into equal parts. She will plant corn in $\frac{1}{5}$ of the garden. Which fraction is equivalent to $\frac{1}{5}$? TEKS 4.3.C

Ⓐ $\frac{2}{15}$

Ⓑ $\frac{3}{12}$

Ⓒ $\frac{2}{10}$

Ⓓ $\frac{4}{5}$

18. Olivia cut a board into 8 equal pieces. She used $\frac{5}{8}$ of the pieces. Which shows $\frac{5}{8}$ written as a sum of unit fractions? TEKS 4.3.A

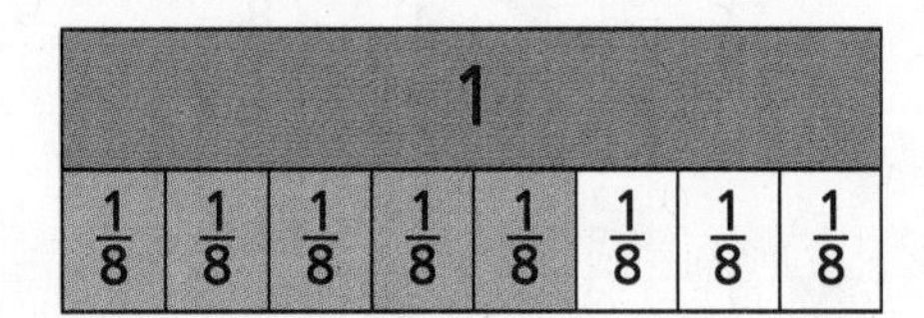

Ⓐ $\frac{1}{8}+\frac{1}{8}+\frac{1}{8}$

Ⓑ $\frac{1}{8}+\frac{1}{8}+\frac{1}{8}+\frac{1}{8}+\frac{1}{8}$

Ⓒ $\frac{1}{8}+\frac{1}{8}$

Ⓓ $\frac{1}{8}+\frac{1}{8}+\frac{1}{8}+\frac{1}{8}$

19. Robert grew $1\frac{3}{4}$ inches last year. Which shows $1\frac{3}{4}$ written as a sum of fractions? TEKS 4.3.B

Ⓐ $\frac{1}{4}+\frac{1}{4}+\frac{1}{4}$

Ⓑ $\frac{1}{4}+\frac{1}{4}$

Ⓒ $\frac{1}{4}+\frac{1}{4}+\frac{1}{4}+\frac{1}{4}+\frac{3}{4}$

Ⓓ $1+\frac{1}{4}+\frac{1}{4}$

Name ____________________

TEKS Number and Operations—4.3.D

MATHEMATICAL PROCESSES 4.1.C, 4.1.D, 4.1.E, 4.1.G

4.1 Compare Fractions Using Benchmarks

Essential Question How can you use benchmarks to compare fractions?

Unlock the Problem (Real World)

Zach made a popcorn snack. He mixed $\frac{5}{8}$ gallon of popcorn with $\frac{1}{2}$ gallon of dried apple rings. Did he use more dried apple rings or more popcorn?

Activity Compare $\frac{5}{8}$ and $\frac{1}{2}$.

Materials ■ fraction strips

Use fraction strips to compare $\frac{5}{8}$ and $\frac{1}{2}$. Record on the model below.

$\frac{1}{2}$	$\frac{1}{2}$			$\frac{1}{2}$			
$\frac{5}{8}$	$\frac{1}{8}$	$\frac{1}{8}$	$\frac{1}{8}$	$\frac{1}{8}$	$\frac{1}{8}$	$\frac{1}{8}$	$\frac{1}{8}$	$\frac{1}{8}$

$\frac{5}{8}$ ◯ $\frac{1}{2}$

So, Zach used more ____________.

Math Talk Mathematical Processes

Explain how the number of eighth-size parts in $\frac{5}{8}$ is related to the number of eighth-size parts you need to make $\frac{1}{2}$.

Benchmarks A **benchmark** is a known size or amount that helps you understand a different size or amount. You can use $\frac{1}{2}$ as a benchmark to help you compare fractions.

1. How many eighths are equivalent to $\frac{1}{2}$?

____

2. How can you compare $\frac{5}{8}$ and $\frac{1}{2}$ without using a model?

____

____

____

Example Use benchmarks to compare fractions.

A family hiked the same mountain trail. Evie and her father hiked $\frac{5}{12}$ of the trail before they stopped for lunch. Jill and her mother hiked $\frac{9}{10}$ of the trail before they stopped for lunch. Who hiked farther before lunch?

Compare $\frac{5}{12}$ and $\frac{9}{10}$ to the benchmark $\frac{1}{2}$.

STEP 1 Compare $\frac{5}{12}$ to $\frac{1}{2}$.

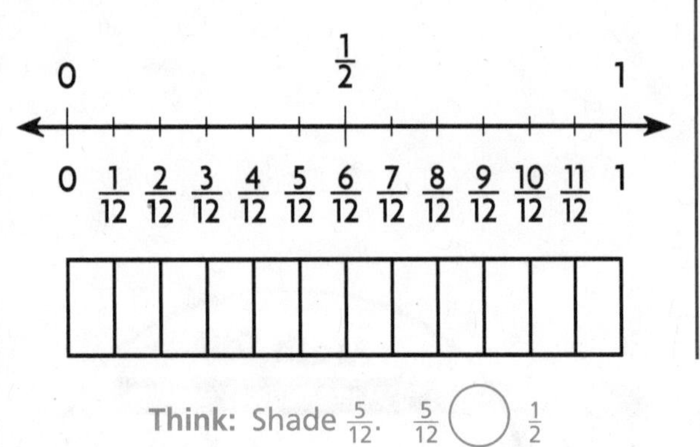

Think: Shade $\frac{5}{12}$. $\frac{5}{12}$ ◯ $\frac{1}{2}$

STEP 2 Compare $\frac{9}{10}$ to $\frac{1}{2}$.

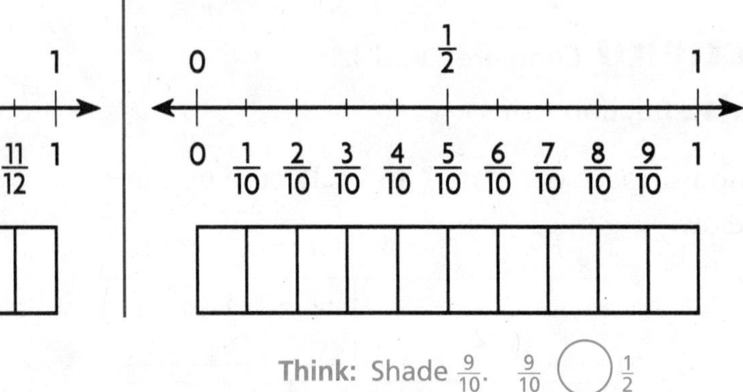

Think: Shade $\frac{9}{10}$. $\frac{9}{10}$ ◯ $\frac{1}{2}$

Since $\frac{5}{12}$ is ____________ than $\frac{1}{2}$ and is $\frac{9}{10}$ ____________ than $\frac{1}{2}$, you know that $\frac{5}{12}$ ◯ $\frac{9}{10}$.

So, ____________________ hiked farther before lunch.

Share and Show

MATH BOARD

1. Compare $\frac{2}{5}$ and $\frac{1}{8}$. Write < or >.

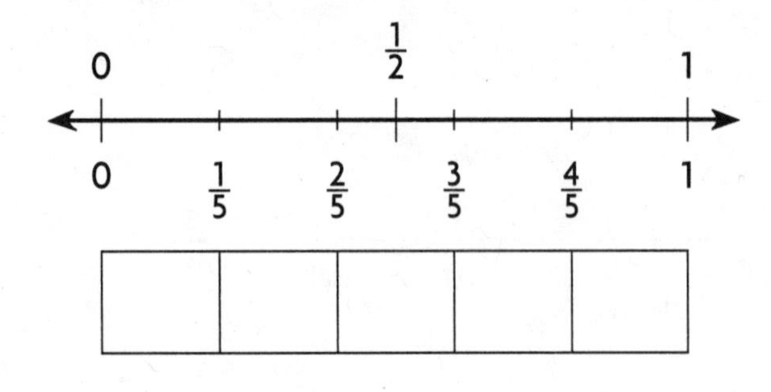

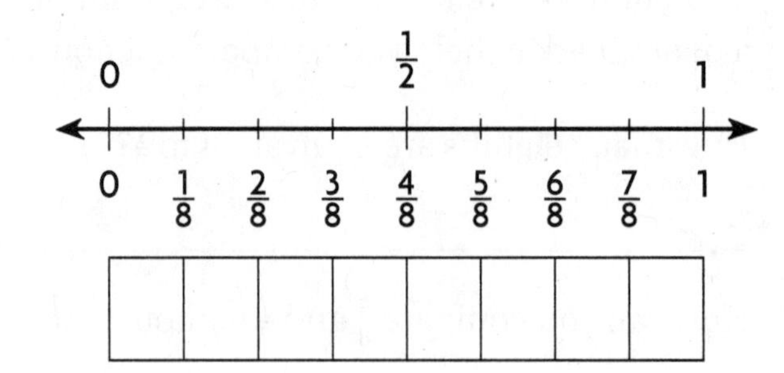

$\frac{2}{5}$ ◯ $\frac{1}{8}$

Compare. Write < or >.

2. $\frac{1}{2}$ ◯ $\frac{4}{6}$

3. $\frac{3}{10}$ ◯ $\frac{1}{2}$

4. $\frac{11}{2}$ ◯ $\frac{4}{8}$

5. $\frac{5}{8}$ ◯ $\frac{2}{5}$

Name ____________________

H.O.T. **Algebra** **Find a numerator that makes the statement true.**

6. $\frac{2}{4} < \frac{\square}{6}$

7. $\frac{8}{10} > \frac{\square}{8}$

8. $\frac{10}{12} > \frac{\square}{4}$

9. $\frac{2}{5} < \frac{\square}{10}$

10. When two fractions are between 0 and $\frac{1}{2}$, how do you know which fraction is greater? **Explain.**

____

____

Problem Solving Real World

11. A group of students ate $\frac{5}{12}$ of a large pepperoni pizza and $\frac{8}{10}$ of a large cheese pizza. Did they eat more pepperoni pizza or cheese pizza?

____

2. **H.O.T.** Saundra ran $\frac{7}{12}$ of a mile. Lamar ran $\frac{3}{4}$ of a mile. Who ran farther? **Explain.**

____

____

____

13. **H.O.T.** **What's the Question?** Selena ran farther than Manny.

____

____

____

14. Mary made a small pan of ziti and a small pan of lasagna. She cut the ziti into 8 equal parts and the lasagna into 9 equal parts. Her family ate $\frac{2}{3}$ of the lasagna. If her family ate more lasagna than ziti, what fraction of the ziti could have been eaten?

____

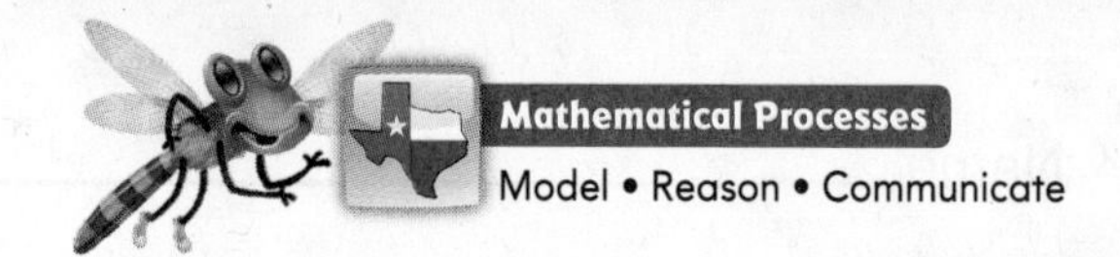

Daily Assessment Task

Fill in the bubble completely to show your answer.

15. **Use Diagrams** Some monkeys live high up in trees. Two monkeys are climbing a tree. One monkey climbed up $\frac{5}{6}$ of the tree. The other monkey climbed up $\frac{7}{8}$ of the tree. Which statement about $\frac{5}{6}$ and $\frac{7}{8}$ is true?

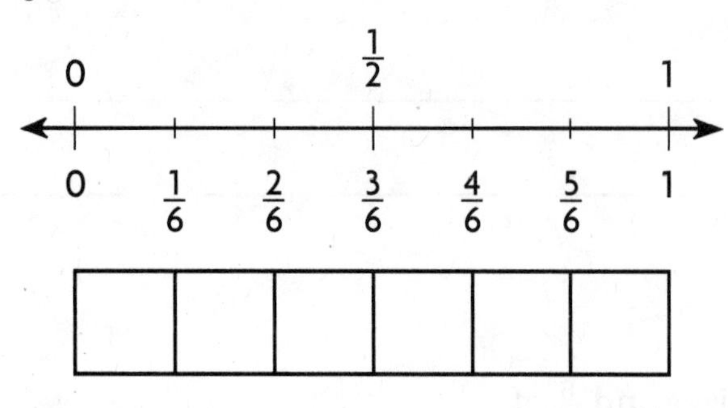

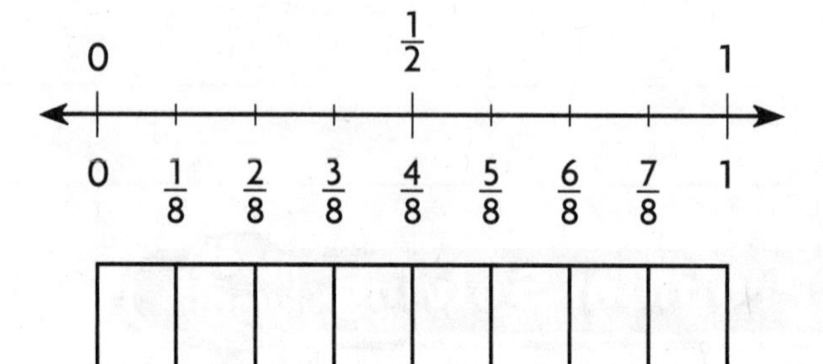

Ⓐ $\frac{5}{6} > \frac{7}{8}$ Ⓒ $\frac{5}{6} < \frac{7}{8}$

Ⓑ $\frac{7}{8} < \frac{5}{6}$ Ⓓ $\frac{5}{6} = \frac{7}{8}$

16. Maggie did $\frac{5}{12}$ of her homework before dinner. Her brother did $\frac{4}{10}$ of his homework. Which statement is true about the fractions $\frac{5}{12}$ and $\frac{4}{10}$?

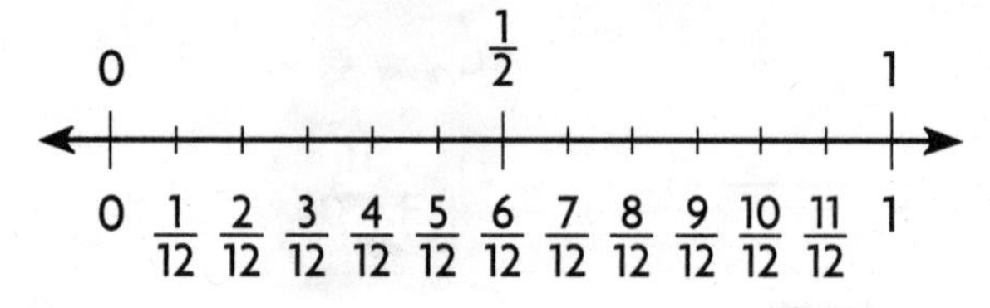

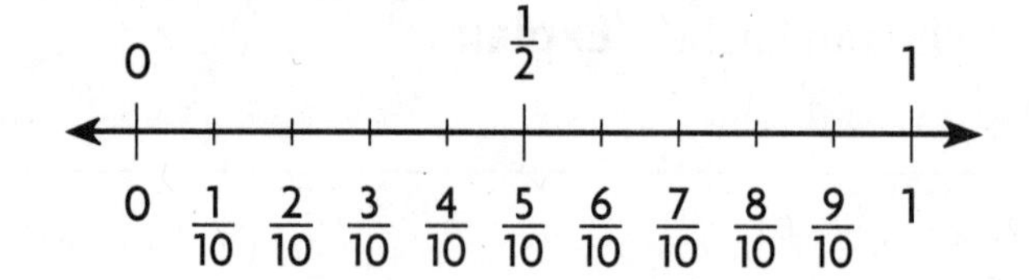

Ⓐ $\frac{5}{12} < \frac{4}{10}$ Ⓒ $\frac{5}{12} > \frac{4}{10}$

Ⓑ $\frac{4}{10} = \frac{1}{2}$ Ⓓ $\frac{5}{12} > \frac{1}{2}$

17. **Multi-Step** If you know that $\frac{2}{6} < \frac{1}{2}$ and $\frac{3}{4} > \frac{1}{2}$, what do you know about $\frac{2}{6}$ and $\frac{3}{4}$?

Ⓐ $\frac{3}{4} = \frac{1}{2}$ Ⓑ $\frac{2}{6} > \frac{3}{4}$ Ⓒ $\frac{2}{6} > \frac{1}{2}$ Ⓓ $\frac{2}{6} < \frac{3}{4}$

TEXAS Test Prep

18. Todd is using the benchmark $\frac{1}{2}$ to compare fractions. Which statement is NOT correct?

Ⓐ $\frac{5}{6} < \frac{1}{2}$ Ⓒ $\frac{5}{6} > \frac{1}{2}$

Ⓑ $\frac{3}{6} = \frac{1}{2}$ Ⓓ $\frac{5}{6} \neq \frac{1}{2}$

Name ______________________

4.1 Compare Fractions Using Benchmarks

1. How many sixths are equivalent to $\frac{1}{2}$?

____

2. How can you compare $\frac{7}{10}$ and $\frac{1}{2}$ without using a model?

____

____

Compare. Write $<$ or $>$.

3. $\frac{8}{10} \bigcirc \frac{3}{8}$

4. $\frac{1}{3} \bigcirc \frac{7}{12}$

5. $\frac{2}{6} \bigcirc \frac{7}{8}$

6. $\frac{3}{4} \bigcirc \frac{1}{2}$

7. $\frac{6}{6} \bigcirc \frac{1}{3}$

8. $\frac{4}{5} \bigcirc \frac{1}{6}$

Find a numerator that makes the statement true.

9. $\frac{2}{4} > \frac{\square}{8}$

10. $\frac{5}{10} < \frac{\square}{8}$

11. $\frac{3}{6} > \frac{\square}{12}$

12. $\frac{2}{8} < \frac{\square}{10}$

Problem Solving

13. Leticia read $\frac{4}{5}$ of her book and Grace read $\frac{6}{10}$ of her book. Who read more of her book, Leticia or Grace? **Explain.**

____

____

14. Kyle made brownies and a cake. He cut the brownies into 6 equal parts and the cake into 8 equal parts. His family ate $\frac{3}{4}$ of the cake. If his family ate more cake than brownies, what fraction of the brownies could have been eaten?

____

____

Lesson Check

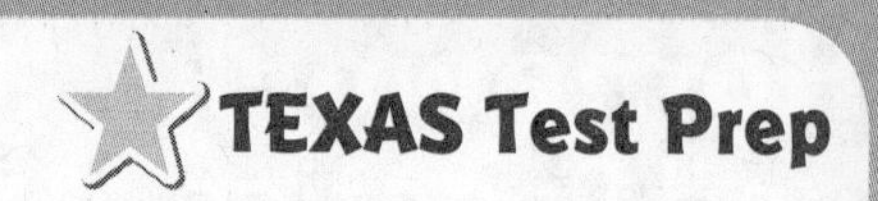

Fill in the bubble completely to show your answer.

15. Which symbol completes the following statement?

$$\frac{5}{8} \bigcirc \frac{9}{10}$$

Ⓐ $=$

Ⓑ $\neq$

Ⓒ $<$

Ⓓ $>$

16. Garrett is using the benchmark $\frac{1}{2}$ to compare fractions. Which statement is NOT true?

Ⓐ $\frac{4}{8} = \frac{1}{2}$

Ⓑ $\frac{3}{8} \neq \frac{1}{2}$

Ⓒ $\frac{3}{8} < \frac{1}{2}$

Ⓓ $\frac{3}{8} > \frac{1}{2}$

17. Rob's paper route is $\frac{8}{10}$ mile long. Lin's route is $\frac{3}{4}$ mile long. What is true about $\frac{8}{10}$ and $\frac{3}{4}$?

Ⓐ $\frac{3}{4} > \frac{8}{10}$

Ⓑ $\frac{8}{10} < \frac{3}{4}$

Ⓒ $\frac{8}{10} > \frac{3}{4}$

Ⓓ $\frac{8}{10} = \frac{3}{4}$

18. Tia compares $\frac{11}{12}$ and $\frac{2}{3}$. Which statement is true?

Ⓐ $\frac{2}{3} = \frac{11}{12}$

Ⓑ $\frac{2}{3} > \frac{11}{12}$

Ⓒ $\frac{11}{12} < \frac{2}{3}$

Ⓓ $\frac{2}{3} < \frac{11}{12}$

19. Multi-Step Sandra is making crafts from leftover ribbons. She needs a ribbon longer than $\frac{2}{3}$ yard to make a bow. Which length of ribbon could she use for the bow?

Ⓐ $\frac{3}{4}$ yard

Ⓑ $\frac{2}{6}$ yard

Ⓒ $\frac{1}{5}$ yard

Ⓓ $\frac{4}{7}$ yard

20. Multi-Step Jessie has several bottles of used paint. He has three bottles of blue paint. The first bottle is $\frac{1}{8}$ full, the second bottle is $\frac{1}{4}$ full, and the third bottle is $\frac{1}{4}$ full. He has one bottle of yellow paint that is $\frac{1}{2}$ full. Which of the following correctly compares the blue paint to the yellow paint?

Ⓐ $\frac{3}{8} = \frac{1}{2}$

Ⓑ $\frac{5}{8} > \frac{1}{2}$

Ⓒ $\frac{3}{8} > \frac{1}{2}$

Ⓓ $\frac{5}{8} < \frac{1}{2}$

Name ______________________________

4.2 Compare Fractions

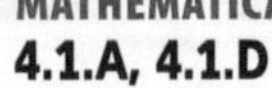

TEKS Number and Operations—4.3.D
MATHEMATICAL PROCESSES 4.1.A, 4.1.D

Essential Question How can you compare fractions?

Unlock the Problem Real World

Hands On

Every year, Avery's school has a fair. This year, $\frac{3}{8}$ of the booths had face painting and $\frac{1}{4}$ of the booths had sand art. Were there more booths with face painting or sand art?

Compare $\frac{3}{8}$ and $\frac{1}{4}$.

One Way Use equivalent fractions with the same denominator.

When two fractions have the same denominator, they have equal-size parts. You can compare the number of parts.

THINK

Think: 8 is a multiple of both 4 and 8. Use 8 as a denominator.

$$\frac{1}{4} = \frac{1 \times \square}{4 \times \square} = \frac{\square}{8}$$

$\frac{3}{8}$ already has 8 as a denominator.

MODEL AND RECORD

Shade the model. Then compare.

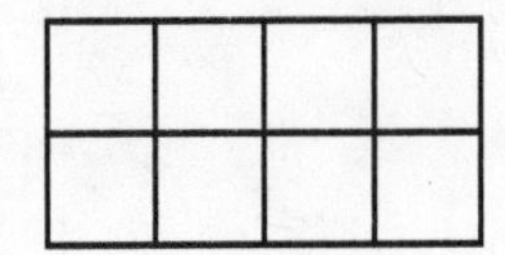
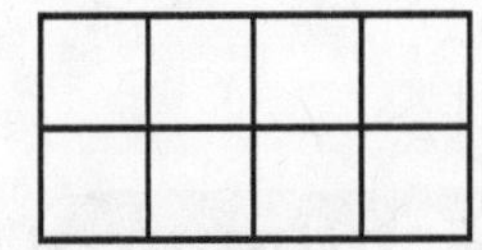

$\frac{3}{8}$ ◯ $\frac{2}{8}$

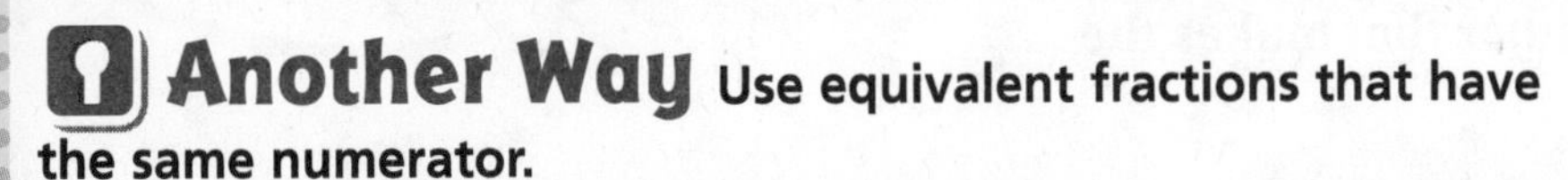

Another Way Use equivalent fractions that have the same numerator.

When two fractions have the same numerator, they represent the same number of parts. You can compare the size of the parts.

THINK

Think: 3 is a multiple of both 3 and 1. Use 3 as a numerator.

$\frac{3}{8}$ already has 3 as a numerator.

$$\frac{1}{4} = \frac{1 \times \square}{4 \times \square} = \frac{3}{\square}$$

MODEL AND RECORD

Shade the model. Then compare.

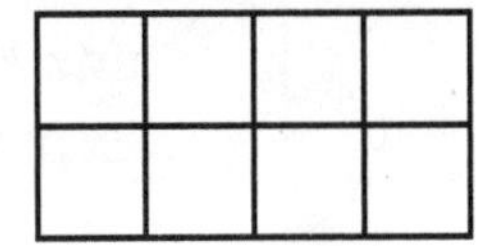
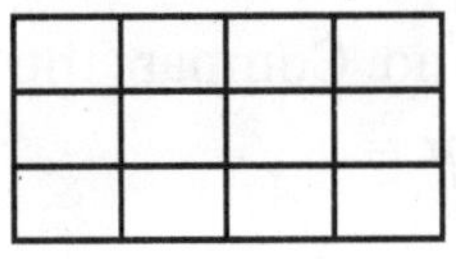

$\frac{3}{8}$ ◯ $\frac{3}{12}$

Since $\frac{3}{8}$ ◯ $\frac{1}{4}$, there were more booths with ____________.

Share and Show

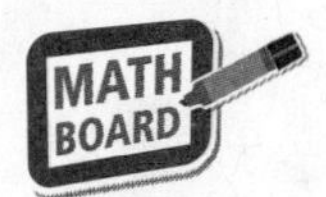

1. Compare $\frac{2}{5}$ and $\frac{1}{10}$.

Think: Use _______ as a denominator.

$\frac{2}{5} = \frac{\square \times \square}{\square \times \square} = \frac{\square}{\square}$

$\frac{1}{10}$

Think: 4 tenth-size parts ◯ 1 tenth-size part.

$\frac{2}{5} \bigcirc \frac{1}{10}$

2. Compare $\frac{6}{10}$ and $\frac{3}{4}$.

Think: Use _______ as a numerator.

$\frac{6}{10}$

$\frac{3}{4} = \frac{\square \times \square}{\square \times \square} = \frac{\square}{\square}$

Think: A tenth-size part ◯ an eighth-size part.

$\frac{6}{10} \bigcirc \frac{3}{4}$

Compare. Write <, >, or =.

3. $\frac{7}{8} \bigcirc \frac{2}{8}$

4. $\frac{5}{12} \bigcirc \frac{3}{6}$

5. $\frac{4}{10} \bigcirc \frac{4}{6}$

6. $\frac{6}{12} \bigcirc \frac{2}{4}$

Math Talk
Mathematical Processes
Explain why using the same numerator or the same denominator can help you compare fractions.

Problem Solving

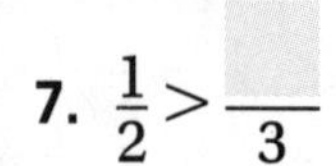

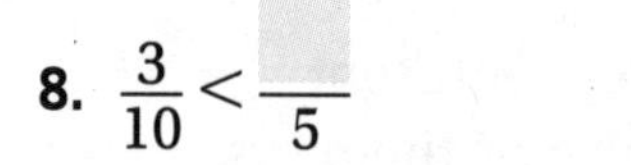

Algebra **Find a number that makes the statement true.**

7. $\frac{1}{2} > \frac{\square}{3}$

8. $\frac{3}{10} < \frac{\square}{5}$

9. $\frac{5}{12} < \frac{\square}{3}$

10. $\frac{2}{3} > \frac{4}{\square}$

11. **Multi-Step** Lafayette has one book that weighs $\frac{5}{8}$ pound and another that weighs $\frac{2}{3}$ pound. Compare the weights using <, >, or =.

____

12. **Multi-Step** Gena, Freddie, and Hank went running. Gena ran $\frac{1}{3}$ mile, Freddie ran $\frac{4}{7}$ mile, and Hank ran $\frac{2}{5}$ mile. Who ran the farthest? **Explain** your reasoning.

____

____

____

Name ______________________________

Problem Solving | Real World

13. H.O.T. **Multi-Step** Jerry is making a strawberry smoothie. Which statement about the recipe is true?

Strawberry Smoothie

3 ice cubes

$\frac{3}{4}$ cup milk

$\frac{2}{6}$ cup cottage cheese

$\frac{8}{12}$ cup strawberries

$\frac{1}{4}$ teaspoon vanilla

$\frac{1}{8}$ teaspoon sugar

Ⓐ The amount of strawberries is greater than the amount of milk.

Ⓑ The amount of milk is less than the amount of cottage cheese.

Ⓒ The amount of strawberries is equal to the amount of cottage cheese.

Ⓓ The amount of vanilla is greater than the amount of sugar.

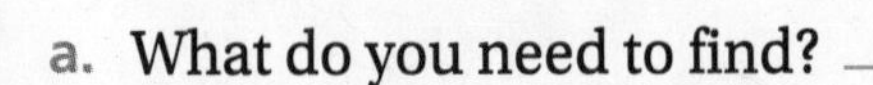

a. What do you need to find? ______________________________

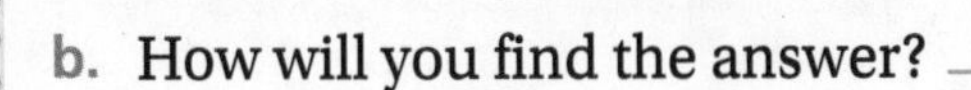

b. How will you find the answer? ______________________________

____

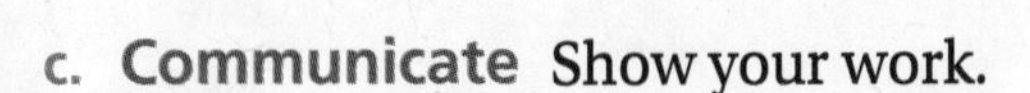

c. **Communicate** Show your work.

d. Fill in the bubble for the correct answer choice above.

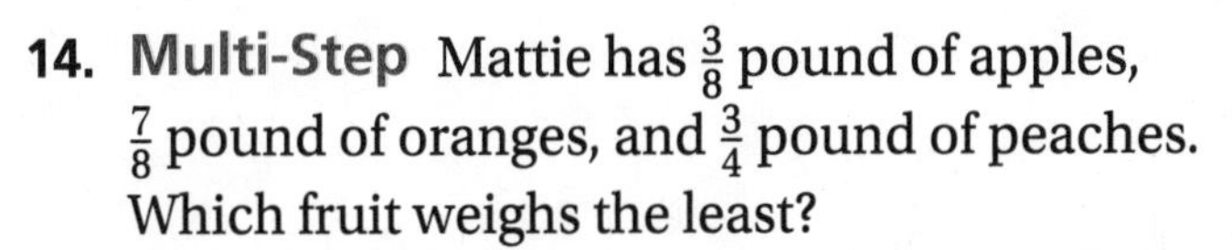

14. **Multi-Step** Mattie has $\frac{3}{8}$ pound of apples, $\frac{7}{8}$ pound of oranges, and $\frac{3}{4}$ pound of peaches. Which fruit weighs the least?

Ⓐ They weigh the same

Ⓑ oranges

Ⓒ apples

Ⓓ peaches

15. One kite reached a height of $\frac{1}{4}$ mile. The other kite reached a height of $\frac{3}{16}$ mile. What can you say about the two heights?

Ⓐ $\frac{1}{4}$ mile = $\frac{3}{16}$ mile

Ⓑ $\frac{3}{16}$ mile > $\frac{1}{4}$ mile

Ⓒ $\frac{1}{4}$ mile > $\frac{3}{16}$ mile

Ⓓ $\frac{1}{4}$ mile < $\frac{3}{16}$ mile

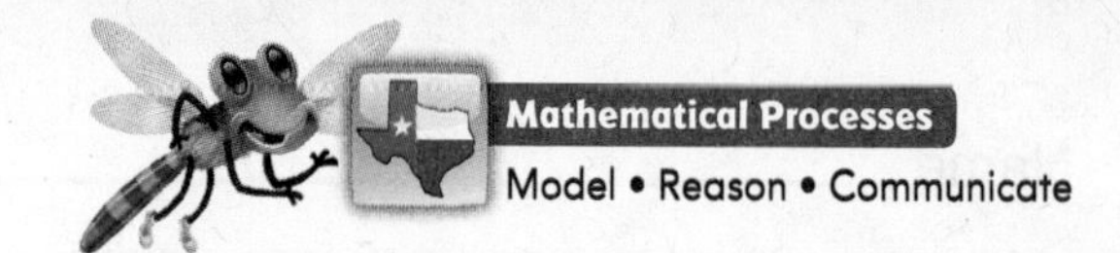

Daily Assessment Task

Fill in the bubble completely to show your answer.

16. Apply Students decorated their piñatas with paint, flowers, feathers, and glitter. They used $\frac{3}{4}$ bottle of green glitter and $\frac{5}{8}$ bottle of silver glitter. Which shows how the amounts of green and silver glitter compare?

Ⓐ $\frac{3}{4} < \frac{5}{8}$

Ⓑ $\frac{3}{4} > \frac{5}{8}$

Ⓒ $\frac{5}{8} > \frac{3}{4}$

Ⓓ $\frac{3}{4} = \frac{5}{8}$

17. Stephen ran $\frac{1}{4}$ mile and Tara ran $\frac{2}{5}$ mile. Which shows how $\frac{2}{5}$ and $\frac{1}{4}$ compare?

Ⓐ $\frac{1}{4} = \frac{2}{5}$

Ⓑ $\frac{2}{5} > \frac{1}{4}$

Ⓒ $\frac{2}{5} < \frac{1}{4}$

Ⓓ $\frac{1}{4} > \frac{2}{5}$

18. Multi-Step Students cut a pepperoni pizza into 12 equal slices and ate 5 slices. They cut a veggie pizza into 6 equal slices and ate 4 slices. Which statement compares the amounts of each pizza that were eaten?

Ⓐ $\frac{12}{5} < \frac{6}{4}$

Ⓑ $\frac{5}{17} > \frac{4}{10}$

Ⓒ $\frac{5}{12} > \frac{4}{6}$

Ⓓ $\frac{4}{6} > \frac{5}{12}$

TEXAS Test Prep

19. Simon studied $\frac{7}{8}$ hour, Marci studied $\frac{7}{12}$ hour, and John studied $\frac{15}{16}$ hour. Which one of the following comparisons is true?

Ⓐ $\frac{15}{16} > \frac{7}{8}$ and $\frac{7}{8} > \frac{7}{12}$

Ⓑ $\frac{7}{12} > \frac{7}{8}$ and $\frac{7}{8} > \frac{15}{16}$

Ⓒ $\frac{7}{12} < \frac{7}{8}$ and $\frac{7}{8} > \frac{15}{16}$

Ⓓ $\frac{15}{16} > \frac{7}{12}$ and $\frac{7}{12} > \frac{7}{8}$

Name ________________________

4.2 Compare Fractions

Compare. Write <, >, or =.

1. $\frac{1}{3} \bigcirc \frac{1}{4}$

2. $\frac{4}{5} \bigcirc \frac{8}{10}$

3. $\frac{3}{4} \bigcirc \frac{2}{4}$

4. $\frac{3}{10} \bigcirc \frac{2}{4}$

5. $\frac{75}{100} \bigcirc \frac{8}{10}$

6. $\frac{4}{6} \bigcirc \frac{2}{3}$

Find a number that makes the statement true.

7. $\frac{1}{2} < \frac{\square}{8}$

8. $\frac{3}{10} > \frac{\square}{20}$

9. $\frac{4}{5} > \frac{2}{\square}$

10. $\frac{1}{2} < \frac{5}{\square}$

11. $\frac{4}{5} > \frac{\square}{10}$

12. $\frac{2}{3} > \frac{3}{\square}$

Problem Solving

13. At the yard sale, $\frac{3}{4}$ of the items for sale were toys and $\frac{5}{8}$ of the items for sale were books. Were there more toys or books for sale? **Explain.**

____

____

14. A smoothie recipe calls for $\frac{3}{4}$ cup of milk and $\frac{2}{3}$ cup of yogurt. Does the recipe call for more milk or yogurt? **Explain.**

____

____

15. A puppy weighs $\frac{7}{18}$ pound and a kitten weighs $\frac{4}{9}$ pound. Which weighs more? **Explain.**

____

____

16. Tully ran $\frac{7}{10}$ mile and Maggie ran $\frac{3}{5}$ mile. Who ran farther? **Explain.**

____

____

Lesson Check

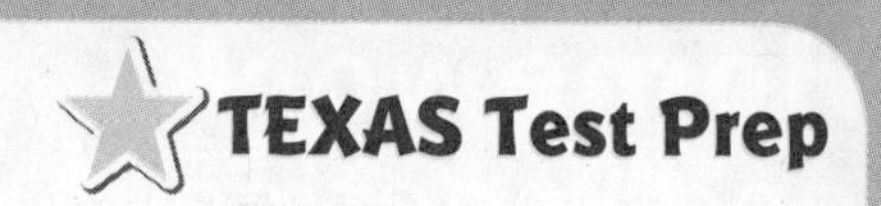

Fill in the bubble completely to show your answer.

17. Which number makes this statement true?

$$\frac{2}{7} > \frac{\square}{5}$$

Ⓐ 2

Ⓑ 3

Ⓒ 4

Ⓓ 1

18. The Garcia family ate $\frac{8}{12}$ of a pizza. What is $\frac{8}{12}$ in simplest form?

Ⓐ $\frac{2}{3}$

Ⓑ $\frac{8}{12}$

Ⓒ $\frac{1}{4}$

Ⓓ $\frac{4}{6}$

19. Jamie mixed $\frac{2}{3}$ bottle of cranberry juice and $\frac{5}{6}$ bottle of orange juice. Which shows how to compare $\frac{2}{3}$ and $\frac{5}{6}$?

Ⓐ $\frac{2}{3} < \frac{5}{6}$

Ⓑ $\frac{5}{6} < \frac{2}{3}$

Ⓒ $\frac{5}{6} = \frac{2}{3}$

Ⓓ $\frac{2}{3} > \frac{5}{6}$

20. Stephan practiced $\frac{9}{10}$ hour on Saturday and $\frac{3}{4}$ hour on Sunday. Which statement compares $\frac{9}{10}$ and $\frac{3}{4}$?

Ⓐ $\frac{3}{4} = \frac{9}{10}$

Ⓑ $\frac{3}{4} > \frac{9}{10}$

Ⓒ $\frac{9}{10} < \frac{3}{4}$

Ⓓ $\frac{9}{10} > \frac{3}{4}$

21. **Multi-Step** Angie, Blake, Carlos, and Daisy went running. Angie ran $\frac{1}{3}$ mile, Blake ran $\frac{3}{5}$ mile, Carlos ran $\frac{7}{10}$ mile, and Daisy ran $\frac{1}{2}$ mile. Who ran the farthest?

Ⓐ Angie

Ⓑ Blake

Ⓒ Carlos

Ⓓ Daisy

22. Carmen is hanging framed pictures on her wall. One picture weighs $\frac{4}{7}$ pound and another weighs $\frac{3}{4}$ pound. Which statement correctly compares the weights?

Ⓐ $\frac{8}{14} = \frac{3}{4}$

Ⓑ $\frac{4}{7} < \frac{3}{4}$

Ⓒ $\frac{8}{14} > \frac{3}{4}$

Ⓓ $\frac{4}{7} > \frac{3}{4}$

Name ______________________________

4.3 Compare and Order Fractions

TEKS Number and Operations—4.3.D, 4.3.G
MATHEMATICAL PROCESSES 4.1.A, 4.1.B, 4.1.D

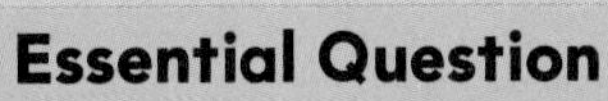

Essential Question How can you order fractions?

Unlock the Problem (Real World)

Jody has equal-size bins for the recycling center. She filled $\frac{3}{5}$ of a bin with plastics, $\frac{1}{12}$ of a bin with paper, and $\frac{9}{10}$ of a bin with glass. Which bin is the most full?

- Underline what you need to find.
- Circle the fractions you will compare.

Example 1 Locate and label $\frac{3}{5}$, $\frac{1}{12}$, and $\frac{9}{10}$ on the number line.

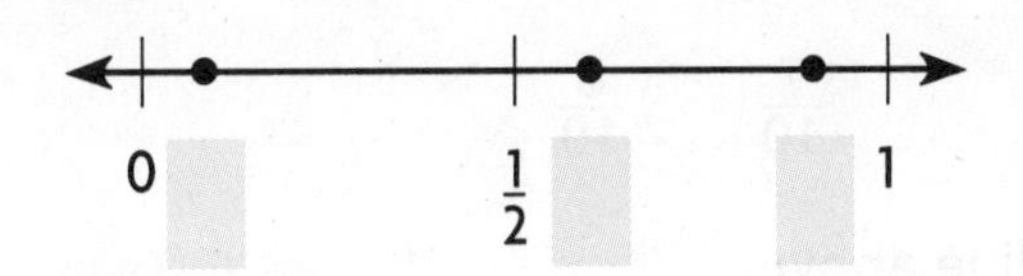

Math Idea

Sometimes it is not reasonable to find the exact location of a point on a number line. Benchmarks can help you find approximate locations.

STEP 1 Compare each fraction to $\frac{1}{2}$.

$\frac{3}{5}$ ◯ $\frac{1}{2}$ $\quad$ $\frac{1}{12}$ ◯ $\frac{1}{2}$ $\quad$ $\frac{9}{10}$ ◯ $\frac{1}{2}$

______ and ______ are both greater than $\frac{1}{2}$.

______ is less than $\frac{1}{2}$.

Label $\frac{1}{12}$ on the number line above.

STEP 2 Compare $\frac{3}{5}$ and $\frac{9}{10}$.

Think: Use 10 as a denominator.

$\frac{3}{5} = \frac{\square \times \square}{\square \times \square} = \frac{\square}{\square}$

Since $\frac{6}{10}$ ◯ $\frac{9}{10}$, you know that $\frac{3}{5}$ ◯ $\frac{9}{10}$.

Label $\frac{3}{5}$ and $\frac{9}{10}$ on the number line above.

The fraction the greatest distance from 0 has the greatest value.

The fraction with the greatest value is ______.

So, the bin with ____________ is the most full.

Math Talk Mathematical Processes

Explain how to write $\frac{3}{5}$ and $\frac{9}{10}$ as decimals in hundredths and compare their distances from 0.

- **Explain** how to write $\frac{3}{5}$ and $\frac{9}{10}$ as decimals in tenths and compare their distances from 0.

____

____

0 $\quad$ $\frac{1}{2}$ $\quad$ $\frac{3}{5}$ → $\frac{6}{10}$ $\quad$ $\frac{9}{10}$ $\quad$ 1

Example 2

Write $\frac{7}{10}$, $\frac{1}{3}$, $\frac{7}{12}$, and $\frac{8}{10}$ in order from least to greatest.

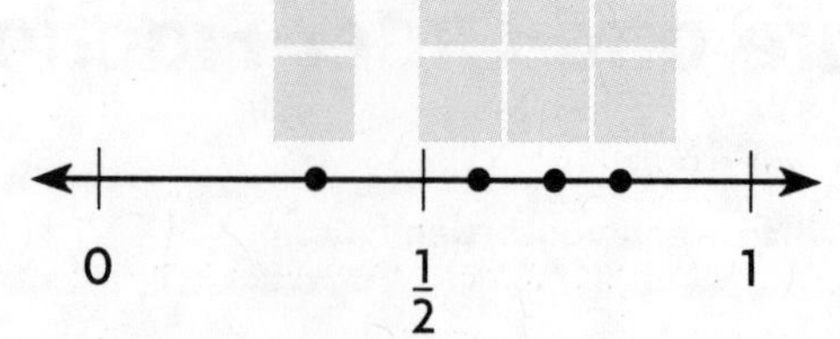

0 $\frac{1}{2}$ 1

STEP 1 Compare each fraction to $\frac{1}{2}$.

List fractions that are less than $\frac{1}{2}$: ______________

List fractions that are greater than $\frac{1}{2}$: ______________

The fraction with the least value is ______.

Locate and label $\frac{1}{3}$ on the number line above.

STEP 2 Compare $\frac{7}{10}$ to $\frac{7}{12}$ and $\frac{8}{10}$.

Think: $\frac{7}{10}$ and $\frac{7}{12}$ have equal numerators.

$\frac{7}{10} \bigcirc \frac{7}{12}$

Think: $\frac{7}{10}$ and $\frac{8}{10}$ have equal denominators.

$\frac{7}{10} \bigcirc \frac{8}{10}$

Locate and label $\frac{7}{10}$, $\frac{7}{12}$, and $\frac{8}{10}$ on the number line above.

The fractions in order from least to greatest are ______________.

So, _____ < _____ < _____ < _____.

Math Talk

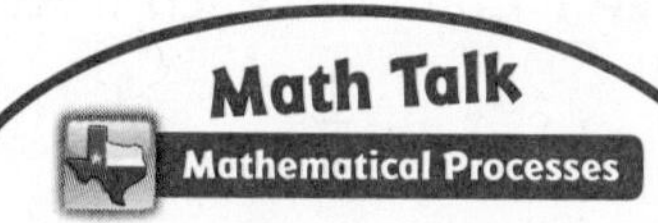

Explain how benchmarks can help you order fractions.

Share and Show

1. Locate and label points on the number line to help you write $\frac{3}{10}$, $\frac{11}{12}$, and $\frac{5}{8}$ in order from least to greatest.

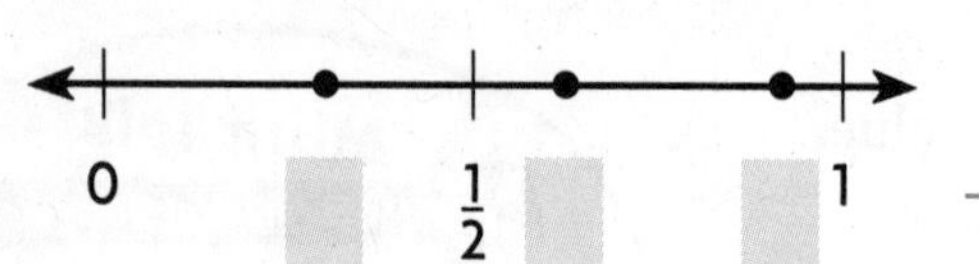

____

Write the fractions in order from least to greatest.

2. $\frac{1}{4}, \frac{5}{8}, \frac{1}{2}$ ______________

3. $\frac{3}{5}, \frac{2}{3}, \frac{3}{10}, \frac{4}{5}$ ______________

4. $\frac{3}{4}, \frac{7}{12}, \frac{5}{12}$ ______________

H.O.T. Algebra **Write a numerator that makes the statement true.**

5. $\frac{1}{2} < \frac{\square}{10} < \frac{4}{5}$

6. $\frac{1}{4} < \frac{5}{12} < \frac{\square}{6}$

7. $\frac{\square}{8} < \frac{3}{4} < \frac{7}{8}$

Name ____________________

Problem Solving (Real World)

8. H.O.T. **Multi-Step** Nancy, Lionel, and Mavis ran in a 5-kilometer race. The table shows their finish times. In what order did Nancy, Lionel, and Mavis finish the race?

Finish line

5-Kilometer Race Results

Name	Time
Nancy	$\frac{2}{3}$ hour
Lionel	$\frac{7}{12}$ hour
Mavis	$\frac{3}{4}$ hour

a. What do you need to find?

____

____

b. What information do you need to solve the problem?

____

____

c. What information is not necessary?

____

d. How will you solve the problem?

____

____

e. Show the steps to solve the problem.

f. Complete the sentences.

The runner who finished first is ________.

The runner who finished second is ________.

The runner who finished third is ________.

9. **Multi-Step** Alma used 3 beads to make a necklace. The lengths of the beads are $\frac{5}{6}$ inch, $\frac{5}{12}$ inch, and $\frac{1}{3}$ inch. What are the lengths in order from shortest to longest?

____

10. H.O.T. **Apply** Portia has done $\frac{3}{7}$ of her English homework, $\frac{6}{7}$ of her math homework, and $\frac{6}{11}$ of her geography homework. Which subject is most complete? Which subject does she have the most left to do?

____

Mathematical Processes
Model • Reason • Communicate

Daily Assessment Task

Fill in the bubble completely to show your answer.

11. **Use Diagrams** Students voted for their favorite hat on Crazy Hat Day. An alien baseball cap got $\frac{1}{4}$ of the votes, a flower power hat got $\frac{5}{8}$ of the votes, and an animal look-alike hat got $\frac{1}{12}$ of the votes. Which shows the fractions written in order from least to greatest?

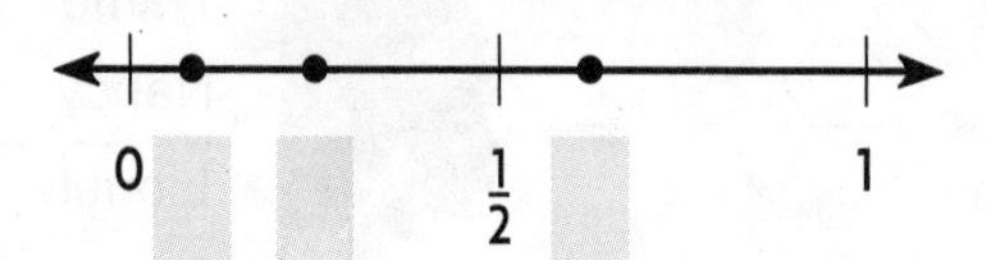

Ⓐ $\frac{1}{12} < \frac{5}{8} < \frac{1}{4}$
Ⓑ $\frac{1}{12} < \frac{1}{4} < \frac{5}{8}$
Ⓒ $\frac{5}{8} < \frac{1}{4} < \frac{1}{12}$
Ⓓ $\frac{1}{4} < \frac{1}{12} < \frac{5}{8}$

12. **Multi-Step** The fourth grade gym class ran a relay. The first runner ran $\frac{4}{5}$ mile, the second runner ran $\frac{3}{10}$ mile, the third runner ran $\frac{1}{5}$ mile and the fourth runner ran $\frac{7}{10}$ mile. Compare $\frac{4}{5}$, $\frac{3}{10}$, $\frac{1}{5}$, and $\frac{7}{10}$. Which fraction represents the greatest distance?

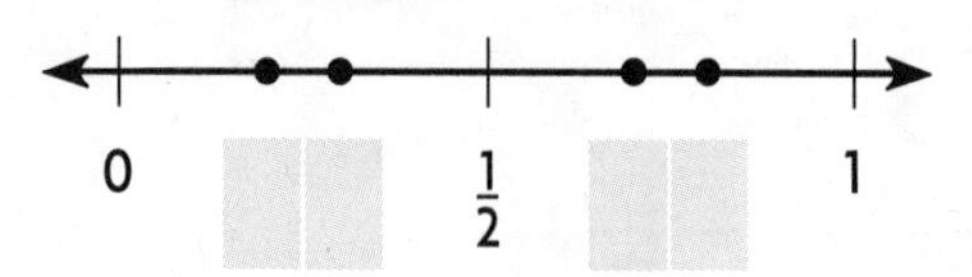

Ⓐ $\frac{4}{5}$
Ⓑ $\frac{3}{10}$
Ⓒ $\frac{1}{5}$
Ⓓ $\frac{7}{10}$

13. **Multi-Step** The three puppies at the animal shelter weighed $\frac{2}{3}$ pound, $\frac{5}{6}$ pound, and $\frac{7}{12}$ pound. Compare $\frac{2}{3}$, $\frac{5}{6}$, and $\frac{7}{12}$. Which shows the fractions written in order from least to greatest?

Ⓐ $\frac{2}{3} < \frac{7}{12} < \frac{5}{6}$
Ⓑ $\frac{2}{3} < \frac{5}{6} < \frac{7}{12}$
Ⓒ $\frac{7}{12} < \frac{5}{6} < \frac{2}{3}$
Ⓓ $\frac{7}{12} < \frac{2}{3} < \frac{5}{6}$

TEXAS Test Prep

14. A recipe for Trail Mix includes $\frac{3}{10}$ cup of sunflower seeds, $\frac{1}{2}$ cup of raisins, and $\frac{3}{8}$ cup of granola. Which list shows the amounts from least to greatest?

Ⓐ $\frac{1}{2}$ cup, $\frac{3}{8}$ cup, $\frac{3}{10}$ cup
Ⓑ $\frac{3}{8}$ cup, $\frac{3}{10}$ cup, $\frac{1}{2}$ cup
Ⓒ $\frac{3}{10}$ cup, $\frac{3}{8}$ cup, $\frac{1}{2}$ cup
Ⓓ $\frac{3}{10}$ cup, $\frac{1}{2}$ cup, $\frac{3}{8}$ cup

Homework and Practice

TEKS Number and Operations—4.3.D, 4.3.G
MATHEMATICAL PROCESSES 4.1.A, 4.1.B, 4.1.D

Name ______________________

4.3 Compare and Order Fractions

Write the fractions in order from least to greatest.

1. $\frac{2}{8}, \frac{2}{4}, \frac{2}{6}$

____

2. $\frac{2}{5}, \frac{1}{3}, \frac{5}{6}$

____

Write a numerator that makes the statement true.

3. $\frac{7}{12} < \frac{\square}{3} < \frac{3}{4}$

4. $\frac{\square}{10} < \frac{9}{15} < \frac{4}{5}$

Problem Solving

5. Walt, Dalia, and Kyra ran a race. The table shows their finish times. In what order did Walt, Dalia, and Kyra finish the race?

____

____

6. Walt's friend Paul also ran in the race. Who finished first, Walt or Paul?

____

Finish line

5-Kilometer Race Results

Name	Time
Walt	$\frac{4}{5}$ hour
Dalia	$\frac{2}{3}$ hour
Kyra	$\frac{5}{6}$ hour
Paul	$\frac{3}{10}$ hour

Lesson Check

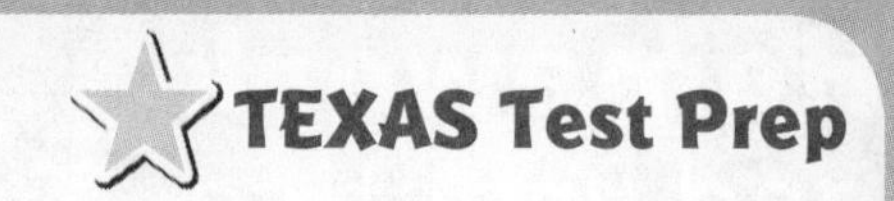

Fill in the bubble completely to show your answer.

7. A recipe for ice cream includes $\frac{3}{4}$ cup milk, $\frac{1}{3}$ cup cream, and $\frac{1}{8}$ cup sugar. Which shows the amounts from least to greatest?

   Ⓐ $\frac{1}{3}$ cup, $\frac{3}{4}$ cup, $\frac{1}{8}$ cup

   Ⓑ $\frac{1}{8}$ cup, $\frac{3}{4}$ cup, $\frac{1}{3}$ cup

   Ⓒ $\frac{3}{4}$ cup, $\frac{1}{3}$ cup, $\frac{1}{8}$ cup

   Ⓓ $\frac{1}{8}$ cup, $\frac{1}{3}$ cup, $\frac{3}{4}$ cup

8. Order the fractions from least to greatest.

   $\frac{4}{5}, \frac{1}{3}, \frac{7}{10}, \frac{3}{5}$

   Ⓐ $\frac{1}{3} < \frac{3}{5} < \frac{7}{10} < \frac{4}{5}$

   Ⓑ $\frac{3}{5} < \frac{1}{3} < \frac{4}{5} < \frac{7}{10}$

   Ⓒ $\frac{7}{10} < \frac{3}{5} < \frac{1}{3} < \frac{4}{5}$

   Ⓓ $\frac{4}{5} < \frac{7}{10} < \frac{1}{3} < \frac{3}{5}$

9. Order the fractions from least to greatest.

   $\frac{2}{3}, \frac{1}{4}, \frac{5}{12}, \frac{3}{4}$

   Ⓐ $\frac{1}{4}, \frac{2}{3}, \frac{5}{12}, \frac{3}{4}$

   Ⓑ $\frac{3}{4}, \frac{5}{12}, \frac{2}{3}, \frac{1}{4}$

   Ⓒ $\frac{1}{4}, \frac{5}{12}, \frac{2}{3}, \frac{3}{4}$

   Ⓓ $\frac{1}{4}, \frac{5}{12}, \frac{3}{4}, \frac{2}{3}$

10. Three potatoes weigh $\frac{1}{4}$ pound, $\frac{5}{8}$ pound, and $\frac{1}{2}$ pound. Which shows the weights from least to greatest?

    Ⓐ $\frac{1}{4}$ pound, $\frac{5}{8}$ pound, $\frac{1}{2}$ pound

    Ⓑ $\frac{1}{2}$ pound, $\frac{1}{4}$ pound, $\frac{5}{8}$ pound

    Ⓒ $\frac{5}{8}$ pound, $\frac{1}{2}$ pound, $\frac{1}{4}$ pound

    Ⓓ $\frac{1}{4}$ pound, $\frac{1}{2}$ pound, $\frac{5}{8}$ pound

11. **Multi-Step** Selma used stones to outline her garden. The lengths of the stones are $\frac{1}{3}$ foot, $\frac{7}{12}$ foot, and $\frac{3}{4}$ foot. What are the lengths in order from shortest to longest?

    Ⓐ $\frac{7}{12}$ foot, $\frac{3}{4}$ foot, $\frac{1}{3}$ foot

    Ⓑ $\frac{1}{3}$ foot, $\frac{7}{12}$ foot, $\frac{3}{4}$ foot

    Ⓒ $\frac{3}{4}$ foot, $\frac{7}{12}$ foot, $\frac{1}{3}$ foot

    Ⓓ $\frac{7}{12}$ foot, $\frac{1}{3}$ foot, $\frac{3}{4}$ foot

12. **Multi-Step** Ms. Mohan bought cheese for a recipe. She bought $\frac{5}{6}$ pound of cheddar cheese, $\frac{1}{4}$ pound of Swiss cheese, and $\frac{3}{8}$ pound of American cheese. What are the amounts in order from least to greatest?

    Ⓐ $\frac{5}{6}$ pound, $\frac{1}{4}$ pound, $\frac{3}{8}$ pound

    Ⓑ $\frac{3}{8}$ pound, $\frac{5}{6}$ pound, $\frac{1}{4}$ pound

    Ⓒ $\frac{1}{4}$ pound, $\frac{3}{8}$ pound, $\frac{5}{6}$ pound

    Ⓓ $\frac{3}{8}$ pound, $\frac{1}{4}$ pound, $\frac{5}{6}$ pound

Name ______________________________

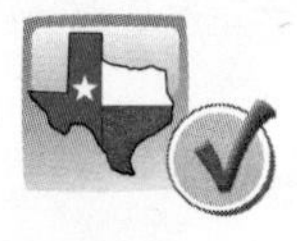

Module 4 Assessment

Vocabulary

Vocabulary
benchmark
numerator
simplest form

Choose the best term from the box.

1. A ____________________ is a known size or amount that helps you understand another size or amount. (p. 113)

Concepts and Skills

Compare. Write <, > or =. TEKS 4.3.D

2. $\frac{7}{8} \bigcirc \frac{7}{12}$

3. $\frac{10}{12} \bigcirc \frac{5}{6}$

4. $\frac{1}{2} \bigcirc \frac{3}{10}$

5. $\frac{1}{4} \bigcirc \frac{2}{3}$

6. $\frac{2}{3} \bigcirc \frac{4}{7}$

7. $\frac{5}{14} \bigcirc \frac{10}{14}$

8. $\frac{1}{4} \bigcirc \frac{4}{7}$

9. $\frac{6}{8} \bigcirc \frac{1}{3}$

Write the fractions in order from least to greatest. TEKS 4.3.D

10. $\frac{2}{3}, \frac{3}{4}, \frac{1}{6}$

____

11. $\frac{7}{10}, \frac{4}{5}, \frac{1}{2}, \frac{4}{12}$

____

Write the fraction or decimal to show their distances from zero. TEKS 4.3.G

12.

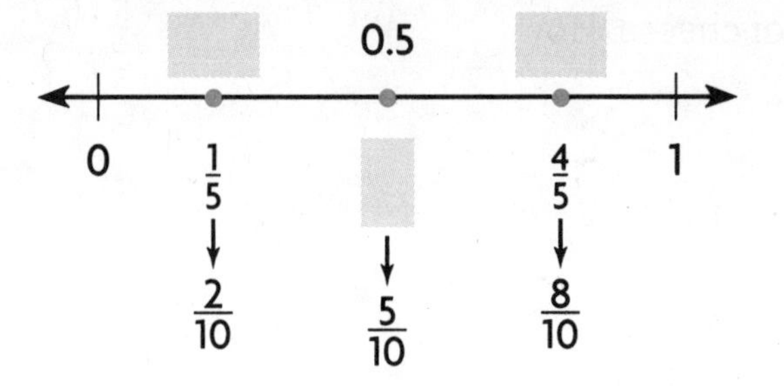

13.

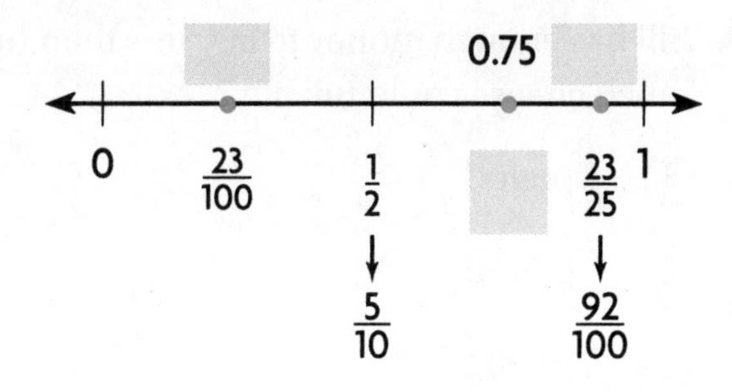

Fill in the bubble completely to show your answer.

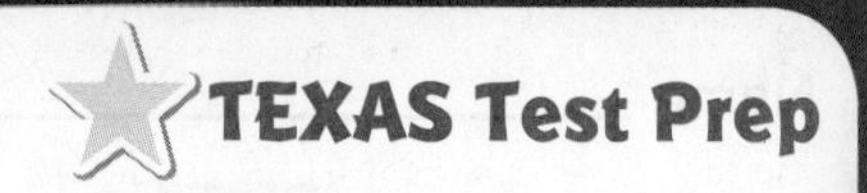

14. Paco needs more than $\frac{3}{8}$ yard of twine to build a model ship. How much twine could he buy? TEKS 4.3.D

Ⓐ $\frac{3}{10}$ yard

Ⓑ $\frac{1}{4}$ yard

Ⓒ $\frac{3}{5}$ yard

Ⓓ $\frac{1}{8}$ yard

15. Rachel, Nancy, and Diego were in a fishing competition. Rachel's fish was $\frac{7}{8}$ foot long, Nancy's fish was $\frac{1}{4}$ foot long, and Diego's fish was $\frac{1}{2}$ foot long. Which shows the correct comparison of the lengths of Rachel and Diego's fish? TEKS 4.3.D

Ⓐ $\frac{1}{4}$ foot $= \frac{7}{8}$ foot

Ⓑ $\frac{1}{2}$ foot $> \frac{7}{8}$ foot

Ⓒ $\frac{1}{2}$ foot $= \frac{7}{8}$ foot

Ⓓ $\frac{1}{2}$ foot $< \frac{7}{8}$ foot

16. Amy needs $\frac{6}{8}$ gallon of fruit juice to make punch. She needs an equal amount of sparkling water. How much sparkling water does she need? TEKS 4.3.D

Ⓐ $\frac{2}{3}$ gallon

Ⓑ $\frac{1}{2}$ gallon

Ⓒ $\frac{2}{8}$ gallon

Ⓓ $\frac{3}{4}$ gallon

17. Bill has enough money to buy less than $\frac{1}{2}$ pound of cheese. How much cheese could Bill buy? TEKS 4.3.D

Ⓐ $\frac{4}{6}$ pound

Ⓑ $\frac{5}{8}$ pound

Ⓒ $\frac{1}{3}$ pound

Ⓓ $\frac{3}{4}$ pound

Name ___________________________________

5.1 Add and Subtract Parts of a Whole

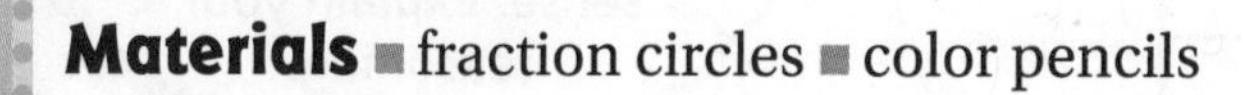

When can you add or subtract parts of a whole?

Investigate

Materials ■ fraction circles ■ color pencils

Ms. Clark has the following pie pieces left over from a bake sale.

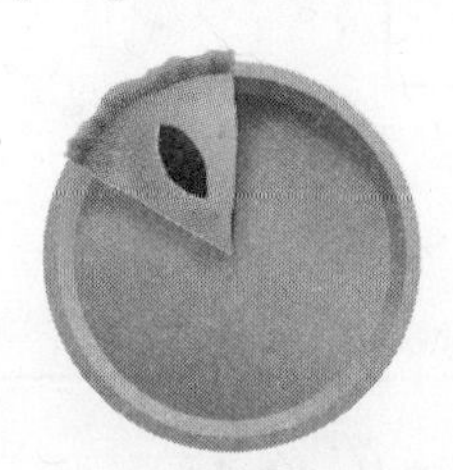

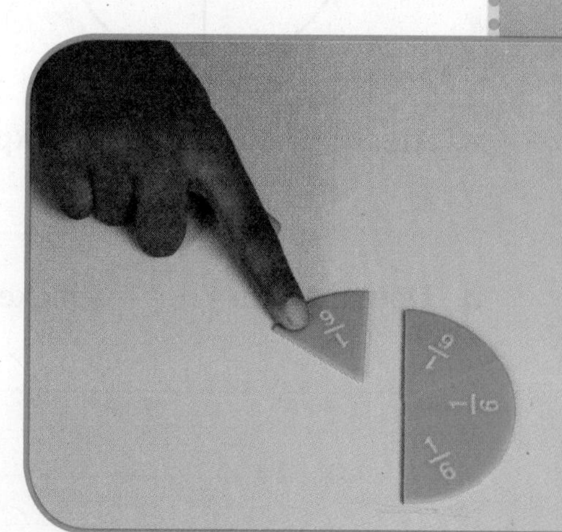

She will combine the pieces so they are on the same dish. How much pie will be on the dish?

A. Model the problem using fraction circles. Draw a picture of your model. Then write the sum.

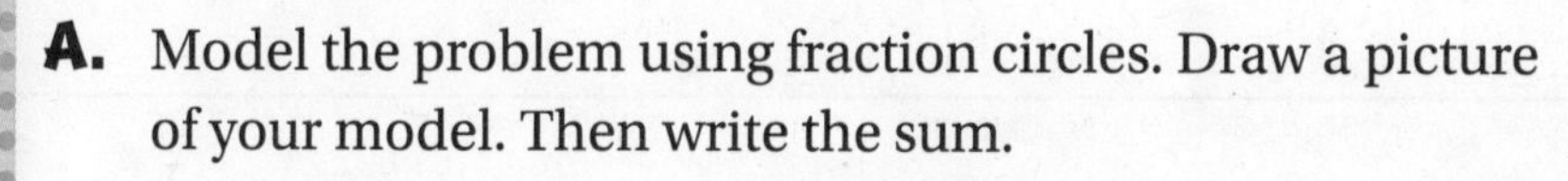

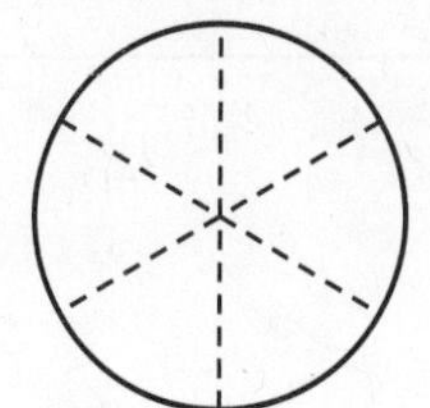 + 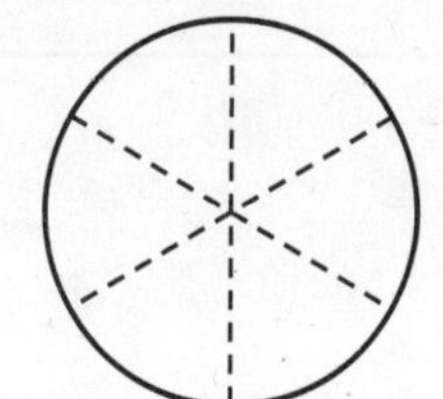 = 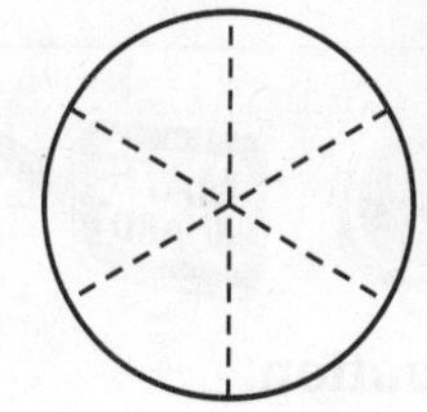

__________ + __________ = __________

So, __________ of a pie is on the dish.

B. Suppose Ms. Clark eats 2 pieces of the pie. How much pie will be left on the dish? Model the problem using fraction circles. Draw a picture of your model. Then write the difference.

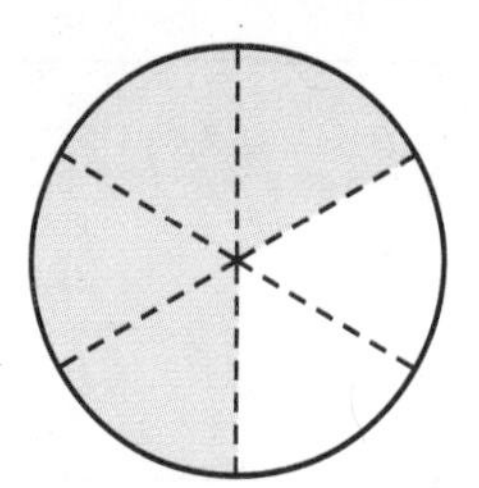

__________ − __________ = __________

So, __________ of the pie is left on the dish.

Make Connections

You can only join or separate parts that refer to the same whole.

Suppose Randy has $\frac{1}{4}$ of a round cake and $\frac{1}{4}$ of a square cake.

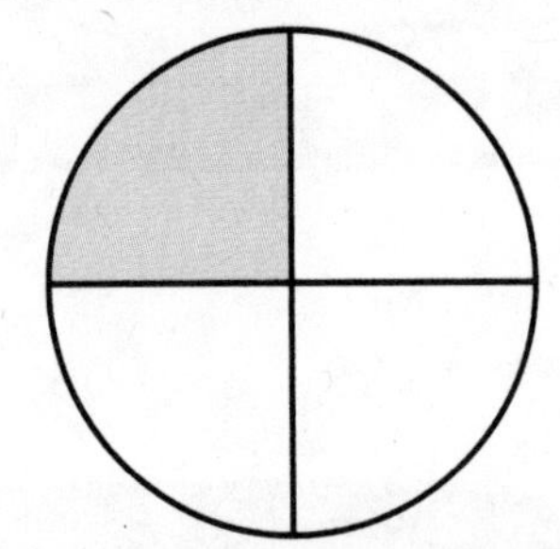

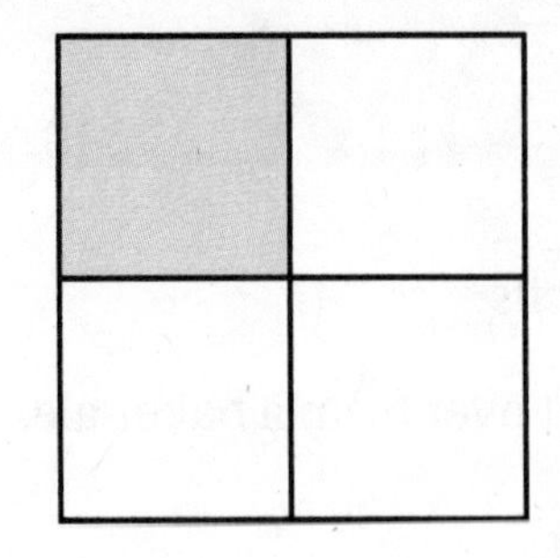

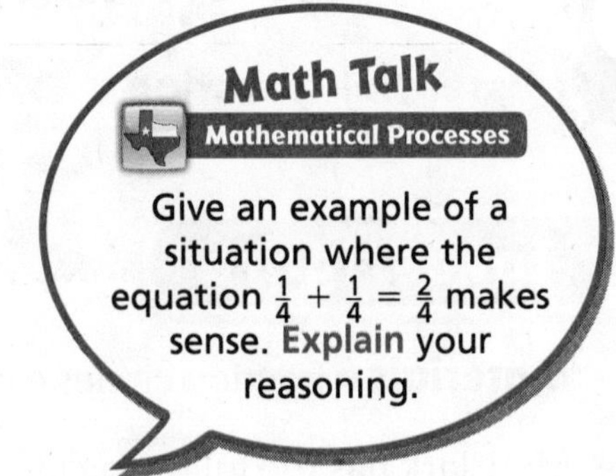

a. Are the wholes the same? **Explain.**

____

b. Does the sum $\frac{1}{4} + \frac{1}{4} = \frac{2}{4}$ make sense in this situation? **Explain.**

____

____

____

Share and Show

Use the model to write an equation.

1.

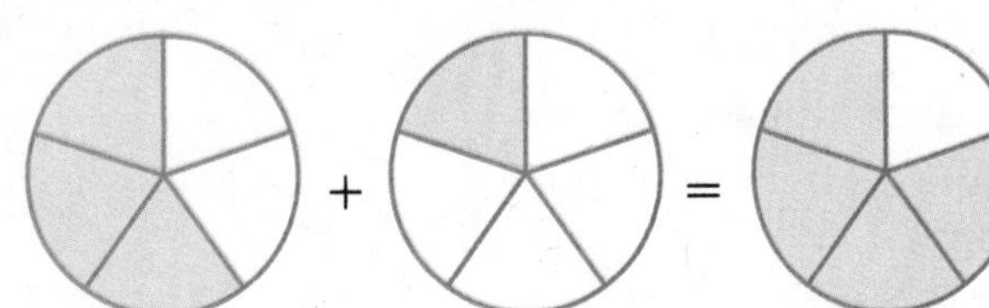

____

2.

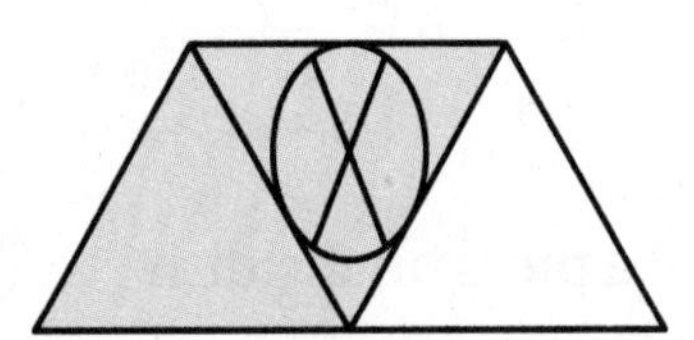

____

3. **Multi-Step** Sean has $\frac{1}{5}$ of a cupcake and $\frac{1}{5}$ of a large cake.

a. Are the wholes the same? **Explain.**

____

b. Does the sum $\frac{1}{5} + \frac{1}{5} = \frac{2}{5}$ make sense in this situation? **Explain.**

____

Name ___________________________

Use the model to solve the equation.

4. $\frac{3}{4} - \frac{1}{4} =$ ______

1			
$\frac{1}{4}$	$\frac{1}{4}$	$\frac{1}{4}$	$\frac{1}{4}$

5. $\frac{5}{6} + \frac{1}{6} =$ ______

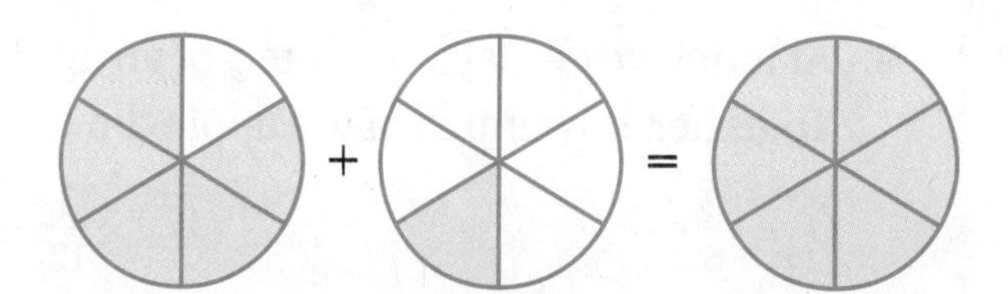

Problem Solving Real World

H.O.T. Sense or Nonsense?

6. Samantha and Kim used different models to help find $\frac{1}{3} + \frac{1}{3}$. Whose model makes sense? Whose model is nonsense? **Explain** your reasoning below each model.

Samantha's Model

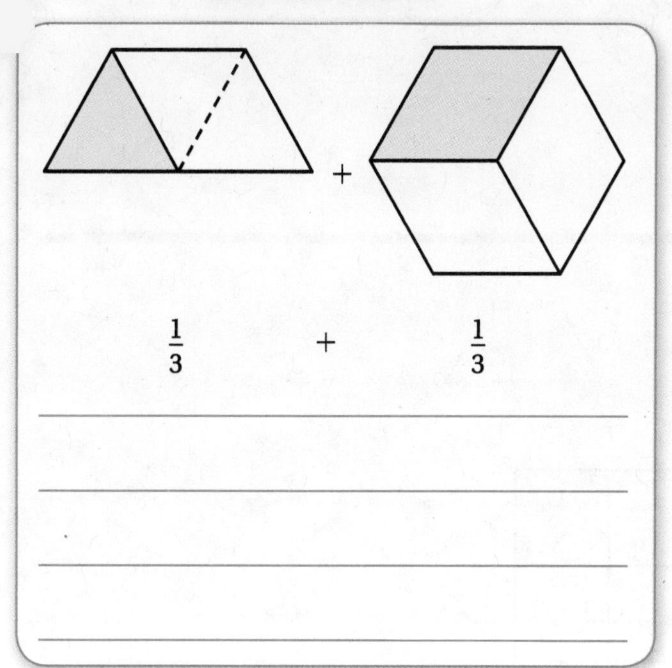

Kim's Model

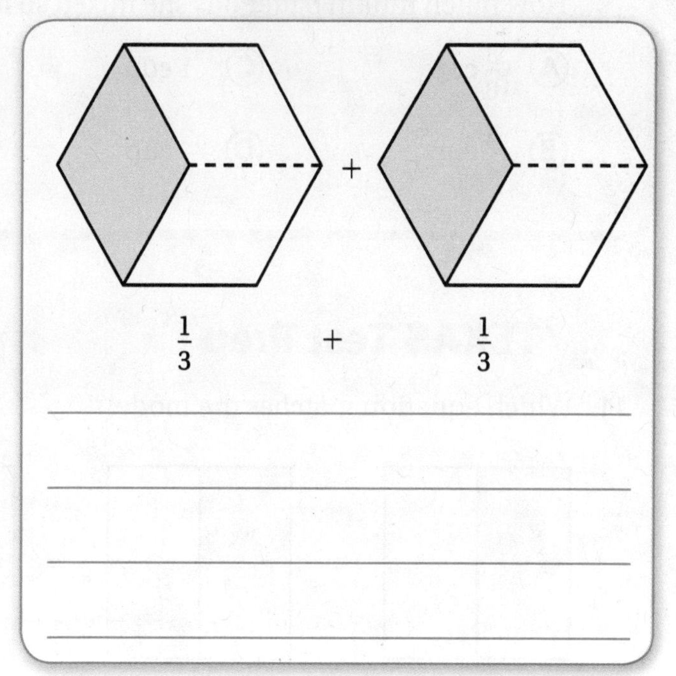

7. **H.O.T. Justify** If there is $\frac{4}{6}$ of a pie on a plate, what part of the pie is missing from the plate? Write an equation to justify your answer.

____

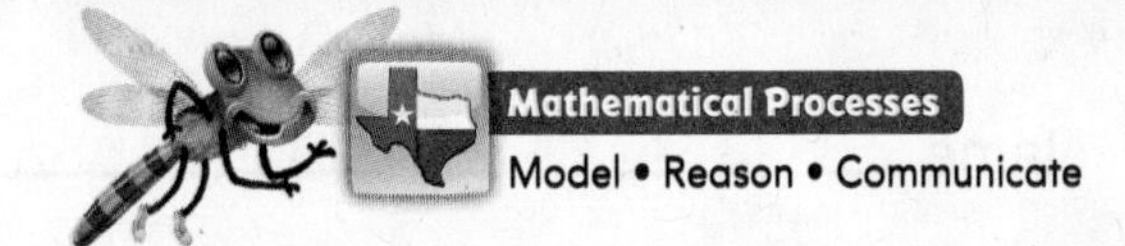

Daily Assessment Task

Fill in the bubble completely to show your answer.
Use models to solve.

8. At lunch yesterday, Ryan ate $\frac{2}{6}$ of an apple and I ate $\frac{2}{6}$ of the apple. Together, how much of the apple did we eat?

Ⓐ $\frac{2}{6}$
Ⓑ $\frac{4}{6}$
Ⓒ $\frac{2}{12}$
Ⓓ $\frac{4}{12}$

9. At the start of art class, Logan had $\frac{7}{12}$ of a block of clay. After class, $\frac{5}{12}$ of the block was left. What fraction of the block did Logan use during class?

Ⓐ $\frac{7}{12}$
Ⓑ $\frac{12}{12}$
Ⓒ $\frac{5}{12}$
Ⓓ $\frac{2}{12}$

10. **Multi-Step** Samantha is mixing batter for muffins. She mixes $\frac{2}{4}$ cup of flour and $\frac{1}{4}$ cup of sugar. Then she adds $\frac{1}{4}$ cup of milk. How much muffin batter has she mixed so far?

Ⓐ $\frac{3}{8}$ cup
Ⓑ $\frac{2}{4}$ cup
Ⓒ 1 cup
Ⓓ $\frac{3}{4}$ cup

TEXAS Test Prep

11. Which equation matches the model?

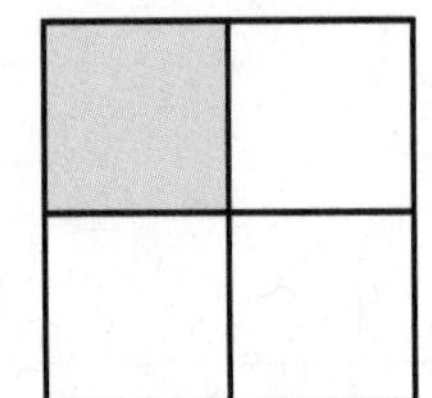 + 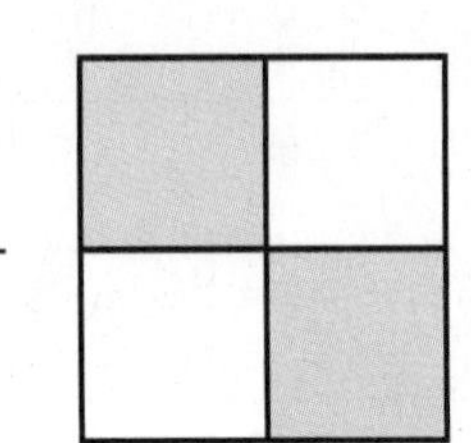 = 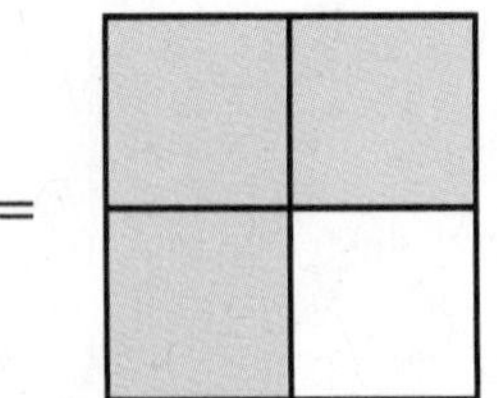

Ⓐ $\frac{1}{4}+\frac{3}{4}=\frac{4}{4}$
Ⓑ $\frac{1}{4}+\frac{2}{4}=\frac{3}{4}$
Ⓒ $\frac{3}{4}+\frac{2}{4}=\frac{5}{4}$
Ⓓ $\frac{1}{8}+\frac{2}{8}=\frac{3}{8}$

Homework and Practice

Name ____________________

5.1 Add and Subtract Parts of a Whole

Use the model to write an equation.

1. + =

____

2.

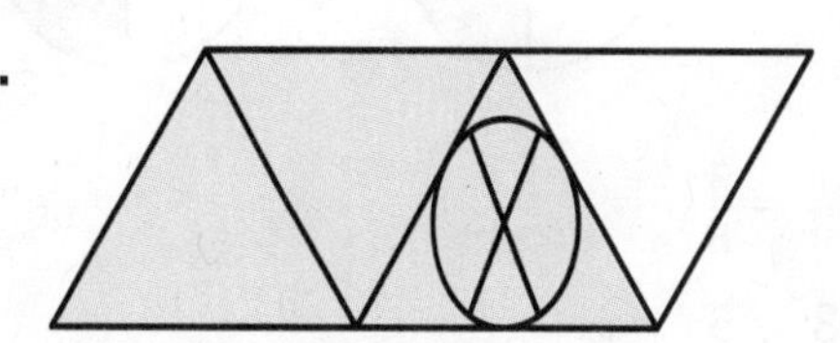

____

Use the model to solve the equation.

3.

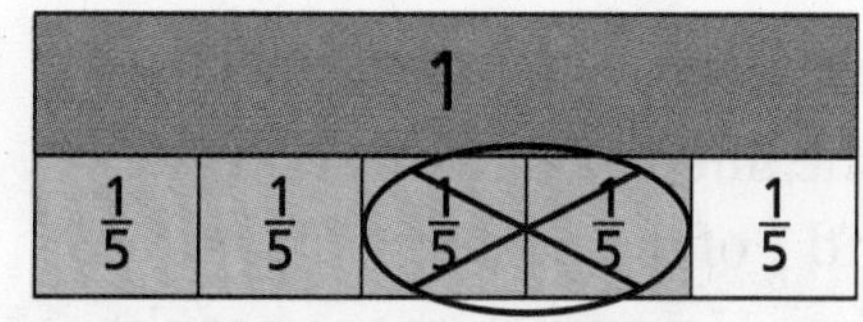

____

4.

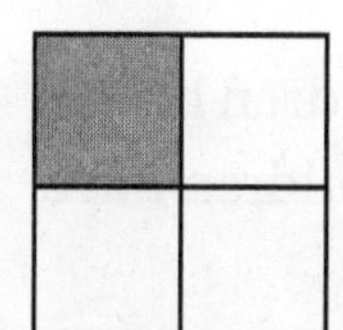

+

=

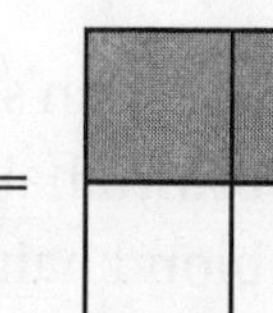

____

5. If there is $\frac{6}{8}$ of a pizza on a plate, what part of the pizza is missing from the plate? Write an equation to justify your answer.

____

____

Problem Solving Real World

6. If there is $\frac{3}{8}$ of a pizza on a plate, what part of the pizza is missing from the plate? Write an equation to justify your answer.

____

7. Maria is making cupcakes. She fills $\frac{4}{12}$ of the cups with chocolate batter and $\frac{7}{12}$ of the cups with vanilla batter. How many of the cups has Maria filled? Write an equation to justify your answer.

____

Lesson Check

TEXAS Test Prep

Fill in the bubble completely to show your answer.

8. Which equation matches the model?

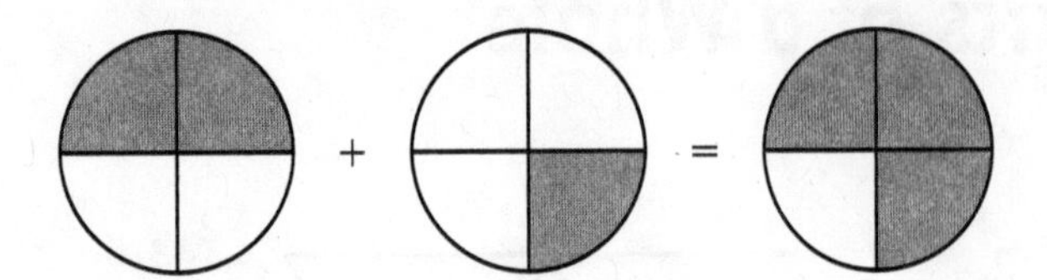

Ⓐ $\frac{2}{8} + \frac{1}{8} = \frac{3}{8}$

Ⓑ $\frac{2}{4} + \frac{3}{4} = \frac{5}{4}$

Ⓒ $\frac{2}{4} + \frac{1}{4} = \frac{3}{4}$

Ⓓ $\frac{1}{4} + \frac{3}{4} = \frac{4}{4}$

9. Which equation matches the model?

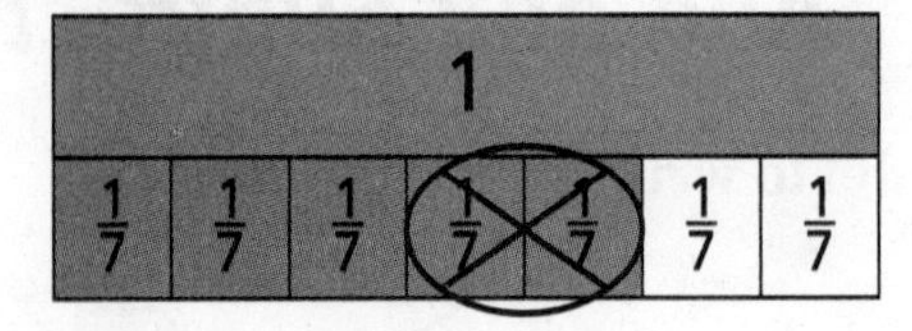

Ⓐ $\frac{5}{7} - \frac{2}{7} = \frac{3}{7}$

Ⓑ $\frac{7}{7} - \frac{5}{7} = \frac{2}{7}$

Ⓒ $\frac{7}{7} - \frac{2}{7} = \frac{5}{7}$

Ⓓ $\frac{5}{7} - \frac{3}{7} = \frac{2}{7}$

10. In Dylan's family $\frac{5}{6}$ of the children have brown hair. The rest of the children have blond hair.

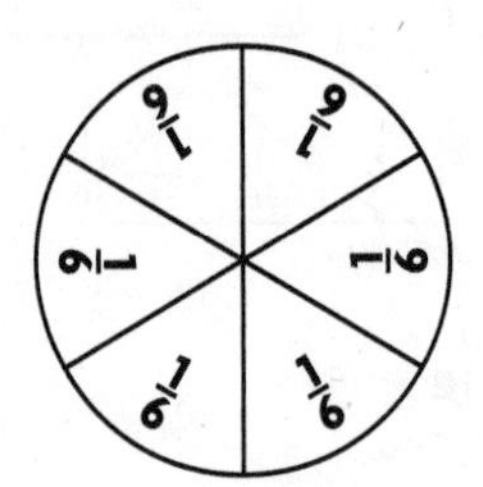

What fraction of the children has blond hair?

Ⓐ $\frac{4}{6}$

Ⓑ $\frac{2}{6}$

Ⓒ $\frac{3}{6}$

Ⓓ $\frac{1}{6}$

11. Miranda made a poster for her science project. She filled $\frac{3}{8}$ of the poster with photos and $\frac{4}{8}$ of the poster with written information. How much space has she filled on her poster so far?

Ⓐ $\frac{7}{8}$

Ⓑ $\frac{1}{8}$

Ⓒ $\frac{6}{8}$

Ⓓ $\frac{2}{8}$

12. Multi-Step Carrie's dance class learned $\frac{1}{5}$ of a new dance on Monday, and $\frac{2}{5}$ of the dance on Tuesday. What fraction of the dance is left for the class to learn on Wednesday?

Ⓐ $\frac{4}{5}$

Ⓑ $\frac{3}{5}$

Ⓒ $\frac{2}{5}$

Ⓓ $\frac{1}{5}$

13. Multi-Step Mrs. Simon planted $\frac{4}{12}$ of her flowers in her front yard, $\frac{3}{12}$ of her flowers in her back yard, and $\frac{2}{12}$ of her flowers on the side of her house. What fraction of her flowers has she planted so far?

Ⓐ $\frac{2}{12}$

Ⓑ $\frac{9}{12}$

Ⓒ $\frac{3}{12}$

Ⓓ $\frac{10}{12}$

Name ______________________________

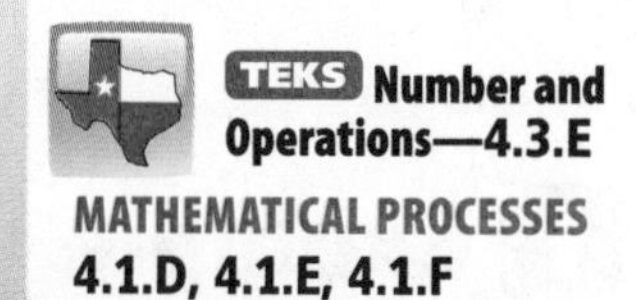

5.2 Add Fractions Using Models

Essential Question How can you add fractions with like denominators using models?

Unlock the Problem

Ms. Clark made a loaf of bread. She used $\frac{1}{8}$ of the bread for a snack and $\frac{5}{8}$ of the bread for lunch. How much bread did she use for a snack and lunch?

One Way Use a picture.

$\frac{1}{8}$ is ______ eighth-size piece of bread.

$\frac{5}{8}$ is ______ eighth-size pieces of bread.

Shade 1 eighth-size piece. Then shade 5 eighth-size pieces.

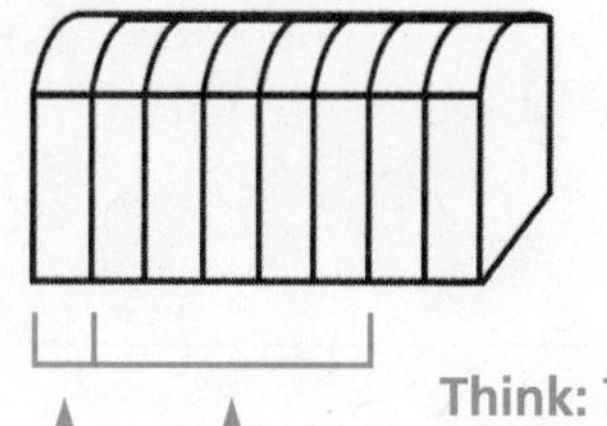

Think: The pieces you shaded represent the pieces Ms. Clark used.

So, Ms. Clark used ______ eighth-size pieces, or $\frac{\square}{8}$ of the bread.

Another Way Use fraction strips.

The 1 strip represents the whole loaf.

Each $\frac{1}{8}$ part represents 1 eighth-size piece of bread.

Shade $\frac{1}{8}$. Then shade $\frac{5}{8}$.

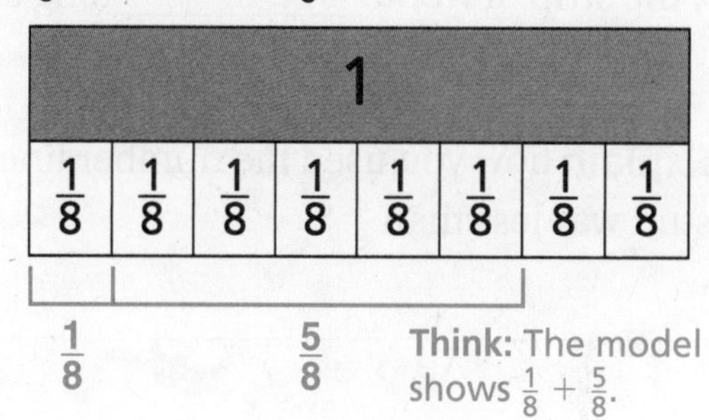

Think: The model shows $\frac{1}{8} + \frac{5}{8}$.

How many $\frac{1}{8}$-size parts are shaded? ______

Write the sum. $\frac{1}{8} + \frac{5}{8} = \frac{\square}{8}$

So, Ms. Clark used ______ of the bread.

Math Talk Mathematical Processes

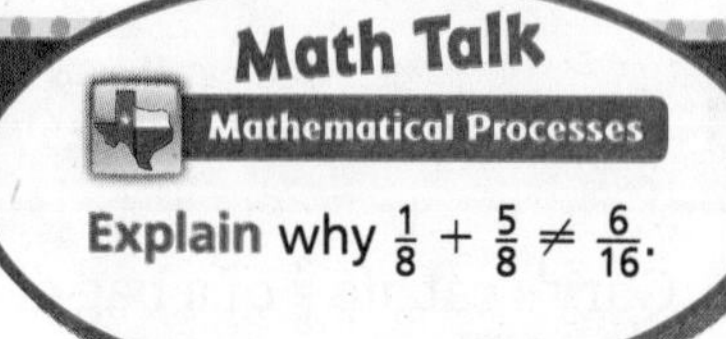

Explain why $\frac{1}{8} + \frac{5}{8} \neq \frac{6}{16}$.

1. **Explain** how the numerator of the sum is related to the fraction strip model.

____

____

2. **Explain** how the denominator of the sum is related to the fraction strip model.

____

Example

Jacob needs two strips of wood to make masts for a miniature sailboat. One mast will be $\frac{3}{6}$ foot long. The other mast will be $\frac{2}{6}$ foot long. He has a strip of wood that is $\frac{4}{6}$ foot long. Is this strip of wood long enough to make both masts?

Shade the model to show $\frac{3}{6} + \frac{2}{6}$.

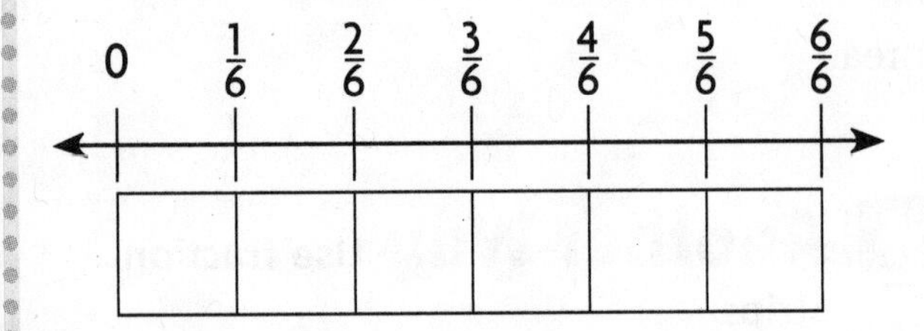

Write the sum. $\frac{3}{6} + \frac{2}{6} = \frac{\square}{6}$

Is the sum less than or greater than $\frac{4}{6}$? ____________

So, the strip of wood ____________ long enough to make both masts.

3. **Explain** how you used the number line to determine if the sum was less than $\frac{4}{6}$.

____

____

4. **What if** each mast was $\frac{2}{6}$ foot long? Could Jacob use the strip of wood to make both masts? **Explain.**

____

Share and Show

1. Gary's cat ate $\frac{3}{5}$ of a bag of cat treats in September and $\frac{1}{5}$ of the same bag of cat treats in October. What part of the bag of cat treats did Gary's cat eat in both months?

Use the model to find the sum $\frac{3}{5} + \frac{1}{5}$.

How many fifth-size pieces are shown? ______

$\frac{3}{5} + \frac{1}{5} = \frac{\square}{5}$ of a bag

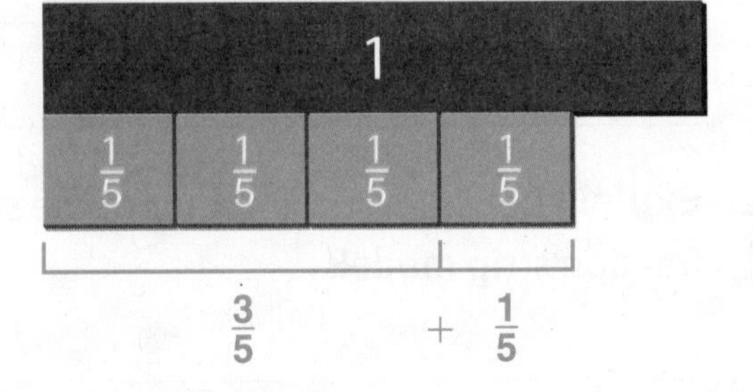

Name ___________________________

Use the model to find the sum.

2\.

1			
$\frac{1}{4}$	$\frac{1}{4}$	$\frac{1}{4}$	$\frac{1}{4}$

$\frac{1}{4}$ + $\frac{2}{4}$

$\frac{1}{4} + \frac{2}{4} =$ ______

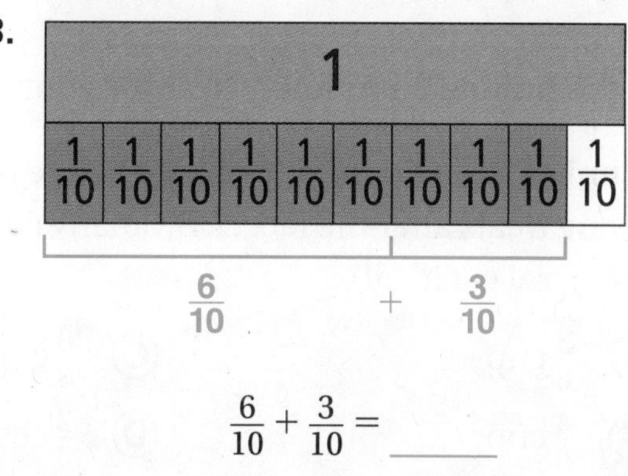

3\. $\frac{6}{10} + \frac{3}{10} =$ ______

Find the sum. Use models to help.

4\. $\frac{3}{6} + \frac{3}{6} =$ ______

5\. $\frac{5}{8} + \frac{2}{8} =$ ______

6\. $\frac{1}{3} + \frac{1}{3} =$ ______

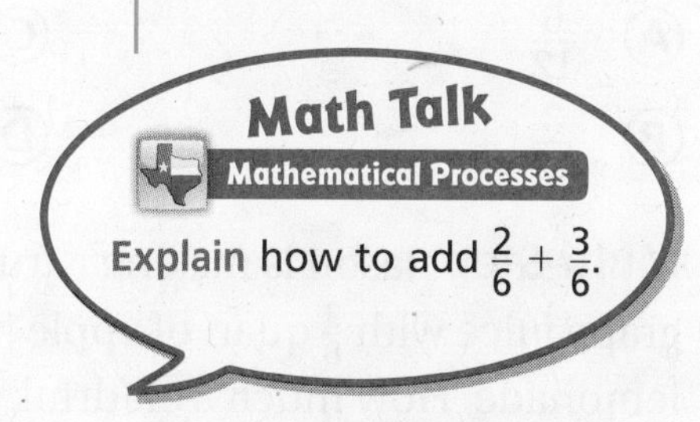

Problem Solving Real World

7\. **Write Math** ▶ **Use Math Language** Jin is putting colored sand in a jar. She filled $\frac{2}{10}$ of the jar with blue sand and $\frac{4}{10}$ of the jar with pink sand. Describe one way to model the part of the jar filled with sand.

____

____

8\. **H.O.T.** **Reasoning** A sum has five addends. Each addend is a unit fraction. The sum is 1. What are the addends?

____

9\. **H.O.T.** **Multi-Step** Mike ate $\frac{2}{12}$ of the pizza for dinner. His mom ate $\frac{1}{12}$ of the pizza. Mike's dad ate $\frac{3}{12}$ of the pizza. If Mike's sister ate $\frac{2}{12}$ of the pizza, what part of the pizza did Mike and his family eat? Write the answer in simplest form.

____

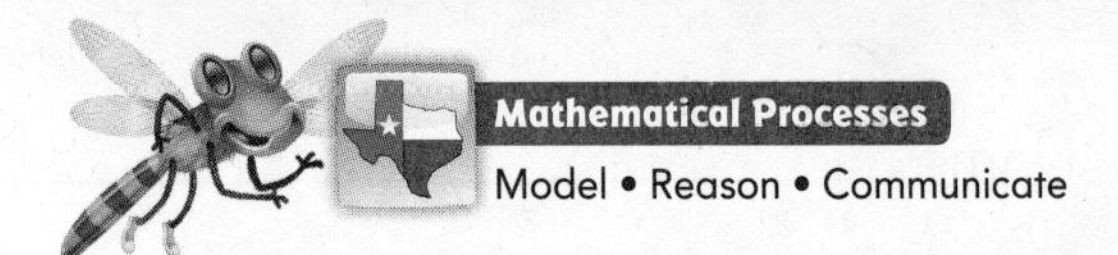

Daily Assessment Task

Fill in the bubble completely to show your answer.

10. Schnitzel gets $\frac{1}{8}$ cup of dog treats before the race. He gets $\frac{2}{8}$ cup of dog treats after the race. How many cups of dog treats does Schnitzel get in all?

Ⓐ $\frac{3}{8}$ cup
Ⓑ $\frac{4}{8}$ cup
Ⓒ $\frac{8}{8}$ cup
Ⓓ $\frac{2}{8}$ cup

11. Kelly has a seashell collection. Of them, $\frac{5}{12}$ of the shells are white and $\frac{2}{12}$ of the shells are pink. What fraction of the seashells in Kelly's collection are white or pink?

Ⓐ $\frac{6}{12}$
Ⓑ $\frac{3}{12}$
Ⓒ $\frac{7}{12}$
Ⓓ $\frac{12}{12}$

12. **Multi-Step** Jason is making a fruit drink. He mixes $\frac{2}{8}$ quart of grape juice with $\frac{3}{8}$ quart of apple juice. Then he adds $\frac{1}{8}$ quart of lemonade. How much fruit drink does Jason make?

Ⓐ $\frac{4}{8}$ quart
Ⓑ $\frac{5}{8}$ quart
Ⓒ $\frac{8}{8}$ quart
Ⓓ $\frac{6}{8}$ quart

TEXAS Test Prep

13. Jamal is making some dessert. He adds $\frac{2}{8}$ cup of milk to the ingredients. He then adds another $\frac{3}{8}$ cup of milk after the ingredients are mixed. How much total milk did Jamal use in the recipe? Use fraction strips or a number line.

Ⓐ $\frac{1}{8}$
Ⓑ $\frac{4}{8}$
Ⓒ $\frac{5}{8}$
Ⓓ $\frac{6}{8}$

Name ____________

5.2 Add Fractions Using Models

Use the model to find the sum.

1.

1					
$\frac{1}{6}$	$\frac{1}{6}$	$\frac{1}{6}$	$\frac{1}{6}$	$\frac{1}{6}$	$\frac{1}{6}$

$\frac{2}{6}$ + $\frac{3}{6}$

$\frac{2}{6} + \frac{3}{6} =$ ______

2.

1							
$\frac{1}{8}$	$\frac{1}{8}$	$\frac{1}{8}$	$\frac{1}{8}$	$\frac{1}{8}$	$\frac{1}{8}$	$\frac{1}{8}$	$\frac{1}{8}$

$\frac{4}{8}$ + $\frac{2}{8}$

$\frac{4}{8} + \frac{2}{8} +$ ______

Find the sum. Use models to help.

3. $\frac{2}{4} + \frac{1}{4} =$ ______

4. $\frac{5}{7} + \frac{2}{7} =$ ______

5. $\frac{1}{5} + \frac{2}{5} =$ ______

6. $\frac{4}{9} + \frac{3}{9} =$ ______

Problem Solving Real World

7. Leigh is layering cookie ingredients in a jar. She fills $\frac{3}{8}$ of the jar with flour and then $\frac{1}{8}$ of the jar with sugar. How much of the jar has Lee filled so far? Draw a model to find the sum.

______

8. Kevin is adding toppings to a pizza. He adds mushrooms to $\frac{2}{6}$ of the pizza and olives to $\frac{3}{6}$ of the pizza. What fraction of the pizza has a topping on it? Draw a model to find the sum.

______

Lesson Check

TEXAS Test Prep

Fill in the bubble completely to show your answer.

9. Jason's rain gauge showed $\frac{1}{4}$ inch of rain on Saturday and $\frac{3}{4}$ inch of rain on Sunday. What is the total amount of rainfall received?

   Ⓐ $\frac{3}{4}$ inch
   Ⓑ $\frac{2}{4}$ inch
   Ⓒ 1 inch
   Ⓓ $\frac{4}{8}$ inch

10. Julie read $\frac{2}{8}$ of her book before lunch and $\frac{5}{8}$ of her book after lunch. What fraction of the book has Julie read?

   Ⓐ $\frac{3}{8}$
   Ⓑ $\frac{7}{8}$
   Ⓒ $\frac{6}{8}$
   Ⓓ $\frac{8}{8}$

11. Frank displays framed photos on a wall. Of the photos, $\frac{5}{12}$ are in wooden frames and $\frac{2}{12}$ are in metal frames. What fraction shows the number of photos that are in either wooden or metal frames?

   Ⓐ $\frac{8}{12}$
   Ⓑ $\frac{3}{12}$
   Ⓒ $\frac{6}{12}$
   Ⓓ $\frac{7}{12}$

12. Anish painted $\frac{5}{10}$ of a fence on Saturday and $\frac{2}{10}$ of the fence on Sunday. How much of the fence was painted by the end of the weekend?

   Ⓐ $\frac{7}{10}$
   Ⓑ $\frac{2}{5}$
   Ⓒ $\frac{3}{10}$
   Ⓓ $\frac{4}{5}$

13. **Multi-Step** Bonnie spent $\frac{2}{10}$ of her money on breakfast and $\frac{3}{10}$ of her money on lunch. Then she spends $\frac{4}{10}$ of her money on dinner. Which fraction shows the amount of money Bonnie has spent today?

   Ⓐ $\frac{7}{10}$
   Ⓑ $\frac{8}{10}$
   Ⓒ $\frac{5}{10}$
   Ⓓ $\frac{9}{10}$

14. **Multi-Step** After one week, $\frac{2}{6}$ of Claire's flowers bloomed. The second week $\frac{1}{6}$ of the flowers bloomed. The third week $\frac{2}{6}$ of the flowers bloomed. Which fraction shows the number of flowers that bloomed?

   Ⓐ $\frac{5}{6}$
   Ⓑ $\frac{4}{6}$
   Ⓒ $\frac{3}{6}$
   Ⓓ $\frac{6}{6}$

Name ______________________________

5.3 Subtract Fractions Using Models

TEKS Number and Operations—4.3.E
MATHEMATICAL PROCESSES 4.1.D

Essential Question

How can you subtract fractions with like denominators using models?

Unlock the Problem (Real World)

A rover needs to travel $\frac{5}{8}$ mile to reach its destination. It has already traveled $\frac{3}{8}$ mile. How much farther does the rover need to travel?

Compare fractions to find the difference.

STEP 1 Shade the model.

Shade the model to show the total distance.

Then shade the model to show how much distance the rover has already covered.

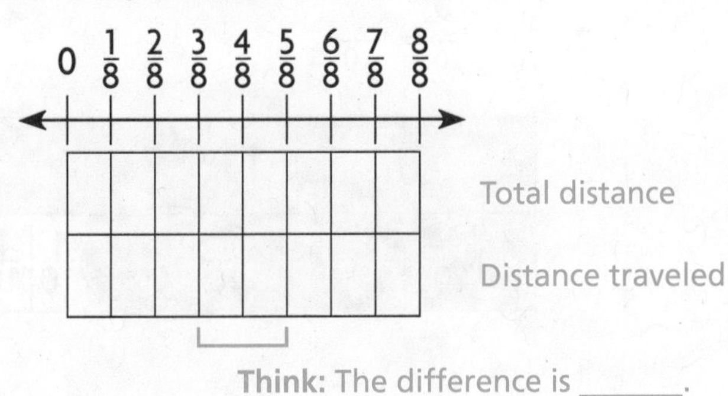

Think: The difference is ______.

STEP 2 Write the difference.

$\frac{5}{8} - \frac{3}{8} = \frac{\square}{8}$

So, the rover needs to travel ______ mile farther.

Another Way Use fraction strips.

Use five $\frac{1}{8}$-size parts to model the whole distance.

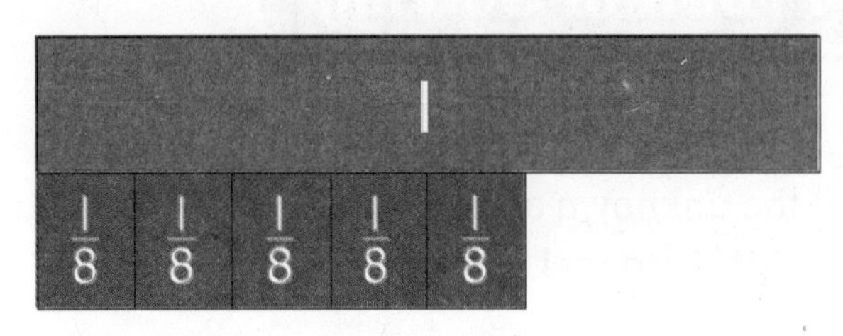

How many $\frac{1}{8}$-size parts should you cross out to model the distance the rover has traveled? ______

How many $\frac{1}{8}$-size parts are left? ______

Write the difference.

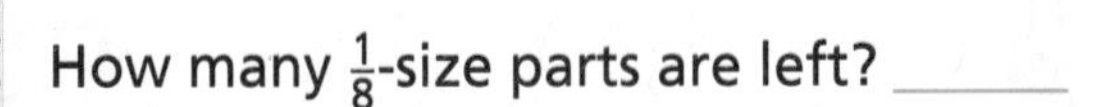

$\frac{5}{8} - \frac{\square}{\square} = \frac{\square}{\square}$

Share and Show

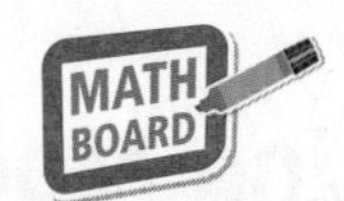

1. Lisa needs $\frac{4}{5}$ pound of shrimp to make shrimp salad. She has $\frac{1}{5}$ pound of shrimp. How much more shrimp does Lisa need to make the salad?

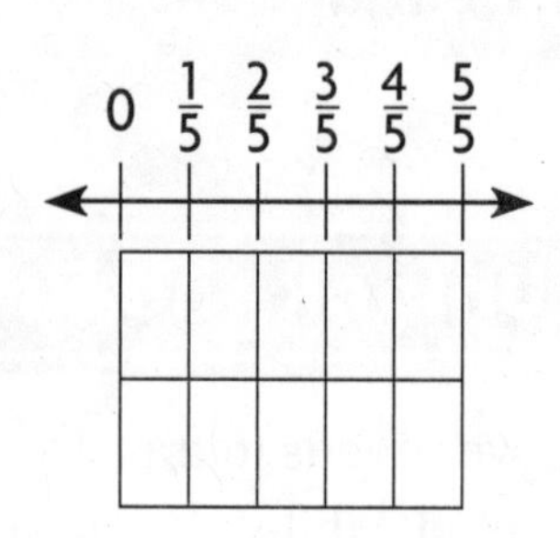

Subtract $\frac{4}{5} - \frac{1}{5}$. Use the model to help.

Shade the model to show how much shrimp Lisa needs.

Then shade the model to show how much shrimp Lisa has. Compare the difference between the two shaded rows.

$\frac{4}{5} - \frac{1}{5} = \frac{\square}{5}$ pound

Lisa needs ______ pound more shrimp.

Use the model to find the difference.

2. $\frac{3}{6} - \frac{2}{6} = \frac{\square}{6}$

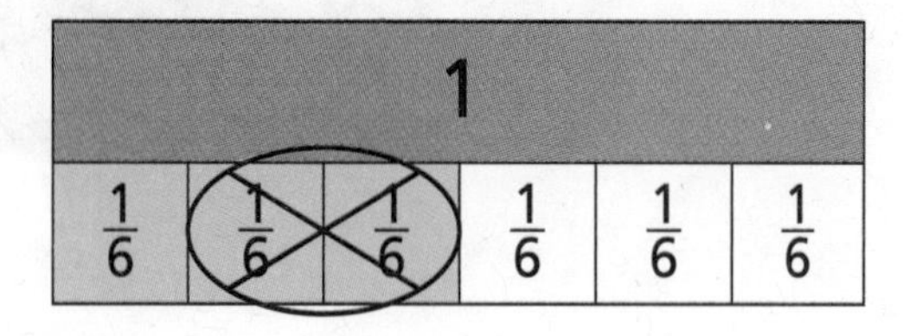

3. $\frac{8}{10} - \frac{3}{10} = \frac{\square}{10}$

1									
$\frac{1}{10}$	$\frac{1}{10}$	$\frac{1}{10}$	$\frac{1}{10}$	$\frac{1}{10}$	$\frac{1}{10}$	$\frac{1}{10}$	$\frac{1}{10}$	$\frac{1}{10}$	$\frac{1}{10}$

Subtract. Use models to help.

4. $\frac{5}{8} - \frac{2}{8} =$ ______

5. $\frac{7}{12} - \frac{2}{12} =$ ______

6. $\frac{3}{4} - \frac{2}{4} =$ ______

Math Talk
Mathematical Processes
Explain why the numerator changes when you subtract fractions with like denominators, but the denominator doesn't.

Problem Solving

7. **H.O.T.** **Explain** how you could find the unknown addend in $\frac{2}{6} + \blacksquare = 1$ without using a model.

____

____

____

Name ______________________________

8. Dani's bean plant grew $\frac{6}{8}$ inch the first week and $\frac{2}{8}$ inch the second week. How much less did Dani's plant grow the second week?

____

Unlock the Problem — Real World

9. H.O.T. **Reasoning Multi-Step** Mrs. Ruiz served a pie for dessert two nights in a row. The drawings below show the pie after her family ate dessert on each night. What fraction of the pie did they eat on the second night?

First night **Second night**

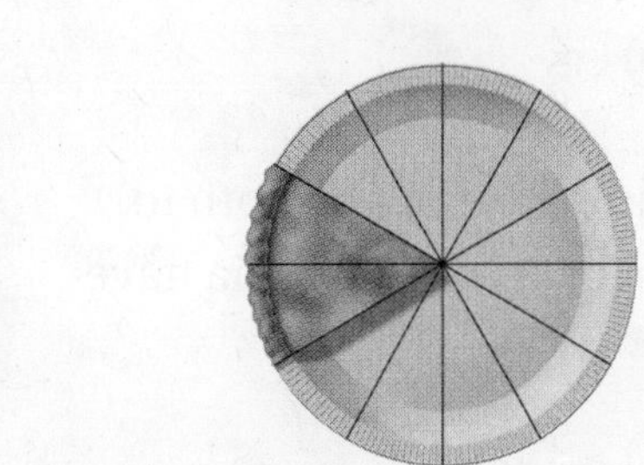

Ⓐ $\frac{2}{12}$ Ⓑ $\frac{5}{12}$ Ⓒ $\frac{7}{12}$ Ⓓ $\frac{10}{12}$

a. What do you need to know? ______________________________

____

b. How can you find the number of pieces eaten on the second night? ______________________________

____

c. **Explain** the steps you used to solve the problem.

____

____

____

____

____

d. Complete the sentences.

After the first night, ______ pieces were left.

After the second night, ______ pieces were left.

So, ______ of the pie was eaten on the second night.

e. Fill in the bubble for the correct answer choice above.

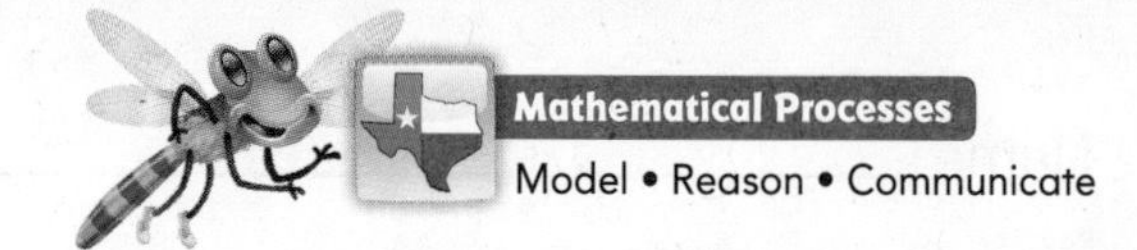

Daily Assessment Task

Fill in the bubble completely to show your answer.

10. Angel is climbing a mountain. He has already climbed $\frac{3}{5}$ of the way. What fraction of the way does Angel have left to climb?

1				
$\frac{1}{5}$	$\frac{1}{5}$	$\frac{1}{5}$	$\frac{1}{5}$	$\frac{1}{5}$

Ⓐ $\frac{2}{5}$ Ⓒ $\frac{3}{5}$

Ⓑ $\frac{1}{2}$ Ⓓ $\frac{2}{3}$

11. Sophia has $\frac{7}{8}$ yard of blue cloth and $\frac{3}{8}$ yard of red cloth to make a kite. How much more blue cloth does Sophia have than red cloth?

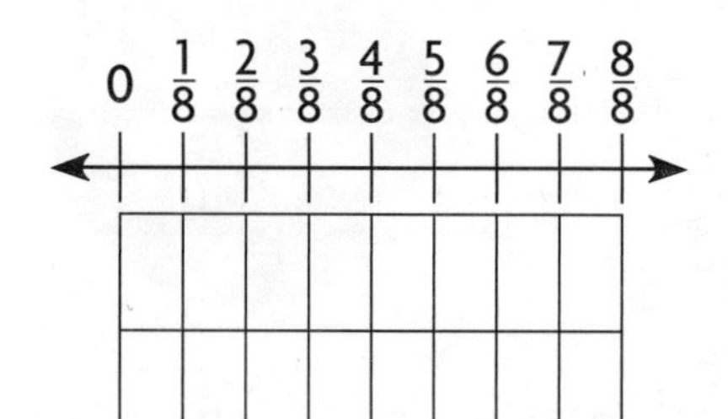

Ⓐ $\frac{3}{8}$ yard Ⓒ $\frac{5}{8}$ yard

Ⓑ $\frac{4}{8}$ yard Ⓓ $\frac{10}{8}$ yard

12. **Multi-Step** David buys $\frac{3}{4}$ pound of bananas. Molly buys $\frac{1}{4}$ pound less of bananas than David. Jude buys $\frac{1}{4}$ pound less of bananas than Molly. How many pounds of bananas does Jude buy?

Ⓐ $\frac{2}{4}$ pound Ⓒ $\frac{1}{4}$ pound

Ⓑ $\frac{1}{3}$ pound Ⓓ $\frac{1}{2}$ pound

TEXAS Test Prep

13. Judi ate $\frac{7}{8}$ of a small pizza and Jack ate $\frac{2}{8}$ of a second small pizza. How much more of a pizza did Judi eat?

Ⓐ $\frac{8}{8}$

Ⓑ 1

Ⓒ $\frac{6}{8}$

Ⓓ $\frac{5}{8}$

Homework and Practice

TEKS Number and Operations—4.3.E
MATHEMATICAL PROCESSES 4.1.D

Name ____________________

5.3 Subtract Fractions Using Models

Use the model to find the difference.

1.

1							
$\frac{1}{8}$	$\frac{1}{8}$	$\frac{1}{8}$	$\frac{1}{8}$	$\frac{1}{8}$	$\frac{1}{8}$	$\frac{1}{8}$	$\frac{1}{8}$

$\frac{4}{8} - \frac{3}{8} =$ ______

2.

1											
$\frac{1}{12}$	$\frac{1}{12}$	$\frac{1}{12}$	$\frac{1}{12}$	$\frac{1}{12}$	$\frac{1}{12}$	$\frac{1}{12}$	$\frac{1}{12}$	$\frac{1}{12}$	$\frac{1}{12}$	$\frac{1}{12}$	$\frac{1}{12}$

$\frac{7}{12} - \frac{4}{12} =$ ______

Subtract. Use models to help.

3. $\frac{5}{7} - \frac{2}{7} =$ ______

4. $\frac{4}{5} - \frac{1}{5} =$ ______

5. $\frac{5}{6} - \frac{3}{6} =$ ______

6. $\frac{8}{10} - \frac{3}{10} =$ ______

Problem Solving Real World

7. Martin's house is $\frac{6}{8}$ mile from his school. If he walks $\frac{4}{8}$ mile, how much further does he need to walk before he reaches the school? Draw a model to find the difference.

______

8. Cynthia is mowing a yard. She has already mowed $\frac{3}{4}$ of the yard. What fraction of the yard does Cynthia have left to mow? Draw a model to find the difference.

______

Lesson Check

TEXAS Test Prep

Fill in the bubble completely to show your answer.

9. Cheri used $\frac{5}{10}$ yard of ribbon to make a bow and $\frac{2}{10}$ yard of ribbon to make a bookmark. How much more ribbon did she use for the bow than she did for the bookmark?

Ⓐ $\frac{7}{10}$

Ⓑ $\frac{4}{10}$

Ⓒ $\frac{5}{10}$

Ⓓ $\frac{3}{10}$

10. Carl had $\frac{7}{12}$ of his cake left after his birthday. Then he and his friend ate $\frac{2}{12}$ of the cake. How much of the cake is left now?

Ⓐ $\frac{5}{12}$

Ⓑ $\frac{9}{12}$

Ⓒ $\frac{6}{12}$

Ⓓ $\frac{4}{12}$

11. Carson needs $\frac{4}{5}$ gallon of paint for his project. He has $\frac{1}{5}$ gallon of paint. How much more paint does Carson need for his project?

Ⓐ $\frac{5}{5}$ gallon

Ⓑ $\frac{2}{5}$ gallon

Ⓒ $\frac{3}{5}$ gallon

Ⓓ $\frac{4}{5}$ gallon

12. Hannah needs to read $\frac{5}{6}$ of a book by Friday to stay on schedule. She has read $\frac{3}{6}$ of the book so far. What fraction of the book does Hannah still need to read?

Ⓐ $\frac{4}{6}$

Ⓑ $\frac{3}{6}$

Ⓒ $\frac{8}{6}$

Ⓓ $\frac{2}{6}$

13. Multi-Step Mrs. Gray sent $\frac{5}{8}$ of her class to the library and $\frac{2}{8}$ of her class to the computer lab. What fraction of the class remained in the classroom?

Ⓐ $\frac{4}{8}$

Ⓑ $\frac{1}{8}$

Ⓒ $\frac{7}{8}$

Ⓓ $\frac{3}{8}$

14. Multi-Step Jarrod planted beans in $\frac{3}{5}$ of his garden. He planted tomatoes in $\frac{1}{5}$ of his garden. What part of the garden does not have tomatoes or beans?

Ⓐ $\frac{1}{5}$

Ⓑ $\frac{2}{5}$

Ⓒ $\frac{3}{5}$

Ⓓ $\frac{4}{5}$

Name ____________________

5.4 Use Benchmarks to Determine Reasonableness

Essential Question How can you find and record sums and differences of fractions?

Unlock the Problem (Real World)

A rover considers many possible paths before choosing the safest path toward its goal. A rover moved $\frac{2}{6}$ yard in a straight line, and then $\frac{5}{6}$ yard around a rock to reach its goal. How far did it travel?

 **Find the sum.**

MODEL IT

Use fraction strips.

Think: The rover moved 2 sixth yard and then 5 sixth yard. Shade 2 sixth-size pieces and then 5 sixth-size pieces.

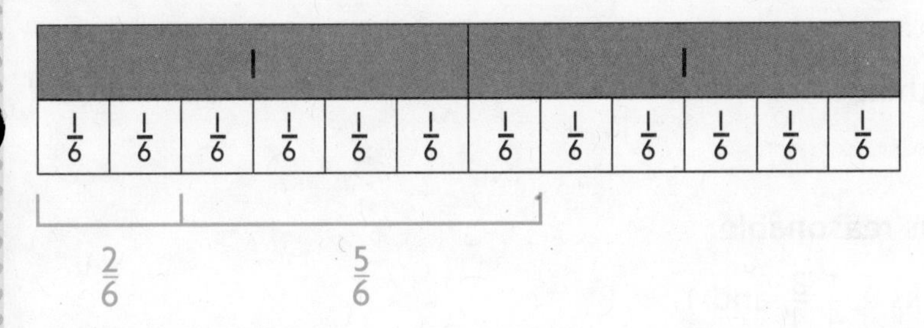

So, the rover traveled ______ yards to reach its goal.

RECORD IT

Write the sum.

______ + ______ = $\frac{7}{6}$

Rename $\frac{7}{6}$ as a mixed number.

Think: The model shows 1 whole yard and 1 sixth yard.

$\frac{7}{6}$ = ______

Math Talk Mathematical Processes

Explain how you know $\frac{5}{6}$ is greater than $\frac{1}{2}$.

 **Determine whether the sum is reasonable.**

Compare the addends to the benchmarks 0, $\frac{1}{2}$, and 1.

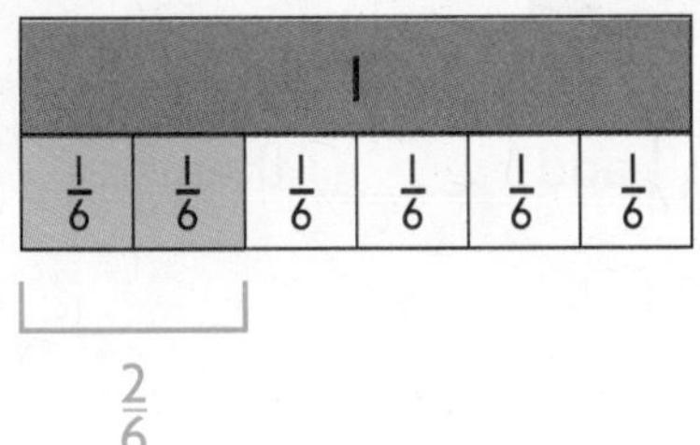

$\frac{2}{6}$ is greater than 0 and less than $\frac{1}{2}$.

The sum is greater than $0 + \frac{1}{2}$ = ______.

The sum is less than $\frac{1}{2} + 1$ = ______.

So, $1\frac{1}{6}$ is a reasonable sum.

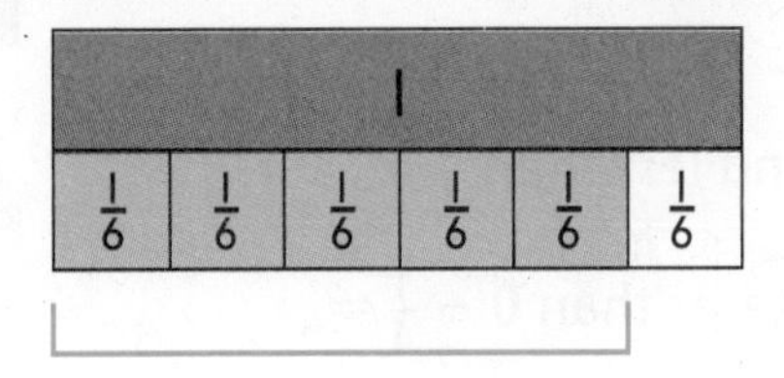

$\frac{5}{6}$ is ________ than $\frac{1}{2}$ and ________ than 1.

Example

A rover must move $\frac{5}{8}$ mile to reach its goal. The rover moves $\frac{1}{8}$ mile toward its goal. How much farther must the rover move to reach its goal?

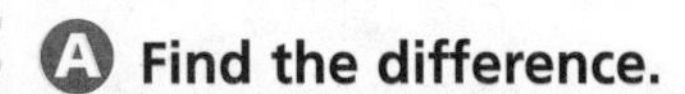

A Find the difference.

MODEL IT

Use fraction strips.

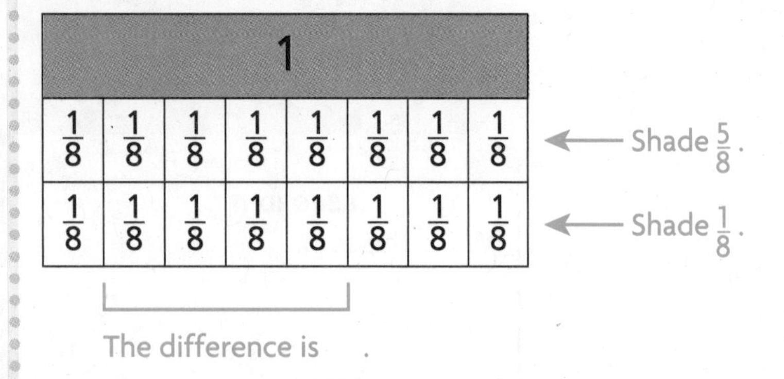

The difference is ___.

RECORD IT

Write the difference.

___ − ___ = $\frac{4}{8}$

So, the rover must move ______ mile farther.

B Determine whether the difference is reasonable.

Compare the fractions to the benchmarks 0, $\frac{1}{4}$, $\frac{3}{4}$, and 1.

1							
$\frac{1}{8}$	$\frac{1}{8}$	$\frac{1}{8}$	$\frac{1}{8}$	$\frac{1}{8}$	$\frac{1}{8}$	$\frac{1}{8}$	$\frac{1}{8}$
$\frac{1}{4}$							

$\frac{1}{8}$ is close to $\frac{1}{4}$.

1							
$\frac{1}{8}$	$\frac{1}{8}$	$\frac{1}{8}$	$\frac{1}{8}$	$\frac{1}{8}$	$\frac{1}{8}$	$\frac{1}{8}$	$\frac{1}{8}$
$\frac{1}{4}$		$\frac{1}{4}$		$\frac{1}{4}$			

$\frac{5}{8}$ is close to $\frac{3}{4}$.

$\frac{1}{8}$ is greater than 0 and less than $\frac{1}{4}$.

$\frac{5}{8}$ is ______ than $\frac{1}{4}$ and ______ than $\frac{3}{4}$.

The difference is greater than $0 + \frac{1}{4} =$ ______.

The difference is less than $\frac{1}{4} + \frac{3}{4} =$ ______.

So, $\frac{4}{8}$ is a reasonable difference.

Name ______________________

Share and Show

1. A rover needs to move $\frac{9}{10}$ mile to a crater. It moves $\frac{4}{10}$ mile toward the crater. How much farther does it need to move to reach the crater?

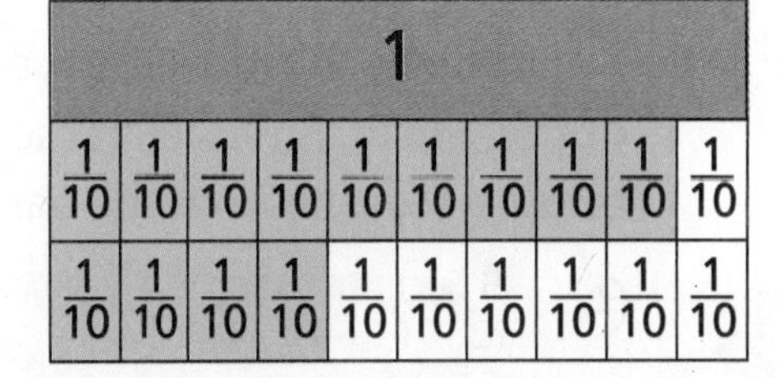

1									
$\frac{1}{10}$	$\frac{1}{10}$	$\frac{1}{10}$	$\frac{1}{10}$	$\frac{1}{10}$	$\frac{1}{10}$	$\frac{1}{10}$	$\frac{1}{10}$	$\frac{1}{10}$	$\frac{1}{10}$
$\frac{1}{10}$	$\frac{1}{10}$	$\frac{1}{10}$	$\frac{1}{10}$	$\frac{1}{10}$	$\frac{1}{10}$	$\frac{1}{10}$	$\frac{1}{10}$	$\frac{1}{10}$	$\frac{1}{10}$

- Model the difference.
- Write the difference.

$\frac{9}{10} - \frac{4}{10} =$ ______________

Add or subtract. Determine whether your answer is reasonable.

2. $\frac{5}{12} + \frac{4}{12} =$ ______________

3. $\frac{4}{6} - \frac{2}{6} =$ ______________

4. $\frac{3}{8} + \frac{7}{8} =$ ______________

Unlock the Problem — Real World

5.  **Apply Multi-Step** In our solar system, $\frac{2}{8}$ of the planets have no moons, $\frac{1}{8}$ have 1 moon, $\frac{1}{8}$ have 2 moons, and $\frac{1}{8}$ have 13 moons. What fraction of the planets have 0, 1, 2, or 13 moons?

Ⓐ $\frac{5}{8}$ Ⓒ $\frac{3}{8}$

Ⓑ $\frac{4}{8}$ Ⓓ $\frac{2}{8}$

a. What do you need to know?

____

b. What information are you given?

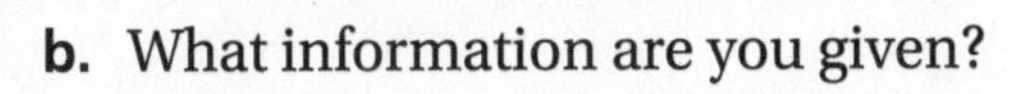

____

____

c. Write the addition problem you will use to solve this problem. ______________

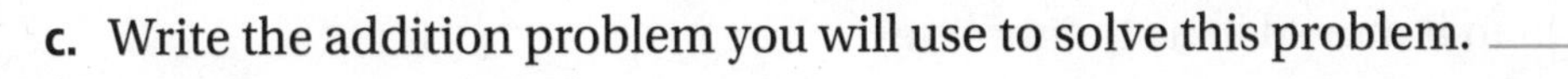

d. Draw a model to help you solve the problem.

e. Fill in the bubble for the correct answer choice above.

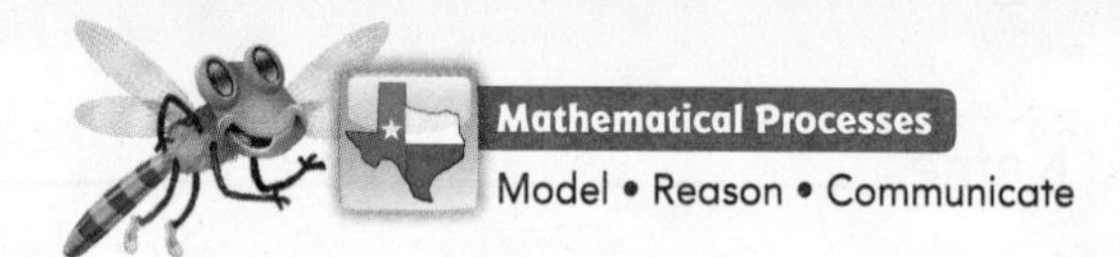

Daily Assessment Task

Fill in the bubble completely to show your answer.

6. Amari times the movement of a banana slug. It moves $\frac{2}{6}$ foot during the first minute. It then moves $\frac{3}{6}$ foot during the second minute. How far does the banana slug move in all?

   Ⓐ $\frac{5}{12}$ foot
   Ⓑ $\frac{1}{6}$ foot
   Ⓒ $\frac{1}{12}$ foot
   Ⓓ $\frac{5}{6}$ foot

7. One day $\frac{3}{8}$ of the students in Jack's class ate toast for breakfast. Another $\frac{1}{8}$ of the students ate oatmeal. Jack added the fractions and found the sum was $\frac{7}{8}$. Which statement best describes the sum $\frac{7}{8}$?

   Ⓐ It is reasonable because $\frac{1}{2} + 0 = \frac{1}{2}$.
   Ⓑ It is reasonable because $\frac{1}{2} + \frac{1}{2} = 1$.
   Ⓒ It is not reasonable because $\frac{1}{2} + 0 = \frac{1}{2}$.
   Ⓓ It is not reasonable because $\frac{1}{2} + \frac{1}{2} = 1$.

8. **Multi-Step** Ms. Ryan buys $\frac{7}{8}$ yard of striped cloth. She uses $\frac{3}{8}$ yard to make a bag. Then she uses $\frac{1}{8}$ yard to make a belt. How much cloth does Ms. Ryan have left to make a hat?

   Ⓐ $\frac{2}{8}$ yard
   Ⓑ $\frac{4}{8}$ yard
   Ⓒ $\frac{3}{8}$ yard
   Ⓓ $\frac{6}{8}$ yard

TEXAS Test Prep

9. Suppose a rover on Mars moved $\frac{2}{6}$ yard in a straight line. Then it moved $\frac{5}{6}$ yard around a rock. How many more yards did the rover move around the rock than it moved in a straight line?

   Ⓐ $\frac{3}{12}$ yard
   Ⓑ $\frac{3}{6}$ yard
   Ⓒ $\frac{7}{12}$ yard
   Ⓓ $1\frac{1}{6}$ yard

TEKS Number and Operations—4.3.F
MATHEMATICAL PROCESSES 4.1.D, 4.1.E, 4.1.F

Name ____________________

5.4 Use Benchmarks to Determine Reasonableness

1. Melina wants to finish $\frac{6}{10}$ of her math homework problems before dinner. She finishes $\frac{4}{10}$ of them. What fraction of her math problems does she still need to complete before dinner?

1									
$\frac{1}{10}$	$\frac{1}{10}$	$\frac{1}{10}$	$\frac{1}{10}$	$\frac{1}{10}$	$\frac{1}{10}$	$\frac{1}{10}$	$\frac{1}{10}$	$\frac{1}{10}$	$\frac{1}{10}$
$\frac{1}{10}$	$\frac{1}{10}$	$\frac{1}{10}$	$\frac{1}{10}$	$\frac{1}{10}$	$\frac{1}{10}$	$\frac{1}{10}$	$\frac{1}{10}$	$\frac{1}{10}$	$\frac{1}{10}$

- Model the difference.
- Write the difference.

$\frac{6}{10} - \frac{4}{10} =$ ____________

Add or subtract. Determine whether your answer is reasonable.

2. $\frac{1}{6} + \frac{4}{6} =$ ____________

3. $\frac{3}{4} - \frac{1}{4} =$ ____________

4. $\frac{9}{12} - \frac{3}{12} =$ ____________

5. $\frac{3}{6} + \frac{2}{6} =$ ____________

Problem Solving Real World

6. In Joe's family, $\frac{2}{6}$ of the people have blue eyes and $\frac{3}{6}$ of the people have brown eyes. What fraction of people has either blue or brown eyes?

____

7. Kim wants to add drawings to $\frac{5}{8}$ of the stories in her journal. So far she has completed drawings for $\frac{2}{8}$ of the stories. How many more stories still need drawings?

____

Lesson Check

Fill in the bubble completely to show your answer.

8. Add. Determine if the answer is reasonable.

$\frac{3}{8} + \frac{2}{8}$

Ⓐ $\frac{4}{8}$

Ⓑ $\frac{3}{8}$

Ⓒ $\frac{5}{8}$

Ⓓ $\frac{1}{8}$

9. Subtract. Determine if the answer is reasonable.

$\frac{10}{12} - \frac{1}{12}$

Ⓐ $\frac{9}{12}$

Ⓑ $\frac{11}{12}$

Ⓒ $\frac{8}{12}$

Ⓓ $\frac{7}{12}$

10. In Martha's class, $\frac{5}{8}$ of the students walk to school and $\frac{1}{8}$ of the students ride the bus. Martha added the fractions and found the sum was $\frac{1}{8}$. Which statement best describes the sum $\frac{1}{8}$?

Ⓐ It is reasonable because $\frac{1}{2} + 0 = \frac{1}{2}$

Ⓑ It is reasonable because $\frac{1}{2} + \frac{1}{2} = 1$

Ⓒ It is not reasonable because $\frac{1}{2} + 0 = \frac{1}{2}$

Ⓓ It is not reasonable because $\frac{1}{2} + \frac{1}{2} = 1$

11. Sabina walks dogs on Saturday. Last Saturday only $\frac{7}{10}$ of the dogs needed to be walked. She walked $\frac{5}{10}$ of them in the morning. What fractional part of the dogs does Sabina need to walk in the afternoon?

Ⓐ $\frac{2}{10}$

Ⓑ $\frac{1}{10}$

Ⓒ $\frac{3}{10}$

Ⓓ $\frac{4}{10}$

12. Multi-Step Luke poured $\frac{3}{4}$ cup yellow paint into a can and $\frac{3}{4}$ cup of blue paint in a can. He mixed the colors to make green paint. Then used $\frac{1}{4}$ cup of the green paint. How much green paint is left?

Ⓐ $\frac{7}{4}$ cup or $1\frac{3}{4}$ cup

Ⓑ $\frac{1}{4}$ cup

Ⓒ $\frac{3}{4}$ cup

Ⓓ $\frac{5}{4}$ cup or $1\frac{1}{4}$ cup

13. Multi-Step Andrew used $\frac{2}{12}$ of a carton of eggs for a cake and $\frac{5}{12}$ of a carton for egg salad. What fraction of the carton is remaining?

Ⓐ $\frac{4}{12}$

Ⓑ $\frac{3}{12}$

Ⓒ $\frac{5}{12}$

Ⓓ $\frac{7}{12}$

Name ____________________

5.5 Add and Subtract Fractions

Essential Question How can you add and subtract fractions with like denominators?

Unlock the Problem

Julie is making a poster for a book report. The directions say to use $\frac{1}{5}$ of the poster to describe the setting, $\frac{2}{5}$ of the poster to describe the characters, and the rest of the poster to describe the plot. What part of the poster will she use to describe the plot?

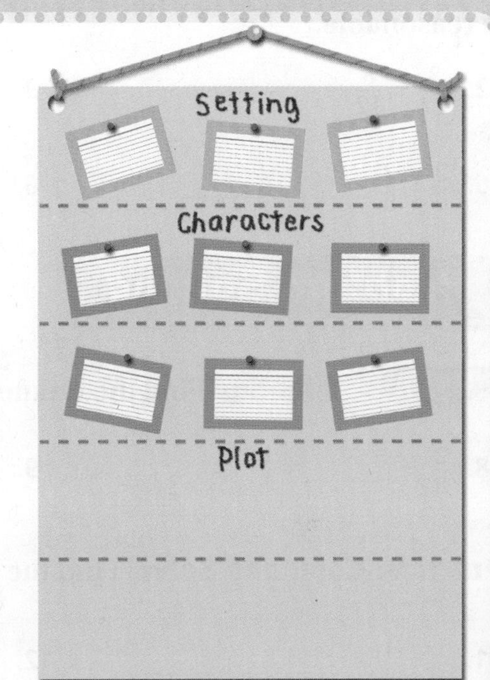

Example Use a model.

Shade ______ to represent the part for the setting.

Shade ______ to represent the part for the characters.

1				
$\frac{1}{5}$	$\frac{1}{5}$	$\frac{1}{5}$	$\frac{1}{5}$	$\frac{1}{5}$

- Write an equation for the part of the poster used for the setting and characters. ______
- What does the part of the model that is not shaded represent?

  ____
- Write an equation for the part of the poster she will use for the plot.

  ____

So, Julie will use ______ of the poster to describe the plot.

Math Talk

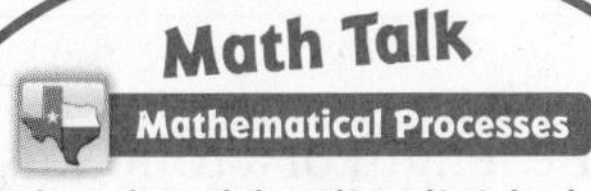

Why should Julie divide her poster into 5 equal parts instead of 3 equal parts? **Explain.**

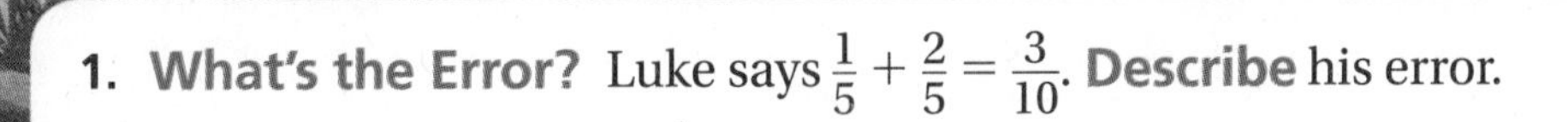

1. **What's the Error?** Luke says $\frac{1}{5} + \frac{2}{5} = \frac{3}{10}$. **Describe** his error.

____

____

____

Share and Show

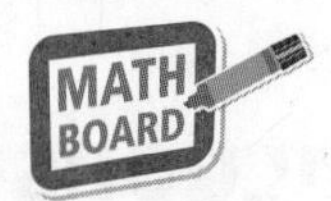

1. 9 twelfth-size parts − 5 twelfth-size parts = ______

$\frac{9}{12} - \frac{5}{12} =$ ______

Find the sum or difference. Determine whether your answer is reasonable.

2. $\frac{3}{12} + \frac{8}{12} =$ ______

3. $\frac{1}{3} + \frac{1}{3} =$ ______

4. $\frac{3}{4} - \frac{1}{4} =$ ______

5. $\frac{2}{6} + \frac{2}{6} =$ ______

6. $\frac{3}{8} + \frac{1}{8} =$ ______

7. $\frac{6}{10} - \frac{2}{10} =$ ______

Problem Solving

H.O.T. **Algebra** **Find the unknown fraction.**

8. $\frac{2}{8} +$ ______ $= \frac{6}{8}$

9. $1 -$ ______ $= \frac{3}{4}$

10. $\frac{4}{5} -$ ______ $= \frac{1}{5}$

Practice: Copy and Solve **Find the sum or difference.**

11. $\frac{1}{4} + \frac{1}{4} =$ ______

12. $\frac{9}{10} - \frac{5}{10} =$ ______

13. $\frac{1}{12} + \frac{7}{12} =$ ______

14. **Use Math Language** **Multi-Step** A city worker is painting a stripe down the center of Main Street. Main Street is $\frac{8}{10}$ mile long. The worker painted $\frac{4}{10}$ mile of the street. **Explain** how to find what part of a mile is left to paint.

______

______

______

15. The length of a rope was $\frac{6}{8}$ yard. Jeff cut the rope into 3 pieces. Each piece is a different length measured in eighths of a yard. What is the length of each piece of rope?

______

Name ________________________

Problem Solving Real World

16. H.O.T. **Sense or Nonsense?** Brian says that when you add or subtract fractions with the same denominator, you can add or subtract the numerators and keep the same denominator. Is Brian correct? **Explain.**

H.O.T. Multi-Step **Sense or Nonsense?**

17. Harry says that $\frac{1}{4} + \frac{1}{4} = \frac{2}{4}$. Jane says $\frac{1}{4} + \frac{1}{4} = \frac{2}{8}$. Whose answer makes sense? Whose answer is nonsense? **Explain** your reasoning.

Harry

$\frac{1}{4} + \frac{1}{4} = \frac{2}{4}$

Jane

$\frac{1}{4} + \frac{1}{4} = \frac{2}{8}$

Harry

Jane

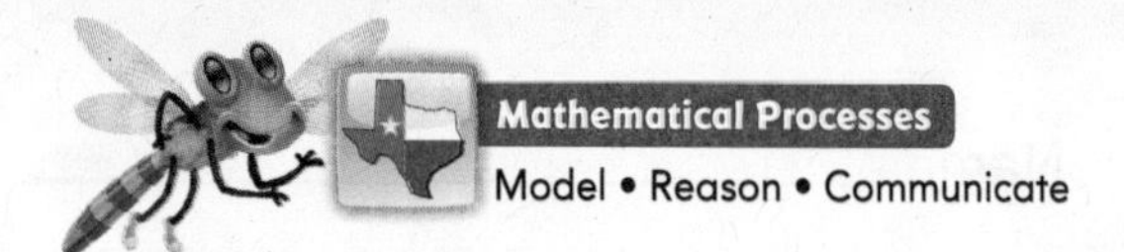

Daily Assessment Task

Fill in the bubble completely to show your answer.

18. The Small family has 1 pie to share for dessert. The parents eat $\frac{1}{6}$ of the pie. The children eat $\frac{4}{6}$ of the pie. What part of the pie does the family eat?

Ⓐ $\frac{6}{6}$

Ⓑ $\frac{5}{12}$

Ⓒ $\frac{5}{6}$

Ⓓ $\frac{3}{12}$

19. Ana rides her bike $\frac{5}{10}$ mile to the park. Then she rides $\frac{3}{10}$ mile to the soccer field. How far does Ana ride her bike?

Ⓐ $\frac{2}{10}$ mile

Ⓑ $\frac{2}{20}$ mile

Ⓒ $\frac{8}{10}$ mile

Ⓓ $\frac{8}{20}$ mile

20. **Multi-Step** Christopher mixes $\frac{3}{8}$ gallon of red paint with $\frac{5}{8}$ gallon of blue paint to make purple paint. He uses $\frac{2}{8}$ gallon of purple paint to paint bookshelves. How much purple paint is left?

Ⓐ $\frac{8}{8}$ gallon

Ⓑ $\frac{4}{8}$ gallon

Ⓒ $\frac{10}{8}$ gallons

Ⓓ $\frac{6}{8}$ gallon

TEXAS Test Prep

21. Otis has 1 cup of granola. He added $\frac{3}{8}$ cup to a bowl of yogurt. How much granola is left?

Ⓐ $\frac{3}{8}$ cup

Ⓑ $\frac{2}{8}$ cup

Ⓒ $\frac{5}{8}$ cup

Ⓓ $\frac{8}{8}$ cup

Homework and Practice

TEKS Number and Operations—4.3.E
Also 4.3.F
MATHEMATICAL PROCESSES 4.1.G

Name ____________________

5.5 Add and Subtract Fractions

Find the sum or difference. Determine whether your answer is reasonable.

1. $\frac{2}{7} + \frac{3}{7} =$ ________

2. $\frac{10}{12} - \frac{6}{12} =$ ________

3. $\frac{8}{9} - \frac{5}{9} =$ ________

4. $\frac{4}{8} + \frac{4}{8} =$ ________

Find the sum or difference.

5. $\frac{4}{7} - \frac{1}{7} =$ ________

6. $\frac{1}{6} + \frac{5}{6} =$ ________

Find the unknown fraction.

7. $\frac{1}{5} +$ ________ $= \frac{4}{5}$

8. $1 -$ ________ $= \frac{2}{4}$

9. $\frac{3}{8} +$ ________ $= 1$

10. $\frac{5}{6} -$ ________ $= \frac{2}{6}$

Problem Solving Real World

11. Jorge's rain gauge showed that it rained $\frac{3}{8}$ inch during the first week of the month. At the end of the second week the gauge was $\frac{7}{8}$ inch full. How much did it rain during the second week?

____

12. Courtney watched a caterpillar crawl on the sidewalk. It crawled $\frac{4}{10}$ yard and stopped. The caterpillar crawled $\frac{5}{10}$ yard further. How far did the caterpillar crawl in all?

____

Lesson Check

TEXAS Test Prep

Fill in the bubble completely to show your answer.

13. At Mary's party, $\frac{4}{8}$ of the guests had chocolate ice cream and $\frac{3}{8}$ of the guests had strawberry ice cream. What fraction of the ice cream was either chocolate or strawberry?

Ⓐ $\frac{1}{16}$

Ⓑ $\frac{7}{8}$

Ⓒ $\frac{1}{8}$

Ⓓ $\frac{7}{16}$

14. The fuel gauge in Mrs. Jensen's car showed $\frac{3}{4}$ of a tank of gas. After driving into the city and back, the gauge showed $\frac{1}{4}$ of a tank of gas. How much gas did Mrs. Jensen use?

Ⓐ $\frac{2}{4}$ tank

Ⓑ 1 tank

Ⓒ $\frac{1}{3}$ tank

Ⓓ $\frac{3}{4}$ tank

15. Craig is folding laundry for his family. In the basket, $\frac{1}{6}$ of the shirts belong to his older brother and $\frac{3}{6}$ of the shirts belong to his younger brother. What fraction of the shirts belong to either his older or younger brother?

Ⓐ $\frac{6}{6}$

Ⓑ $\frac{5}{6}$

Ⓒ $\frac{2}{3}$

Ⓓ $\frac{1}{3}$

16. After sharing with the class, Dana has $\frac{4}{12}$ of her cupcakes left. What fractional part of the cupcakes did she share with the class?

Ⓐ $\frac{2}{3}$

Ⓑ $\frac{1}{4}$

Ⓒ $\frac{3}{4}$

Ⓓ $\frac{1}{3}$

17. **Multi-Step** Josie had 1 gallon of ice cream. She used $\frac{3}{10}$ gallon to make a chocolate milkshake and $\frac{3}{10}$ gallon to make a vanilla milkshake. How much ice cream is left?

Ⓐ $\frac{6}{10}$ gallon

Ⓑ $\frac{4}{10}$ gallon

Ⓒ $\frac{7}{10}$ gallon

Ⓓ $\frac{5}{10}$ gallon

18. **Multi-Step** In Mr. Green's music class, $\frac{3}{12}$ of the students play the guitar and $\frac{4}{12}$ of the students play the violin. The rest of the students play the piano. What fraction of the students play the piano?

Ⓐ $\frac{8}{12}$

Ⓑ $\frac{9}{12}$

Ⓒ $\frac{7}{12}$

Ⓓ $\frac{5}{12}$

Name ______________________________

5.6 Add and Subtract Mixed Numbers

TEKS Number and Operations—4.3.E

MATHEMATICAL PROCESSES 4.1.A, 4.1.D, 4.1.E

Essential Question How can you add and subtract mixed numbers with like denominators?

Unlock the Problem (Real World)

After a party, there were $1\frac{4}{6}$ quesadillas left on one tray and $2\frac{3}{6}$ quesadillas left on another tray. How much of the quesadillas were left?

Example Add mixed numbers.

THINK	MODEL	RECORD
STEP 1 Add the fractional parts of the mixed numbers.	Think: Shade to model $\frac{4}{6} + \frac{3}{6}$. 	$1\frac{4}{6}$ $+ 2\frac{3}{6}$ ――― $\frac{\square}{\square}$
STEP 2 Add the whole-number parts of the mixed numbers.	Think: Shade to model 1 + 2. 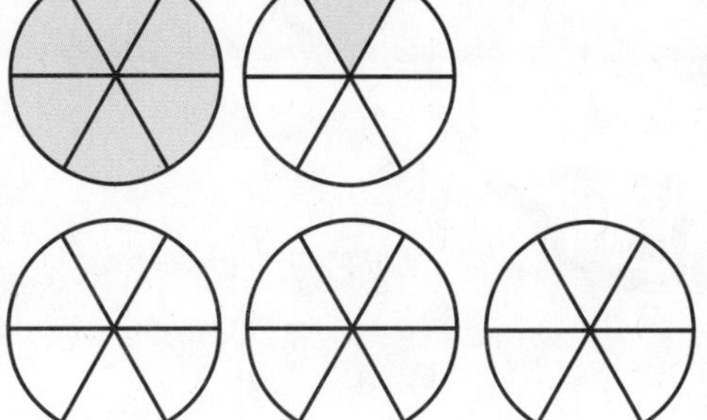	$1\frac{4}{6}$ $+ 2\frac{3}{6}$ ――― $\square\frac{7}{6}$
STEP 3 Rename the sum.	Think: $\frac{7}{6}$ is greater than 1. Group the wholes together to rename the sum. The model shows a total of ____ wholes and ―― left over.	$3\frac{7}{6} = 3 + \frac{6}{6} + \frac{\square}{\square}$ $= 3 + 1 + \frac{\square}{\square} = \square\frac{\square}{\square}$

So, ______ quesadillas were left.

Math Talk Mathematical Processes

When modeling sums such as $\frac{4}{6}$ and $\frac{3}{6}$, why is it helpful to combine parts into wholes when possible? **Explain.**

Example Subtract mixed numbers.

Alejandro had $3\frac{4}{6}$ quesadillas. His family ate $2\frac{3}{6}$ of the quesadillas. How many quesadillas are left?

Find $3\frac{4}{6} - 2\frac{3}{6}$.

MODEL

Shade the model to show $3\frac{4}{6}$.

Then cross out $2\frac{3}{6}$ to model the subtraction.

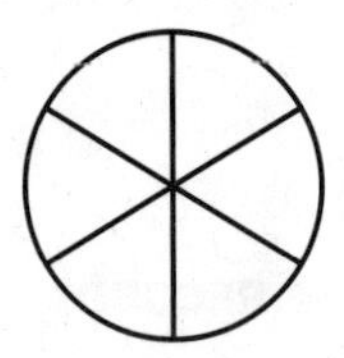
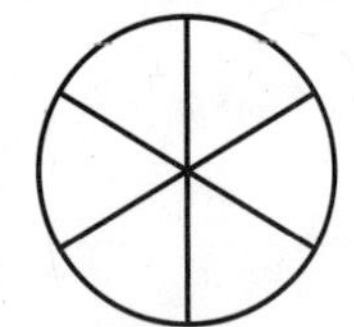
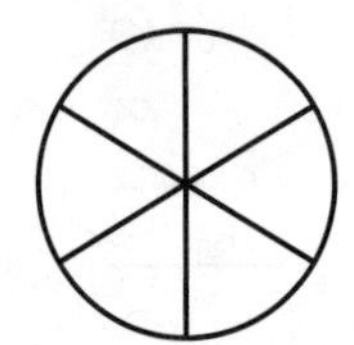
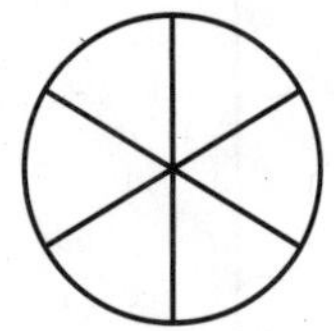

The difference is ______.

RECORD

Subtract the fractional parts of the mixed numbers.

Then subtract the whole-number parts of the mixed numbers.

$$3\frac{4}{6}$$
$$-\ 2\frac{3}{6}$$
$$\rule{1em}{0.4pt}\ \frac{\rule{1em}{0.4pt}}{\rule{1em}{0.4pt}}$$

So, there are ______ quesadillas left.

Share and Show

Write the sum as a mixed number with the fractional part less than 1.

1. $1\frac{1}{6}$ $+3\frac{3}{6}$ Add whole numbers. $\square + \square$ Add fractions. $\square + \square$ $\square + \square = \underline{\qquad}$

2. $1\frac{4}{5}$ $+7\frac{2}{5}$

3. $2\frac{1}{2}$ $+3\frac{1}{2}$

Name ______________________________

Find the difference.

4. $\begin{array}{r} 3\frac{7}{12} \\ -2\frac{5}{12} \\ \hline \end{array}$

5. $\begin{array}{r} 4\frac{2}{3} \\ -3\frac{1}{3} \\ \hline \end{array}$

✓ 6. $\begin{array}{r} 6\frac{9}{10} \\ -3\frac{7}{10} \\ \hline \end{array}$

Math Talk

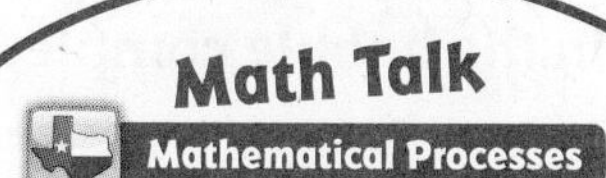

Explain how adding and subtracting mixed numbers is different from adding and subtracting fractions.

Problem Solving Real World

Solve. Write your answer as a mixed number.

Write Math ▶ Show Your Work

7. The driving distance from Alex's house to the museum is $6\frac{7}{10}$ miles. What is the round-trip distance?

____

8. H.O.T. **Apply Multi-Step** The driving distance from the sports arena to Kristina's house is $10\frac{9}{10}$ miles. The distance from the sports arena to Luke's house is $2\frac{7}{10}$ miles. How much greater is the driving distance between the sports arena and Kristina's house than between the sports arena and Luke's house?

____

9. Benji biked from his house to the nature preserve, a distance of $23\frac{4}{5}$ miles. Jade biked from her house to the lake, a distance of $12\frac{2}{5}$ miles. How many fewer miles did Jade bike than Benji?

____

10. H.O.T. **Apply** During the Samson family trip, they drove from home to a ski lodge, a distance of $55\frac{4}{5}$ miles, and then drove an additional $12\frac{4}{5}$ miles to visit friends. If the family drove the same route back home, what was the distance traveled during their trip?

____

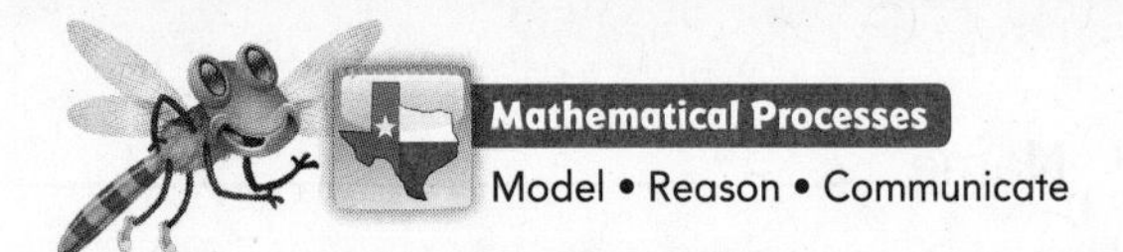

Daily Assessment Task

Fill in the bubble completely to show your answer.

11. A chameleon's body is $1\frac{4}{6}$ feet long. Its tongue is $2\frac{5}{6}$ feet long. How much longer is the chameleon's tongue than its body?

Ⓐ $2\frac{3}{6}$ feet

Ⓑ $1\frac{3}{6}$ feet

Ⓒ $1\frac{1}{6}$ feet

Ⓓ $2\frac{1}{6}$ feet

12. Jill rides her horse $5\frac{6}{12}$ miles on a horse trail. She will ride $4\frac{5}{12}$ miles more to reach the end of the trail. How long is the horse trail?

Ⓐ $1\frac{1}{12}$ miles

Ⓑ $1\frac{11}{12}$ miles

Ⓒ $9\frac{1}{12}$ miles

Ⓓ $9\frac{11}{12}$ miles

13. **Multi-Step** Students bring $8\frac{7}{8}$ gallons of lemonade to a picnic. They drink $5\frac{2}{8}$ gallons with lunch. Then they drink $2\frac{1}{8}$ gallons with an afternoon snack. How much lemonade is left?

Ⓐ $3\frac{5}{8}$ gallons

Ⓑ $6\frac{3}{4}$ gallons

Ⓒ $5\frac{3}{4}$ gallons

Ⓓ $1\frac{1}{2}$ gallons

TEXAS Test Prep

14. Jeff used $4\frac{7}{8}$ cups of orange juice and $3\frac{1}{8}$ cups of pineapple juice to make a tropical punch. How much more orange juice than pineapple juice did Jeff use?

Ⓐ $\frac{3}{4}$ cup

Ⓑ $1\frac{3}{4}$ cups

Ⓒ $1\frac{7}{8}$ cups

Ⓓ 8 cups

Homework and Practice

TEKS Number and Operations—4.3.E
MATHEMATICAL PROCESSES 4.1.A, 4.1.D, 4.1.E

Name ____________________

5.6 Add and Subtract Mixed Numbers

Write the sum as a mixed number with the fractional part less than 1.

1. $8\frac{1}{3} + 3\frac{2}{3}$

2. $5\frac{4}{8} + 3\frac{5}{8}$

3. $7\frac{4}{6} + 4\frac{3}{6}$

4. $3\frac{5}{12} + 4\frac{2}{12}$

Find the difference.

5. $7\frac{3}{4} - 2\frac{2}{4}$

6. $3\frac{5}{10} - 1\frac{3}{10}$

7. $5\frac{7}{12} - 4\frac{1}{12}$

8. $5\frac{7}{8} - 2\frac{3}{8}$

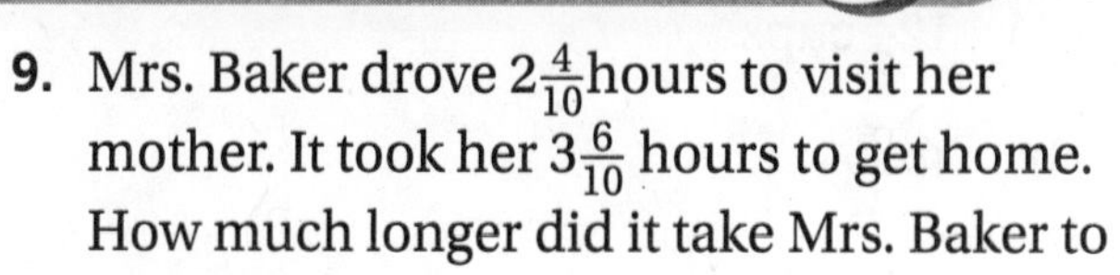

9. Mrs. Baker drove $2\frac{4}{10}$ hours to visit her mother. It took her $3\frac{6}{10}$ hours to get home. How much longer did it take Mrs. Baker to get home?

10. Monica's recipe calls for $2\frac{3}{4}$ cup of water and $3\frac{3}{4}$ cup of milk. What is the total amount of liquid in the recipe?

Lesson Check

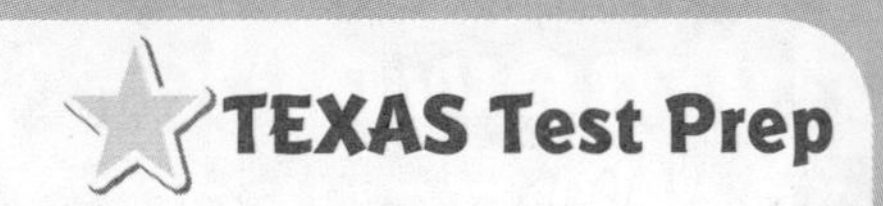

Fill in the bubble completely to show your answer.

11. Kimberly's kite tail is $5\frac{5}{6}$ feet long. Margaret's kite tail is $4\frac{3}{6}$ feet long. How much longer is Kimberly's kite tail than Margaret's kite tail?

Ⓐ $1\frac{2}{3}$ feet

Ⓑ $1\frac{1}{3}$ feet

Ⓒ $2\frac{1}{3}$ feet

Ⓓ $2\frac{2}{3}$ feet

12. Wayne recorded his exercise for two months. He walked $2\frac{8}{10}$ miles the first day. He walked $1\frac{5}{10}$ miles the second day. What is the total distance he walked during the two days?

Ⓐ $4\frac{3}{10}$ miles

Ⓑ $4\frac{2}{10}$ miles

Ⓒ $3\frac{3}{10}$ miles

Ⓓ $3\frac{2}{10}$ miles

13. Kris used $7\frac{5}{12}$ inches of tape to wrap her brother's gift and $6\frac{9}{12}$ inches of tape to wrap her sister's gift. What is the total amount of tape Kris used to wrap the gifts?

Ⓐ $13\frac{1}{6}$ inches

Ⓑ $14\frac{1}{6}$ inches

Ⓒ $13\frac{1}{12}$ inches

Ⓓ $14\frac{1}{12}$ inches

14. The mall is $6\frac{6}{10}$ miles from Miranda's house. The nearest grocery store is $4\frac{2}{10}$ miles from her house. How much farther is the mall than the grocery store from Miranda's house?

Ⓐ $2\frac{2}{5}$ miles

Ⓑ $4\frac{4}{5}$ miles

Ⓒ $2\frac{4}{5}$ miles

Ⓓ $8\frac{2}{5}$ miles

15. **Multi-Step** A tank has $5\frac{3}{4}$ gallons of water in it. Today, $4\frac{1}{4}$ gallons of the water is used. Then, the tank is filled with another $6\frac{3}{4}$ gallons of water. What is the amount of water in the tank now?

Ⓐ $8\frac{1}{4}$ gallons

Ⓑ $1\frac{1}{2}$ gallons

Ⓒ $8\frac{1}{4}$ gallons

Ⓓ $1\frac{3}{4}$ gallons

16. **Multi-Step** For a candy recipe, Karen will need $4\frac{3}{8}$ cups of dark chocolate chips, $5\frac{5}{8}$ cups milk chocolate chips, and $3\frac{4}{8}$ cups white chocolate chips. What is the total amount of chips needed for the candy recipe?

Ⓐ $12\frac{1}{2}$ cups

Ⓑ $12\frac{2}{3}$ cups

Ⓒ $13\frac{2}{3}$ cups

Ⓓ $13\frac{1}{2}$ cups

Name ______________________________

5.7 Use Properties of Addition

TEKS Number and Operations—4.3.E
MATHEMATICAL PROCESSES 4.1.D, 4.1.E, 4.1.F

Essential Question

How can properties help you add fractions with like denominators?

Connect You can use properties of addition to help you add fractions.

Commutative Property: $\frac{3}{5} + \frac{1}{5} = \frac{1}{5} + \frac{3}{5}$

Associative Property: $(1\frac{2}{9} + \frac{2}{9}) + \frac{7}{9} = 1\frac{2}{9} + (\frac{2}{9} + \frac{7}{9})$

Remember

Parentheses ( ) tell which operation to do first.

Unlock the Problem

Jane and her teammates are training for their track meet. On the first day of practice, they run $2\frac{4}{8}$ miles around the track. On the second day, they run $2\frac{1}{8}$ miles. On the last day of practice before the meet, they run $\frac{7}{8}$ mile. How many miles did Jane and her teammates run to train for their track meet?

Use the Associative Property.

Day 1 + Day 2 + Day 3

$\left(2\frac{4}{8} + 2\frac{1}{8}\right) + \frac{7}{8} = \square + (\square + \square)$

Write the number sentence to represent the problem. Use the Associative Property to group fractions that can be added mentally.

$= \square + \square$

Add the fractions in parentheses.

$= \square$

Then add.

So, Jane and her teammates ran ______ miles to prepare for their track meet.

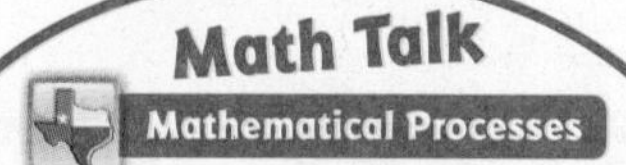

Math Talk Mathematical Processes

Explain why grouping the fractions differently makes it easier to find the sum.

- **Explain** why you would not group $2\frac{4}{8}$ and $\frac{7}{8}$ together in parentheses.

____

____

____

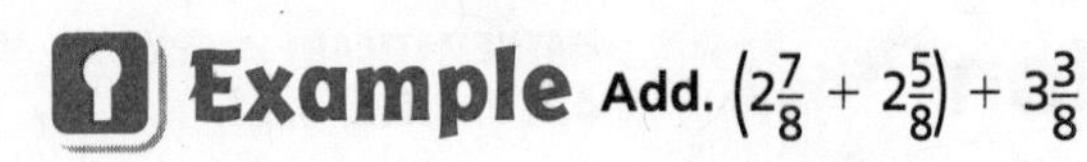

Example Add. $\left(2\frac{7}{8} + 2\frac{5}{8}\right) + 3\frac{3}{8}$

Use the Associative Property.

$\left(2\frac{7}{8} + 2\frac{5}{8}\right) + 3\frac{3}{8} = \square + \left(\square + \square\right)$ Use the Associative Property to group fractions that can be added mentally.

$= \square + \square$ Add the fractions in the parentheses.

$= \square$ Then add.

Try This!

Subtraction is not commutative or associative. When you subtract, perform operations in parentheses first. Then subtract from left to right.

a. $5\frac{8}{12} - \frac{2}{12} - \frac{1}{12} =$ ______ $- \frac{1}{12} =$ ______

b. $\left(5\frac{8}{12} - \frac{2}{12}\right) - \frac{1}{12} =$ ______ $- \frac{1}{12} =$ ______

c. $5\frac{8}{12} - \left(\frac{2}{12} - \frac{1}{12}\right) = 5\frac{8}{12} -$ ______ $=$ ______

Explain how you can use your answers to parts b and c to conclude that subtraction is not associative.

____

____

Share and Show

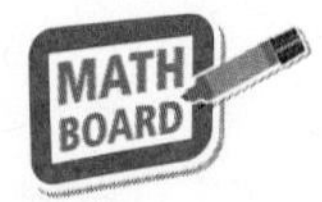

Use the properties and mental math to solve. Write your answer in simplest form.

1. $\left(2\frac{5}{8} + \frac{1}{8}\right) + \frac{7}{8}$

2. $\frac{7}{12} + \left(\frac{5}{12} + \frac{2}{12}\right)$

3. $3\frac{1}{4} + \left(2\frac{3}{4} + 6\frac{2}{4}\right)$

Name ______________________

Problem Solving Real World

Use the map to solve 4–5.

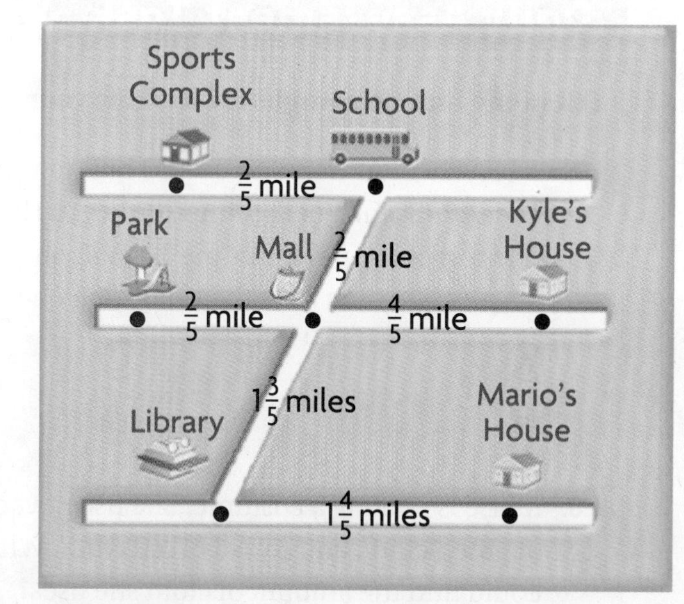

4. **Multi-Step** In the morning, Julie rides her bike from the sports complex to the school. In the afternoon, she rides from the school to the mall, and then to Kyle's house. How far does Julie ride her bike?

____

5. **H.O.T.** On one afternoon, Mario walks from his house to the library. That evening, Mario walks from the library to the mall, and then to Kyle's house. **Describe** how you can use the properties to find how far Mario walks.

____

____

____

____

6. **H.O.T.** **Analyze** Explain how you would use the Associative Property to help you solve this problem. $(6\frac{2}{8} + 5\frac{3}{8}) + 1\frac{5}{8}$

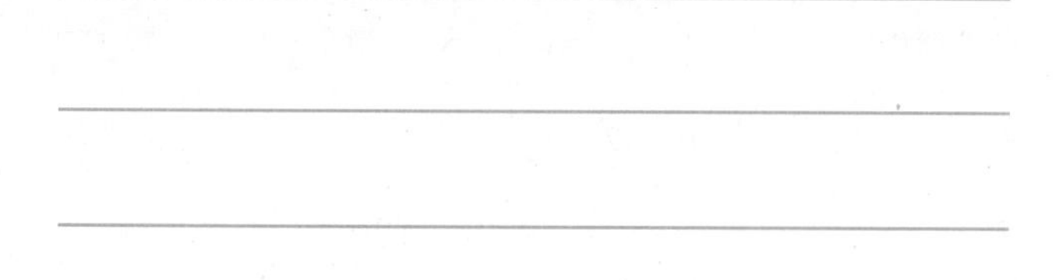

Write Math ▶ **Show Your Work**

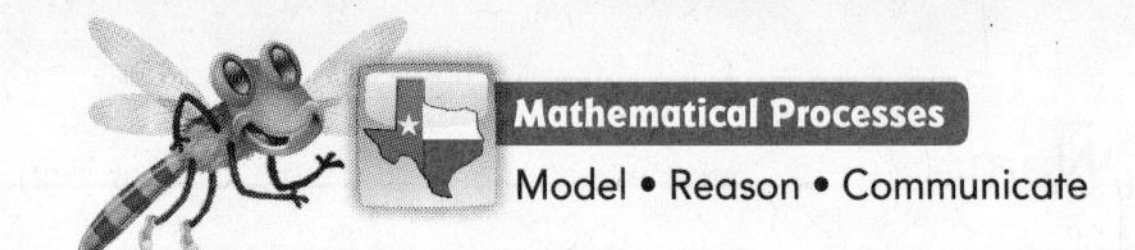

Daily Assessment Task

Fill in the bubble completely to show your answer.

7. A bicycle rider trains on Type 3 hills for $\frac{3}{8}$ of his practice time, Type 2 hills for $\frac{1}{8}$ of the time, and Type HC hills for $\frac{3}{8}$ of the time. The rest of the practice time is spent on flat ground. What part of his practice time does the rider train on hills?

Ⓐ $\frac{4}{8}$ Ⓒ $\frac{6}{8}$

Ⓑ $\frac{7}{8}$ Ⓓ $\frac{8}{8}$

8. Marie is making a costume. She uses $\frac{2}{4}$ yard of blue cloth, $\frac{1}{4}$ yard of green cloth, and $\frac{1}{4}$ yard of red cloth. Which shows a way Marie could find the amount of cloth she uses?

Ⓐ $\frac{2}{4} + (\frac{1}{4} + \frac{1}{4})$ Ⓒ $\frac{3}{4} + (\frac{1}{4} + \frac{1}{4})$

Ⓑ $\frac{2}{4} + (\frac{2}{4} + \frac{1}{4})$ Ⓓ $\frac{1}{4} + (\frac{1}{4} + \frac{1}{4})$

9. **Multi-Step** Otis needs 1 pound of apples to make an apple pie. He has $\frac{3}{12}$ pound of yellow apples, $\frac{4}{12}$ pound of red apples, and $\frac{3}{12}$ pound of green apples. How many more pounds of apples does he need?

Ⓐ $\frac{6}{12}$ pound Ⓒ $\frac{10}{12}$ pound

Ⓑ $\frac{7}{12}$ pound Ⓓ $\frac{2}{12}$ pound

TEXAS Test Prep

10. Bill got an answer of $\frac{8}{10}$ to the problem $(\frac{9}{10} - \frac{4}{10}) - \frac{3}{10}$. Which statement shows the error he made?

Ⓐ He did not subtract all the numbers.

Ⓑ He subtracted $(\frac{9}{10} - \frac{4}{10})$ first.

Ⓒ He regrouped as $\frac{9}{10} - (\frac{4}{10} - \frac{3}{10})$.

Ⓓ He subtracted from left to right.

Homework and Practice

TEKS Number and Operations—4.3.E
MATHEMATICAL PROCESSES 4.1.D, 4.1.E, 4.1.F

Name ________________

5.7 Use Properties of Addition

Use the properties and mental math to solve. Write your answer in simplest form.

1. $\frac{1}{5} + \left(\frac{4}{5} + \frac{2}{5}\right)$

2. $\left(\frac{3}{9} + \frac{5}{9}\right) + \frac{4}{9}$

3. $\left(\frac{2}{3} + \frac{2}{3}\right) + \frac{1}{3}$

4. $4\frac{2}{6} + \left(2\frac{4}{6} + 3\frac{3}{6}\right)$

5. $\left(2\frac{3}{4} + 1\frac{3}{4}\right) + 3\frac{1}{4}$

6. $1\frac{2}{7} + \left(3\frac{5}{7} + 3\frac{4}{7}\right)$

Problem Solving Real World

Use the map for 7–8.

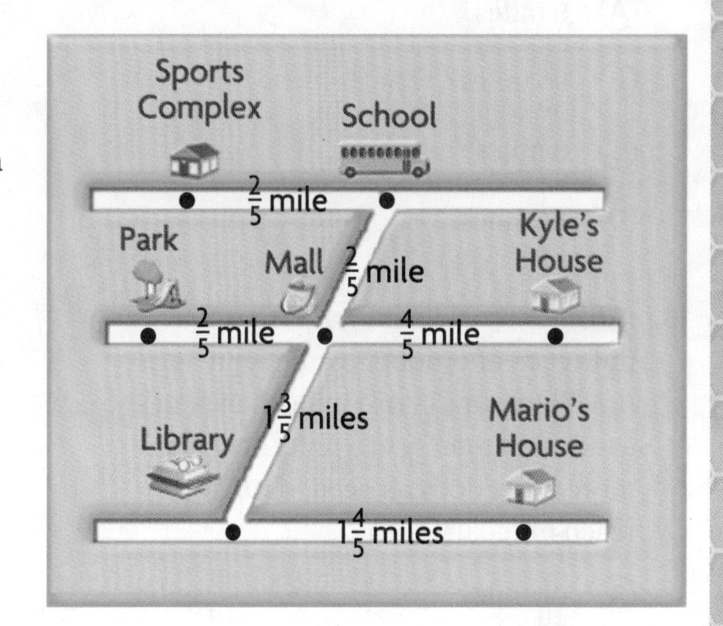

7. On Saturday, Mario walked from his house to the library. Later that day, he walked from the library to the mall, and then to the park. How far did Mario walk on Saturday?

____

8. Kyle rode his bike from the library to the mall. Later he rode from the mall to school, and then to the sports complex. How far did Kyle ride his bike?

____

Lesson Check

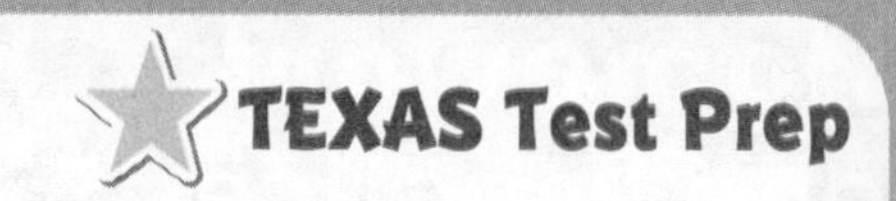

Fill in the bubble completely to show your answer.

9. Robin is studying for a history test. She studies for $\frac{3}{4}$ hour on both Friday and Saturday and $1\frac{1}{4}$ hour on Sunday. Robin writes $(\frac{3}{4} + \frac{3}{4}) + 1\frac{1}{4}$ to find the amount of time she studied. Which shows another way Robin could find the amount of time she studied?

Ⓐ $\frac{3}{4} + (\frac{3}{4} + \frac{3}{4})$

Ⓑ $\frac{3}{4} + (\frac{3}{4} + \frac{1}{4})$

Ⓒ $\frac{3}{4} + (1\frac{1}{4} + 1\frac{1}{4})$

Ⓓ $\frac{3}{4} + (\frac{3}{4} + 1\frac{1}{4})$

10. At Hill School, the fourth grade classes each had a pizza party. Mr. Dean's class ate $5\frac{3}{8}$ pizzas, Mrs. Sander's class ate $4\frac{5}{8}$ pizzas, and Mrs. Carter's class ate $5\frac{5}{8}$ pizzas. What is the total amount of pizza eaten by all three classes?

Ⓐ $14\frac{7}{8}$ pizzas

Ⓑ $14\frac{1}{2}$ pizzas

Ⓒ $15\frac{5}{8}$ pizzas

Ⓓ 15 pizzas

11. The distance from Jill's house to the grocery store is $3\frac{7}{10}$ miles. The distance from the grocery store to the bank is $\frac{2}{10}$ mile. The distance from the bank to the gym is $5\frac{1}{10}$ miles. If Jill drives from her house to the bank and then to the gym, how far has she traveled?

Ⓐ 9 miles

Ⓑ $9\frac{1}{5}$ miles

Ⓒ 8 miles

Ⓓ $8\frac{1}{5}$ miles

12. At lunchtime, Dale's Diner served a total of $2\frac{2}{6}$ pots of vegetable soup, $3\frac{5}{6}$ pots of chicken soup, and $4\frac{3}{6}$ pots of tomato soup. How many pots of soup were served in all?

Ⓐ $9\frac{2}{3}$ pots

Ⓑ $10\frac{2}{3}$ pots

Ⓒ $10\frac{1}{3}$ pots

Ⓓ $9\frac{1}{3}$ pots

13. Multi-Step William wants to run a mile each afternoon to train for a race. If William runs $\frac{3}{10}$ of a mile, then $\frac{4}{10}$ of a mile and then $\frac{2}{10}$ of a mile, how many more miles does he need to run to reach his goal?

Ⓐ $\frac{6}{10}$ mile

Ⓑ $\frac{9}{10}$ mile

Ⓒ $\frac{1}{10}$ mile

Ⓓ $\frac{7}{10}$ mile

14. Grace has $2\frac{1}{3}$ yards of red fabric, $2\frac{2}{3}$ yards of blue fabric, and $1\frac{2}{3}$ yards of green fabric. How much fabric does Grace have?

Ⓐ $6\frac{2}{3}$ yards

Ⓑ $7\frac{2}{3}$ yards

Ⓒ $5\frac{2}{3}$ yards

Ⓓ $3\frac{1}{3}$ yards

Name ________________

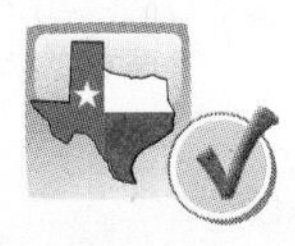

Module 5 Assessment

Concepts and Skills

Use the model to write an equation. TEKS 4.3.E

1.

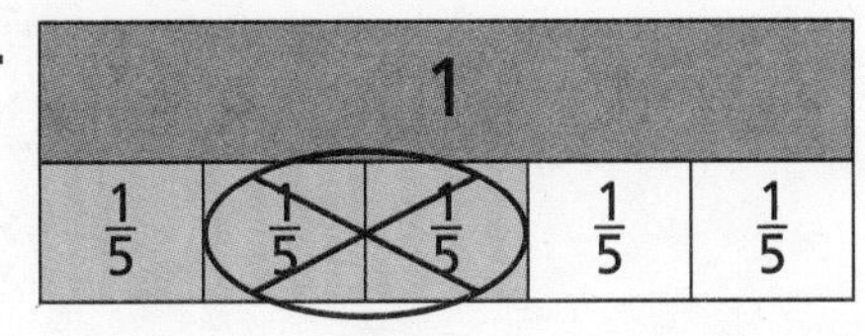

____

2.

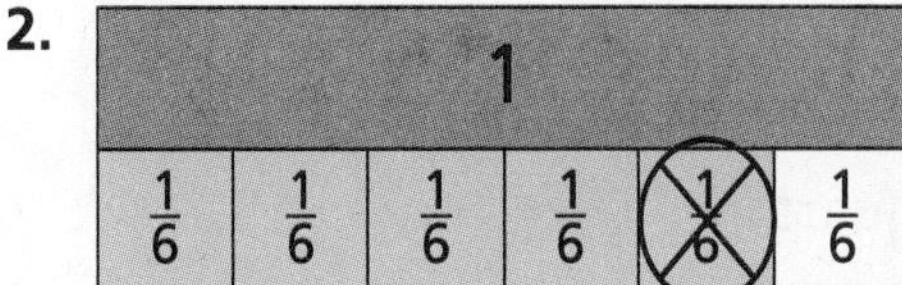

____

Use the model to find the sum. TEKS 4.3.E

3. $\frac{3}{8} + \frac{2}{8} =$ ________

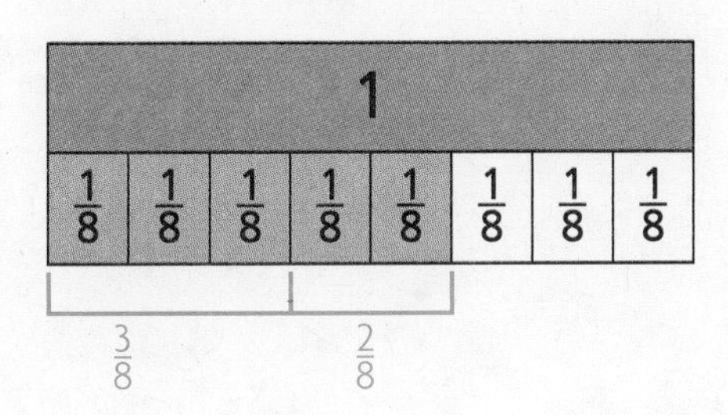

4. $\frac{4}{10} + \frac{5}{10} =$ ________

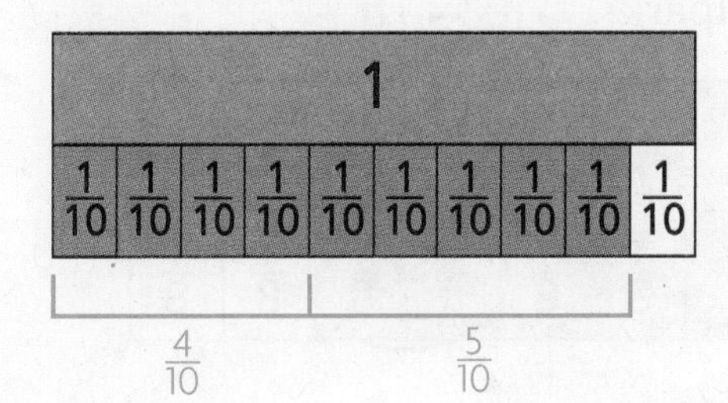

Use the model to find the difference. TEKS 4.3.E

5. $\frac{5}{6} - \frac{3}{6} = \frac{\square}{6}$

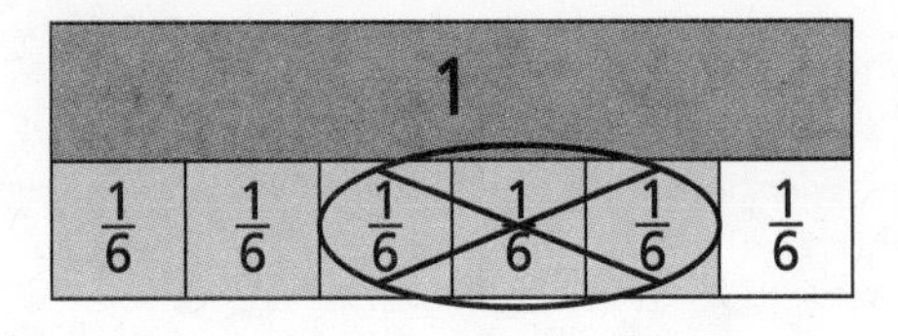

6. $\frac{7}{10} - \frac{4}{10} = \frac{\square}{10}$

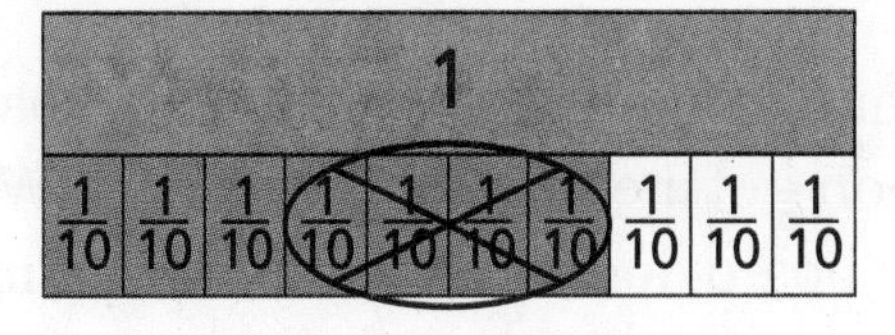

Find the sum or difference. Use fraction strips or a number line. TEKS 4.3.E

7. $\frac{9}{12} - \frac{7}{12} =$ ________

8. $\frac{2}{3} + \frac{1}{3} =$ ________

9. $\frac{1}{5} + \frac{3}{5} =$ ________

10. $\frac{2}{6} + \frac{2}{6} =$ ________

11. $\frac{4}{4} - \frac{2}{4} =$ ________

12. $\frac{7}{8} - \frac{4}{8} =$ ________

Fill in the bubble completely to show your answer.

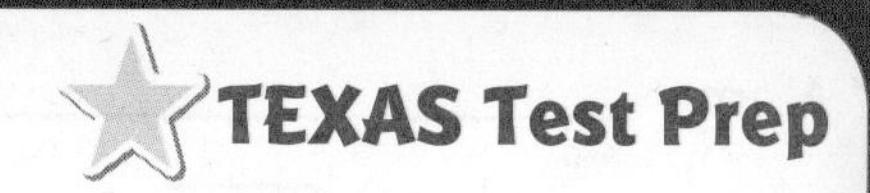

13. Tyrone mixed $\frac{7}{12}$ quart of red paint with $\frac{1}{12}$ quart of yellow paint. How much paint does Tyrone have in the mixture? TEKS 4.3.E

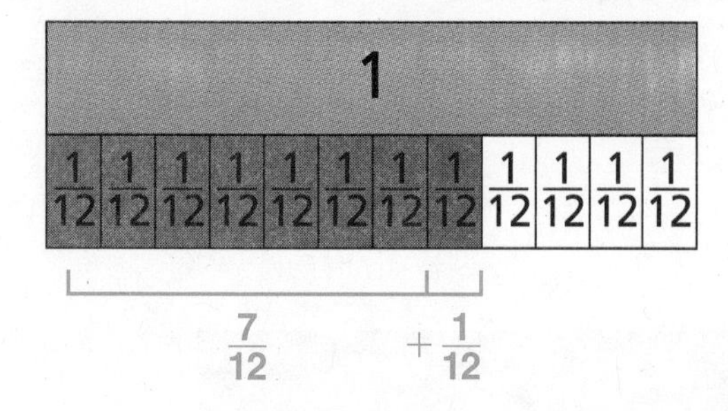

Ⓐ $\frac{8}{24}$ quart

Ⓑ $\frac{6}{12}$ quart

Ⓒ $\frac{8}{12}$ quart

Ⓓ $\frac{12}{12}$ quart

14. Jorge lives $\frac{6}{8}$ mile from school and $\frac{2}{8}$ mile from a ballpark. How much farther does Jorge live from school than from the ballpark? TEKS 4.3.E

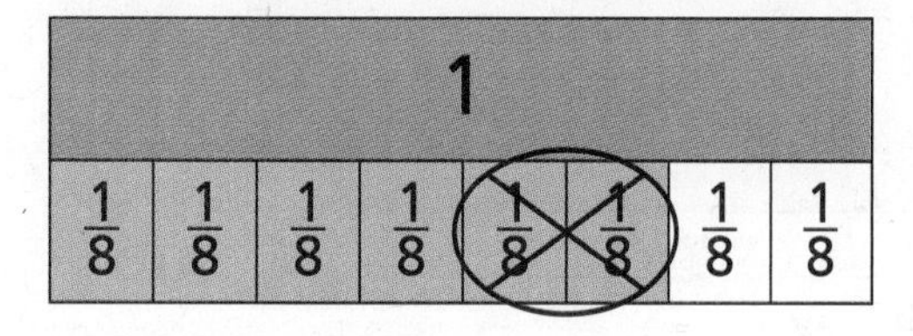

Ⓐ $\frac{4}{16}$ mile

Ⓑ $\frac{4}{8}$ mile

Ⓒ $\frac{8}{8}$ mile

Ⓓ 8 miles

15. Eloise hung artwork on $\frac{2}{5}$ of a bulletin board. She hung math papers on $\frac{1}{5}$ of the same bulletin board. What part of the bulletin board does not have artwork or math papers? Use models to help. TEKS 4.3.E

Ⓐ $\frac{1}{10}$

Ⓑ $\frac{3}{5}$

Ⓒ $\frac{3}{10}$

Ⓓ $\frac{2}{5}$

Name ______________________

Unit 1 Assessment

Vocabulary

Choose the best term from the box.

Vocabulary
unit fraction
benchmark
decimal

1. A ______________ is a known size or amount that helps you understand another size or amount. (p. 113)

2. A ______________ always has a numerator of 1. (p. 99)

Concepts and Skills

Write the decimal shown by the model. The flat represents 1 unit. TEKS 4.2.E

3. 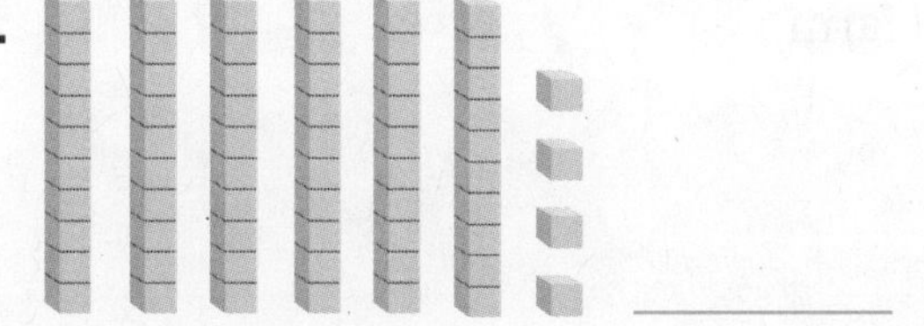 ________

4. 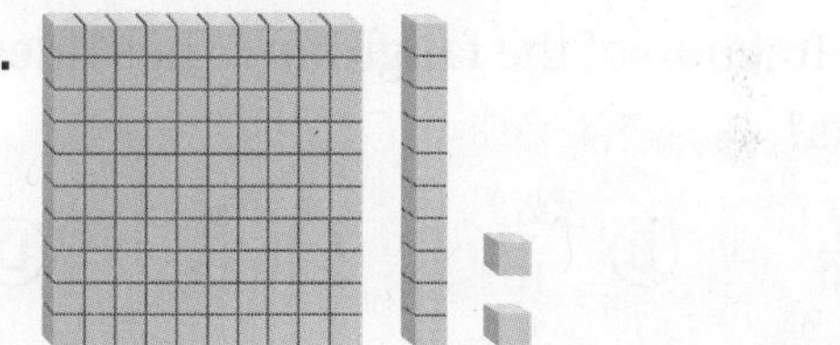 ________

Compare. Write <, >, or =. Shade the model to help. TEKS 4.2.F

5. 0.45 ◯ 0.84

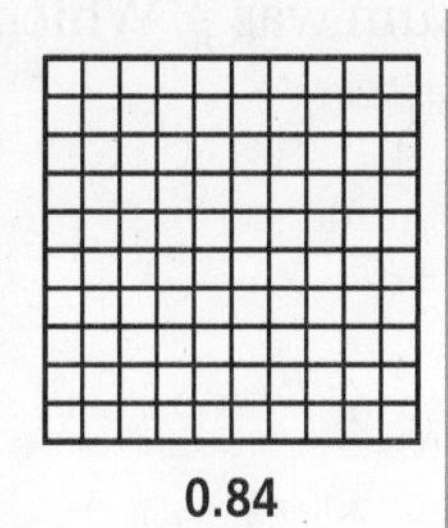

0.45 0.84

6. 0.74 ◯ 0.74

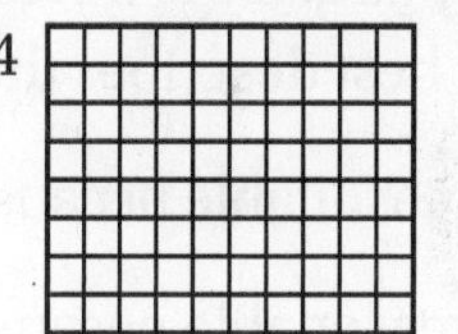

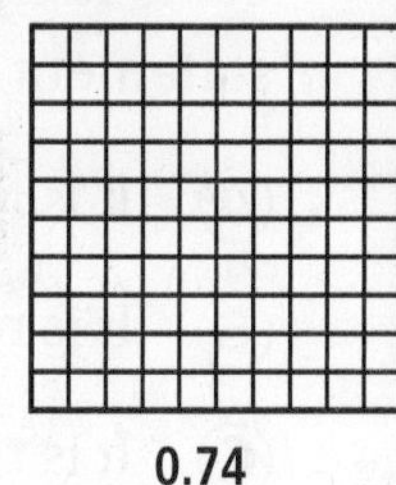

0.74 0.74

Write the fraction in simplest form. TEKS 4.3.C

7. $\frac{6}{9}$ ________

8. $\frac{4}{10}$ ________

9. $\frac{8}{12}$ ________

10. $\frac{3}{15}$ ________

Use the properties and mental math to find the sum. Write your answer in simplest form. TEKS 4.3.E

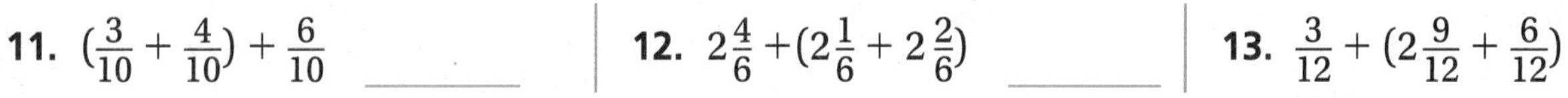

11. $(\frac{3}{10} + \frac{4}{10}) + \frac{6}{10}$ ________

12. $2\frac{4}{6} + (2\frac{1}{6} + 2\frac{2}{6})$ ________

13. $\frac{3}{12} + (2\frac{9}{12} + \frac{6}{12})$ ________

Fill in the bubble completely to show your answer.

TEXAS Test Prep

14. Pam paid for her lunch with the amount of money shown below.

How much money did Pam spend on lunch, written as a decimal and as a fraction in terms of money? TEKS 4.2.E

Ⓐ 2.73; $2\frac{73}{100}$

Ⓑ 2.78; $2\frac{78}{100}$

Ⓒ 2.7; $2\frac{7}{100}$

Ⓓ 2 .77; $2\frac{77}{100}$

15. Miguel's class went to the state fair. The fairground is divided into sections. Rides are in $\frac{6}{10}$ of the fairground. Games are in $\frac{2}{10}$ of the fairground. Farm exhibits are in $\frac{1}{10}$ of the fairground. Which fraction of the fairgrounds has rides, games, and farm exhibits? TEKS 4.3.E

Ⓐ $\frac{3}{10}$ Ⓑ $\frac{9}{10}$ Ⓒ $\frac{8}{10}$ Ⓓ $\frac{4}{10}$

16. In Kelly's class, $\frac{1}{4}$ of the students said that blue was their favorite color. Another $\frac{1}{4}$ of the students said yellow was their favorite color. Kelly added the fractions and found the sum was $\frac{3}{8}$. Which statement best describes the sum $\frac{3}{8}$? TEKS 4.3.F

Ⓐ It is reasonable because $\frac{1}{2} + 0 = \frac{1}{2}$.

Ⓑ It is reasonable because $\frac{1}{4} + \frac{1}{2} = 1$.

Ⓒ It is not reasonable because $\frac{1}{4} + \frac{1}{4} = \frac{1}{2}$.

Ⓓ It is not reasonable because $\frac{1}{2} + \frac{1}{2} = 1$.

17. Pike National Forest located in California has a total area of 871,495 acres. What is the area rounded to the nearest thousand? TEKS 4.2.D

Ⓐ 800,000

Ⓑ 870,000

Ⓒ 871,000

Ⓓ 900,000

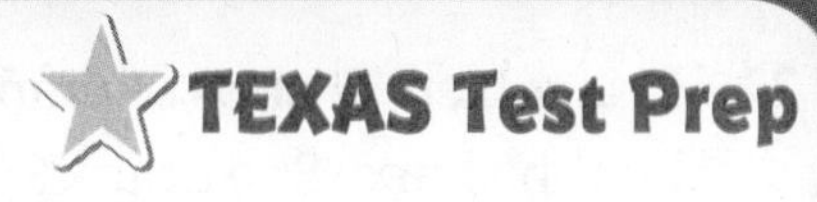

18. Carson shaded a model to represent the parts of the books he read this weekend. Which decimal written in standard and expanded form represents the parts of the books he read? TEKS 4.2.E

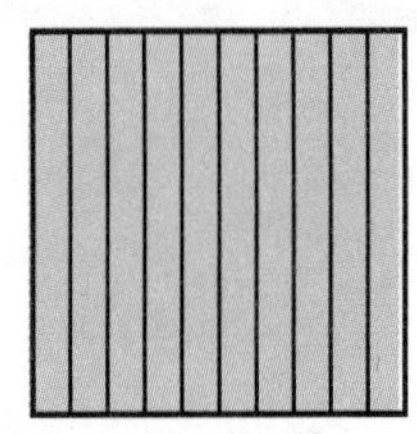
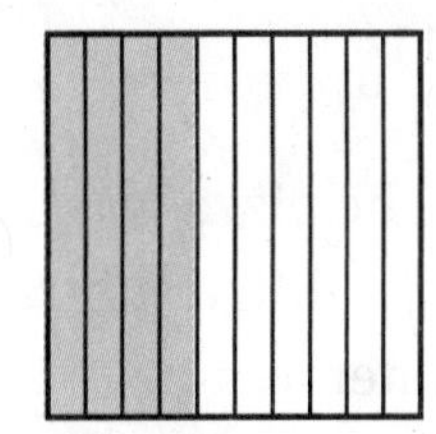

Ⓐ 4.4; 4 + 0.4

Ⓑ 0.44; 0.4 + 0.04

Ⓒ 1.4; 1 + 0.4

Ⓓ 1.14; 1 + 0.1 + 0.04

19. Pablo is training for a marathon. He ran $5\frac{4}{8}$ miles on Friday, $6\frac{1}{8}$ miles on Saturday, and $7\frac{2}{8}$ miles on Sunday. How many miles did he run on all three days? TEKS 4.3.E

Ⓐ $1\frac{5}{8}$ miles

Ⓑ $12\frac{1}{8}$ miles

Ⓒ $18\frac{4}{8}$ miles

Ⓓ $18\frac{7}{8}$ miles

20. The total attendance for all baseball games for 2011 was 78,588,004. Which number below is greater than 78,588,004? TEKS 4.2.C

Ⓐ 75,858,004

Ⓑ 78,585,041

Ⓒ 78,588,014

Ⓓ 78,587,001

21. Erica's high score on her new video game is 31,000 points. Maria's high score is $\frac{1}{10}$ of Erica's. How do you write Maria's score in expanded form? TEKS 4.2.A, 4.2.B

Ⓐ 30 + 1

Ⓑ 3,000 + 100

Ⓒ 300 + 1

Ⓓ 30,000 + 1,000

22. Lisa mixed $4\frac{4}{6}$ cups of orange juice with $3\frac{1}{6}$ cups of milk to make a health shake. She drank $3\frac{3}{6}$ cups of the health shake. How much of the health shake did Lisa not drink? TEKS 4.3.E

Ⓐ $\frac{2}{3}$ Ⓑ $4\frac{2}{6}$ Ⓒ $7\frac{5}{6}$ Ⓓ $11\frac{2}{6}$

23. At Mika's party, there was 1 pepperoni pizza. The pizza was cut into 8 slices. Two people each ate a slice of pizza. Mika subtracted to find out how much pizza was left. Which statement best describes the difference $\frac{6}{8}$? TEKS 4.3.F

Ⓐ It is reasonable because $1 - \frac{3}{4} = \frac{1}{4}$.

Ⓑ It is reasonable because $1 - \frac{1}{4} = \frac{3}{4}$.

Ⓒ It is not reasonable because $\frac{3}{4} - \frac{1}{4} = \frac{1}{2}$.

Ⓓ It is not reasonable because $\frac{1}{4} + \frac{1}{4} = \frac{1}{2}$.

24. Ann needs $\frac{2}{8}$ gallon of fruit juice and $\frac{4}{8}$ gallon of orange juice to make punch. She needs an amount of sparkling water that is equal to the amount of fruit juice and orange juice combined. In simplest form, how much sparkling water does she need? TEKS 4.3.C

Ⓐ $\frac{2}{8}$ gallon

Ⓑ $\frac{3}{4}$ gallon

Ⓒ $\frac{1}{2}$ gallon

Ⓓ Not here

25. The table shows the distances of some places in town from the school. Are any of the places shown in the table the same distance from the school? **Explain** how you know. TEKS 4.3.C

Distance from School

Place	Distance
Library	$\frac{3}{5}$ mile
Post Office	$\frac{1}{2}$ mile
Park	$\frac{3}{4}$ mile
Town Hall	$\frac{8}{10}$ mile

____

____

____

____

Unit 2

Number and Operations: Whole Number and Decimal Operations

Show What You Know

Check your understanding of important skills.

Name ______________________________

▶ 3-Digit Subtraction Within 1,000 **Find the difference.**

1. $\begin{array}{r} 626 \\ -\ \ \ 8 \\ \hline \end{array}$

2. $\begin{array}{r} 744 \\ -\ 36 \\ \hline \end{array}$

3. $\begin{array}{r} 413 \\ -\ 37 \\ \hline \end{array}$

4. $\begin{array}{r} 681 \\ -422 \\ \hline \end{array}$

5. $\begin{array}{r} 247 \\ -105 \\ \hline \end{array}$

6. $\begin{array}{r} 624 \\ -\ 69 \\ \hline \end{array}$

7. $\begin{array}{r} 599 \\ -195 \\ \hline \end{array}$

8. $\begin{array}{r} 691 \\ -337 \\ \hline \end{array}$

▶ Practice Multiplication Facts **Find the product.**

9. $8 \times 7 =$ ______

   $7 \times 8 =$ ______

10. $4 \times 6 =$ ______

    $6 \times 4 =$ ______

11. $3 \times 5 =$ ______

    $5 \times 3 =$ ______

12. $6 \times 9 =$ ______

    $9 \times 6 =$ ______

▶ Model Division with Arrays **Draw to complete each array. Then complete the number sentence.**

13. ■ ■ ■ ■

    $8 \div 4 =$ ______

14. ■
■
■

    $21 \div 3 =$ ______

GO DIGITAL Assessment Options: Soar to Success Math

Vocabulary Builder

▶ Visualize It

Sort the words into the Venn diagram.

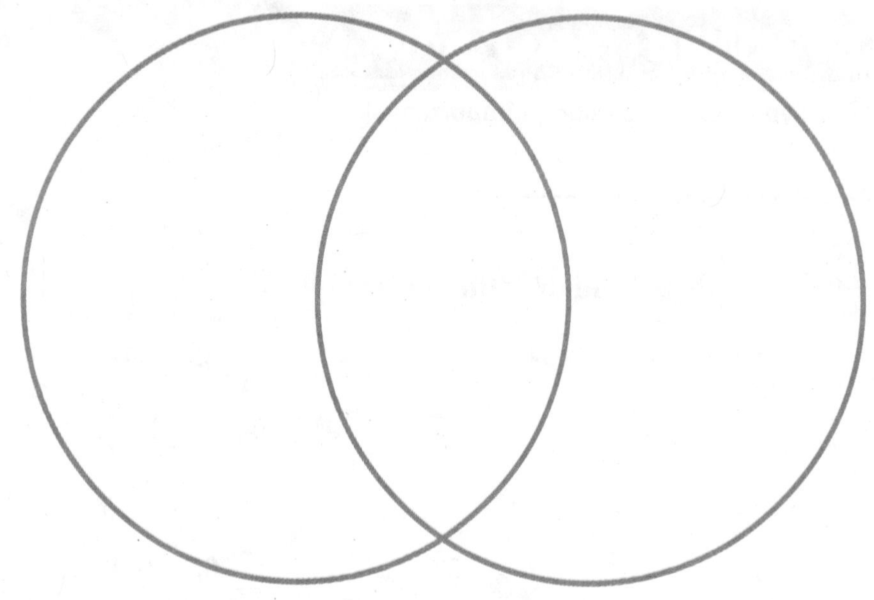

Review Words
divide
dividend
division
divisor
factor
multiple
multiplication
product
quotient

Preview Words
compatible numbers
Distributive Property
partial product
partial quotient
remainder

▶ Understand Vocabulary

Write the word that answers the riddle.

1. I am the method of dividing in which multiples of the divisor are subtracted from the dividend and then the quotients are added together. ____________

2. I am the number that is to be divided in a division problem. ____________

3. I am the amount left over when a number cannot be divided equally. ____________

4. I am the method of multiplying in which the ones, tens, hundreds, and so on are multiplied separately and then the products are added together. ____________

• Interactive Student Edition
• Multimedia *e*Glossary

Name ______________________________

Vocabulary

Sometimes when you multiply greater numbers, you can **estimate** the **product** by rounding factors to the greatest place value.

A movie theater is expanding its 218 seats to three times that number. About how many seats will the theater have?

Fill in the chart to estimate the product of 3×218.

Step 1: Round 218 to the nearest hundred.	218 ⟶ ________ 3×218 is close to ________
Step 2: Multiply.	If $3 \times 2 = 6$, then $3 \times 200 =$ ________
So, the movie theater will have about ________ seats.	

Fill in the chart to estimate the product of 24×49.

Step 1: Round 49 to the nearest ten and 24 to the nearest ten.	49 ⟶ ________ 24 ⟶ ________ 24×49 is close to ________
Step 2: Multiply.	If $2 \times 5 = 10$, then $20 \times 50 =$ ________
So, the product of 24×49 is about ________.	

Writing Write down a 1-digit and a 4-digit number and estimate the product.

____

____

Reading Look for this book in your library. *Great Estimations*, by Bruce Goldstone

Get Ready **Game**

Digit Division

Object of the Game Create a division problem with the smallest remainder.

Materials

- 3 sets of 1–9 number cards
- One number cube labeled with digits 2, 3, 4, 5, 6, and 9

Set Up

Shuffle the number cards. Label a number cube with the digits 2, 3, 4, 5, 6, and 9.

Number of Players 2

How to Play

1. Player 1 picks three number cards. Player 2 tosses the number cube. Each player makes a dividend from the digits on the number cards. Players divide by the number on the number cube.

2. Players earn points equal to the remainder. If the remainder is 0, the player earns no points.

3. Play continues until there are no more number cards. The points are added up, and the player with the lowest total wins the game.

Name ______________________

6.1 Add Whole Numbers

TEKS Number and Operations—4.4.A
Also 4.4.G
MATHEMATICAL PROCESSES
4.1.A, 4.1.C

Essential Question How can you add whole numbers?

Unlock the Problem (Real World)

Alaska is the largest state in the United States by area. Its land area is 570,374 square miles and its water surface area is 86,051 square miles. Find the total area of Alaska.

- Underline what you are asked to find.
- Circle the information you will use.

▲ The area of Alaska is outlined in the photo above.

Find the sum.

Add. 570,374 + 86,051

Think: It is important to line up the addends by place value when adding two numbers.

STEP 1 Add the ones.

Add the tens. Regroup.

12 tens = 1 hundred ______ tens

$$\begin{array}{r} \overset{1}{} \\ 570{,}374 \\ +\ 86{,}051 \\ \hline \square \end{array}$$

STEP 2 Add the hundreds.

Add the thousands.

$$\begin{array}{r} 570{,}374 \\ +\ 86{,}051 \\ \hline \square 25 \end{array}$$

STEP 3 Add the ten thousands.

Regroup.

15 ten thousands =

1 hundred thousand ______ ten thousands

$$\begin{array}{r} 570{,}374 \\ +\ 86{,}051 \\ \hline \square 6{,}425 \end{array}$$

STEP 4 Add the hundred thousands.

$$\begin{array}{r} 570{,}374 \\ +\ 86{,}051 \\ \hline \square 56{,}425 \end{array}$$

So, the total area of Alaska is __________ square miles.

Math Talk Mathematical Processes

Explain how you know when to regroup when adding.

Estimate You can estimate to tell whether an answer is reasonable. To estimate a sum, round each addend before you add.

Example Estimate. Then find the sum.

Juneau has an area of 2,717 square miles. Valdez has an area of 222 square miles. What is their combined area?

A Estimate. Use the grid to help you align the addends by place value.

2,717 → 3,000 Round to the nearest thousand.

222 → + ______ Round to the nearest hundred.

So, the combined area of Juneau and Valdez is about ______ square miles.

B Find the sum.

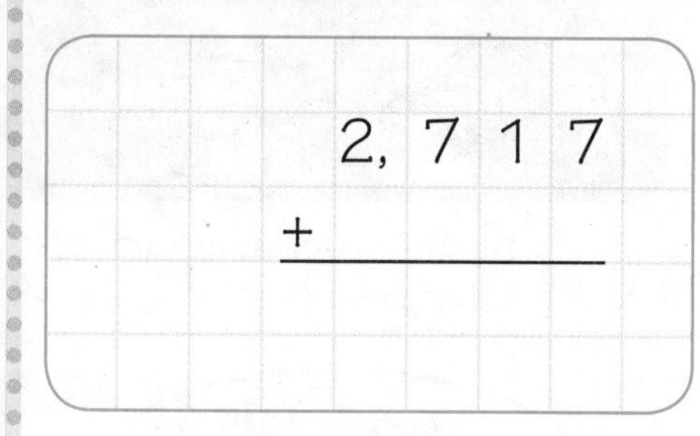

Think: Begin by adding the ones.

ERROR Alert

Remember to align the addends by place value.

So, the combined area of Juneau and Valdez is ______ square miles.

- Is the sum reasonable? **Explain.**

____

Share and Show

1. Use the grid to find 738,901 + 162,389.

Use the grid to align the addends by place value.

Name ___________________________

Estimate. Then find the sum.

2. Estimate: __________

$$\begin{array}{r} 72{,}931 \\ +\ 18{,}563 \\ \hline \end{array}$$

3. Estimate: __________

$$\begin{array}{r} 432{,}068 \\ +\ 239{,}576 \\ \hline \end{array}$$

4. Estimate: __________

$$\begin{array}{r} 64{,}505 \\ +\ 38{,}972 \\ \hline \end{array}$$

Math Talk — Mathematical Processes

Explain how you know your answer for Exercise 2 is reasonable.

Problem Solving — Real World

Use the table for 5–8.

Major Cities of Alaska

City	Population*
Anchorage	286, 174
Fairbanks	35,252
Juneau	30,796

*2009 U.S. Census Bureau estimates

5. Evaluate Reasonableness Use estimation to show your answer is reasonable. What is the combined population of Fairbanks and Juneau?

____

____

6. H.O.T. Pose a Problem Look at Problem 5. Write and solve a similar problem.

____

____

____

7. H.O.T. Multi-Step Evaluate Reasonableness What is the combined population of the three major Alaskan cities? Estimate to verify your answer.

____

8. Write Math Multi-Step The digit 5 occurs two times in the population of Fairbanks. What is the value of each 5? **Explain** your answer.

____

____

____

Write Math ▸ Show Your Work

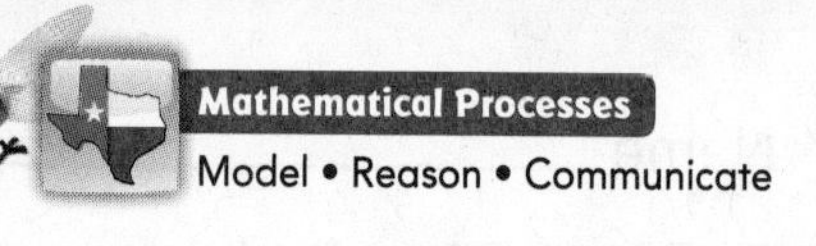

Daily Assessment Task

Fill in the bubble completely to show your answer.

9. The water slide is the most popular ride at Water World. In the first year, 34,573 visitors rode the water slide. In the second year, 56,364 visitors rode the water slide. How many visitors rode the water slide in the first two years?

Ⓐ 80,837
Ⓑ 90,137
Ⓒ 90,937
Ⓓ 81,937

10. A sports store had 17,631 customers in May. The number of customers in June was 4,385 more than the store had in May. How many customers did the store have in June?

Ⓐ 21,016
Ⓑ 11,916
Ⓒ 61,481
Ⓓ 22,016

11. **Multi-Step** A rock band played on Friday night, Saturday night, and Sunday afternoon. On each of the two nights, 11,452 people bought tickets to see the band. On Sunday afternoon, 10,310 people bought tickets. In all, how many people bought tickets to see the band?

Ⓐ 22,904
Ⓑ 32,114
Ⓒ 33,214
Ⓓ 21,762

TEXAS Test Prep

12. Alaska's Glacier Bay National Park had 418,911 visitors in 2008. The park had 25,742 more visitors in 2009 than in 2008. How many people visited the park in 2008 and 2009 combined?

Ⓐ 862,564
Ⓑ 852,564
Ⓒ 863,564
Ⓓ 963,564

Homework and Practice

TEKS Number and Operations—4.4.A
Also 4.4.G
MATHEMATICAL PROCESSES 4.1.A, 4.1.C

Name ________________

6.1 Add Whole Numbers

Use the grid to find the sum.

1. 382,654 + 436,807

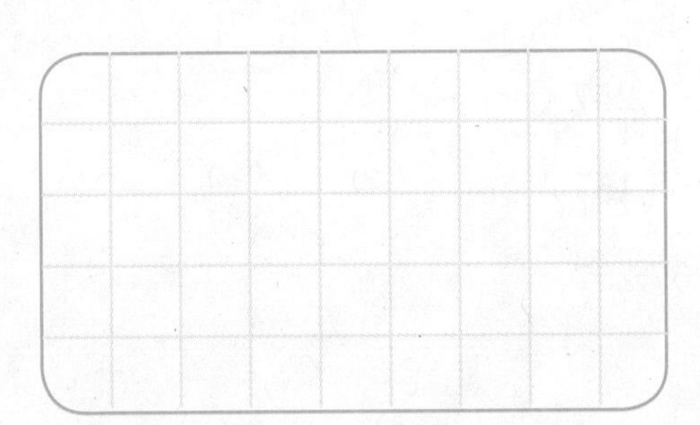

2. 634,731 + 182,169

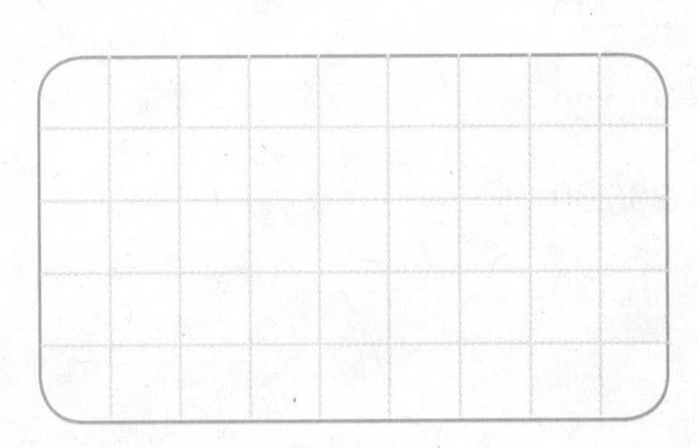

Estimate. Then find the sum.

3. Estimate: __________

$$\begin{array}{r} 36{,}204 \\ +\ 40{,}918 \\ \hline \end{array}$$

4. Estimate: __________

$$\begin{array}{r} 206{,}834 \\ +\ 194{,}268 \\ \hline \end{array}$$

5. Estimate: __________

$$\begin{array}{r} 636{,}291 \\ +\ 280{,}329 \\ \hline \end{array}$$

6. Estimate: __________

$$\begin{array}{r} 86{,}432 \\ +\ 51{,}078 \\ \hline \end{array}$$

Problem Solving Real World

Use the table for 7–8.

7. What is the combined population of Austin and Fort Worth? Estimate to verify your answer.

____

8. What is the combined population of Fort Worth and El Paso? Estimate to verify your answer.

____

Major Cities of Texas

City	Population*
Houston	2,099,541
San Antonio	1,327,407
Dallas	1,197,816
Austin	970,390
Fort Worth	741,206
El Paso	649,121

*2010 U.S. Census Bureau

Lesson Check

Fill in the bubble completely to show your answer.

9. A department store had 17,296 customers in November and 21,034 customers in December. How many customers did the store have in November and December combined?

Ⓐ 38,220
Ⓑ 38,320
Ⓒ 28,230
Ⓓ 38,330

10. A recycling center collected 28,473 cans during its first year of operation. In the second year, the center collected 39,784 cans. How many cans were collected in the first two years?

Ⓐ 58,157
Ⓑ 68,257
Ⓒ 68,157
Ⓓ 67,257

11. The Megaplex Movie Theater sold 47,328 tickets on Saturday. On Sunday, the theater sold 39,573 tickets. What is the total number of tickets sold on Saturday and Sunday?

Ⓐ 86,901
Ⓑ 86,801
Ⓒ 76,901
Ⓓ 76,801

12. During one month, 208,350 people visited the Alamo. The next month 197,695 visited the site. How many people visited the Alamo during these two months?

Ⓐ 405,945
Ⓑ 405,045
Ⓒ 395,945
Ⓓ 406,045

13. **Multi-Step** For the first football game of the season, 62,732 fans attended. The number of fans at the second game was 469 more than at the first game. What is the total number of fans that attended the first two games?

Ⓐ 124,623
Ⓑ 124,933
Ⓒ 125,933
Ⓓ 125,923

14. **Multi-Step** Daisy's Flower Shop sold 135,649 flowers during its first year. The second year, the shop sold an additional 9,754 flowers. How many flowers did the shop sell in these two years?

Ⓐ 280,952
Ⓑ 281,052
Ⓒ 281,042
Ⓓ 280,052

Name ________________________________

6.2 Subtract Whole Numbers

TEKS Number and Operations—4.4.A
Also 4.4.G
MATHEMATICAL PROCESSES
4.1.A, 4.1.C

Essential Question How can you subtract whole numbers?

Unlock the Problem (Real World)

Mt. Bear and Mt. Bona are two mountains in Alaska. Mt. Bear is 14,831 feet tall and Mt. Bona is 16,421 feet tall. How much taller is Mt. Bona than Mt. Bear?

Estimate. 16,000 − 15,000 = ________

Subtract. 16,421 − 14,831

▲ Mt. Bear and Mt. Bona are in the St. Elias Mountain Range located in the Wrangell-St. Elias National Park and Preserve in Alaska.

STEP 1 Subtract the ones.

Regroup to subtract the tens.

4 hundreds 2 tens =

3 hundreds ______ tens

```
  312
 16,421
-14,831
```

STEP 2 Regroup to subtract the hundreds.

6 thousands 3 hundreds =

5 thousands ______ hundreds

```
   13
  5 312
 16,421
-14,831
     90
```

STEP 3 Subtract the thousands.

Subtract the ten thousands.

```
   13
  5 312
 16,421
-14,831
   ,590
```

So, Mt. Bona is ________ feet taller than Mt. Bear. Since ________ is close to the estimate of ________, the answer is reasonable.

Share and Show

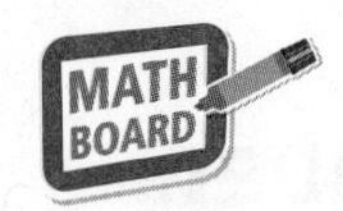

1. Subtract. Use the grid to record the problem.

637,350 − 43,832

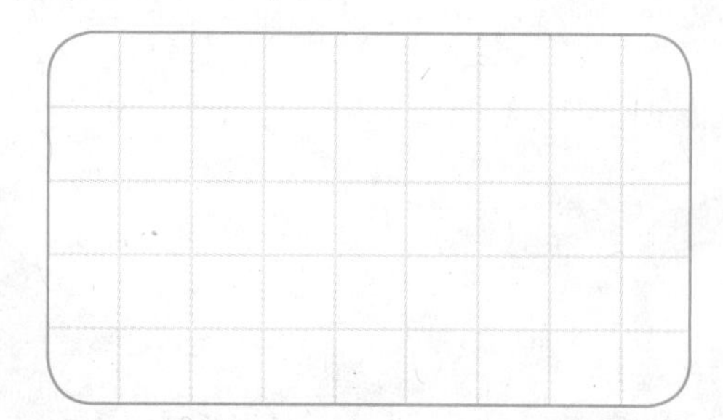

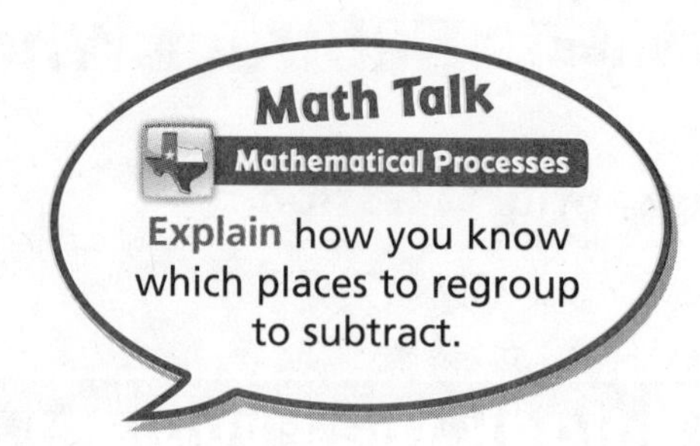

Estimate. Then find the difference.

2. Estimate: ______

$$\begin{array}{r} 14,659 \\ -\ 11,584 \\ \hline \end{array}$$

3. Estimate: ______

$$\begin{array}{r} 456,912 \\ -\ \ 37,800 \\ \hline \end{array}$$

4. Estimate: ______

$$\begin{array}{r} 407,001 \\ -\ 184,652 \\ \hline \end{array}$$

Problem Solving

Practice: Copy and Solve **Subtract. Add to check.**

5. 653,809 − 256,034

6. 258,197 − 64,500

7. 496,004 − 398,450

8. 500,000 − 145,609

H.O.T. **Algebra** **Find the missing digit.**

9.
$$\begin{array}{r} 6,532 \\ -\ 4,1\square 5 \\ \hline 2,407 \end{array}$$

10.
$$\begin{array}{r} \square 08,665 \\ -\ 659,420 \\ \hline 149,245 \end{array}$$

11.
$$\begin{array}{r} 697,320 \\ -\ 432,\square 08 \\ \hline 264,712 \end{array}$$

Name ______________________________

Problem Solving

H.O.T. What's the Error?

12. Maryland has an area of 12,407 square miles. Texas has an area of 268,601 square miles. How much larger is Texas than Maryland?

Read how Janice solved the problem. Find her error.

Texas: 268,601 square miles
Maryland: 12,407 square miles
I can subtract to find the difference.

$$\begin{array}{r} 268{,}601 \\ -12{,}407 \\ \hline 144{,}531 \end{array}$$

Describe Janice's error. Then solve the problem.

So, Texas is ______________ square miles larger than Maryland.

Use the table for 13–15.

13. **Evaluate Reasonableness** How many more acres were grown in 1996 than in 1986? Estimate to check the reasonableness of your answer.

____

____

14. H.O.T. **Multi-Step** What is the difference between the greatest number of acres and the least number of acres used for growing oranges?

____

15. **Multi-Step Apply** Grapefruit was grown on 144,416 acres in 1996. What is the total number of acres for oranges and grapefruit in 1996?

____

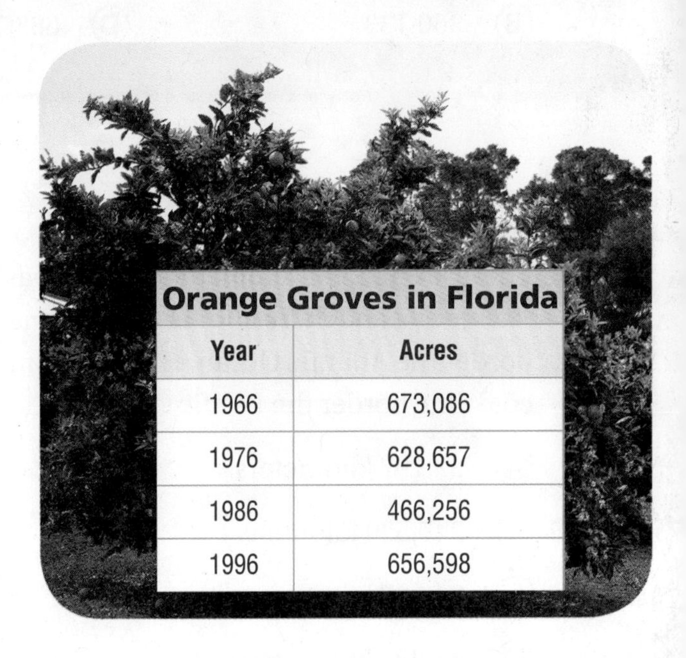

Orange Groves in Florida

Year	Acres
1966	673,086
1976	628,657
1986	466,256
1996	656,598

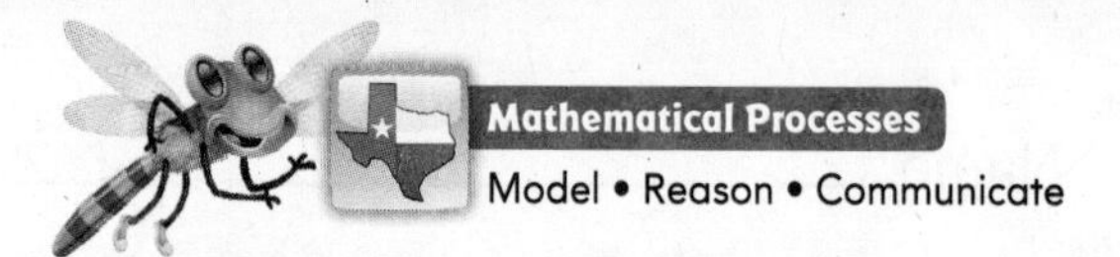

Daily Assessment Task

Fill in the bubble completely to show your answer.

16. A team of artists finished a movie with 129,600 frames. Their next movie will have 172,800 frames. How many more frames will their next movie have than their first movie?

Ⓐ 143,200
Ⓑ 53,200
Ⓒ 43,200
Ⓓ 157,200

17. A company sold 257,296 phones in December. It sold 163,804 phones in January. How many fewer phones did the company sell in January than in December?

Ⓐ 114,692
Ⓑ 94,692
Ⓒ 194,492
Ⓓ 93,492

18. **Multi-Step** This year, 426,731 people visited a water park. Last year, 102,865 fewer people visited the park. The year the park opened, 84,007 fewer people visited the park than last year. How many people visited the water park the year it opened?

Ⓐ 249,869
Ⓑ 360,133
Ⓒ 239,859
Ⓓ 683,796

TEXAS Test Prep

19. There are 135,663 kilometers of U.S. coastline that border the Pacific Ocean. There are 111,866, kilometers of U.S. coastline that border the Atlantic Ocean. How many more kilometers of U.S. coastline border the Pacific Ocean?

Ⓐ 23,797 kilometers
Ⓑ 247,539 kilometers
Ⓒ 24,807 kilometers
Ⓓ 24,203 kilometers

Name ______________________________

6.3 PROBLEM SOLVING • Comparison Problems with Addition and Subtraction

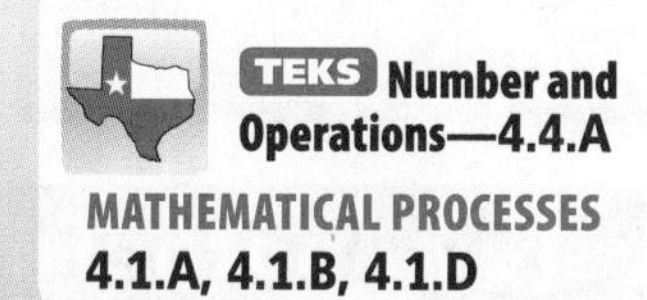

TEKS Number and Operations—4.4.A

MATHEMATICAL PROCESSES 4.1.A, 4.1.B, 4.1.D

Essential Question

How can you use the strategy *draw a diagram* to solve comparison problems with addition and subtraction?

Unlock the Problem

Real World

Hot air balloon festivals draw large crowds of people. The attendance on the first day of one festival was 17,350. On the second day the attendance was 18,925. How many more people attended the hot air balloon festival on the second day?

Use the graphic organizer to help you solve the problem.

Read		Plan
What do I need to find?	**What information am I given?**	**What is my plan or strategy?**
Write what you need to find. ______________ ______________ ______________ ______________	______________ people attended on the first day, ______________ people attended on the second day.	What strategy can you use? ______________ ______________ ______________ ______________

Solve

I can draw a strip diagram and write an equation to represent the problem.

18,925

17,350

18,925 − 17,350 = ________

So, ________ more people attended the festival on the second day.

Try Another Problem

During an event, a hot air balloon traveled a distance of 5,110 feet during the first trip. During the second trip, it traveled 850 feet more than it traveled during the first trip. How far did it travel during the second trip?

Read		Plan
What do I need to find?	**What information am I given?**	**What is my plan or strategy?**

Solve

- Is your answer reasonable? **Explain** how you know.

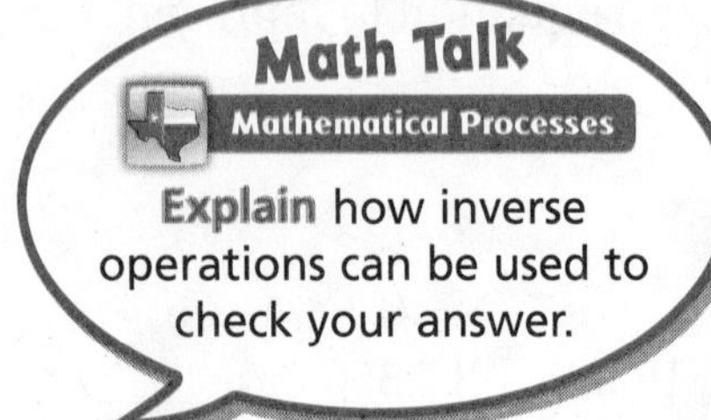

Name ______________________________

Share and Show

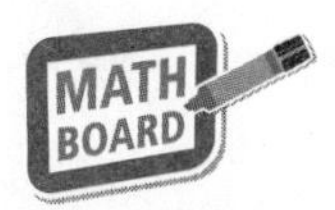

1. Hot air balloons are able to fly at very high altitudes. A world record height of 64,997 feet was set in 1988. In 2005, a new record of 68,986 feet was set. How many feet higher was the 2005 record than the 1988 record?

First, draw a diagram to show the problem.

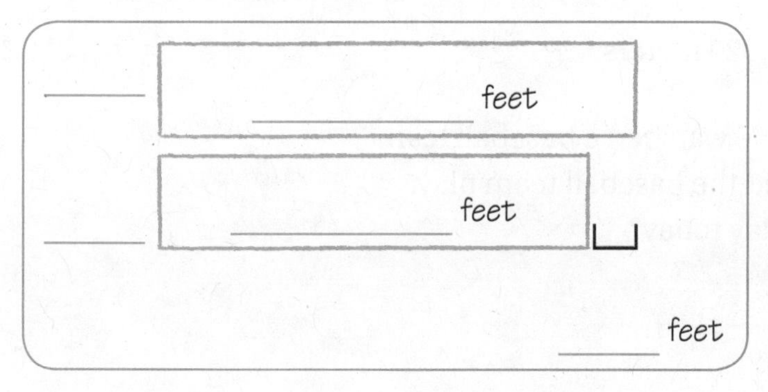

Next, write the problem you need to solve.

____

Last, solve the problem.

So, the 2005 record was __________ feet higher than the 1988 record.

2. H.O.T. **What if** a new world altitude record of 70,000 feet was set? How many feet higher would the new record be than the 2005 record?

____

Unlock the Problem Tips

- Use the Problem Solving Ma Board.
- Underline important facts.
- Choose a strategy you know.

Write Math ▶ Show Your ork

Problem Solving Real World

3. H.O.T. **Multi-Step** There were 665 hot air balloon pilots at a hot air balloon race. There were 1,550 more ground crew members than there were pilots. How many pilots and ground crew members were there all together?

____

4. **Apply** Last year, the ticket sales for a commercial hot air balloon ride were $109,076. This year, the ticket sales were $125,805. How much more were the ticket sales this year?

____

Daily Assessment Task

Fill in the bubble completely to show your answer.

5. A tower on the Great Wall of China is 9,660 meters from a fort. The tower is 28,980 meters from a castle. How many more meters is the tower from the castle than the tower is from the fort?

Ⓐ 19,320 meters
Ⓑ 38,640 meters
Ⓒ 12,540 meters
Ⓓ 21,320 meters

6. **Use Diagrams** Yesterday, 65,231 people watched a baseball team play. Today, 6,701 fewer people watched the baseball team play. How many people watched the team play today?

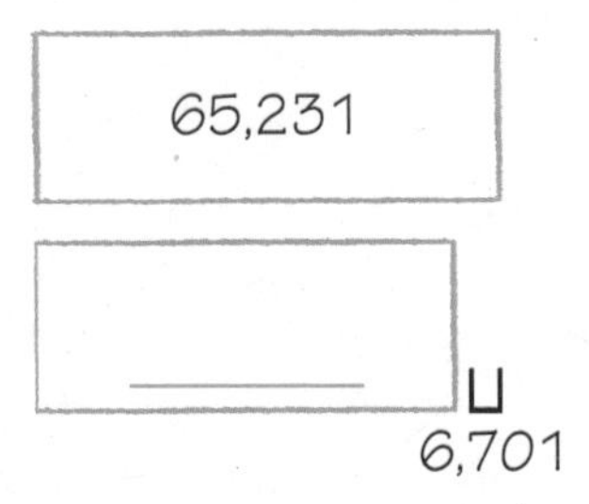

Ⓐ 71,932
Ⓑ 58,530
Ⓒ 61,530
Ⓓ 61,932

7. **Multi-Step** A plane flies 2,342 miles on Monday. On Tuesday, it flies 586 more miles than on Monday. What is the total number of miles the plane flies on Monday and Tuesday?

Ⓐ 1,756 miles
Ⓑ 2,928 miles
Ⓒ 4,098 miles
Ⓓ 5,270 miles

TEXAS Test Prep

8. Rusty wants to buy a small hot air balloon. The cost of training for a license is $2,750. The cost of buying the balloon is $21,200 more than the cost of training. How much will Rusty pay for the balloon and the training?

Ⓐ $23,950
Ⓑ $36,700
Ⓒ $26,700
Ⓓ $26,600

Homework and Practice

TEKS Numbers and Operations—4.4.A
MATHEMATICAL PROCESSES 4.1.A, 4.1.B, 4.1.D

Name ____________________

6.3 PROBLEM SOLVING • Comparison Problems with Addition and Subtraction

Use the information in the table for 1–3.

Balloonist	Distance in Feet
Abby	47,149
Jake	46,394
Diana	41,507
Kunal	32,766
Martin	29,912

Total Distance Traveled in One Day

1. How much farther did Abby's balloon travel than Jake's balloon?

Think: How can a strip diagram help represent the problem? What equation can be written?

Abby 47,149

Jake 46,394

47,149 − 46,394 = ________ feet.

2. Which balloonist traveled 11,595 feet farther than Martin? Draw a strip diagram and write a number sentence to solve the problem.

____

3. What is the difference between the greatest distance traveled and the least distance traveled?

________ feet

Problem Solving Real World

4. At the balloon festival, 1,539 people volunteered. Then, 253 more people volunteered. How many people volunteered for the event?

____

5. A vendor at the balloon festival sold 10,450 shirts the first year and 11,232 shirts the following year. How many more shirts were sold in the second year than in the first year?

____

Lesson Check

TEXAS Test Prep

Fill in the bubble completely to show your answer.

6. Last week, 52,341 people attended the football game. This week, 7,769 fewer people attended the football game.

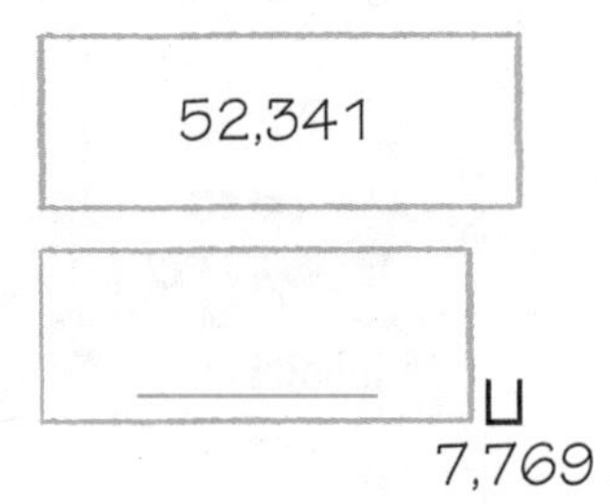

How many people attended the game this week?

Ⓐ 54,572
Ⓑ 50,110
Ⓒ 44,572
Ⓓ 60,110

7. A bookstore made $7,499 in book sales and $4,829 in magazine sales.

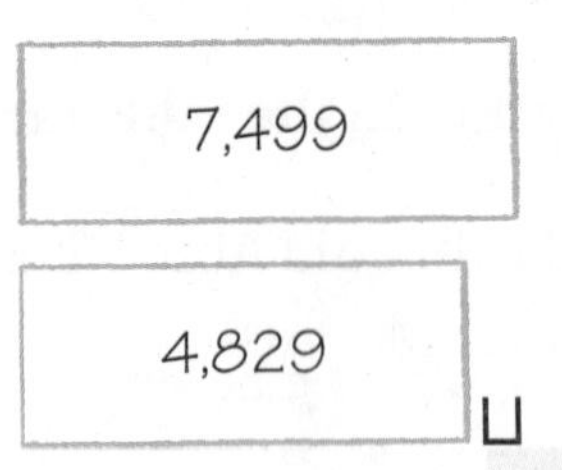

How much more did the store collect in book sales than it did in magazine sales?

Ⓐ $11,328
Ⓑ $3,760
Ⓒ $12,328
Ⓓ $2,670

8. The attendance at the theater during June was 37,135. In July, 3,353 fewer people attended the theater. How many people attended the theater in July?

Ⓐ 40,448
Ⓑ 33,782
Ⓒ 34,482
Ⓓ 4,685

9. A sports store collected $53,285 for sporting equipment in the summer. During the winter, the company collected $89,135 for sporting equipment. How much more did the store collect in the winter than in the summer?

Ⓐ $35,850
Ⓑ $142,420
Ⓒ $35,980
Ⓓ $35,950

10. Multi-Step There were 36,491 visitors to the water park last month. This month there were 1,873 more visitors than last month. What is the total number of visitors for both months?

Ⓐ 74,855
Ⓑ 38,364
Ⓒ 64,755
Ⓓ 37,263

11. Multi-Step Marcia drove her car 19,543 miles the first year she owned it. The second year, she drove it 759 miles more than the first year. What is the total number of miles she drove after owning the car for two years?

Ⓐ 38,835 miles
Ⓑ 39,845 miles
Ⓒ 19,292 miles
Ⓓ 20,302 miles

Name ______________________________

6.4 Add Decimals

Essential Question How can place value help you add decimals?

Unlock the Problem Real World

Henry recorded the amount of rain that fell over 2 hours. In the first hour, Henry measured 2.35 centimeters of rain. In the second hour, he measured 1.82 centimeters of rain.

Henry estimated that about 4 centimeters of rain fell in 2 hours. What is the total amount of rain that fell? How can you use this estimate to decide if your answer is reasonable?

Add. 2.35 + 1.82

- Add the hundredths first.

  5 hundredths + 2 hundredths = ______ hundredths.

- Then add the tenths and ones. Regroup as needed.

  3 tenths + 8 tenths = ______ tenths. Regroup.

  2 ones + 1 one + 1 regrouped one = ______ ones.

- Record the sum for each place value.

$$\begin{array}{r} 2.35 \\ +\ 1.82 \\ \hline \end{array}$$

Draw a quick picture to check your work.

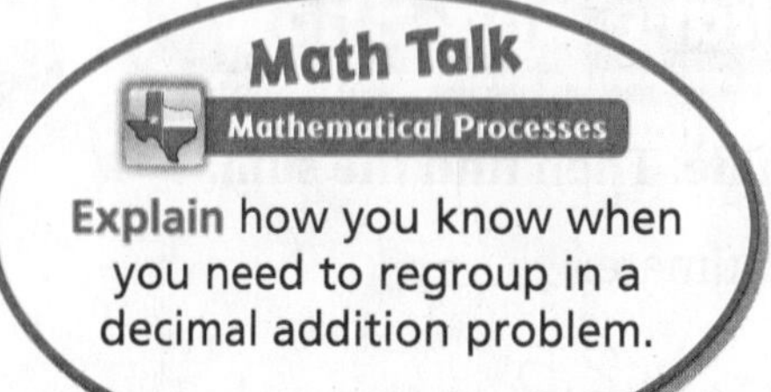

So, ______ centimeters of rain fell.

Since ______ is close to the estimate, 4, the answer is reasonable.

Equivalent Decimals When adding decimals, you can use equivalent decimals to help keep the numbers aligned in each place. Add zeros to the right of the last digit as needed, so that the addends have the same number of decimal places.

Try This! **Estimate. Then find the sum.**

STEP 1

Estimate the sum.

$$20.4 + 13.76$$

$$\downarrow \qquad \downarrow$$

Estimate: $20 + 14 =$ ______

STEP 2

Find the sum.

Add the hundredths first.
Then, add the tenths, ones, and tens.
Regroup as needed.

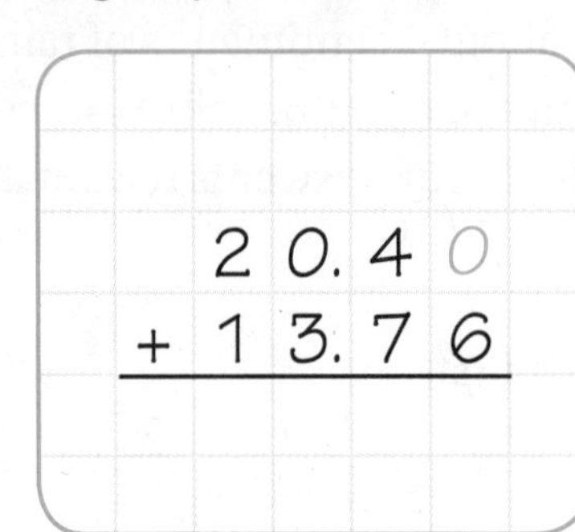

Think: 20.4 = 20.40

20.40 + 13.76 = ____________

- Is your answer reasonable? **Explain.**

____

Share and Show

Estimate. Then find the sum.

1. Estimate: ______

   $$\begin{array}{r} 2.5 \\ +\ 4.6 \\ \hline \end{array}$$

2. Estimate: ______

   $$\begin{array}{r} 8.75 \\ +\ 6.43 \\ \hline \end{array}$$

3. Estimate: ______

   $$\begin{array}{r} 2.03 \\ +\ 7.89 \\ \hline \end{array}$$

4. Estimate: ______

   6.34 + 3.8 = ____________

5. Estimate: ______

   0.63 + 0.6 = ____________

Math Talk

Mathematical Processes

Explain why it is important to remember to line up the place values in each number when adding or subtracting decimals.

Name ______________________________

Problem Solving Real World

6. H.O.T. **Multi-Step** A city received 4.65 centimeters of rain in the first two weeks of August. During the rest of the month it rained 3.68 centimeters more than it had the first two weeks. What is the total rainfall in centimeters for the month of August?

- (A) 8.33 centimeters
- (B) 12.01 centimeters
- (C) 12.98 centimeters
- (D) 11.99 centimeters

a. What do you need to find? ______________________________

b. What information are you given? ______________________________

____

c. How will you use addition to find the total number of centimeters of rain that fell? ______________________________

____

____

d. Show how you solved the problem.

e. Fill in the bubble for the correct answer choice above.

7. **Apply** Tania measured the growth of her plant each week. The first week, the plant's height measured 2.65 decimeters. During the second week, Tania's plant grew 0.38 decimeter. How tall was Tania's plant at the end of the second week?

- (A) 2.27 decimeters
- (B) 3.03 decimeters
- (C) 3.23 decimeters
- (D) 3.93 decimeters

8. H.O.T. **Multi-Step** Maggie had $35.13. Then her mom gave her $7.50 each of the two times she watched her younger brother. How much money does Maggie have now?

- (A) $41.63
- (B) $42.63
- (C) $41.63
- (D) $50.13

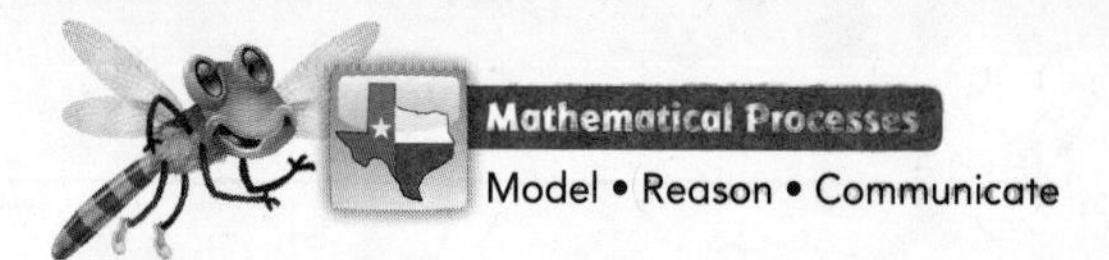

Daily Assessment Task

Fill in the bubble completely to show your answer.

9. A king's crown has a ruby that is 4.9 carats and a sapphire that is 5.32 carats. What is the total number of carats on the king's crown?

Ⓐ 9.41 carats

Ⓑ 9.22 carats

Ⓒ 10.22 carats

Ⓓ 11.12 carats

10. Josh bought 1.75 pounds of apples and 2.4 pounds of oranges. How many pounds of apples and oranges did he buy in all?

Ⓐ 2.15 pounds

Ⓑ 4.15 pounds

Ⓒ 1.99 pounds

Ⓓ 3.75 pounds

11. **Multi-Step Evaluate** Sean runs 2.62 miles. Lisa runs 3.02 miles. Shannon runs 2.78 miles. Max runs 3.8 miles. Which two people run for a total of 5.4 miles?

Ⓐ Sean and Shannon

Ⓑ Lisa and Max

Ⓒ Lisa and Shannon

Ⓓ Sean and Max

TEXAS Test Prep

12. When Mandy got a puppy, it weighed three and eighty-five hundredths pounds. After a month, it weighed ninety-five hundredths more than when she got it. How much did the puppy weigh at the end of the month?

Ⓐ 480 pounds

Ⓑ 4.70 pounds

Ⓒ 4.80 pounds

Ⓓ 3.70 pounds

Homework and Practice

TEKS Number and Operations—4.4A
MATHEMATICAL PROCESSES 4.1.B, 4.1.E

Name ______

6.4 Add Decimals

Estimate. Then find the sum.

1. Estimate: ______

$$\begin{array}{r} 3.4 \\ +\ 2.7 \\ \hline \end{array}$$

2. Estimate: ______

$$\begin{array}{r} 5.26 \\ +\ 9.75 \\ \hline \end{array}$$

3. Estimate: ______

$$\begin{array}{r} 3.09 \\ +\ 8.89 \\ \hline \end{array}$$

4. Estimate: ______

$$\begin{array}{r} 7.30 \\ +\ 1.84 \\ \hline \end{array}$$

5. Estimate: ______

5.29 + 6.78 = ______

6. Estimate: ______

6.2 + 2.36 = ______

7. Estimate: ______

9.2 + 3.04 = ______

8. Estimate: ______

7.08 + 2.9 = ______

9. Estimate: ______

7.86 + 2.9 = ______

10. Estimate: ______

4.3 + 2.49 = ______

Problem Solving Real World

11. Monique's dog weighs 10.6 pounds. Her cat weighs 8.4 pounds. What is the combined total weight of Monique's pets?

______

12. Monique spent $8.49 on dog food and $7.99 on cat food. What is the total amount Monique spent on food for her pets?

______

Lesson Check

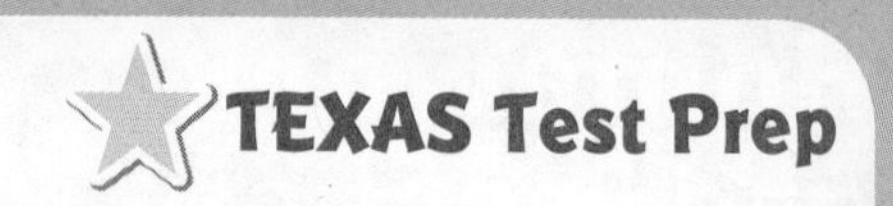

Fill in the bubble completely to show your answer.

13. Joseph ran 3.75 miles around the track. After resting, Joseph ran an additional 2.9 miles. What is the total distance Joseph ran?

Ⓐ 3.94 miles

Ⓑ 6.65 miles

Ⓒ 4.04 miles

Ⓓ 5.65 miles

14. On the first day of school, Cassandra measured 1.37 meters tall. During the school year, Cassandra grew 0.06 meters. How tall was Cassandra at the end of the school year?

Ⓐ 1.33 meters

Ⓑ 1.31 meters

Ⓒ 1.43 meters

Ⓓ 1.42 meters

15. Walter measured the growth of a plant for his science project. At the end of the first week, the plant was 9.54 centimeters tall. During the second week, the plant grew 2.68 centimeters. How tall was Walter's plant at the end of the second week?

Ⓐ 11.22 centimeters

Ⓑ 12.12 centimeters

Ⓒ 11.12 centimeters

Ⓓ 12.22 centimeters

16. The distance from Jeff's house to his uncle's house is 12.58 miles. If Jeff travels another 9.49 miles, he will reach his grandmother's house. What is the distance from Jeff's house to his grandmother's house?

Ⓐ 22.07 miles

Ⓑ 21.97 miles

Ⓒ 21.07 miles

Ⓓ 22.08 miles

17. **Multi-Step** Kyle earned $9.50 per week for two weeks in a row helping his brother mow lawns. His brother paid him an additional $3.75 to clean the mower. What is the total amount Kyle earned?

Ⓐ $12.75

Ⓑ $19.00

Ⓒ $22.75

Ⓓ $13.25

18. **Multi-Step** Mrs. McDonald spent $24.65 at a yard sale on Saturday. On Sunday, she went to another yard sale and spent $14.95 more than she did on Saturday. What is the total amount that Mrs. McDonald spent at both yard sales?

Ⓐ $38.60

Ⓑ $64.25

Ⓒ $39.60

Ⓓ $63.25

Name ______________________________

6.5 Subtract Decimals

TEKS Number and Operations—4.4.A

MATHEMATICAL PROCESSES 4.1.A, 4.1.D, 4.1.E

Essential Question How can place value help you subtract decimals?

Unlock the Problem Real World

Hannah has 3.36 kilograms of apples and 2.28 kilograms of oranges. Hannah estimates she has about 1 more kilogram of apples than oranges. How many more kilograms of apples than oranges does Hannah have? How can you use this estimate to decide if your answer is reasonable?

- What operation will you use to solve the problem?

____

- Circle Hannah's estimate and check that your answer is reasonable.

Subtract. 3.36 − 2.28

- Subtract the hundredths first. If there are not enough hundredths, regroup 1 tenth as 10 hundredths.

  ______ hundredths − 8 hundredths = 8 hundredths

- Then subtract the tenths and ones. Regroup as needed.

  ______ tenths − 2 tenths = 0 tenths

  ______ ones − 2 ones = 1 one

- Record the difference for each place value.

$$\begin{array}{r} 3.36 \\ -\ 2.28 \\ \hline \end{array}$$

Draw a quick picture to check your work.

So, Hannah has ____________ more kilograms of apples than oranges.

Since ____________ is close to 1, the answer is reasonable.

Math Talk Mathematical Processes

Explain how you know when to regroup in a decimal subtraction problem.

Share and Show

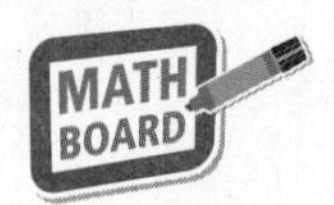

Estimate. Then find the difference.

1. Estimate: ______

$$\begin{array}{r} 5.83 \\ -2.18 \\ \hline \end{array}$$

2. Estimate: ______

$$\begin{array}{r} 4.45 \\ -1.86 \\ \hline \end{array}$$

✓ 3. Estimate: ______

$$\begin{array}{r} 4.03 \\ -2.25 \\ \hline \end{array}$$

Find the difference. Check your answer.

4.

$$\begin{array}{r} 0.70 \\ -0.43 \\ \hline \end{array}$$

5.

$$\begin{array}{r} 13.2 \\ -8.04 \\ \hline \end{array}$$

✓ 6.

$$\begin{array}{r} 15.8 \\ -9.67 \\ \hline \end{array}$$

Problem Solving

Find the difference.

7. three and seventy-two hundredths subtracted from five and eighty-one hundredths

______

8. one and six hundredths subtracted from eight and thirty-two hundredths

______

H.O.T. **Algebra** **Write the unknown number for n.**

9. $5.28 - 3.4 = n$

$n =$ ______

10. $n - 6.47 = 4.32$

$n =$ ______

11. $11.57 - n = 7.51$

$n =$ ______

Practice: Copy and Solve **Find the difference.**

12. $8.42 - 5.14$

13. $16.46 - 13.87$

14. $34.27 - 17.51$

15. $15.83 - 11.45$

16. $12.74 - 10.54$

17. $48.21 - 13.65$

Name ____________________

Problem Solving (Real World)

18. H.O.T. **Multi-Step** In peanut butter, how many more grams of protein and fat combined are there than grams of carbohydrates? Use the label at the right.

PEANUT BUTTER Nutrition Facts	
Serving Size 2 Tbsp (32.0 g)	
Amount Per Serving	
Calories	190
Calories from Fat	190
	% Daily Value*
Total Fat 16g	**25%**
Saturated Fat 3g	**18%**
Polyunsaturated Fat 4.4g	
Monounsaturated Fat 7.8g	
Cholesterol 0mg	**0%**
Sodium 5mg	**0%**
Total Carbohydrates 6.2g	**2%**
Dietary Fiber 1.9g	**8%**
Sugars 2.5g	**8%**
Protein 8.1g	
*Based on a 2,000 calorie diet	

a. What do you need to know?

____

____

b. How will you use subtraction to find how many more grams of protein and fat there are than grams of carbohydrates?

____

____

c. Show how you solved the problem.

d. Complete each sentence.

The peanut butter has ______ grams of protein and ______ grams of fat for a total of ______ grams.

The peanut butter has ______ grams of carbohydrates.

There are ______ more grams of protein and fat than grams of carbohydrates in the peanut butter.

19. H.O.T. **Reasoning** Kyle is building a block tower. Right now the tower stands 0.89 meter tall. How much higher does the tower need to be to reach a height of 1.74 meters?

____

20. **Multi-Step Analyze** Karin made punch for her party. She used 2.50 liters of orange juice and 1.75 liters of ginger ale. She had 2.35 liters of punch left over. How many liters of punch was used for her party?

____

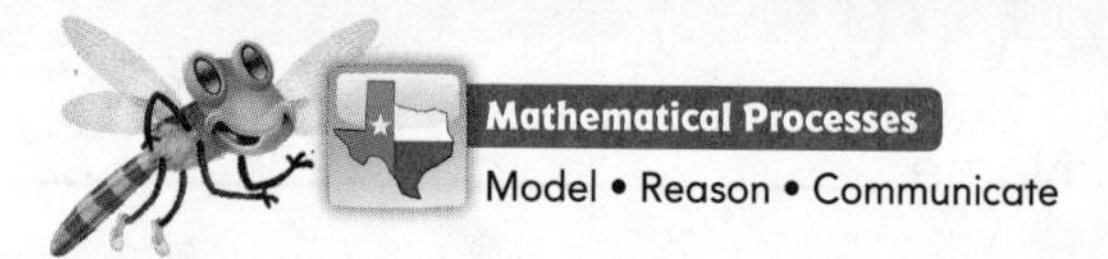

Daily Assessment Task

Fill in the bubble completely to show your answer.

21. Adrian made a poster for his math project. The capital letters on his poster are 4.29 centimeters high. The lowercase letters are 1.97 centimeters high. How much taller are the capital letters than the lowercase letters?

Ⓐ 6.26 centimeters

Ⓑ 3.72 centimeters

Ⓒ 5.16 centimeters

Ⓓ 2.32 centimeters

22. Evaluate Michael's tomato plant was 9.6 centimeters tall when he planted it. It is 21.7 centimeters tall now. How much did the tomato plant grow?

Ⓐ 18.3 centimeters

Ⓑ 28.1 centimeters

Ⓒ 12.1 centimeters

Ⓓ 31.3 centimeters

23. Multi-Step Marty bought 2.07 pounds of potato salad. She ate 0.25 pound. Her brother ate 0.38 pound. How much potato salad was left?

Ⓐ 0.63 pound

Ⓑ 2.70 pounds

Ⓒ 1.82 pounds

Ⓓ 1.44 pounds

TEXAS Test Prep

24. Allie is 158.7 centimeters tall. Her older brother is 3.55 centimeters taller than she is. Her younger brother is 9.53 centimeters shorter than her older brother. How tall is Allie's younger brother?

Ⓐ 162.25 centimeters

Ⓑ 147.7 centimeters

Ⓒ 171.78 centimeters

Ⓓ 152.72 centimeters

Homework and Practice

Name ____________________

6.5 Subtract Decimals

Estimate. Then find the difference.

1. Estimate: ______

$$\begin{array}{r} 4.08 \\ -\ 1.74 \\ \hline \end{array}$$

2. Estimate: ______

$$\begin{array}{r} 13.54 \\ -\ 6.7 \\ \hline \end{array}$$

Find the difference. Check your answer.

3. $$\begin{array}{r} 16.05 \\ -\ 1.5 \\ \hline \end{array}$$

4. $$\begin{array}{r} 21.4 \\ -\ 16.97 \\ \hline \end{array}$$

Find the unknown number for *n*.

5. $7.3 - n = 1.9$

$n =$ ______

6. $n - 8.12 = 11.52$

$n =$ ______

Find the difference.

7. $14.36 - 12.65$

8. $69.32 - 32.46$

Problem Solving Real World

9. John compared the labels of two brands of peanut butter. Brand X has 16.2 grams of fat. Brand Y has 12.7 grams of fat. How much more fat does Brand X contain than Brand Y?

____

10. Sandra ran 63.6 kilometers. Philip ran 8 kilometers less than Sandra. How many kilometers did Philip run?

____

Lesson Check

TEXAS Test Prep

Fill in the bubble completely to show your answer.

11. Erin had $33.65 in her savings account. She spent $9.99 on a new scarf. How much does Erin have left in her savings account?

Ⓐ $23.65

Ⓑ $43.64

Ⓒ $33.66

Ⓓ $23.66

12. Carolyn lives 14.57 miles from the mall. Roberto lives 9.08 miles from the mall. How much farther does Carolyn live from the mall than Roberto?

Ⓐ 5.59 miles

Ⓑ 5.49 miles

Ⓒ 23.65 miles

Ⓓ 23.55 miles

13. One year it rained 59.89 inches in Port Arthur, Texas. The same year it rained 18.69 inches in Lubbock, Texas. How much more rainfall did Port Arthur receive than Lubbock?

Ⓐ 41.20 inches

Ⓑ 40.60 inches

Ⓒ 58.02 inches

Ⓓ 78.58 inches

14. Kaitlin and Will both entered pumpkins in a pumpkin growing competition. Kaitlin's pumpkin weighed 54.43 pounds, and Will's pumpkin weighed 72.11 pounds. How much more did Will's pumpkin weigh than Kaitlin's pumpkin?

Ⓐ 28.78 pounds

Ⓑ 28.68 pounds

Ⓒ 22.32 pounds

Ⓓ 17.68 pounds

15. **Multi-Step** Juan is building bike ramps. The first ramp is 20.32 centimeters high. The second ramp is 5.08 centimeters shorter than the first ramp. The third ramp is 3.81 centimeters shorter than the second ramp. What is the height of the third ramp?

Ⓐ 10.16 centimeters

Ⓑ 16.51 centimeters

Ⓒ 11.43 centimeters

Ⓓ 15.24 centimeters

16. **Multi-Step** Mr. Campbell bought 4.53 kilograms of ice for the picnic. He placed 2.27 kilograms of ice in the soda chest and 0.45 kilograms of ice in the punch bowl. How much ice does Mr. Campbell have left?

Ⓐ 1.36 kilograms

Ⓑ 1.81 kilograms

Ⓒ 4.08 kilograms

Ⓓ 2.72 kilograms

Name ____________________

Module 6 Assessment

Concepts and Skills

Estimate. Then find the sum. TEKS 4.4.A, 4.4.G

1. Estimate: __________

$$\begin{array}{r} 5{,}239 \\ +\ 1{,}056 \\ \hline \end{array}$$

2. Estimate: __________

$$\begin{array}{r} 24{,}032 \\ +\ 18{,}636 \\ \hline \end{array}$$

3. Estimate: __________

$$\begin{array}{r} 728{,}625 \\ +\ 211{,}582 \\ \hline \end{array}$$

4. Estimate: __________

$$\begin{array}{r} 264{,}185 \\ +\ 38{,}642 \\ \hline \end{array}$$

Estimate. Then find the difference. TEKS 4.4.A, 4.4.G

5. Estimate: __________

$$\begin{array}{r} 4{,}328 \\ -\ 2{,}147 \\ \hline \end{array}$$

6. Estimate: __________

$$\begin{array}{r} 35{,}128 \\ -\ 27{,}728 \\ \hline \end{array}$$

7. Estimate: __________

$$\begin{array}{r} 639{,}714 \\ -\ 323{,}471 \\ \hline \end{array}$$

8. Estimate: __________

$$\begin{array}{r} 175{,}932 \\ -\ 28{,}731 \\ \hline \end{array}$$

Find the sum. TEKS 4.4.A

9. $\begin{array}{r} 12.87 \\ +\ 5.75 \\ \hline \end{array}$

10. $\begin{array}{r} 32.64 \\ +\ 18.78 \\ \hline \end{array}$

11. $\begin{array}{r} 19.28 \\ +\ 2.54 \\ \hline \end{array}$

12. 14.36 + 7.87 __________

13. 0.25 + 0.77 __________

14. 6.75 + 8.49 __________

Find the difference. TEKS 4.4.A

15. $\begin{array}{r} 9.2 \\ -\ 0.4 \\ \hline \end{array}$

16. $\begin{array}{r} 10.5 \\ -\ 6.8 \\ \hline \end{array}$

17. $\begin{array}{r} 0.75 \\ -\ 0.28 \\ \hline \end{array}$

18. $\begin{array}{r} 6.7 \\ -\ 3.8 \\ \hline \end{array}$

19. $\begin{array}{r} 8.17 \\ -\ 3.81 \\ \hline \end{array}$

20. $\begin{array}{r} 12.27 \\ -\ 6.94 \\ \hline \end{array}$

Fill the bubble in completely to show your answer.

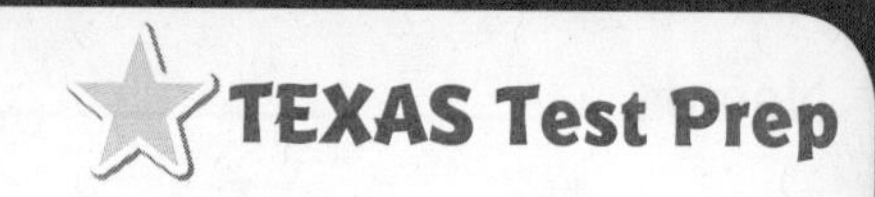

21. During October, Chad's website had 12,014 visitors and Pamela's website had 11,987 visitors. Kim's website had 6,347 more visitors than Pamela's website. How many visitors did all three websites have during October? TEKS 4.4.A

Ⓐ 30,348

Ⓑ 5,667

Ⓒ 42,335

Ⓓ 18,334

22. The town of Spring Lake has a population of 30,155 during the summer, a population of 13,876 during the winter, and a population of 22,654 during the fall. How many more people spend time in Spring Lake during the summer and winter combined than during the fall? TEKS 4.4.A

Ⓐ 8,778

Ⓑ 44,031

Ⓒ 7,501

Ⓓ 21,377

23. The Smiths are on a summer road trip. They travel 10.9 hours the first day, 8.6 hours the second day, and 12.4 hours the final day. How may hours does the Smith family travel during the three-day trip? TEKS 4.4.A

Ⓐ 31.9 hours

Ⓑ 3.8 hours

Ⓒ 23.3 hours

Ⓓ 19.5 hours

24. During one week, Morgan jogged 51.2 kilometers, Karen jogged 53.52 kilometers, and Kelly jogged 6 kilometers less than Morgan. How many more kilometers did Karen jog that week than Kelly? TEKS 4.4.A

Ⓐ 104.72 kilometers

Ⓑ 8.32 kilometers

Ⓒ 45.2 kilometers

Ⓓ 57.2 kilometers

Name ______________________________

7.1 Multiply Tens, Hundreds, and Thousands

TEKS Number and Operations—4.4.B
Also 4.4.H

MATHEMATICAL PROCESSES
4.1.A, 4.1.C, 4.1.E

Essential Question

How does understanding place value help you multiply tens, hundreds, and thousands?

Unlock the Problem (Real World)

Each car on a train has 200 seats. How many seats are on a train with 8 cars?

Find 8×200.

One Way Draw a quick picture.

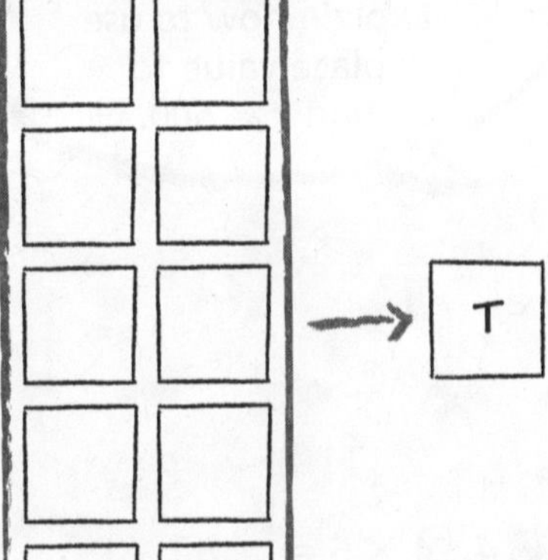

Think: 10 hundreds = 1,000

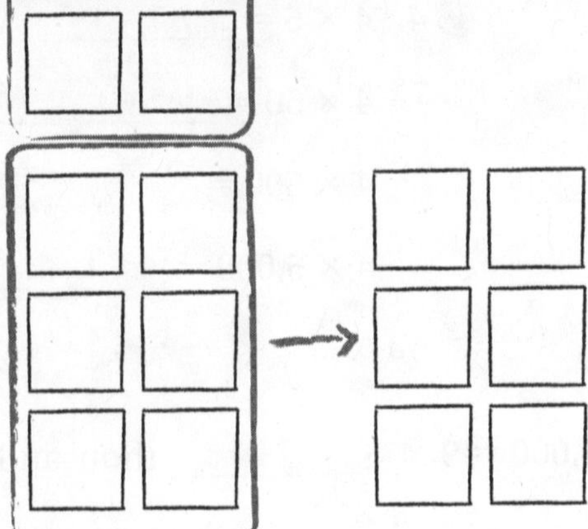

Think: 6 hundreds = 600

$1{,}000 + 600 =$ ______

Another Way Use place value.

$8 \times 200 = 8 \times$ ______ hundreds

$=$ ______ hundreds

$=$ ______ Think: 16 hundreds is 1 thousand, 6 hundreds.

So, there are ______ seats on a train with 8 cars.

Math Talk

Mathematical Processes

Explain how finding 8×2 can help you find 8×200.

 Use patterns.

Basic fact:

$3 \times 7 = 21$ ← basic fact

$3 \times 70 = 210$

$3 \times 700 =$ ______

$3 \times 7{,}000 =$ ______

Basic fact with a zero:

$8 \times 5 = 40$ ← basic fact

$8 \times 50 = 400$

$8 \times 500 =$ ______

$8 \times 5{,}000 =$ ______

Share and Show

1. Use the drawing to find 2×500.

$2 \times 500 =$ ______

Complete the pattern.

2. $3 \times 8 = 24$

   $3 \times 80 =$ ______

   $3 \times 800 =$ ______

   $3 \times 8{,}000 =$ ______

3. $6 \times 2 = 12$

   $6 \times 20 =$ ______

   $6 \times 200 =$ ______

   $6 \times 2{,}000 =$ ______

4. $4 \times 5 =$ ______

   $4 \times 50 =$ ______

   $4 \times 500 =$ ______

   $4 \times 5{,}000 =$ ______

Find the product.

5. $6 \times 500 = 6 \times$ ______ hundreds

   $=$ ______ hundreds

   $=$ ______

6. $9 \times 5{,}000 = 9 \times$ ______ thousands

   $=$ ______ thousands

   $=$ ______

H.O.T. Algebra **Find the missing factor.**

7. ______ $\times 9{,}000 = 63{,}000$

8. $7 \times$ ______ $= 56{,}000$

9. $8 \times$ ______ $= 3{,}200$

Name ______________________

Unlock the Problem

10. HOT **Multi-Step Apply** Joe's Fun and Sun rents beach chairs. The store rented 300 beach chairs each month in April and in May. The store rented 600 beach chairs each month from June through September. How many beach chairs did the store rent during the 6 months?

Ⓐ 1,200 Ⓒ 3,000

Ⓑ 2,400 Ⓓ 5,400

a. What do you need to know? ______________________

____

b. How will you find the number of beach chairs? ______________________

____

c. Show the steps you use to solve the problem.

d. Complete the sentences.

For April and May, a total of ______ beach chairs were rented.

For June through September, a total of ______ beach chairs were rented.

Joe's Fun and Sun rented ______ beach chairs during the 6 months.

e. Fill in the bubble for the correct answer choice above.

11. HOT **Use Math Language** How does the number of zeros in the product of 8 and 5,000 compare to the number of zeros in the factors? **Explain.**

____

____

Mathematical Processes
Model • Reason • Communicate

Daily Assessment Task

Fill in the bubble completely to show your answer.

12. True Blue plans to decorate backpacks. They will make a profit of $6 for each backpack they decorate. How much profit will they make all together if they decorate and sell 300 backpacks?

Ⓐ $300

Ⓑ $1,800

Ⓒ $180

Ⓓ $600

13. A whistle company packs 4,000 whistles in each box that it sends to stores. How many whistles are in 8 boxes?

Ⓐ 240

Ⓑ 24,000

Ⓒ 32,000

Ⓓ 3,200

14. **Multi-Step** Joshua spends 20 hours walking dogs. He also spends 2 hours on each garden he weeds. He weeds 50 gardens. How much time does Joshua spend walking dogs and weeding gardens?

Ⓐ 90 hours

Ⓑ 100 hours

Ⓒ 70 hours

Ⓓ 120 hours

TEXAS Test Prep

15. Carmen has three books of 20 stamps and five books of 10 stamps. How many stamps does she have?

Ⓐ 110

Ⓑ 60

Ⓒ 50

Ⓓ 100

Name ______________________________

7.2 Estimate Products

Essential Question

How can you estimate products by rounding and determine if exact answers are reasonable?

Unlock the Problem (Real World)

An African elephant can reach as high as 23 feet with its trunk. It uses its trunk to pick up objects that weigh up to 3 times as much as a 165-pound person. About how much weight can an African elephant pick up with its trunk?

- Cross out the information you will not use.
- Circle the numbers you will use.
- How will you use the numbers to solve the problem?

____

One Way Estimate by rounding.

STEP 1 Round the greater factor to the nearest hundred.

3×165

↓

3×200

STEP 2 Use mental math.

Think: $3 \times 200 = 3 \times 2$ hundreds

$= 6$ hundreds

$=$ ______

So, an African elephant can pick up about 600 pounds with its trunk.

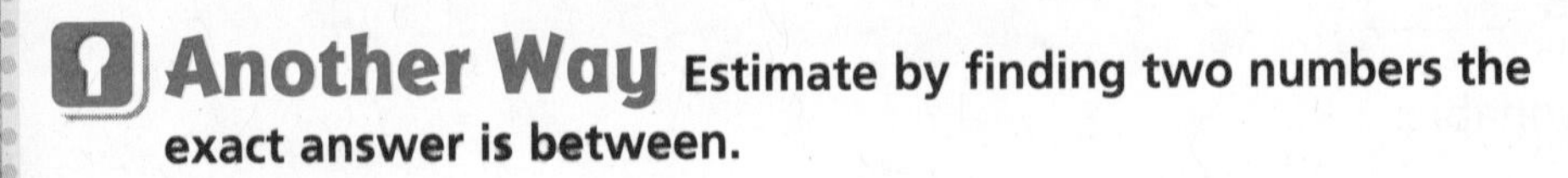

Another Way Estimate by finding two numbers the exact answer is between.

3×165

↓

$3 \times 100 =$ ______

3×165

↓

$3 \times 200 =$ ______

Think: 165 is between 100 and 200. Use those numbers to estimate.

So, the African elephant can pick up between 300 and 600 pounds.

An African elephant is the largest living land mammal.

1. Is 200 less than or greater than 165? ______________________

2. So, would the product of 3 and 165 be less than or greater than 600? ______________________

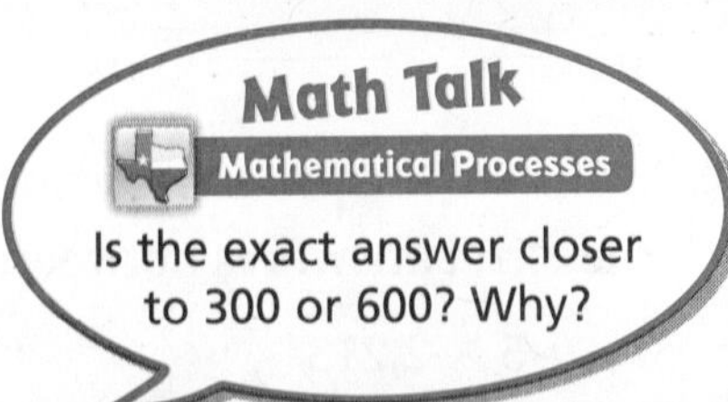

Describe Reasonableness You can estimate a product to find whether an exact answer is reasonable.

Tell whether an exact answer is reasonable.

Eva's horse eats 86 pounds each week. Eva solved the equation below to find how much feed she needs for 4 weeks.

$4 \times 86 = \blacksquare$

Eva says she needs 344 pounds of feed.
Is her answer reasonable?

One Way Estimate.

4×86

↓ Think: Round to the nearest ten.

_____ × _____ = _____

344 is close to 360.

Another Way Find two numbers the exact answer is between.

4×86

↓

_____ × _____ = _____

4×86

↓

_____ × _____ = _____

_____ is between _____ and _____.

So, 344 pounds of feed is reasonable.

Share and Show

1. Estimate the product by rounding to the nearest thousand.

   $5 \times 2,213$

   ↓

   _____ × _____ = _____

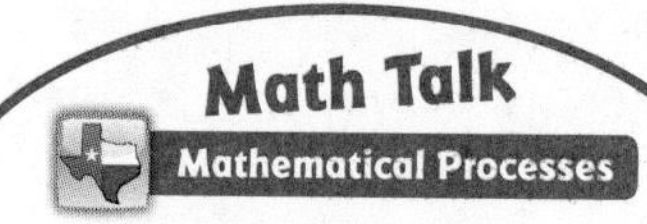

Is an exact answer of 11,065 reasonable? Explain.

2. Estimate the product by finding two numbers the exact answer is between.

   $5 \times 2,213$

   _____ × _____ = _____

   $5 \times 2,213$

   _____ × _____ = _____

Name ______________________

Tell whether the exact answer is reasonable.

3. Kira needs to make color copies of a horse show flyer. The printer can make 24 copies in 1 minute. Kira says the printer makes 114 copies in 6 minutes.

4. Jones Elementary is having a car wash to raise money for a community horse trail. Each car wash ticket costs $8. Tiara says the school will receive $1,000 if 125 tickets are sold.

Problem Solving Real World

Tell whether the exact answer is reasonable.

5. Mrs. Hense sells a roll of coastal Bermuda horse hay for $58. She says she will make $174 if she sells 3 rolls.

6. Mr. Brown sells horse supplies. A pair of riding gloves sells for $16. He says he will make $144 if he sells 9 pairs.

H.O.T. **Predict whether the exact answer will be *less than or greater than* the estimate. Explain your answer.**

7. **Justify** The food stand at the zoo sold 2,514 pounds of hamburger last month. The average cost of a pound of hamburger is $2. Jeremy estimates that about $6,000 worth of hamburger was sold last month.

8. **Evaluate Reasonableness** A zoo bought 2,240 pounds of fresh food for the bears this month. The average cost of a pound of food is $4. Jeremy estimates that about $8,000 was spent on fresh food for the bears this month.

Daily Assessment Task

Fill in the bubble completely to show your answer.

9. Some scientists think the honey mushroom is 2,400 years old. Other scientists think it could be about 4 times as old. Which is the best estimate that other scientists think the age of the honey mushroom could be?

Ⓐ 16,000 years old

Ⓑ 8,000 years old

Ⓒ 4,000 years old

Ⓓ 12,000 years old

10. Alan scores 7,895 points in the first level of a computer game. He scores 5 times as many points in the second level. Which estimate is closest to the number of points Alan scores in the second level?

Ⓐ about 50,000

Ⓑ about 45,000

Ⓒ about 35,000

Ⓓ about 40,000

11. **Multi-Step** Students in the third grade sell 265 tickets to the school play. Students in the fourth grade sell 3 times as many tickets as the third grade students. The number of tickets sold by fourth-grade students is between which two estimates?

Ⓐ 0 and 300

Ⓑ 300 and 600

Ⓒ 600 and 900

Ⓓ 900 and 1,200

TEXAS Test Prep

2. Miranda needs to copy some papers. She has 182 pages that she needs to copy. She needs 6 copies of each page. About how many pages will Miranda copy?

Ⓐ 2,000

Ⓑ 1,400

Ⓒ 600

Ⓓ 1,200

Name ____________________

7.3 Multiply Using the Distributive Property

TEKS Number and Operations—4.4.D
Also 4.4.B

MATHEMATICAL PROCESSES
4.1.C, 4.1.D, 4.1.E

Essential Question How can you use the Distributive Property to multiply a 2-digit number by a 1-digit number?

Investigate

Materials ■ color pencils ■ grid paper

You can use the Distributive Property to break apart numbers to make them easier to multiply.

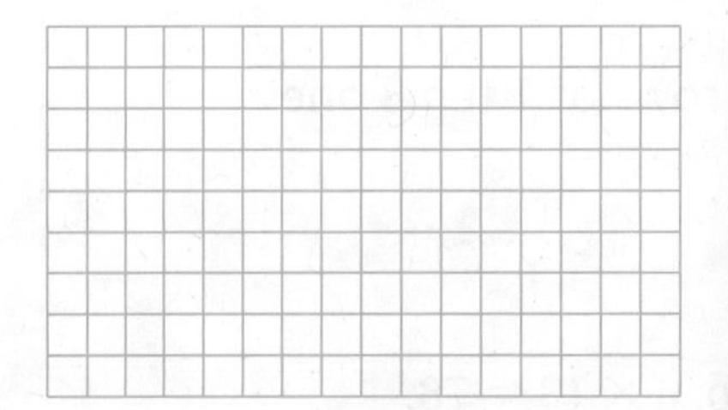

The **Distributive Property** states that multiplying a sum by a number is the same as multiplying each addend by the number and then adding the products.

A. Outline a rectangle on the grid to model 6×13.

B. Think of 13 as $5 + 8$. Break apart the model to show $6 \times (5 + 8)$. Label and shade the smaller rectangles. Use two different colors.

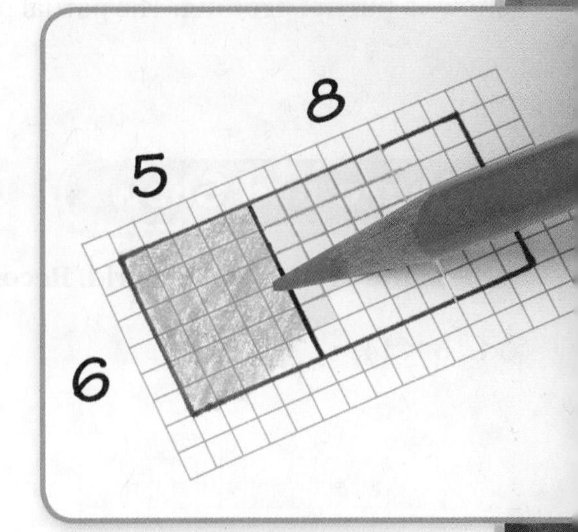

Use the Distributive Property. Find the product each smaller rectangle represents. Then find the sum of the products. Record your answers.

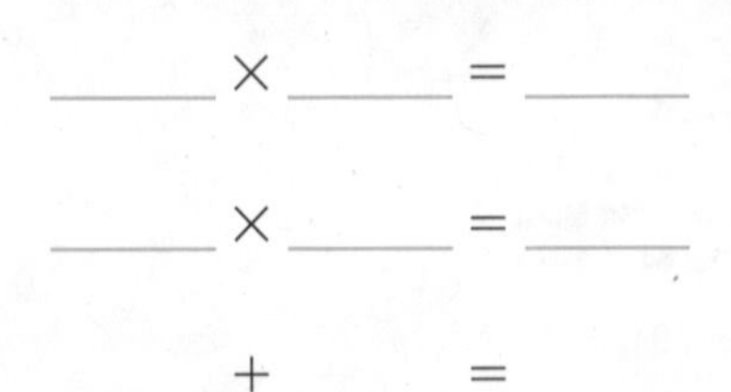

____ × ____ = ____

____ × ____ = ____

____ + ____ = ____

C. Model 6×13 again. Think of 13 as a different sum. Break apart the model to show 6 × (____ + ____). Find the product each smaller rectangle represents. Then find the sum of the products. Record your answers.

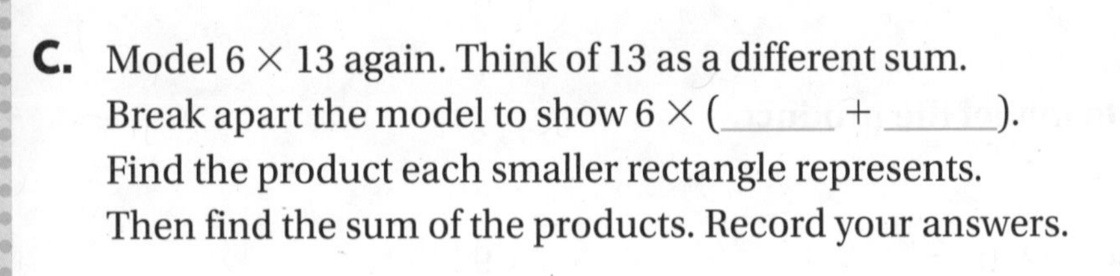

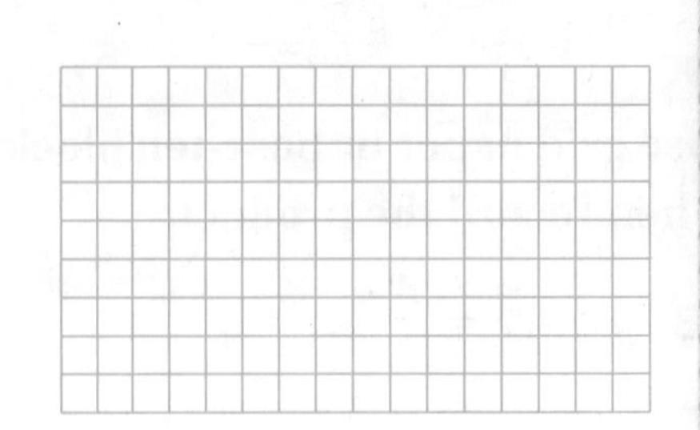

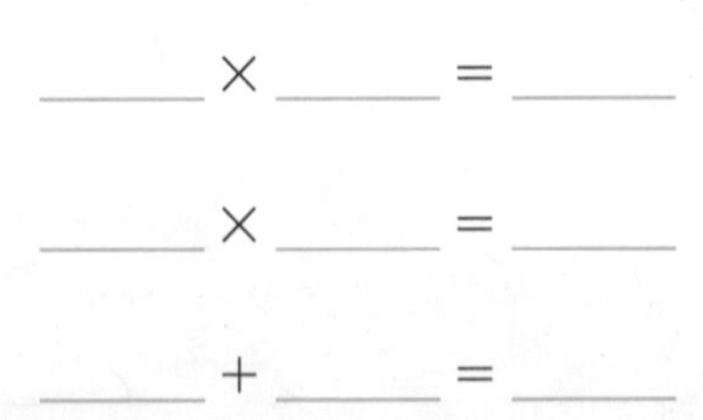

____ × ____ = ____

____ × ____ = ____

____ + ____ = ____

Make Connections

Another way to model the problem is to use base-ten blocks to show tens and ones.

STEP 1 Use base-ten blocks to model 6×13.

6 rows of 1 ten 3 ones

STEP 2 Break the model into tens and ones.

($6 \times$ 1 ten) ($6 \times$ 3 ones)

(6×10) (6×3)

_____ _____

STEP 3 Add the tens and the ones to find the product.

$(6 \times 10) + (6 \times 3)$

$60 + 18$

_____

So, $6 \times 13 = 78$.

In Step 2, the model is broken into two parts. Each part shows a **partial product**. The partial products are 60 and 18.

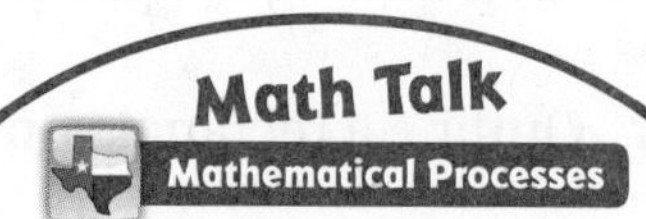

How does breaking apart the model into tens and ones make finding the product easier?

Share and Show

Model the product on the grid. Record the product.

1. $5 \times 14 =$ _____

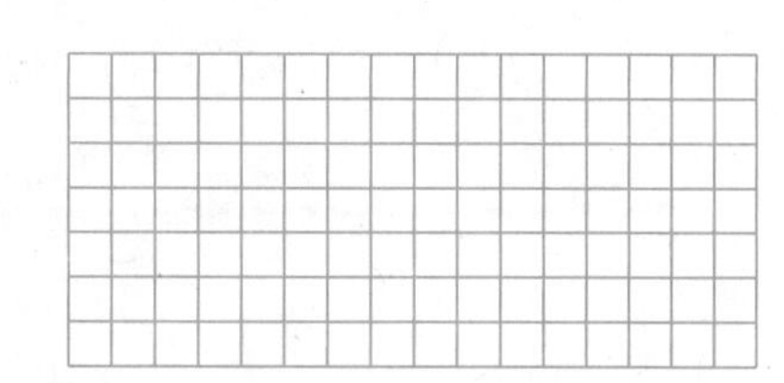

2. $4 \times 16 =$ _____

Use grid paper or base-ten blocks to model the product. Then record the product.

3. $7 \times 12 =$ _____

4. $5 \times 16 =$ _____

5. $9 \times 13 =$ _____

6. H.O.T. **Evaluate** To find 7×23, is it easier to break apart the factor, 23, as $20 + 3$ or $15 + 8$? **Explain.**

____

____

Name ______________________

Problem Solving Real World

Pose a Problem

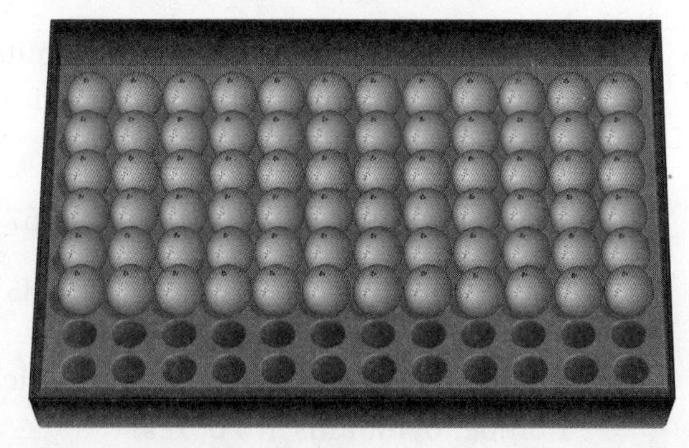

7. **Evaluate** Kyle went to a fruit market. The market sells a wide variety of fruits and vegetables. The picture at the right shows a display of oranges.

   Write a problem that can be solved using the picture.

Pose a problem.	**Solve your problem.**

8. **H.O.T.** **Multi-Step Use Math Language** Describe how you could change the problem by changing the number of rows of oranges and the number of empty spaces in the picture. Then solve the problem.

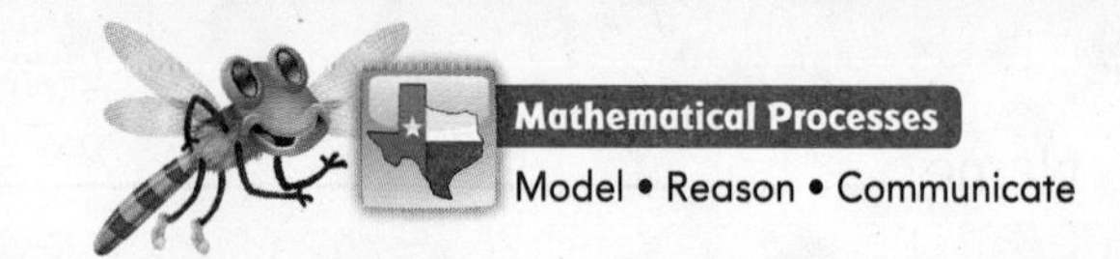

Daily Assessment Task

Fill in the bubble completely to show your answer.

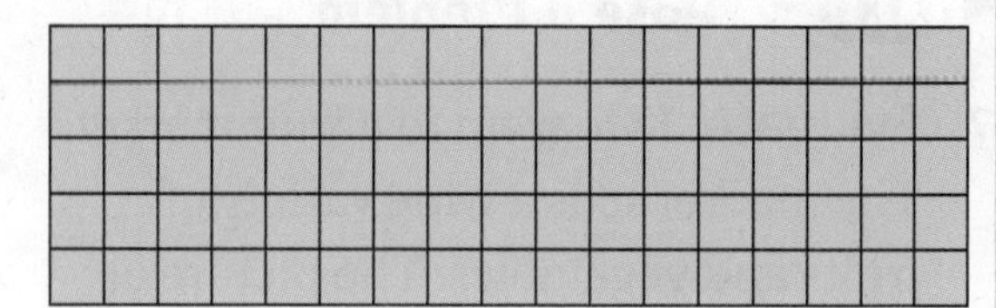

9. Ryan plays with his robo-pup 17 minutes each day. How many minutes will Ryan play with his robo-pup in 5 days?

Ⓐ 34 minutes
Ⓑ 22 minutes
Ⓒ 57 minutes
Ⓓ 85 minutes

10. There are 13 muffins in each box. Which shows the total number of muffins in 4 boxes?

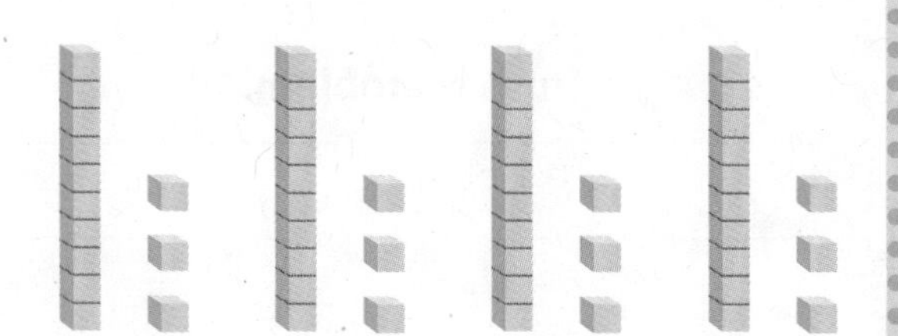

Ⓐ $(4 \times 10) + (4 \times 3) = 52$

Ⓑ $(4 \times 10) + 3 = 43$

Ⓒ $4 + (10 \times 3) = 34$

Ⓓ $(4 + 10) + (4 + 3) = 21$

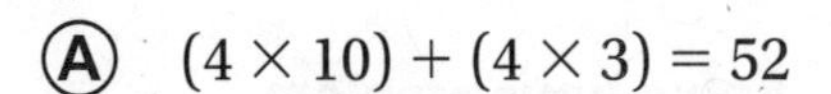

11. Multi-Step Ava and Mia are setting up chairs for the play. Ava sets up 6 rows of chairs with 14 chairs in each row. Mia sets up 5 rows of chairs with 16 chairs in each row. How many more chairs does Ava set up than Mia?

Ⓐ 4
Ⓑ 5
Ⓒ 6
Ⓓ 14

TEXAS Test Prep

12. Brenda has already handed out 17 programs for the play. Before the play is over, she needs to have handed out a total that is 4 times that many programs. How many programs does Brenda have left to hand out before the end of the play?

Ⓐ 21
Ⓑ 63
Ⓒ 80
Ⓓ 51

Homework and Practice

TEKS Number and Operations—4.4.D
Also 4.4.B
MATHEMATICAL PROCESSES 4.1.C, 4.1.D, 4.1.E

Name ______________________

7.3 Multiply Using the Distributive Property

Model the problem on the grid. Record the product.

1. $7 \times 13 =$ ______________

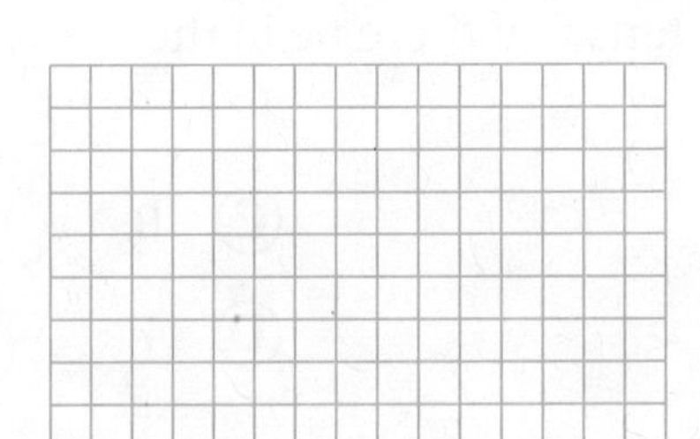

2. $5 \times 15 =$ ______________

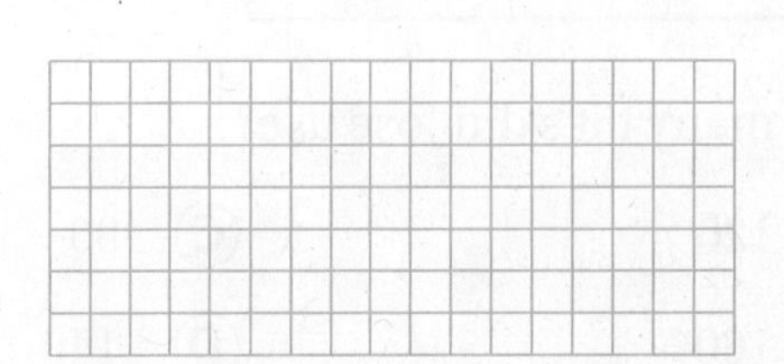

Use grid paper or base-ten blocks to model the product. Then record the product.

3. $3 \times 14 =$ ______________

4. $8 \times 16 =$ ______________

5. $9 \times 12 =$ ______________

6. $5 \times 14 =$ ______________

7. $7 \times 11 =$ ______________

8. $2 \times 18 =$ ______________

Problem Solving

Jeannie has a flat of daisies. She has planted some of them in her garden.

Write a problem that can be solved using the picture.

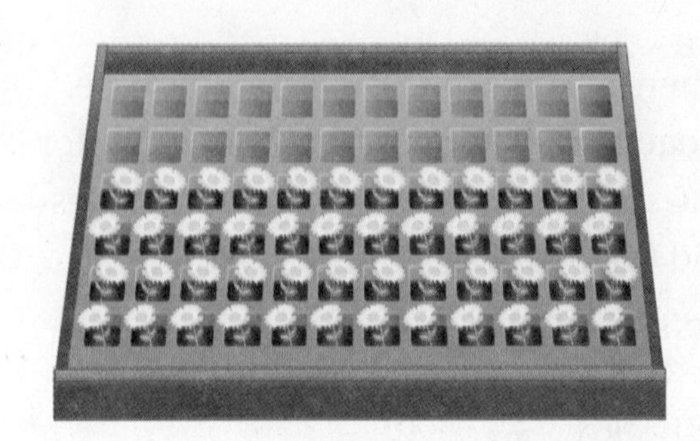

9. Pose a problem.

____

____

____

10. Solve your problem.

____

____

____

Lesson Check

TEXAS Test Prep

Fill in the bubble completely to show your answer.

11. The shaded part of the model shows how José tiled his floor.

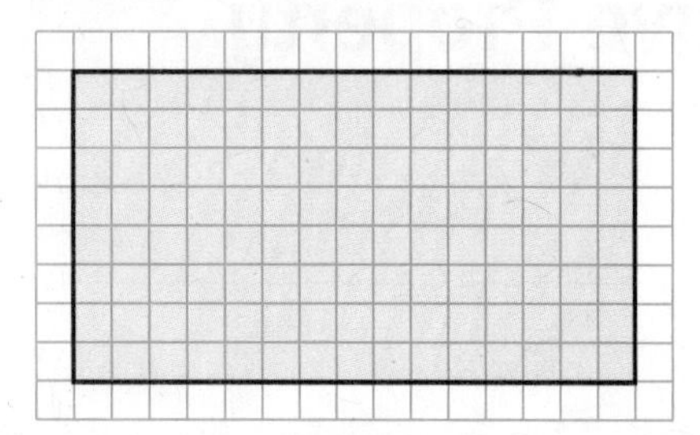

How many tiles did José use?

Ⓐ 120
Ⓑ 160
Ⓒ 80
Ⓓ 140

12. The model below represents the expression 6×16.

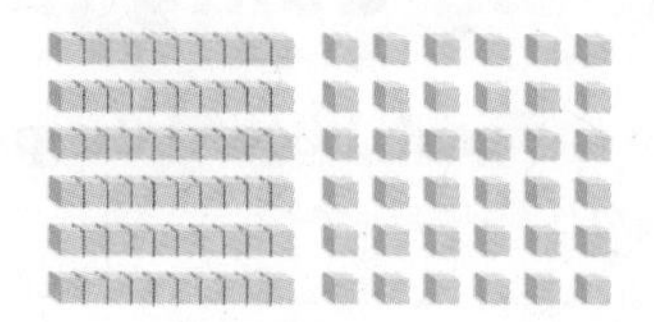

How many tens will there be in the final product?

Ⓐ 4
Ⓑ 3
Ⓒ 9
Ⓓ 7

13. Will collects military medals. He has 5 cases of medals. Each case holds 18 medals. How many medals does Will have?

Ⓐ 75
Ⓑ 95
Ⓒ 80
Ⓓ 90

14. Yolando has 12 inches of ribbon. She needs 6 times as much ribbon than what she has. How many inches of ribbon does Yolanda need?

Ⓐ 74 inches
Ⓑ 62 inches
Ⓒ 60 inches
Ⓓ 72 inches

15. There are 24 bottles of water in a case. Coach Rinaldo buys 4 cases of water for the school field day. How many bottles did Coach Rinaldo buy?

Ⓐ 86
Ⓑ 96
Ⓒ 88
Ⓓ 90

16. **Multi-Step** Peyton bought 4 cartons of eggs with 12 eggs in each carton. Chloe bought 3 cartons of eggs with 18 eggs in each carton. Which statement is true?

Ⓐ Chloe bought more eggs than Peyton.
Ⓑ Together Chloe and Peyton bought 96 eggs.
Ⓒ Peyton bought 6 more eggs than Chloe.
Ⓓ Both girls bought the same number of eggs.

Name ______________________________

7.4 Multiply Using Expanded Form

Essential Question How can you use expanded form to multiply a multidigit number by a 1-digit number?

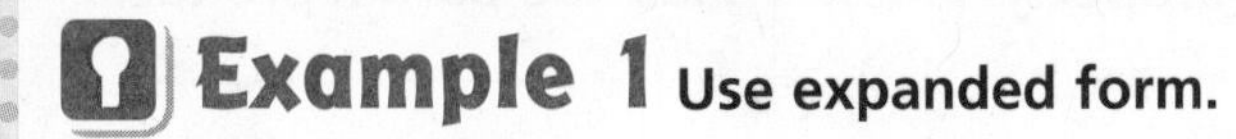

Unlock the Problem

Example 1 Use expanded form.

Multiply. 5×143

$5 \times 143 = 5 \times (\_\_\_\_ + \_\_\_\_ + \_\_\_\_)$ Write 143 in expanded form.

$= (5 \times 100) + (\_\_\_\_ \times \_\_\_\_) + (\_\_\_\_ \times \_\_\_\_)$ Use the Distributive Property.

	SHADE THE MODEL	THINK AND RECORD
STEP 1	Model: 5 by 100, 40, 3	Multiply the hundreds. $(5 \times 100) + (5 \times 40) + (5 \times 3)$ $\_\_\_\_ + (5 \times 40) + (5 \times 3)$
STEP 2	Model: 5 by 100, 40, 3	Multiply the tens. $(5 \times 100) + (5 \times 40) + (5 \times 3)$ $500 + \_\_\_\_ + (5 \times 3)$
STEP 3	Model: 5 by 100, 40, 3	Multiply the ones. $(5 \times 100) + (5 \times 40) + (5 \times 3)$ $500 + 200 + \_\_\_\_$
STEP 4	Model: 5 by 100, 40, 3	Add the partial products. 500 200 + 15

So, $5 \times 143 = \_\_\_\_$.

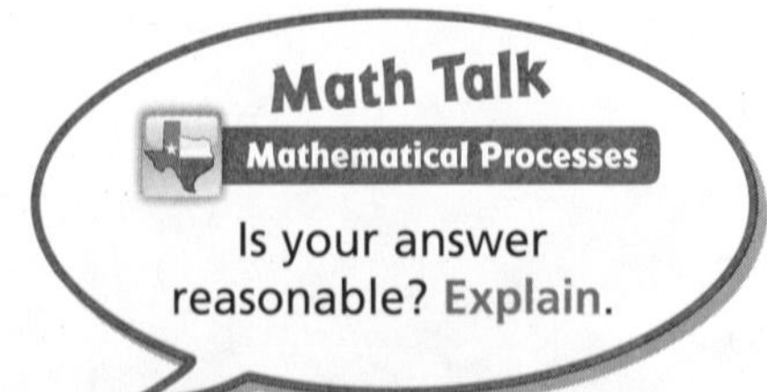

Example 2 Use expanded form.

The gift shop at the animal park orders 3 boxes of toy animals. Each box has 1,250 toy animals. How many toy animals does the shop order?

Multiply. $3 \times 1,250$

STEP 1

Write 1,250 in expanded form. Use the Distributive Property.

$3 \times 1,250 = 3 \times (\_\_\_\_ + \_\_\_\_ + \_\_\_\_)$

$= (3 \times 1,000) + (\_\_\_\_ \times \_\_\_\_) + (\_\_\_\_ \times \_\_\_\_)$

STEP 2

Add the partial products.

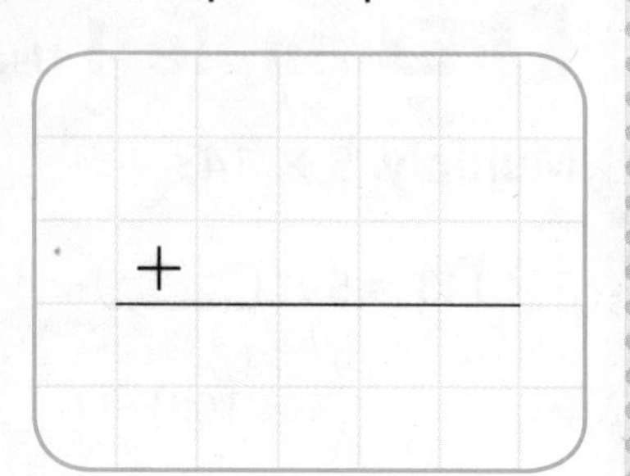

So, the shop ordered ________ animals.

Share and Show

1. Find 4×213. Use expanded form.

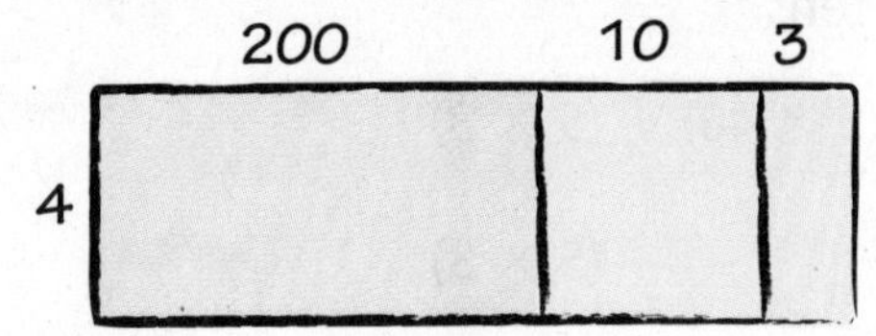

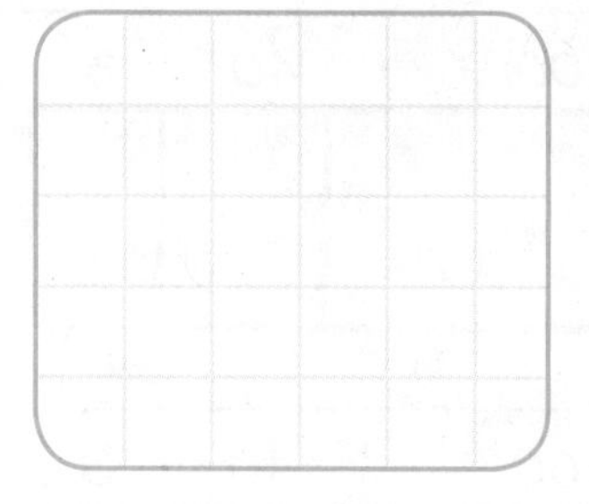

$4 \times 213 = \_\_\_\_ \times (\_\_\_\_ + \_\_\_\_ + \_\_\_\_)$

$= (\_\_\_\_ \times \_\_\_\_) + (\_\_\_\_ \times \_\_\_\_) + (\_\_\_\_ \times \_\_\_\_)$ Use the Distributive Property.

$= \_\_\_\_ + \_\_\_\_ + \_\_\_\_$

$= \_\_\_\_$

Record the product. Use expanded form to help.

2. $4 \times 59 = \_\_\_\_$

3. $3 \times 288 = \_\_\_\_$

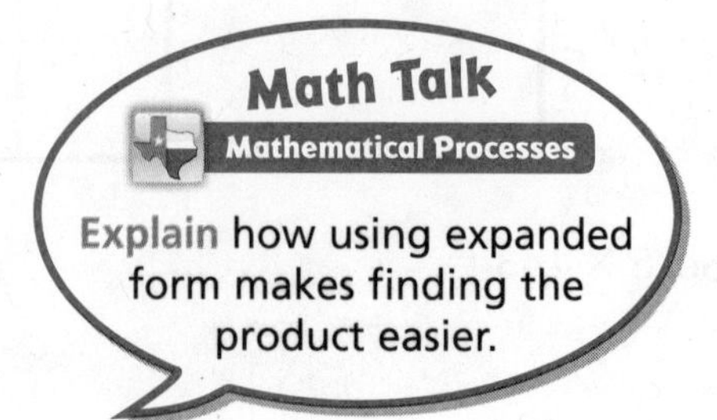

Name ______________________________

Problem Solving Real World

Use the table for 4–6.

Sacco Nursery Plant Sale		
Tree	Regular Price	Discounted Price (4 or more)
Flowering Cherry	$59	$51
Italian Cypress	$79	$67
Muskogee Crape Myrtle	$39	$34
Royal Empress	$29	$25

Write Math ▶ Show Your Work

4. What is the total cost of 3 Italian cypress trees?

____

5. H.O.T. **Multi-Step What's the Error?** Tanya says that the difference in the cost of 4 flowering cherry trees and 4 Muskogee crape myrtles is $80. Is she correct? **Explain.**

____

____

____

6. H.O.T. **Multi-Step** What is the cost of 4 Royal Empress and 3 Muskogee Crape Myrtle?

____

7. **Use Math Language** What is the greatest possible product of a 2-digit number and a 1-digit number? **Explain** how you know.

____

____

____

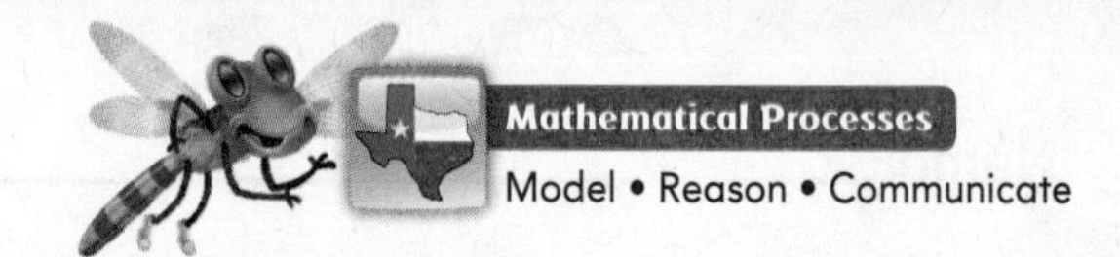

Daily Assessment Task

Fill in the bubble completely to show your answer.

8. Sara uses 5 rolls of tape to make a flower. Each roll has 344 inches of tape. How many inches of tape does Sara use to make the flower?

Ⓐ 349 inches
Ⓑ 1,504 inches
Ⓒ 1,544 inches
Ⓓ 1,720 inches

9. A worker at an office supply store orders 5 large boxes of pencils. Each box contains 6,120 pencils. Which shows one way to find the number of pencils the worker orders?

Ⓐ $(5 \times 600) + (5 \times 10) + (5 \times 2)$
Ⓑ $(5 \times 6{,}000) + (5 \times 100) + (5 \times 2)$
Ⓒ $(5 \times 6{,}000) + (5 \times 100) + (5 \times 20)$
Ⓓ $(5 \times 6{,}000) + (5 \times 10) + (5 \times 2)$

10. **Multi-Step** A hotel has 128 rooms on each floor. There are 4 floors in all. If 334 of the rooms in the hotel have been cleaned, how many rooms still need to be cleaned?

Ⓐ 178
Ⓑ 206
Ⓒ 384
Ⓓ 512

TEXAS Test Prep

11. Which expression shows how to multiply 5×381 by using place value and expanded form?

Ⓐ $(5 \times 3) + (5 \times 8) + (5 \times 1)$
Ⓑ $(5 \times 300) + (5 \times 80) + (5 \times 100)$
Ⓒ $(5 \times 300) + (5 \times 80) + (5 \times 1)$
Ⓓ $(5 \times 300) + (5 \times 80) + (5 \times 10)$

TEKS Number and Operations—4.4.D
Also 4.4.B, 4.4.H
MATHEMATICAL PROCESSES 4.1.C, 4.1.F, 4.1.G

Name ______________________

7.4 Multiply Using Expanded Form

Record the product. Use expanded form to help.

1. $5 \times 73 =$ ______________

2. $6 \times 241 =$ ______________

Problem Solving

Use the table for 3–6.

Sam's Sweaters Sale!		
Sweaters	Regular Price	Sale Price (3 or more)
Turtleneck	$44	$36
Zip-front	$119	$98
V-neck	$78	$65
Button-front	$54	$43

3. What is the cost of 2 v-neck sweaters?

____

4. What is the cost of 5 button-front sweaters?

____

5. What is the cost of 4 v-neck sweaters and 2 zip-front sweaters?

____

6. Ben wants to buy 3 zip-front sweaters and 3 turtleneck sweaters. He says he will pay $225 more for the zip-front sweaters than for the turtleneck sweaters. Is he correct? **Explain.**

____

7. What is the greatest possible product of a 3-digit number and a 1-digit number? **Explain** how you know.

____

Lesson Check

TEXAS Test Prep

Fill in the bubble completely to show your answer.

8. A jeweler has 36 inches of silver chain. She needs 5 times that much to make some necklaces. How much silver chain does the jeweler need to make her necklaces?

Ⓐ 150 inches

Ⓑ 41 inches

Ⓒ 90 inches

Ⓓ 180 inches

9. Gretchen walks her dog 3 times a day. Each time she walks the dog, she walks 1,760 yards. How many yards does she walk her dog in 1 day?

Ⓐ 528 yards

Ⓑ 3,390 yards

Ⓒ 5,280 yards

Ⓓ 3,228 yards

10. Angela needs 144 blocks for each layer of a block tower. How many blocks does she need to make a tower 8 layers tall?

Ⓐ 1,152

Ⓑ 720

Ⓒ 1,064

Ⓓ 1,048

11. Which expression shows how to multiply 9×856 using place value and expanded form?

Ⓐ $(9 \times 800) + (9 \times 50) + (9 \times 6)$

Ⓑ $(9 \times 8) + (9 \times 5) + (9 \times 6)$

Ⓒ $(8 \times 90) + (5 \times 90) + (6 \times 90)$

Ⓓ $(9 \times 80) + (9 \times 50) + (9 \times 60)$

12. **Multi-Step** Jennifer bought 4 packages of tacks. There are 48 tacks in a package. She used 160 of the tacks to put up posters. How many tacks does she have left?

Ⓐ 12

Ⓑ 320

Ⓒ 32

Ⓓ 120

13. Jamal is making 8 wooden rails. Each rail is 42 inches long. How many inches of board does Jamal need to make all the rails?

Ⓐ 238 inches

Ⓑ 336 inches

Ⓒ 342 inches

Ⓓ 34 inches

Name ______________________________

7.5 Multiply Using Partial Products

Essential Question How can you use place value and partial products to multiply by a 1-digit number?

Unlock the Problem

Connect How can you use what you know about the Distributive Property to break apart numbers to find products of 3-digit and 1-digit numbers?

- How can you write 182 as a sum of hundreds, tens, and ones?

____

Use place value and partial products.

Multiply. 6 × 182 **Estimate.** 6 × 200 = __________

SHADE THE MODEL | **THINK AND RECORD**

STEP 1

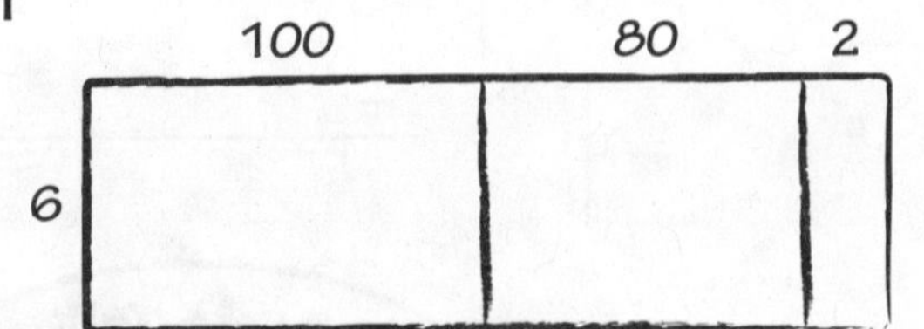

$$\begin{array}{r} 182 \\ \times\ 6 \\ \hline \square \end{array}$$

← Multiply the hundreds.
6 × 1 hundred = 6 hundreds

STEP 2

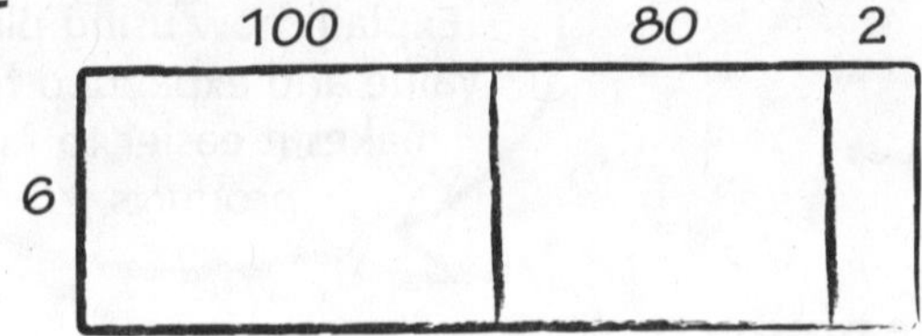

$$\begin{array}{r} 182 \\ \times\ 6 \\ \hline 600 \\ \square \end{array}$$

← Multiply the tens.
6 × 8 tens = 48 tens

STEP 3

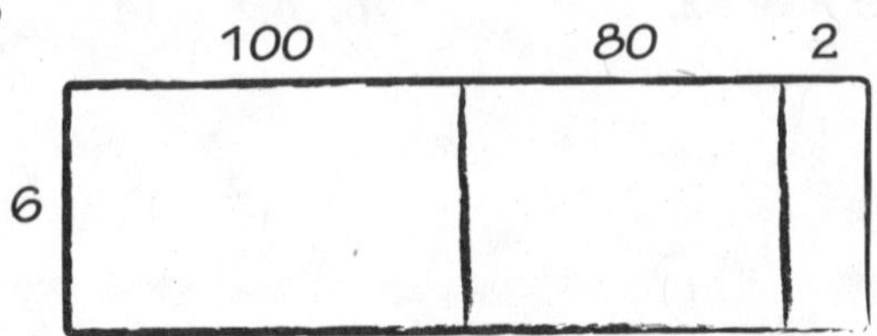

$$\begin{array}{r} 182 \\ \times\ 6 \\ \hline 600 \\ 480 \\ \square \end{array}$$

← Multiply the ones.
6 × 2 ones = 12 ones

STEP 4

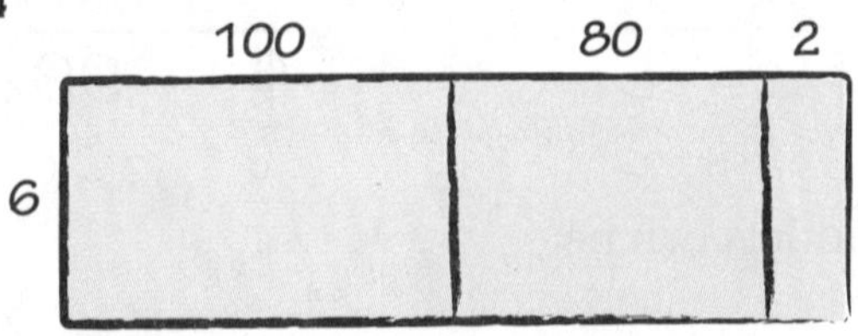

$$\begin{array}{r} 182 \\ \times\ 6 \\ \hline 600 \\ 480 \\ +\ 12 \\ \hline \end{array}$$

← Add the partial product

Math Talk Mathematical Processes

How can you use the Distributive Property to find 4 × 257?

So, 6 × 182 = __________. Since __________ is close to the estimate of 1,200, it is reasonable.

Share and Show

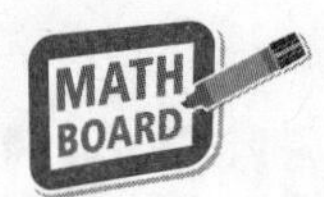

1. Use the model to find 2 × 137.

100 30 7

2

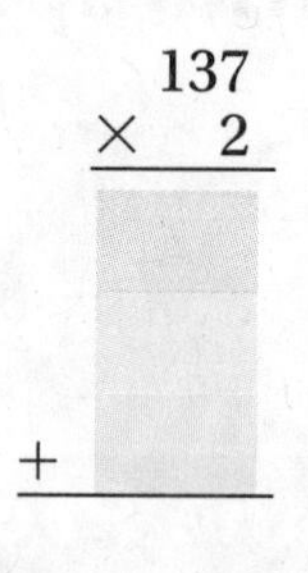

Estimate. Then record the product.

2. Estimate: ______

  1 9 0
× 3
+

3. Estimate: ______

  4 7 1
× 4
+

4. Estimate: ______

  $ 3, 4 3 9
× 7
+

Math Talk
Mathematical Processes
Explain how using place value and expanded form makes it easier to find products.

Problem Solving

Practice: Copy and Solve **Estimate. Then record the product.**

5. 2 × 78
6. 2 × $210
7. 9 × $682
8. 8 × 8,145

Algebra **Find the missing digit.**

9. ▢5 × 7 = 455

10. 248 × 3 = ▢44

11. $395 × ▢ = $2,370

12. 3,748 × 4 = $1▢,992

13. **Write Math** ▶ **Explain** how modeling partial products can be used to find the products of greater numbers.

Name ________________________________

Problem Solving Real World

14. Look at the picture. Kylie has 832 songs on her portable media player. Lance has 3 times as many songs. How many fewer songs can Lance add to his player than Kylie can add to hers?

Up To 9,000 Songs

Battery Life For Audio: 22 Hours

____

15. **Multi-Step** James wants to buy the new portable media player shown. He has 5 times as many songs as Susan. Susan has 1,146 songs. Will all of his songs fit on the portable media player? How many songs does James have?

____

16. **H.O.T.** **Multi-Step** The sum of a 3-digit number and a 1-digit number is 217. The product of the numbers is 642. If one number is between 200 and 225, what are the numbers?

____

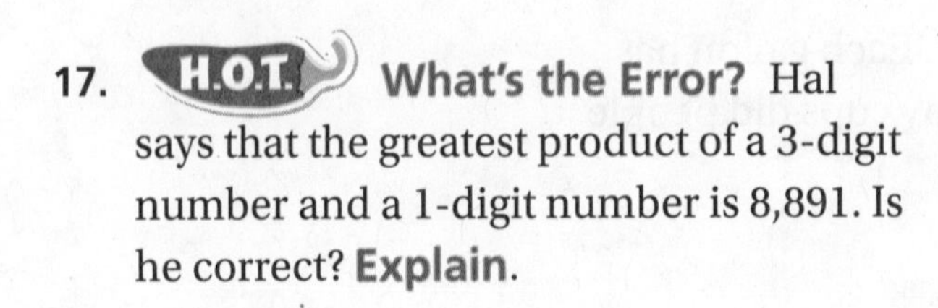

17. **H.O.T.** **What's the Error?** Hal says that the greatest product of a 3-digit number and a 1-digit number is 8,891. Is he correct? **Explain.**

____

____

Write Math ▶ **Show Your Work**

Daily Assessment Task

Fill in the bubble completely to show your answer.

18. A guide charges $128 to take a group of people on a tour of an island. How much will the guide charge to take 4 groups of the same size on tours?

Ⓐ $256
Ⓑ $412
Ⓒ $192
Ⓓ $512

19. Kalista works 164 hours each month. How many hours does she work in 8 months?

Ⓐ 1,282 hours
Ⓑ 1,312 hours
Ⓒ 1,476 hours
Ⓓ 1,600 hours

20. **Multi-Step** A trip from El Paso to Dallas, Texas, is 638 miles. A trip from Dallas to Atlanta, Georgia, is 780 miles. If you always go through Dallas, how long is a trip from El Paso to Atlanta and then back to El Paso?

Ⓐ 1,418 miles
Ⓑ 1,560 miles
Ⓒ 2,836 miles
Ⓓ 3,226 miles

TEXAS Test Prep

21. Mrs. Jackson bought 6 gallons of juice for a party. Each gallon has 16 cups. If 3 cups of juice were left over, how many cups did people drink at the party?

Ⓐ 93 cups
Ⓑ 48 cups
Ⓒ 78 cups
Ⓓ 13 cups

Homework and Practice

Name ______________________

7.5 Multiply Using Partial Products

Estimate. Then record the product.

1. Estimate: __________

$$\begin{array}{r} \$78 \\ \times \quad 7 \\ \hline \end{array}$$

2. Estimate: __________

$$\begin{array}{r} 351 \\ \times \quad 5 \\ \hline \end{array}$$

3. Estimate: __________

$$\begin{array}{r} 2{,}209 \\ \times \quad 4 \\ \hline \end{array}$$

4. 3×56

____

5. $6 \times \$315$

____

6. $8 \times 1{,}253$

____

Find the missing digit.

7.

$$\begin{array}{r} \square 2 \\ \times \quad 8 \\ \hline 576 \end{array}$$

8.

$$\begin{array}{r} 473 \\ \times \quad 2 \\ \hline \square 46 \end{array}$$

9.

$$\begin{array}{r} 3{,}051 \\ \times \quad \square \\ \hline 9{,}153 \end{array}$$

Problem Solving

Four friends are having a contest. They will see who is the first to load 8,000 songs on their media player.

10. Jeannie has loaded 467 songs. Paul has loaded 4 times as many songs as Jeannie. How many more songs has Paul loaded than Jeannie?

____

11. Juro has loaded 1,632 songs. Jessica has loaded 5 times as many. How many songs does Jessica have? Is it enough to win the contest? **Explain.**

____

____

Lesson Check

TEXAS Test Prep

Fill in the bubble completely to show your answer.

12. A store bought 9 cases of light bulbs. There are 48 light bulbs in a case. How many light bulbs does the store buy?

Ⓐ 108

Ⓑ 432

Ⓒ 362

Ⓓ 392

13. The Wilson family is flying to Dallas for a wedding. Airplane tickets cost $372 each. How much will 6 tickets cost?

Ⓐ $1,854

Ⓑ $2,022

Ⓒ $1,612

Ⓓ $2,232

14. Hugo drives 208 miles to and from work each week. How many miles does he drive in 4 weeks?

Ⓐ 112 miles

Ⓑ 1,120 miles

Ⓒ 832 miles

Ⓓ 8,032 miles

15. Which is the best estimate of the product of $4,306 \times 7$?

Ⓐ 2,800

Ⓑ 28,000

Ⓒ 2,100

Ⓓ 35,000

16. Multi-Step Coach Ramirez bought 8 cases of bottled water for a road race. There are 24 bottles in each case. After the race, 34 bottles of water were left. How many bottles were used at the race?

Ⓐ 192

Ⓑ 158

Ⓒ 248

Ⓓ 10

17. Multi-Step The sum of a three-digit number and a one-digit number is 160. The product of the two numbers is 624. What are the two numbers?

Ⓐ 156 and 4

Ⓑ 151 and 9

Ⓒ 78 and 8

Ⓓ 155 and 5

Name ______________________________

7.6 Multiply Using Mental Math

Essential Question How can you use mental math and properties to help you multiply numbers?

Unlock the Problem

Properties of Multiplication can make multiplication easier.

There are 4 sections of seats in the Playhouse Theater. Each section has 7 groups of seats. Each group has 25 seats. How many seats are there in the theater?

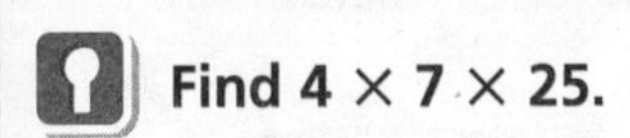

Find $4 \times 7 \times 25$.

$4 \times 7 \times 25 = 4 \times 25 \times 7$ Commutative Property

$= \_\_\_\_\_\_ \times 7$ Think: $4 \times 25 = 100$

$= \_\_\_\_\_\_$ Think: $100 \times 7 = 700$

So, there are 700 seats in the theater.

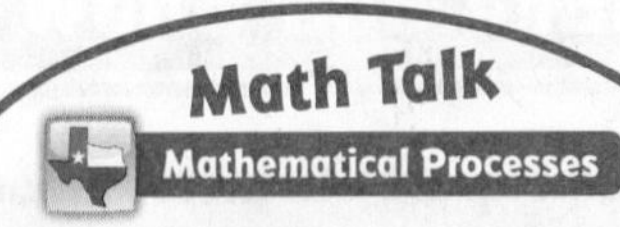

How could knowing 4×25 help you find 6×25?

Try This! **Use mental math and properties.**

A **Find $(6 \times 10) \times 10$.**

$(6 \times 10) \times 10 = 6 \times (10 \times 10)$ Associative Property

$= 6 \times \_\_\_\_\_\_$

$= \_\_\_\_\_\_$

B **Find $(4 \times 9) \times 250$.**

$(4 \times 9) \times 250 = 250 \times (4 \times 9)$ Commutative Property

$= (250 \times 4) \times 9$ Associative Property

$= \_\_\_\_\_\_ \times 9$

$= \_\_\_\_\_\_$

Remember

The Associative Property states that you can group factors in different ways and get the same product. Use parentheses to group the factors you multiply first.

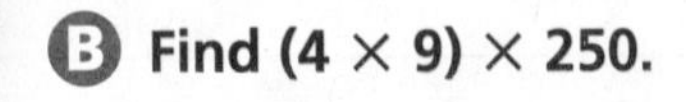

More Strategies Choose the strategy that works best with the numbers in the problems.

Examples

A Use addition.

Multiply. 4×625

Think: 625 is 600 plus 25.

$4 \times 625 = 4 \times (600 + 25)$

$= (4 \times 600) + (4 \times 25)$

$=$ ______ $+$ ______

$=$ ______

B Use subtraction.

Multiply. 5×398

Think: 398 is 2 less than 400.

$5 \times 398 = 5 \times (400 - 2)$

$= (5 \times$ ______ $) - (5 \times 2)$

$= 2{,}000 -$ ______

$=$ ______

Share and Show

1. Break apart the factor 112 to find 7×112 by using mental math and addition.

   $7 \times 112 = 7 \times ($ ______ $+ 12)$

   $=$ ____________

   $=$ ____________

   $=$ ____________

Math Talk

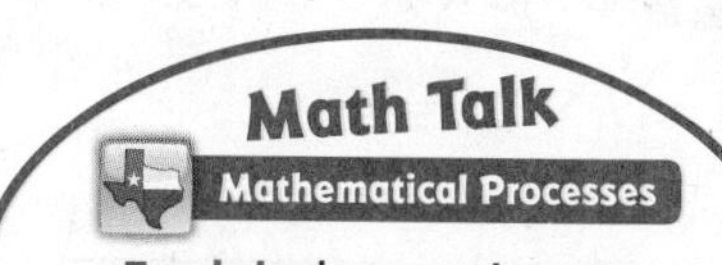

Explain how using an addition strategy is related to using a subtraction strategy.

Find the product. Tell which strategy you used.

2. $4 \times 6 \times 50$ ____________

3. 5×420 ____________

4. 6×298 ____________

Problem Solving

Practice: Copy and Solve **Use a strategy to find the product.**

5. 16×400

6. $3 \times 31 \times 10$

7. 3×199

8. $3 \times 1{,}021$

H.O.T. Algebra **Use mental math to find the unknown number.**

9. $21 \times 40 = 840$, so $21 \times 42 =$ ______.

10. $9 \times 60 = 540$, so $9 \times 59 =$ ______.

Name ________________________________

Problem Solving Real World

Use the table for 11–13.

Arena Ticket Prices Per Game

Section	Full Season	15-Game Plan	Gate Price
K	$44	$46	$48
L	$30	$32	$35
M	$25	$27	$30
N	$20	$22	$25

11. Three hundred people buy tickets at the gate for Section N. How much money is collected for Section N at the gate?

____

12. H.O.T. **Multi-Step Reasoning** When the full season tickets first went on sale, 2,000 Full Season tickets sold for Section N. Two weeks after the tickets first went on sale, another 1,500 full season tickets were sold for Section N. How much money was spent on full season tickets for Section N in total? How much more money was spent when the tickets first went on sale than after the first two weeks?

____

13. Tina and 3 of her friends buy the full season plan for Section M. If there are 45 games in the full season, how much money do they spend?

____

14. H.O.T. **Multi-Step What's the Error?** Louisa says that $40 \times 3{,}210$ is 12,840. **Describe** and correct her error.

____

____

____

____

Write Math ▶ **Show Your Work**

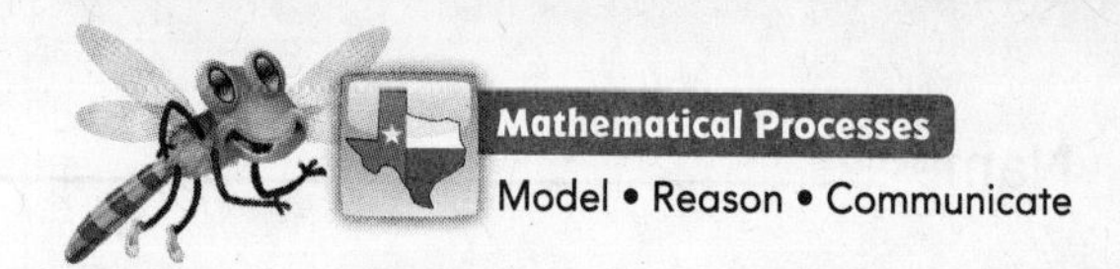

Daily Assessment Task

Fill in the bubble completely to show your answer.

15. A customer wants to buy 4 model sets for $109 each. Matt uses mental math to find the total cost. How much should Matt charge the customer?

Ⓐ $113
Ⓑ $409
Ⓒ $436
Ⓓ $440

16. There are 5 shelves for tennis balls. Each can holds 3 tennis balls. There are 20 cans on each shelf. The work below shows how Isabelle finds the total number of tennis balls. Which strategy does she use?

$$5 \times 3 \times 20 = 5 \times 20 \times 3$$
$$= 100 \times 3$$
$$= 300$$

Ⓐ Associative Property
Ⓑ Commutative Property
Ⓒ Distributive Property
Ⓓ Halving and Doubling

17. **Multi-Step** Mr. Jackson buys 5 boxes of clay for camp. Each box has 12 different color packs. Each pack costs $6. How much does Mr. Jackson spend on clay?

Ⓐ $72
Ⓑ $36
Ⓒ $30
Ⓓ $360

TEXAS Test Prep

18. Which of the following shows a strategy to use to find 3×198?

Ⓐ $(3 \times 200) - (3 \times 2)$
Ⓑ $(3 \times 200) + (3 \times 2)$
Ⓒ $(3 \times 198) - 6$
Ⓓ $198 - 6$

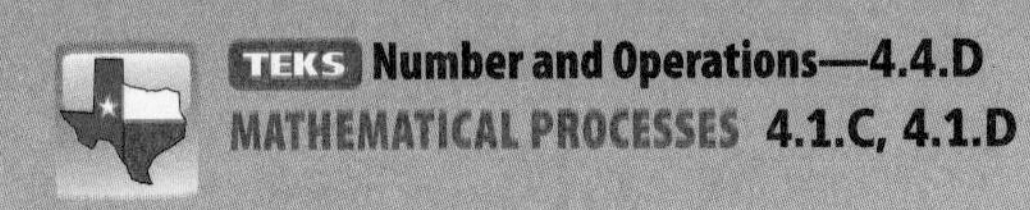

Homework and Practice

Name ______________________

7.6 Multiply Using Mental Math

Use a strategy to find the product.

1. $5 \times 75 \times 2 =$ ____________

2. $6 \times 302 =$ ____________

Use mental math to find the unknown number.

3. $7 \times 80 = 560$, so $14 \times 40 =$ ________

4. $32 \times 30 = 960$, so $32 \times 31 =$ ________

Problem Solving

Use the table for 5–7.

Orchestra Ticket Prices Per Concert		
Section	Season Ticket	Single Ticket
A	$50	$58
B	$40	$48

5. For the first concert, 300 people bought single tickets for section B. How much money was spent on single tickets?

____

6. Raoul buys 2 season tickets for section A. There are 14 concerts in the series. How much money does Raoul spend?

____

7. There are 248 section A season ticket holders and 304 section B season ticket holders at the second concert. How much money was spent by season ticket holders for the second concert?

____

Lesson Check

Fill in the bubble completely to show your answer.

8. Terrance found the product for 9×81 like this:

$$9 \times 81 = (9 \times 80) + (9 \times 1)$$
$$= 720 + 9 = 729$$

Which strategy did he use?

Ⓐ Commutative Property

Ⓑ Associative Property

Ⓒ Distributive Property

Ⓓ halving and doubling

9. Eileen multiplied $40 \times 88 = 3{,}520$. Which of the following has a product of 3,520?

Ⓐ 80×44

Ⓑ 20×44

Ⓒ 176×80

Ⓓ 176×40

10. The Smith's are selling some of their extra chairs. They are selling 4 chairs each for $125. How much will the Smith's make if they sell all the chairs?

Ⓐ $500

Ⓑ $400

Ⓒ $425

Ⓓ $575

11. There are 42 straws in a box. Nathan bought 5 boxes. How many straws did Nathan buy?

Ⓐ 220

Ⓑ 110

Ⓒ 210

Ⓓ 120

12. Multi-Step The science museum sells dinosaur models to schools and libraries for $107 each. The town library buys 3 dinosaur models. The town elementary school buys 5 models. What is the total cost of the models the town buys?

Ⓐ $567

Ⓑ $780

Ⓒ $136

Ⓓ $856

13. Multi-Step Kyle and Karen each bought 5 books of ride tickets at the fair. Each book has 15 tickets. How many tickets did they buy altogether?

Ⓐ 75

Ⓑ 150

Ⓒ 300

Ⓓ 200

Name ___________________________

7.7 PROBLEM SOLVING • Multi-Step Multiplication Problems

TEKS Number and Operations—4.4.D
Also 4.4.H
MATHEMATICAL PROCESSES
4.1.B, 4.1.C, 4.1.E, 4.1.F

Essential Question

When can you use the *draw a diagram* strategy to solve a multi-step multiplication problem?

Unlock the Problem Real World

At the sea park, one section in the stadium has 9 rows with 18 seats in each row. In the center of each of the first 6 rows, 8 seats are in the splash zone. How many seats are not in the splash zone?

Use the graphic organizer to help you solve the problem.

Read

What do I need to find?

I need to find the number of seats that ____________ in the splash zone.

What information am I given?

There are 9 rows with ____________ seats in each row of the section.

There are 6 rows with ____________ seats in each row of the splash zone.

Plan

What is my plan or strategy?

I can ____________ to find both the number of seats in the section and the number of seats in the splash zone.

Solve

I drew a diagram of the section to show 9 rows of 18 seats. In the center, I outlined a section to show the 6 rows of 8 seats in the splash zone.

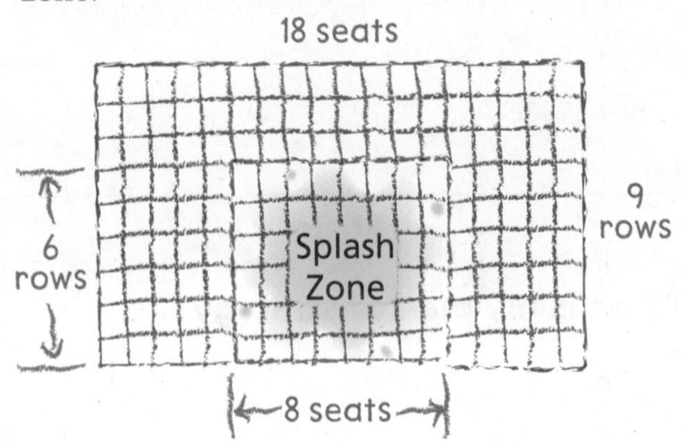

$$\begin{array}{r} 18 \\ \times\ 9 \\ \hline \end{array}$$ ← total number of seats in the section

$$\begin{array}{r} 8 \\ \times\ 6 \\ \hline \end{array}$$ ← seats in the splash zone

1. What else do you need to do to solve the problem?

____

____

Try Another Problem

At the sea park, one section of the shark theater has 8 rows with 14 seats in each row. In the middle of the section, 4 rows of 6 seats are reserved. How many seats are not reserved?

Read	Solve
What do I need to find?	
What information am I given?	
Plan	
What is my plan or strategy?	

2. How did your diagram help you solve the problem?

____

____

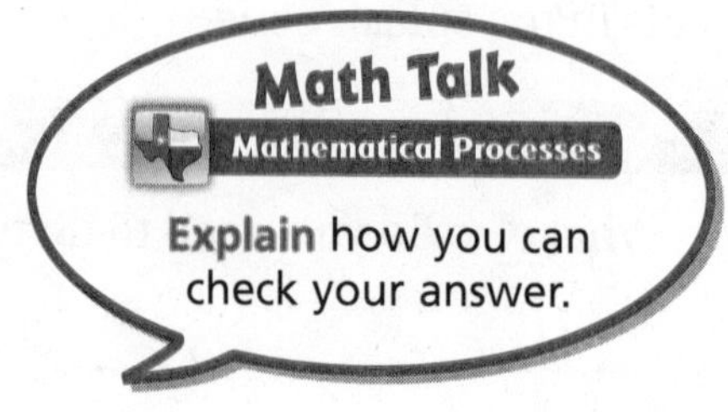

Name ______________________________

Share and Show

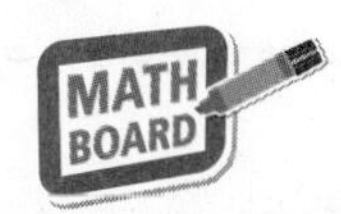

Unlock the Problem Tips

- ✓ Use the Problem Solving MathBoard.
- ✓ Underline important facts.
- ✓ Choose a strategy you know.

✓ 1. The seats in Sections A and B of the stadium are all taken. Section A has 8 rows of 14 seats each. Section B has 6 rows of 16 seats each. How many people are seated in Sections A and B?

First, draw and label a diagram. **Next**, find the number of seats in each section.

Section A　　Section B

Last, find the total number of seats. ________ + ________ = ________

There are ________ people seated in Sections A and B.

✓ 2. **What if** Sections A and B each had 7 rows? How many people would have been seated in Sections A and B?

____

Problem Solving

3. H.O.T. **Analyze** Carol, Ann, and Liz each bought a toy fish. Carol's fish is 10 inches longer than Ann's fish. Liz's fish is 2 inches longer than twice the length of Ann's fish. Ann's fish is 12 inches long. Find the length of each toy.

____

4. H.O.T. **Multi-Step** There are 8 rows of 22 chairs set up for an awards ceremony at the school. In each row, the 2 chairs on each end are reserved for students receiving awards. The rest of the chairs are for guests. How many chairs are there for guests?

____

Write Math ▶ Show Your Work

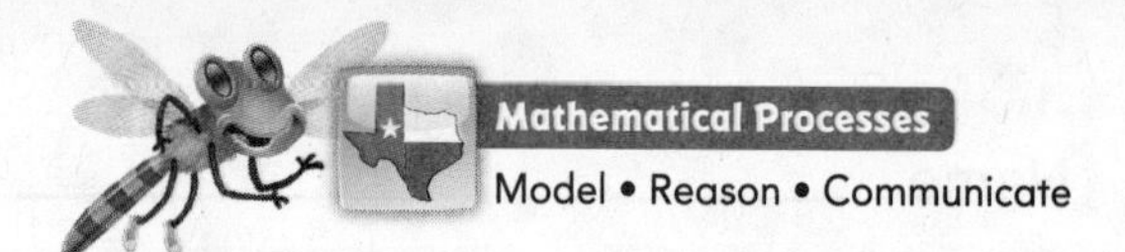

Daily Assessment Task

Fill in the bubble completely to show your answer.

5. **Multi-Step** In one night, a group of 5 mites lay 21 eggs each. A group of 4 mites lay 23 eggs each. How many more eggs did the first set of mites lay?

   Ⓐ 2
   Ⓑ 23
   Ⓒ 13
   Ⓓ 82

6. **Multi-Step** Students make holiday cards and thank you cards to sell at the school fair. They pack 6 boxes with 14 holiday cards in each box. They pack 8 boxes with 12 thank you cards in each box. How many cards do they pack in all?

   Ⓐ 84
   Ⓑ 180
   Ⓒ 96
   Ⓓ 12

7. **Multi-Step** Students and teachers build a new patio at the school. They lay 8 tiles in each of 13 rows. The center section has 7 rows of 4 tiles that are laid by teachers. The students lay the rest of the tiles. How many tiles do students lay?

   Ⓐ 104
   Ⓑ 132
   Ⓒ 76
   Ⓓ 28

TEXAS Test Prep

8. A teacher has 29 students in her class. She gives each student 3 stickers and has no stickers left over. How many stickers did she have?

   Ⓐ 78
   Ⓑ 67
   Ⓒ 87
   Ⓓ 88

TEKS Number and Operations—4.4.D
Also 4.4.H
MATHEMATICAL PROCESSES 4.1.B, 4.1.C, 4.1.E, 4.1.F

Name ______________________

7.7 Multi-Step Multiplication Problems

1. Mr. Snider is tiling a floor. The floor is 16 tiles long and 9 tiles wide. The center section is 12 tiles long and 5 tiles wide. How many tiles are in the border section?

   ____

2. Ben is reading a book that is 48 pages long. Joy is reading one that is 64 pages longer than Ben's. Terry is reading one that is twice as long as Joy's. How many pages are in Joy and Terry's books?

   ____

3. A flower bed has 26 rows of flowers and each row has 8 flowers. One section of the flower bed contains red flowers. There are 8 rows of red flowers. The rest of the flower bed is white flowers. How many white flowers are there?

   ____

4. Ginger sent 18 text messages yesterday. Jerry sent 4 more than twice as many messages as Ginger sent. Kyle sent 15 fewer messages than Jerry. How many text messages did Jerry and Kyle send?

   ____

5. A group of fans at a football game are sitting in 7 rows with 28 in each row. In the center, a section of 14 fans in 3 rows and a section of 11 fans in 3 rows have cards spelling out the team name. How many fans do not have a card?

   ____

6. Patti has some of her action figures in 6 boxes with 36 in each box. She has some in 4 boxes with 15 in each box. How many action figures does Patti have in her collection?

   ____

Lesson Check

TEXAS Test Prep

7. **Multi-Step** Eva sold 7 boxes of granola bars that have 24 bars in each. She sold 5 boxes of fruit bars that have 18 bars in each. How many bars did Eva sell?

   Ⓐ 258
   Ⓑ 42
   Ⓒ 504
   Ⓓ 158

8. **Multi-Step** Laura is making a necklace that is 5 rows of beads wide with 72 beads in each row. There is a center purple section that is 3 rows wide with 54 beads in each row. The rest of the beads are black. How many black beads are there?

   Ⓐ 208
   Ⓑ 198
   Ⓒ 162
   Ⓓ 360

9. **Multi-Step** Craig practiced his drums 4 hours more than twice the number of hours Nicki practiced. Nicki practiced 5 hours less than Marsha practiced. Marsha practiced for 16 hours. How many hours did Craig practice?

   Ⓐ 46 hours
   Ⓑ 40 hours
   Ⓒ 26 hours
   Ⓓ 36 hours

10. **Multi-Step** A quilt is made up of 400 squares. Each section is 16 squares long and 4 squares wide. There are 4 sections that are made of dotted red squares. The rest of the quilt is made of blue squares. How many blue squares are in the quilt?

    Ⓐ 144
    Ⓑ 336
    Ⓒ 256
    Ⓓ 224

11. **Multi-Step** Joyce has seven 12-ounce packages and three 24-ounce packages of frozen strawberries. How many ounces of frozen strawberries does Joyce have?

    Ⓐ 146 ounces
    Ⓑ 156 ounces
    Ⓒ 136 ounces
    Ⓓ 288 ounces

12. **Multi-Step** David planted his apple orchard in 6 rows with 22 trees in each row. He planted his almond orchard in 8 rows with 28 trees in each row. How many more almond trees than apple trees did David plant?

    Ⓐ 92
    Ⓑ 286
    Ⓒ 356
    Ⓓ 102

Name ______________________________

7.8 Multiply 3-Digit and 4-Digit Numbers with Regrouping

TEKS Number and Operations—4.4.D
Also 4.4.G
MATHEMATICAL PROCESSES
4.1.E, 4.1.F

Essential Question How can you use regrouping to multiply?

Unlock the Problem (Real World)

Alley Spring, in Missouri, produces an average of 567 million gallons of water per week. How many gallons of water do the springs produce in 3 weeks?

Multiply. 3×567

Estimate. $3 \times$ __________ = __________

THINK	RECORD
STEP 1 Multiply the ones. 3×7 ones = __________ ones Regroup the 21 ones.	$\overset{2}{567}$ $\times\ 3$ 1 Regroup the 21 ones as 2 tens and 1 one.
STEP 2 Multiply the tens. 3×6 tens = __________ tens Add the regrouped tens. 18 tens + 2 tens = 20 tens Regroup the 20 tens.	22 567 $\times\ 3$ 01 Regroup 20 tens as 2 hundreds 0 tens.
STEP 3 Multiply the hundreds. 3×5 hundreds = __________ hundreds Add the regrouped hundreds. 15 hundreds + 2 hundreds = 17 hundreds	22 567 $\times\ 3$ 1,701 17 hundreds is the same as 1 thousand 7 hundreds.

So, Alley Spring produces __________ gallons of water in 3 weeks.

Example

Use an estimate or an exact answer.

The table shows the prices of three vacation packages. Jake, his parents, and his sister want to choose a package.

Lakefront Vacations

	Adult	Child
Package A	$1,299	$619
Package B	$849	$699
Package C	$699	$484

A About how much would Package C cost Jake's family?

STEP 1

Estimate the cost for 2 adults.

$2 \times \$699$

↓

$2 \times \$700 =$ ______

STEP 2

Estimate the cost for 2 children.

$2 \times \$484$

↓

$2 \times \$500 =$ ______

STEP 3

Add to estimate the total cost.

$$\begin{array}{r} \square \\ + \square \\ \hline \square \end{array}$$

So, Package C would cost Jake's family about ______.

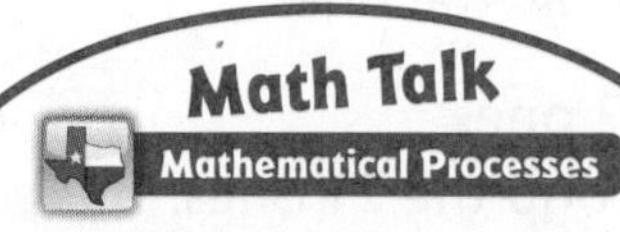

B Jake's family wants to compare the total costs of Packages A and C. Which plan costs more? How much more does it cost?

Package A

Adults	Children	Total Cost
$1,299 × 2 = ____	$619 × 2 = ____	____ + ____ = ____

Package C

Adults	Children	Total Cost
$699 × 2 = ____	$484 × 2 = ____	____ + ____ = ____

Subtract to compare the total costs of the packages.

$$\begin{array}{r} \$3,836 \\ -\ \$2,366 \\ \hline \square \end{array}$$

So, Package ______ would cost ______ more than Package ______.

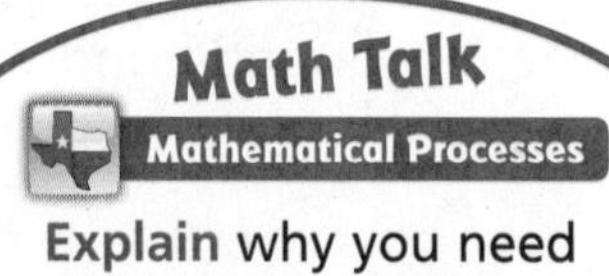

Name ______________________________

Share and Show

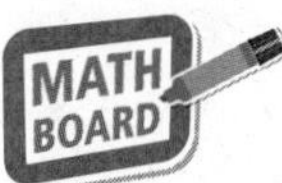

1. Tell what is happening in Step 1 of the problem.

STEP 1	STEP 2	STEP 3	STEP 4
2	42	1 42	1 42
1,274	1,274	1,274	1,274
× 6	× 6	× 6	× 6
4	44	644	7,644

____

____

Estimate. Then find the product.

2. Estimate: __________

$$\begin{array}{r} 603 \\ \times \quad 4 \\ \hline \end{array}$$

✓ 3. Estimate: __________

$$\begin{array}{r} 1,935 \\ \times \quad 7 \\ \hline \end{array}$$

✓ 4. Estimate: __________

$$\begin{array}{r} \$8,326 \\ \times \quad 5 \\ \hline \end{array}$$

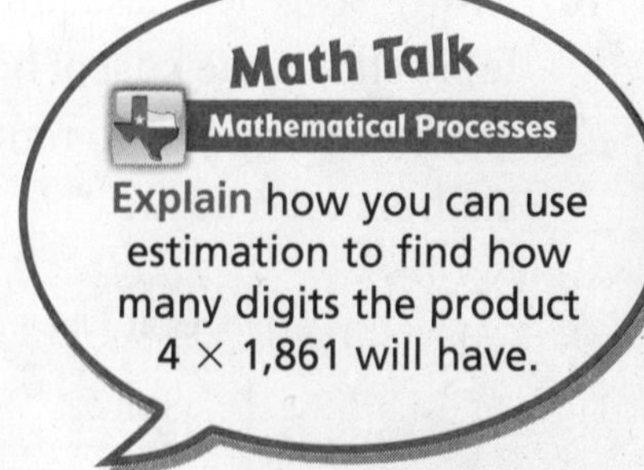

Problem Solving

5. Look at the table. About how many more people visited the park in 2007 than in 2000?

____

6. **H.O.T.** **Use Diagrams** Philadelphia, Pennsylvania, is 2,147 miles from Salt Lake City, Utah, and 2,868 miles from Portland, Oregon. What is the difference in the round-trip distances between Philadelphia and each of the other two cities? **Explain** whether you need an estimate or an exact answer.

____

____

Table Rock State Park Attendance

Year	Number of Visitors
2000	869,736
2007	1,160,031

7. **H.O.T.** **Sense or Nonsense? Multi-Step** Joe says that the product of a 4-digit number and a 1-digit number is always a 4-digit number. Does Joe's statement make sense? **Explain.**

____

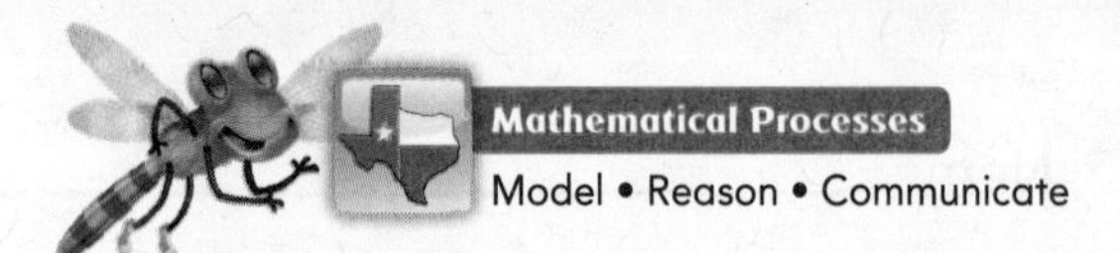

Daily Assessment Task

Fill in the bubble completely to show your answer.

8. Tissue paper comes in packages of 6 sheets. Ms. Rodriguez buys 225 packages of tissue paper. How many sheets of tissue paper does she buy?

Ⓐ 1,220 Ⓒ 1,320

Ⓑ 1,250 Ⓓ 1,350

9. Dan has 1,398 sports cards. Mason has 3 times as many sports cards as Dan. How many sports cards does Mason have?

Ⓐ 4,194 Ⓒ 1,401

Ⓑ 3,974 Ⓓ 466

10. Multi-Step Kayla's family wants to rent a boat for 4 days. The table shows the cost of boats for 1 day. How much more will Kayla's family pay to rent a ski boat for 4 days than to rent a sailboat for 4 days?

Boat Type	Cost for 1 Day
Sailboat	$225
Fishing boat	$210
Ski boat	$288

Ⓐ $63 Ⓒ $900

Ⓑ $252 Ⓓ $1,152

TEXAS Test Prep

11. What number is 150 more than the product of 5 and 4,892?

Ⓐ 24,610

Ⓑ 24,160

Ⓒ 25,610

Ⓓ 24,061

Name ______________________________

7.8 Multiply 3-Digit and 4-Digit Numbers with Regrouping

Estimate. Then find the product.

1. Estimate: ______________

$$\begin{array}{r} 887 \\ \times \quad 6 \\ \hline \end{array}$$

2. Estimate: ______________

$$\begin{array}{r} 2{,}309 \\ \times \quad 8 \\ \hline \end{array}$$

3. Estimate: ______________

$$\begin{array}{r} \$7{,}155 \\ \times \quad 3 \\ \hline \end{array}$$

Problem Solving

4. It is 1,748 miles from Dan's home in Austin, Texas to his sister's home in San Jose, California. It is 1,174 miles to his brother's home near Minneapolis, Minnesota. How many miles more is the trip there and back to Dan's sister's home than the trip there and back to to his brother's home?

____

____

____

5. A theater seats 378 people. There are 2 shows each weekend for 4 weekends. If all of the seats are sold for all performances, how many people will see the shows? Explain whether you need an estimate or an exact answer.

____

____

____

6. Emma says that the product of a 3-digit number and a 1-digit number will be either a 3-digit number or a 4-digit number. Does Emma's statement make sense? **Explain.**

____

____

____

Lesson Check

★ TEXAS Test Prep

Fill in the bubble completely to show your answer.

7. It takes Earth 365 days to orbit the sun. How many days does it take Earth to orbit the sun 3 times?

Ⓐ 1,095 days

Ⓑ 985 days

Ⓒ 995 days

Ⓓ 1,185 days

8. Denver, Colorado is 5,280 feet above sea level. How many feet above sea level is a mountain peak that is 4 times higher above sea level?

Ⓐ 20,820 feet

Ⓑ 5,284 feet

Ⓒ 21,120 feet

Ⓓ 26,140 feet

9. How many thousands are in the estimated product of $4 \times 6{,}817$?

Ⓐ 22

Ⓑ 14

Ⓒ 10

Ⓓ 28

10. Between which two numbers is the product of 9×452?

Ⓐ 3,600 and 4,500

Ⓑ 3,000 and 4,000

Ⓒ 4,800 and 5,400

Ⓓ 2,700 and 3,600

11. **Multi-Step** The secret code for a math competition is 382 less than 5 times 861. What is the code?

Ⓐ 2,771

Ⓑ 4,687

Ⓒ 3,923

Ⓓ 1,049

12. **Multi-Step** Airplane tickets to Fairbanks, Alaska will cost $958 each. Airplane tickets to Vancouver, Canada will cost $734. How much can the four members of the Harrison family save on airfare by vacationing in Vancouver?

Ⓐ $896

Ⓑ $2,936

Ⓒ $224

Ⓓ $906

Name ____________________

Module 7 Assessment

Vocabulary

Choose the best term from the box to complete the sentence.

Vocabulary
Distributive Property
factor
partial products

1. To find the product of a two-digit number and a 1-digit number, you can multiply the tens, multiply the ones, and find the sum of each ____________. (p. 230)

2. The ____________ states that multiplying a sum by a number is the same as multiplying each addend by the number and then adding the products. (p. 229)

Concepts and Skills

Find the product. TEKS 4.4.B

3. $6 \times 10 =$ ________
4. $7 \times 100 =$ ________
5. $9 \times 300 =$ ________
6. $8 \times 7{,}000 =$ ________

Use grid paper or base-ten blocks to model the product. Then record the product. TEKS 4.4.D

7. $6 \times 15 =$ ________
8. $3 \times 18 =$ ________
9. $9 \times 15 =$ ________
10. $8 \times 17 =$ ________

Record the product. Use expanded form to help. TEKS 4.4.D

11. $5 \times 64 =$ ________
12. $3 \times 272 =$ ________

Estimate. Then record the product. TEKS 4.4.D, 4.4.G

13. Estimate: ______
$$\begin{array}{r} 75 \\ \times\ 5 \\ \hline \end{array}$$

14. Estimate: ______
$$\begin{array}{r} 647 \\ \times\ 6 \\ \hline \end{array}$$

15. Estimate: ______
$$\begin{array}{r} 5{,}763 \\ \times\ 3 \\ \hline \end{array}$$

16. Estimate: ______
$$\begin{array}{r} \$4{,}362 \\ \times\ 6 \\ \hline \end{array}$$

Jse a strategy to find the product. TEKS 4.4.D

17. $3 \times 6 \times 10$ ______
18. 12×50 ______
19. 5×115 ______
20. 8×120 ______

Fill in the bubble completely to show your answer.

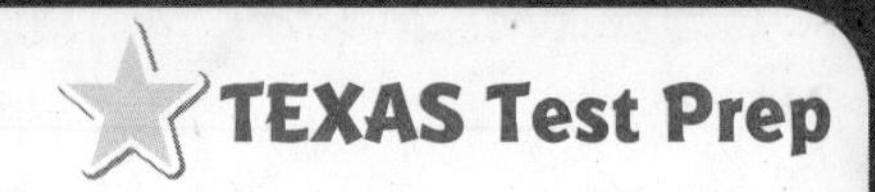

21. Sunset School had 4 performances of their school play during the first week. The auditorium can seat 2,518 people and all of the seats at each performance were filled. During the second week, 7,450 people attended the play. How many people saw the play during the two weeks? TEKS 4.4.D

Ⓐ 10,072
Ⓑ 4,932
Ⓒ 9,968
Ⓓ 17,522

22. The table below shows the number of calories in 1 cup of different kinds of berries. How many more calories are in 4 cups of blackberries than in 4 cups of strawberries? TEKS 4.4.D

Berry Nutrition

Berry	Number of Calories in 1 Cup
Blackberries	62
Blueberries	83
Raspberries	64
Strawberries	46

Ⓐ 16
Ⓑ 184
Ⓒ 64
Ⓓ 248

23. The skating rink rents 184 pairs of skates in a month. About how many pairs of skates does the rink rent in 4 months? TEKS 4.4.G

Record your answer and fill in the bubbles on the grid. Be sure to use the correct place value.

			.		
⓪	⓪	⓪		⓪	⓪
①	①	①		①	①
②	②	②		②	②
③	③	③		③	③
④	④	④		④	④
⑤	⑤	⑤		⑤	⑤
⑥	⑥	⑥		⑥	⑥
⑦	⑦	⑦		⑦	⑦
⑧	⑧	⑧		⑧	⑧
⑨	⑨	⑨		⑨	⑨

Name ______________________________

TEKS Number and Operations—4.4.B
Also 4.4.D
MATHEMATICAL PROCESSES
4.1.C, 4.1.F

8.1 Multiply by Tens

Essential Question

What strategies can you use to multiply by tens?

Unlock the Problem

Real World

Animation for a computer-drawn cartoon requires about 20 frames per second. How many frames would need to be drawn for a 30-second cartoon?

- The phrase "20 frames per second" means 20 frames are needed for each second of animation. How does this help you know what operation to use?

____

____

One Way Use place value.

Multiply. 20×30

You can think of 30 as 3 tens.

$20 \times 30 = 20 \times$ ______ tens

$=$ ______ tens

$= 600$

Remember

The Associative Property states that you can group factors in different ways and get the same product. Use parentheses to group the factors you multiply first.

Another Way Use the Associative Property.

You can think of 30 as 3×10.

$20 \times 30 = 20 \times (3 \times 10)$

$= (20 \times 3) \times 10$

$=$ ______ $\times$ ______

$=$ ______

So, ______ frames would need to be drawn.

Math Talk

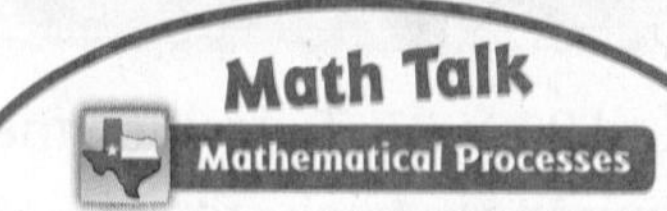

Mathematical Processes

How can you use place value to tell why $60 \times 10 = 600$? Explain.

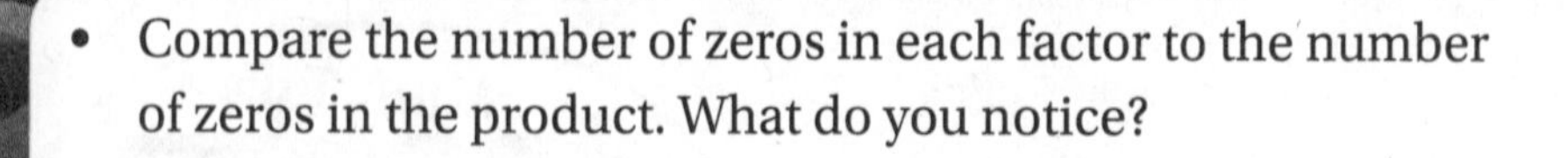

- Compare the number of zeros in each factor to the number of zeros in the product. What do you notice?

____

____

Another Way

Use mental math to find 14×30.

Use the halving-and-doubling strategy.

STEP 1 Find half of 14 to make the problem simpler.

Think: To find half of a number, divide by 2.

$14 \div 2 =$ ________

STEP 2 Multiply.

$7 \times 30 =$ ________

STEP 3 Double 210.

Think: To double a number, multiply by 2.

$2 \times 210 =$ ________

So, $14 \times 30 = 420$.

Try This! **Multiply.**

Use mental math to find 12×40.

Use place value to find 12×40.

Share and Show

1. Find 20×27. Tell which method you chose. **Explain** what happens in each step.

____

____

Choose a method. Then find the product.

2. 10×12
3. 20×20
4. 40×24
5. 11×60

Math Talk

Mathematical Processes

Explain how you can use $30 \times 10 = 300$ to find 30×12.

Name ______________________

Problem Solving

Algebra **Find the unknown digit in the number.**

6. $64 \times 40 = 2{,}56$■

■ = ______

7. $29 \times 50 = 1{,}$⬟50

⬟ = ______

8. 3◆ $\times 47 = 1{,}410$

◆ = ______

Problem Solving

Use the table for 9–10.

Title	Date Released	Frames per Second
The Enchanted Drawing©	1900	20
Little Nemo©	1911	16
Snow White and the Seven Dwarfs©	1937	24
Pinocchio©	1940	19
The Flintstones™	1960–1966	24

9. How many frames did it take to produce 50 seconds of *Pinocchio*?

____

10. Are there fewer frames in 10 seconds of *The Flintstones* or in 14 seconds of *The Enchanted Drawing*? What is the difference in the number of frames?

____

11. H.O.T. The product of my number and twice my number is 128. What is half my number? **Explain** how you solved the problem.

____

____

____

Write Math ▶ **Show Your Work**

12. H.O.T. **Multi-Step** **What's the Error?** Tanya says that the product of a multiple of ten and a multiple of ten will always have only one zero. Is she correct? **Explain.**

____

____

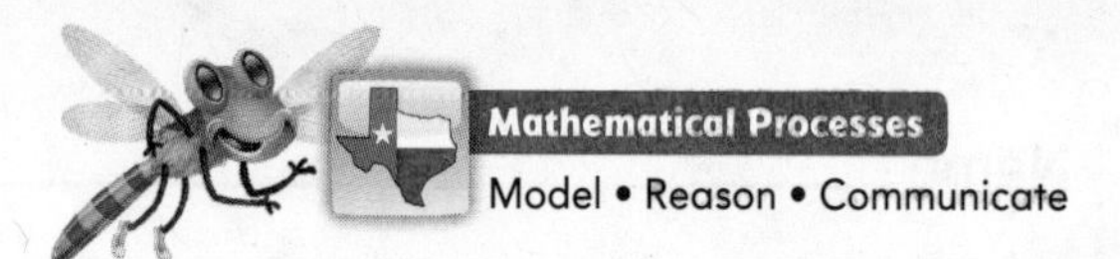

Daily Assessment Task

Fill in the bubble completely to show your answer.

13. A giant kelp plant can grow 60 centimeters per day. About how much can it grow in 30 days?

Ⓐ 180 centimeters

Ⓑ 18,000 centimeters

Ⓒ 1,800 centimeters

Ⓓ 1,200 centimeters

14. Mrs. Sanchez drives a total of 50 miles for work each day. How many miles does she drive in 42 days?

Ⓐ 2,000 miles

Ⓑ 2,010 miles

Ⓒ 210 miles

Ⓓ 2,100 miles

15. **Multi-Step** Alison is getting ready for a math contest. Each day, she works on multiplication problems for 20 minutes and division problems for 10 minutes. How many minutes does Alison practice multiplication and division problems in 15 days?

Ⓐ 300 minutes

Ⓑ 150 minutes

Ⓒ 350 minutes

Ⓓ 450 minutes

TEXAS Test Prep

16. Luis jogs 10 miles a week. He bikes 20 miles a week. How far will he have jogged in 26 weeks?

Ⓐ 30 miles

Ⓑ 200 miles

Ⓒ 260 miles

Ⓓ 520 miles

TEKS Number and Operations—4.4.B
Also 4.4.D
MATHEMATICAL PROCESSES 4.1.C, 4.1.F

Name ______________________

8.1 Multiply by Tens

Choose a method. Then find the product.

1. $30 \times 40 =$ ______
2. $16 \times 20 =$ ______
3. $50 \times 11 =$ ______

Find the unknown digit in the number.

4. $54 \times 30 = 162$■
5. $36 \times 40 = 1$⬟40
6. 2◆ $\times 62 = 1{,}240$

■ = ______ ⬟ = ______ ◆ = ______

Problem Solving

Use the table for 7–8.

Sign Up Now for Lessons!

Sport	Lesson Length (in minutes)
Tennis	40
Golf	60
Swimming	50

7. The tennis instructor teaches 20 lessons each week. How many minutes does she teach?

____

8. Last month, the golf teacher taught 32 lessons. The swimming teacher taught 40 lessons. Which teacher taught for the most minutes? What is the difference in the number of minutes?

____

____

9. The product of half my number times my number is 162. What is twice my number? **Explain** how you solved the problem.

____

____

____

Lesson Check

TEXAS Test Prep

Fill in the bubble completely to show your answer.

10. Julian practices his trombone 30 minutes each day. How many minutes does he practice in 31 days?

    Ⓐ 1,200 minutes
    Ⓑ 610 minutes
    Ⓒ 930 minutes
    Ⓓ 630 minutes

11. There are 50 lollipops in a bag. How many lollipops are there in 12 bags?

    Ⓐ 600
    Ⓑ 512
    Ⓒ 1,100
    Ⓓ 520

12. A factory makes 80 bicycles a day. How many bicycles do they make in 22 days?

    Ⓐ 320
    Ⓑ 1,760
    Ⓒ 1,660
    Ⓓ 844

13. Malala has 20 vases. She puts 12 flowers in each vase. How many flowers does she use?

    Ⓐ 24
    Ⓑ 144
    Ⓒ 440
    Ⓓ 240

14. **Multi-Step** Caroline packs 12 jars of jam in a box. She has 40 boxes. She has 542 jars of jam. How many jars of jam will she have left when all the boxes are full?

    Ⓐ 62
    Ⓑ 42
    Ⓒ 52
    Ⓓ 72

15. **Multi-Step** Sam is going to make 30 copies of the book of puzzles he wrote. The book has 18 pages. He has 500 sheets of paper. How many more sheets of paper does he need?

    Ⓐ 30
    Ⓑ 140
    Ⓒ 40
    Ⓓ 130

Name ________________________________

8.2 Estimate Products

TEKS Number and Operations—4.4.G
Also 4.4.D

MATHEMATICAL PROCESSES
4.1.A, 4.1.G

Essential Question What strategies can you use to estimate products?

Unlock the Problem (Real World)

The Smith family opens the door of their refrigerator 32 times in one day. There are 31 days in May. About how many times is it opened in May?

- Underline any information you will need.

One Way Use rounding and mental math.

Estimate. 32×31

STEP 1 Round each factor.

32×31

↓ ↓

30×30

STEP 2 Use mental math.

$3 \times 3 = 9$ ← basic fact

$30 \times 30 =$ ______

So, the Smith family opens the refrigerator door about 900 times during the month of May.

All 24 light bulbs in the Park family's home are CFL light bulbs. Each CFL light bulb uses 28 watts to produce light. About how many watts will the light bulbs use when turned on all at the same time?

Another Way Use mental math and compatible numbers.

Compatible numbers are numbers that are easy to compute mentally.

Estimate. 24×28

STEP 1 Use compatible numbers.

24×28

↓ ↓

25×30 Think: $25 \times 3 = 75$

STEP 2 Use mental math.

$25 \times 3 = 75$

$25 \times 30 =$ ______

So, about 750 watts are used.

Try This! **Estimate 26 × $79.**

A Round to the nearest ten

26 × $79

↓ ↓

_____ × _____ = _____

26 × $79 is about _____.

B Compatible numbers

26 × $79

↓ ↓

25 × $80 = _____

Think: How can you use 25 × 4 = 100 to help find 25 × 8?

26 × $79 is about _____.

Share and Show

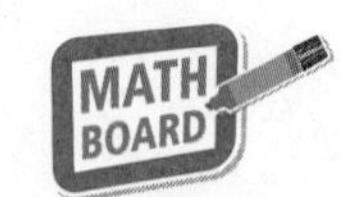

1. To estimate the product of 62 and 28 by rounding, how would you round the factors? What would the estimated product be?

_____

Estimate the product. Choose a method.

2. 96 × 34

3. 47 × $39

4. 78 × 72

Math Talk
Mathematical Processes
Describe how you know if an estimated product will be greater than or less than the exact answer.

Problem Solving

Practice: Copy and Solve **Estimate the product. Choose a method.**

5. 61 × 31

6. 52 × 68

7. 26 × 44

8. 57 × $69

9. 55 × 39

10. 51 × 81

11. 47 × $32

12. 49 × 64

Find two possible factors for the estimated product.

13. 2,800 _____

14. 8,100 _____

15. 5,600 _____

16. 2,400 _____

Name ______________________________

Problem Solving Real World

17. Apply On average, a refrigerator door is opened 38 times each day. Len has two refrigerators in his house. Based on this average, about how many times in a 3-week period are the refrigerator doors opened?

____

18. The cost to run a refrigerator is about $57 each year. About how much will it have cost to run by the time it is 15 years old?

____

19. H.O.T. **Multi-Step** If Mel opens his refrigerator door 36 times every day, about how many times will it be opened in April? Will the exact answer be more than or less than the estimate? **Explain.**

____

____

____

____

Write Math ▶ **Show Your Work**

20. H.O.T. **Explain** why $2,400 and $2,000 are both reasonable estimates for problems A and B below Try This! on page 274.

____

____

____

21. H.O.T. **What's the Question?** The estimated product of two numbers, that are not multiples of ten, is 2,800.

____

____

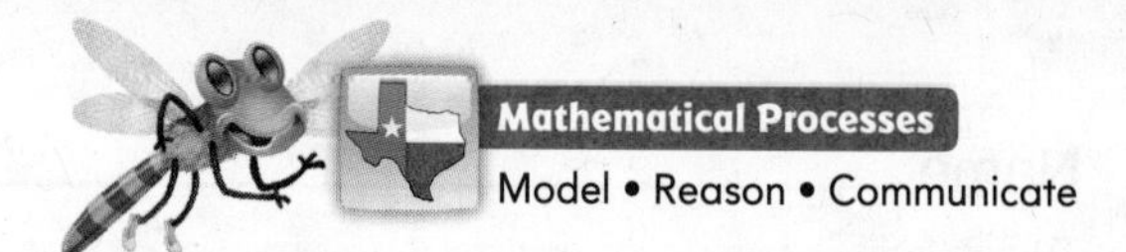

Daily Assessment Task

Fill in the bubble completely to show your answer.

22. A scientist watches a thorny dragon eat ants for 32 minutes. It eats at a rate of up to 45 ants every minute. At this rate, about how many ants does the thorny dragon eat in 32 minutes?

Ⓐ 2,000 ants

Ⓑ 1,500 ants

Ⓒ 1,600 ants

Ⓓ 150 ants

23. Denise uses 24 beads to make 1 beaded necklace. About how many beads does she need to make 42 beaded necklaces?

Ⓐ 1,500 beads

Ⓑ 100 beads

Ⓒ 800 beads

Ⓓ 150 beads

24. **Multi-Step** Mr. Parker jogs for 35 minutes each day. He jogs 5 days in week 1, 6 days in week 2, and 7 days in week 3. About how many minutes does he jog?

Ⓐ 400 minutes

Ⓑ 350 minutes

Ⓒ 200 minutes

Ⓓ 800 minutes

TEXAS Test Prep

25. Which is the best estimate for the product 75×23?

Ⓐ 2,600

Ⓑ 2,200

Ⓒ 160

Ⓓ 1,600

TEKS Number and Operations—4.4.G
Also 4.4.D
MATHEMATICAL PROCESSES 4.1.A, 4.1.G

Name ______________________

8.2 Estimate Products

Estimate the product. Choose a method.

1. 42 × 28 ________

2. 95 × 33 ________

3. 61 × 58 ________

4. 77 × 13 ________

Find two possible factors for the estimated product.

5. 1,600 ________

6. 4,500 ________

7. 6,000 ________

8. 3,200 ________

Problem Solving

9. A bus holds 58 people. For the last away game, 27 bus loads of fans traveled to the game. About how many fans went to the game on the buses?

____

10. The fence posts along Tom's driveway are 96 inches apart. There are 32 fence posts. About how many inches long is the fence?

____

11. Will the exact answer to Problem 9 be more than or less than the estimate? **Explain.**

____

____

12. Nona used compatible numbers to estimate that 25 × 42 is about 1,000. Gerry rounded and estimated that the product is about 1,200. Which estimate is closest to the exact answer? **Explain.**

____

____

____

Lesson Check

TEXAS Test Prep

Fill in the bubble completely to show your answer.

13. Which is the best estimate for the product of 26 × 78?

Ⓐ 2,400

Ⓑ 1,600

Ⓒ 2,000

Ⓓ 1,400

14. For which two factors is the product closest to 4,800?

Ⓐ 24 × 24

Ⓑ 56 × 83

Ⓒ 47 × 66

Ⓓ 92 × 38

15. A store has 12 rows of eye glasses in a display. There are 27 pairs of glasses in each row. Which estimate is closest to the number of pairs of glasses in the store's display?

Ⓐ 300

Ⓑ 240

Ⓒ 360

Ⓓ 200

16. A factory uses 28 screws for each bookcase they make. In one day, they produce 44 bookcases. About how many screws are needed each day?

Ⓐ 1,500

Ⓑ 1,000

Ⓒ 800

Ⓓ 1,200

17. **Multi-Step** A theater has 17 rows of seats on the floor and 11 rows of seats in the balcony. There are 55 seats in each row. Which is the best estimate of the total number of seats in the theater?

Ⓐ 180

Ⓑ 1,500

Ⓒ 2,400

Ⓓ 1,800

18. **Multi-Step** There are 48 beads in a package. Mariah bought 4 packages of blue, 9 packages of gold, 6 packages of red, and 2 packages of silver beads. Which is the best estimate of the total number of beads she bought?

Ⓐ 1,000

Ⓑ 800

Ⓒ 1,200

Ⓓ 2,400

Name ___________________________

Area Models and Partial Products

TEKS Number and Operations—4.4.C
Also 4.4.D, 4.4.H
MATHEMATICAL PROCESSES
4.1.C, 4.1.D

Essential Question How can you use area models and partial products to multiply 2-digit numbers?

Investigate

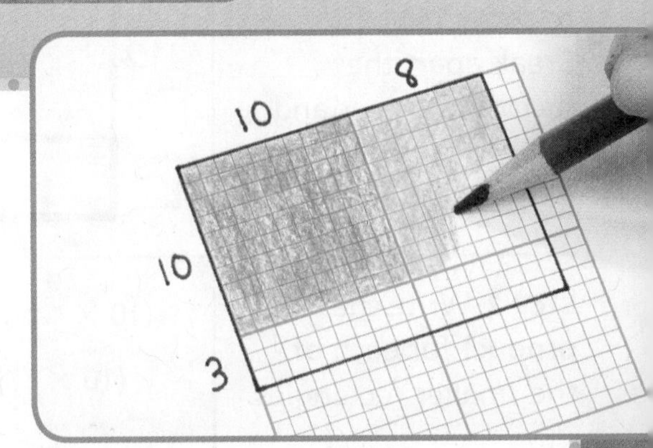

Materials ■ color pencils

How can you use a model to break apart factors and make them easier to multiply?

A. Outline a rectangle on the grid to model 13 × 18. Break apart the model into smaller rectangles to show factors broken into tens and ones. Label and shade the smaller rectangles. Use the colors below.

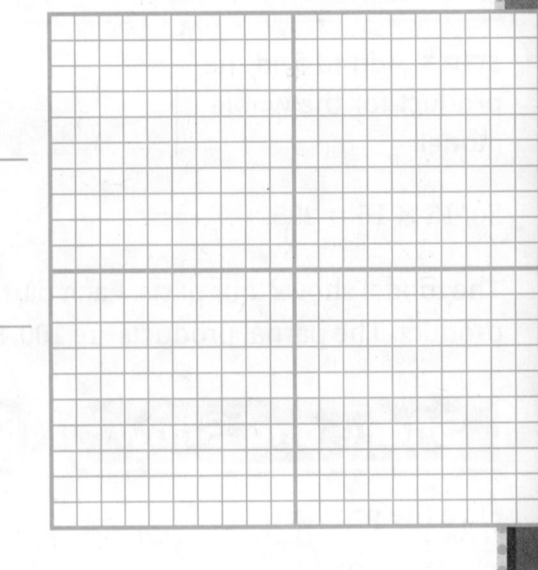

B. Find the product of each smaller rectangle. Then, find the sum of the partial products. Record your answers.

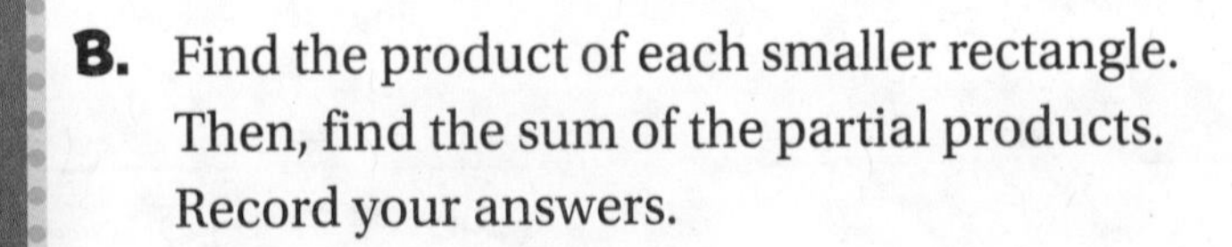

$\_\_\_ = 10 \times 10$

$\_\_\_ = 10 \times 8$

$\_\_\_ = 3 \times 10$

$\_\_\_ = 3 \times 8$

100 + ____ + ____ + ____ = ____

C. Draw the model again. Break apart the whole model to show factors different from those shown the first time. Label and shade the four smaller rectangles and find their products. Record the sum of the partial products to represent the product of the whole model.

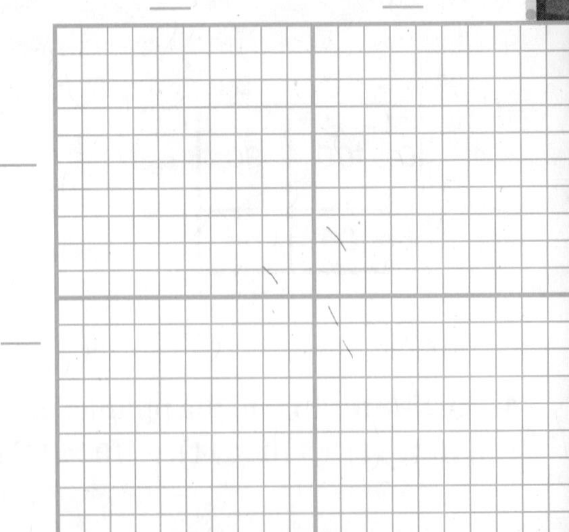

____ + ____ + ____ + ____ = ____

Make Connections

You can draw a simple diagram to model and break apart factors to find a product. Find 15 × 15.

Math Idea

A **perfect square** is a number that has the same number as its two factors. 144 is a perfect square since both of its factors are 12.

STEP 1 Draw a model to show 15 × 15. Break apart the factors into tens and ones to show the partial products.

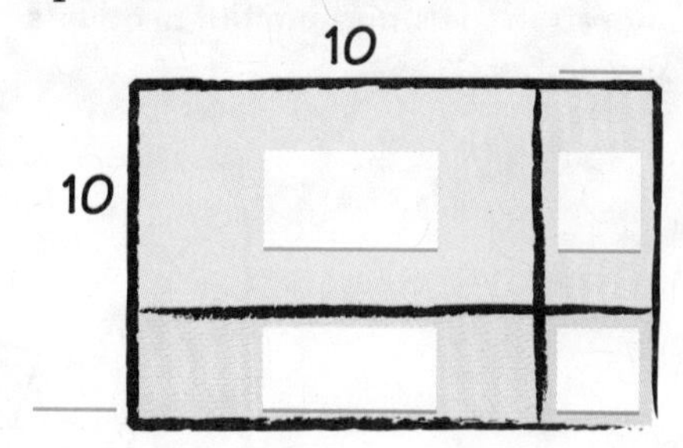

STEP 2 Write the product for each of the smaller rectangles.

(10 × 1 tens)	(10 × 5 ones)	(5 × 1 tens)	(5 × 5 ones)
(10 × 10)	(10 × 5)	(5 × 10)	(5 × 5)

STEP 3 Add to find the product for the whole model.

___ + ___ + ___ + ___ = ___

So, 15 × 15 = 225.

The model shows four parts. Each part represents a partial product. The partial products are 100, 50, 50, and 25.

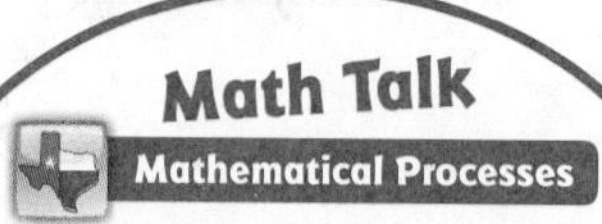

Explain how breaking apart the factors of a perfect square into tens and ones makes finding the product easier.

Share and Show

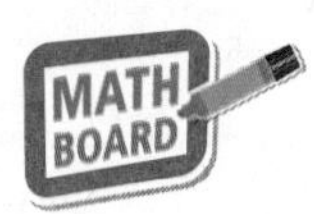

Find the product.

1. 16 × 19 = ___

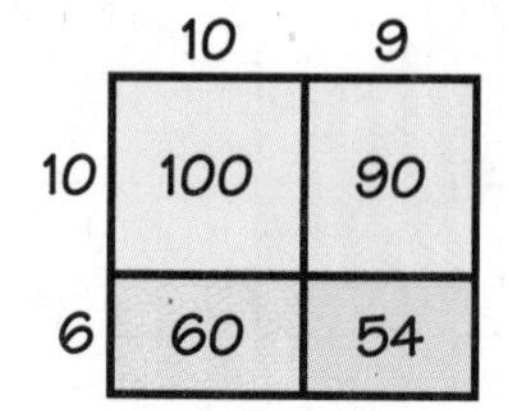

2. 18 × 26 = ___

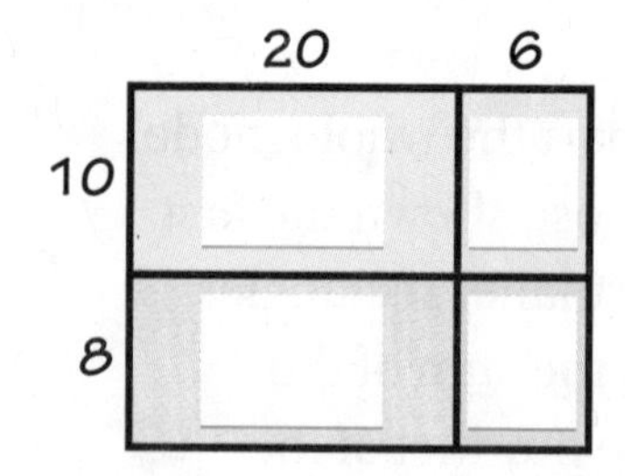

3. 27 × 39 = ___

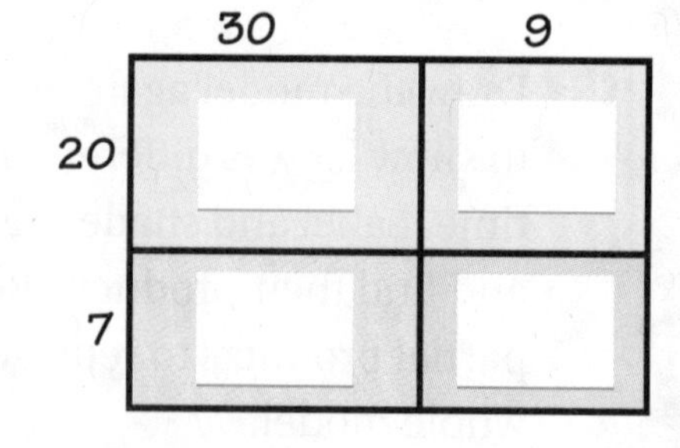

4. Evaluate To find the product of 10 and 33, which is the easier computation, (10 × 11) + (10 × 11) + (10 × 11) or (10 × 30) + (10 × 3)? **Explain.**

___

___

Name ______________________________

Problem Solving

Multi-Step **Sense or Nonsense?**

5. Jamal and Kim used different ways to solve 12×15 by using partial products. Whose answer makes sense? Whose answer is nonsense? **Explain** your reasoning.

Jamal's Work

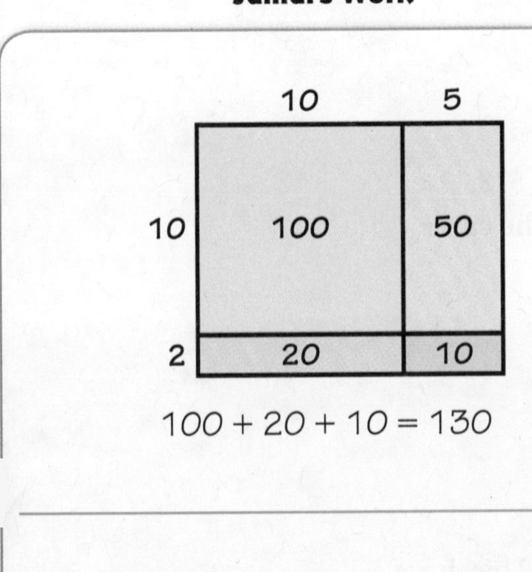

Kim's Work

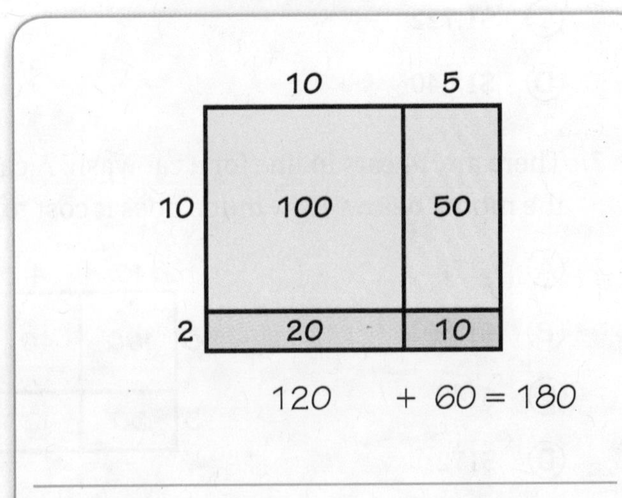

a. For the answer that is nonsense, write an answer that makes sense.

b. **H.O.T.** **Use Diagrams** Look at Kim's method. Can you think of another way Kim could use the model to find the product? **Explain.**

10 5
10 100 50
2 20 10

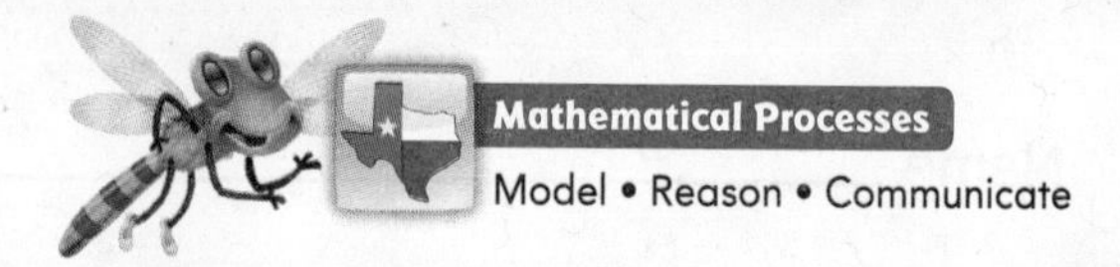

Daily Assessment Task

Fill in the bubble completely to show your answer.

6. A restaurant buys 21 cube-shaped watermelons. Each watermelon costs $82. How much does the restaurant pay for the watermelons?

   Ⓐ $1,720

   Ⓑ $1,680

   Ⓒ $1,722

   Ⓓ $1,640

7. There are 14 cars in line for a car wash. A car wash costs $13. Use the model below. How much does it cost to wash all of the cars?

   Ⓐ $170

   Ⓑ $182

   Ⓒ $142

   Ⓓ $172

	10	4
10	100	40
3	30	12

8. **Multi-Step** Students sell muffins at a school bake sale. They have 12 muffins in each of 15 boxes. They sell 125 muffins. How many muffins are left?

   Ⓐ 65 muffins

   Ⓑ 5 muffins

   Ⓒ 45 muffins

   Ⓓ 55 muffins

TEXAS Test Prep

9. The cost of a ski-lift ticket is $31. How much will 17 tickets cost?

   Ⓐ $48

   Ⓑ $527

   Ⓒ $310

   Ⓓ $217

Homework and Practice

TEKS Number and Operations—4.4.C
Also 4.4.D, 4.4.H
MATHEMATICAL PROCESSES 4.1.C, 4.1.D

Name ________________________

8.3 Area Models and Partial Products

Find the product.

1. $14 \times 18 =$ ______

	10	8
10	100	80
4	40	32

2. $32 \times 16 =$ ______

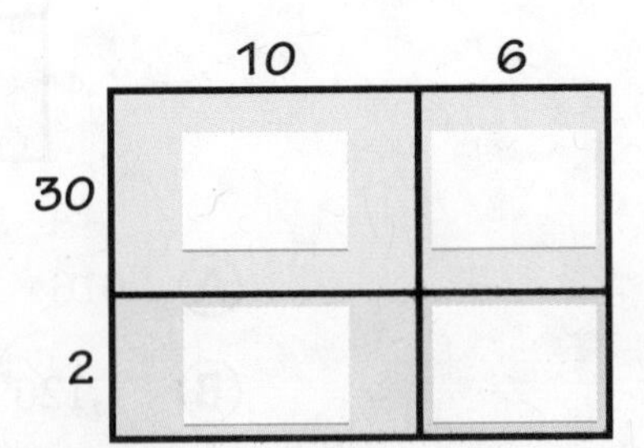

3. $26 \times 22 =$ ______

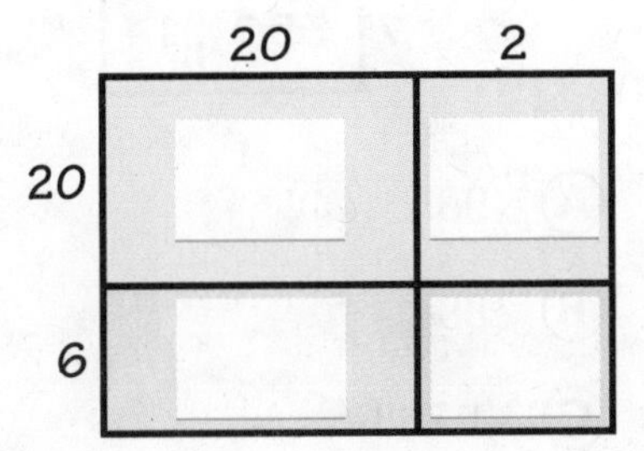

Problem Solving

4. Victor and Carla used different ways to solve 37×23 by using partial products. Whose answer makes sense? Whose answer is nonsense? **Explain** your reasoning.

Victor's Work

	20	3
30	600	90
7	140	21

$690 + 161 + 740 + 111 = 1{,}702$

____

____

____

____

Carla's Work

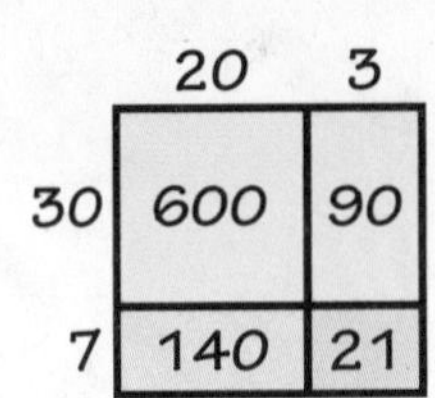

$600 + 140 + 90 + 21 = 851$

____

____

____

____

5. For the answer that is nonsense, write an answer that makes sense.

____

Lesson Check

TEXAS Test Prep

Fill in the bubble completely to show your answer.

6. Use the model. What is the product of 17 × 52?

	50	2
10	500	20
7	350	14

Ⓐ 953

Ⓑ 884

Ⓒ 1,768

Ⓓ 1,190

7. Complete the model. What is the product of 44 × 14?

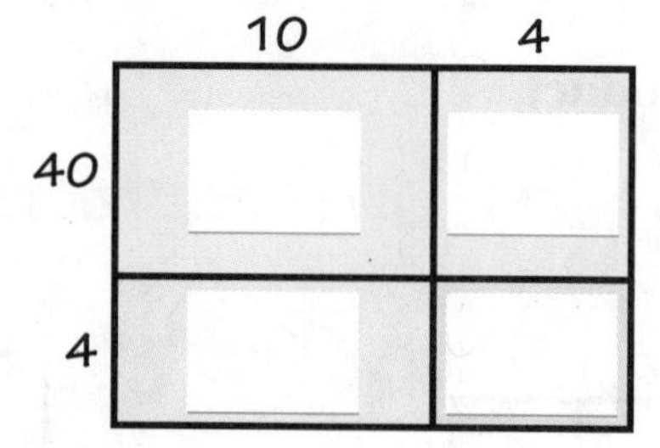

Ⓐ 616

Ⓑ 1,120

Ⓒ 1,232

Ⓓ 516

8. A toy store orders 18 boxes of stuffed animals. There are 35 stuffed animals in a box. How many stuffed animals did the store order?

Ⓐ 630

Ⓑ 1,260

Ⓒ 414

Ⓓ 530

9. Bradley's heart beats 78 times a minute. How many times does it beat in 45 minutes?

Ⓐ 3,170

Ⓑ 3,210

Ⓒ 3,510

Ⓓ 3,470

10. Multi-Step Emma bought 16 packages of rolls for a party. There were 12 rolls in each package. After the party there were 8 rolls left over. How many rolls were eaten?

Ⓐ 192

Ⓑ 138

Ⓒ 200

Ⓓ 184

11. Multi-Step Mr. Ramirez needs 400 paper cups for the school cafeteria. He has 14 packages of paper cups. There are 25 cups in a package. How many more cups does Mr. Ramirez need?

Ⓐ 25

Ⓑ 50

Ⓒ 300

Ⓓ 65

Name ______________________

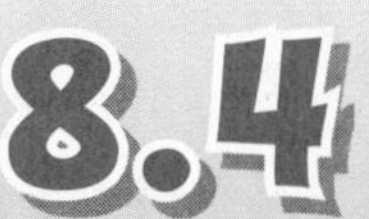

8.4 Multiply Using Partial Products

TEKS Number and Operations—4.4.C, 4.4.D
MATHEMATICAL PROCESSES 4.1.C, 4.1.D, 4.1.E

Essential Question How can you use place value and partial products to multiply 2-digit numbers?

Unlock the Problem

Connect You know how to break apart a model to find partial products. How can you use what you know to find and record a product?

Multiply. 34 × 57 **Estimate.** 30 × 60 = ________

SHADE THE MODEL | THINK AND RECORD

STEP 1

$$\begin{array}{r} 57 \\ \times\ 34 \\ \hline \end{array}$$

← Multiply the tens by the tens. 30 × 5 tens = 150 tens

STEP 2

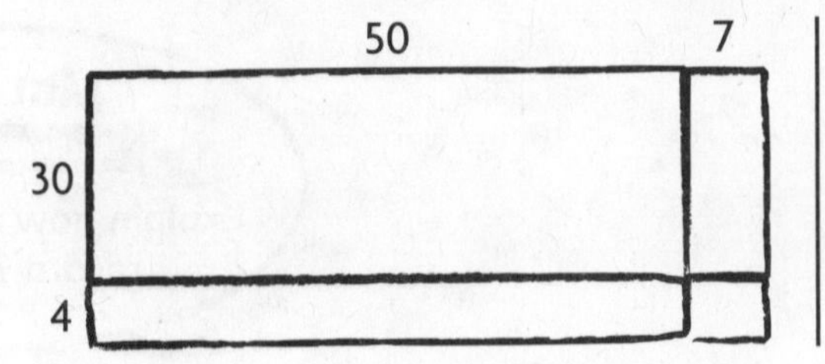

$$\begin{array}{r} 57 \\ \times\ 34 \\ \hline 1{,}500 \end{array}$$

← Multiply the ones by the tens. 30 × 7 ones = 210 ones

STEP 3

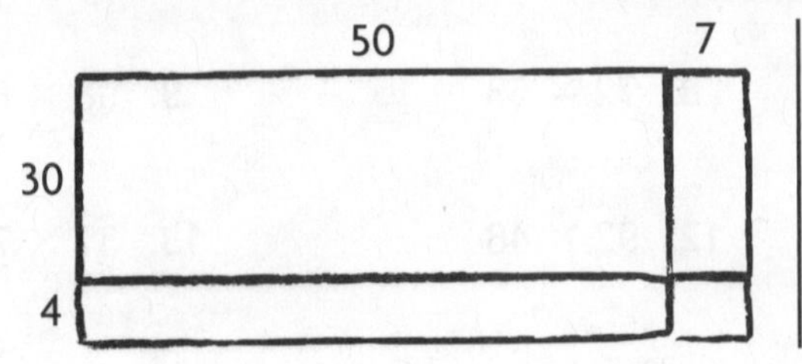

$$\begin{array}{r} 57 \\ \times\ 34 \\ \hline 1{,}500 \\ 210 \end{array}$$

← Multiply the tens by the ones. 4 × 5 tens = 20 tens

STEP 4

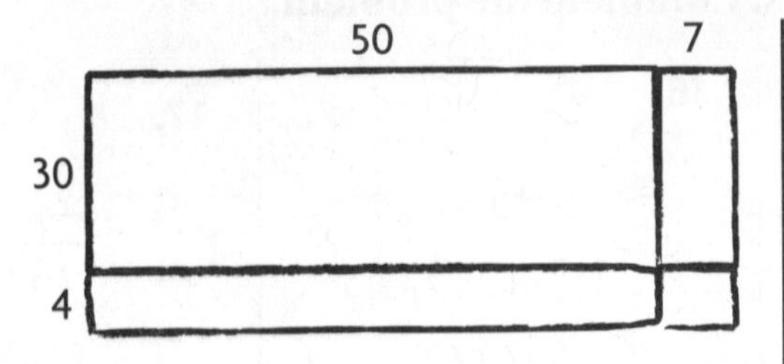

$$\begin{array}{r} 57 \\ \times\ 34 \\ \hline 1{,}500 \\ 210 \\ 200 \\ +\ \quad \\ \hline \end{array}$$

← Multiply the ones by the ones. 4 × 7 ones = 28 ones
← Add the partial products.

So, 34 × 57 = 1,938. Since 1,938 is close to the estimate of 1,800, it is reasonable.

Math Talk

Mathematical Processes

You can write 10 × 4 ones = 40 ones as 10 × 4 = 40. What is another way to write 10 × 3 tens = 30 tens?

Share and Show

1. Find 24 × 34.

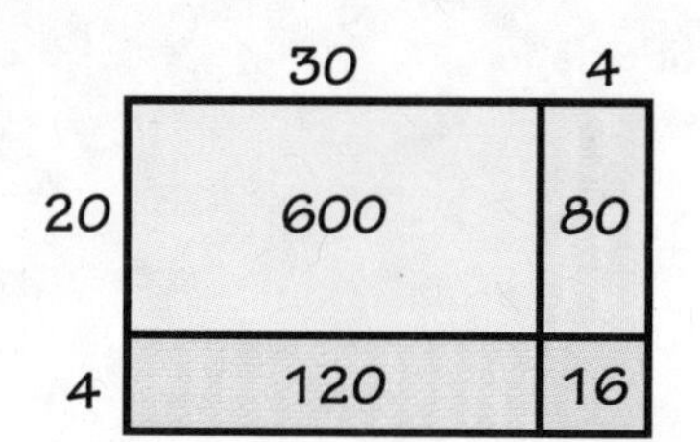


```
   3 4
 × 2 4
```

Record the product.

2.	3.	✓ 4.	✓ 5.
12 × 12	31 × 24	25 × 43	37 × 26

Math Talk

Mathematical Processes

Explain how to model and record 74 × 25.

Problem Solving

Practice: Copy and Solve **Record the product.**

6. 38 × 47
7. 46 × 27
8. 72 × 53
9. 98 × 69
10. 53 × 68
11. 76 × 84
12. 92 × 48
13. 37 × 79

H.O.T. **Algebra** **Find the unknown digits. Complete the problem.**

14.
```
     ▢6
   × ▢4
  1,400
    120
    280
  +  24
  _____
```

15.
```
     ▢2
   × ▢7
  7,200
    180
    560
  +  14
  _____
```

16.
```
     ▢6
   × 5▢
  1,500
    300
     90
  +  18
  _____
```

17.
```
     3▢
   × ▢8
    600
     80
    240
  +  32
  _____
```

Name ______________________________

Problem Solving (Real World)

Use the pictograph for 18–20.

18. **Use Graphs** A fruit-packing warehouse is shipping 15 boxes of grapefruit to a store in St. Louis, Missouri. What is the total weight of the shipment?

____

Pounds of Citrus Fruit per Box

Citrus Fruit	Weight per Box (in pounds)
Grapefruit	● ● ● ● ● ● ● ● ◖
Orange	● ● ● ● ● ● ● ● ●
Tangelo	● ● ● ● ● ● ● ● ●
Tangerine	● ● ● ● ● ● ● ● ● ◖

Key: Each ● = 10 pounds.

19. How much less do 13 boxes of tangelos weigh than 18 boxes of tangerines?

____

20. What is the weight of 12 boxes of oranges?

____

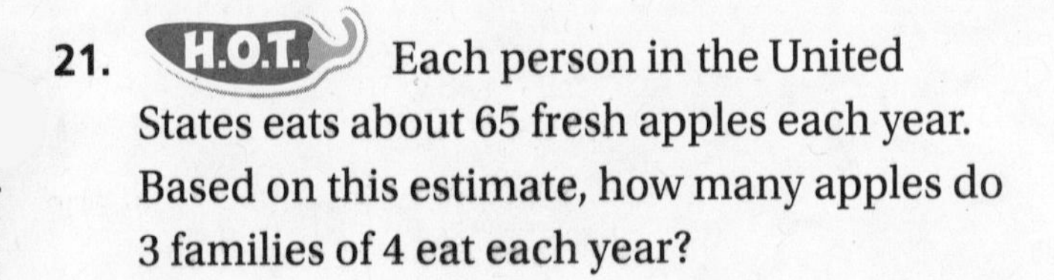

21. H.O.T. Each person in the United States eats about 65 fresh apples each year. Based on this estimate, how many apples do 3 families of 4 eat each year?

____

Math on the Spot

22. H.O.T. **Multi-Step** Martin has 14 packages to ship. Each package weighs 11 pounds. After shipping those 14 packages, he shipped 13 other packages that each weighed 27 pounds. How many pounds of packages did Martin ship? **Explain.**

____

____

23. **Use Math Language** The product of 26×93 is more than 25×93. How much more? **Explain** how you know without multiplying.

____

____

Write Math ▶ **Show Your Work**

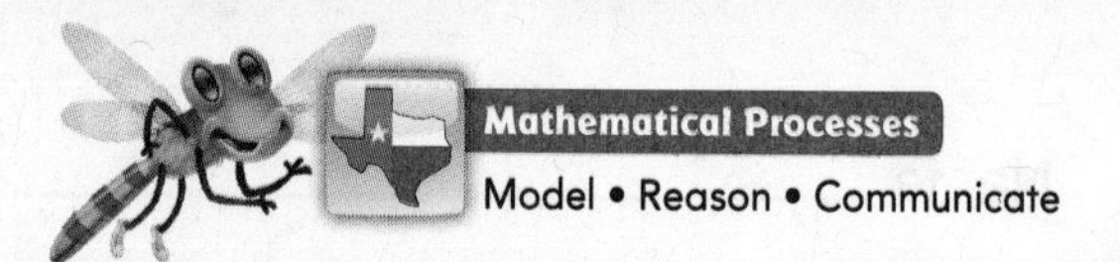

Daily Assessment Task

Fill in the bubble completely to show your answer.

24. A builder is clearing more land. He clears one strip that is 32 feet wide. He needs 28 of these strips cleared. How many feet wide will the cleared land be?

Ⓐ 840 feet

Ⓑ 880 feet

Ⓒ 856 feet

Ⓓ 896 feet

25. Students line up in equal rows for a school picture. There are 41 rows of 16 students. How many students are in the school picture?

Ⓐ 640 students

Ⓑ 656 students

Ⓒ 650 students

Ⓓ 646 students

26. **Multi-Step** Mrs. Parker sells 18 boxes of 45 oranges at the Farmers' Market. She sells 16 boxes of 52 lemons. How many more lemons than oranges does Mrs. Parker sell?

Ⓐ 22 more lemons

Ⓑ 50 more lemons

Ⓒ 42 more lemons

Ⓓ 20 more lemons

TEXAS Test Prep

27. Each row of apple trees has 14 trees. There are 16 rows. How many apple trees are there?

Ⓐ 1,340

Ⓑ 224

Ⓒ 184

Ⓓ 124

Homework and Practice

TEKS Number and Operations—4.4.C, 4.4.D
MATHEMATICAL PROCESSES 4.1.C, 4.1.D, 4.1.E

Name ______________________

8.4 Multiply Using Partial Products

Record the product.

1. $\begin{array}{r} 15 \\ \times 15 \\ \hline \end{array}$

2. $\begin{array}{r} 31 \\ \times 26 \\ \hline \end{array}$

3. $\begin{array}{r} 54 \\ \times 41 \\ \hline \end{array}$

4. $\begin{array}{r} 72 \\ \times 66 \\ \hline \end{array}$

Find the unknown digits. Complete the problem.

5. $\begin{array}{r} \square 3 \\ \times \square 8 \\ \hline 200 \\ 30 \\ 160 \\ +\ 24 \\ \hline \end{array}$

6. $\begin{array}{r} \square 6 \\ \times \square 2 \\ \hline 2{,}000 \\ 240 \\ 100 \\ +\ 12 \\ \hline \end{array}$

7. $\begin{array}{r} 7 \square \\ \times \square 5 \\ \hline 2{,}100 \\ 210 \\ 350 \\ +\ 35 \\ \hline \end{array}$

8. $\begin{array}{r} \square 1 \\ \times 2 \square \\ \hline 1{,}800 \\ 20 \\ 540 \\ +\ 6 \\ \hline \end{array}$

Problem Solving Real World

Use the pictograph for 9–12.

Weight of Dog Food per Bag

Type of Food	Weight per bag (in pounds)
Adult Food	🐕 🐕 🐕 🐕
Puppy Food	🐕 🐕 🐕
Grain Free	🐕 🐕 🐕
Training Treats	🐕 🐕

Key: Each 🐕 = 10 pounds

9. Pet Center ordered 75 bags of training treats. How many pounds did Pet Center order?

____

10. What is the weight of 45 bags of grain free dog food?

____

11. The animal shelter bought 28 bags of puppy food and 36 bags of adult dog food. What is the total weight of their order?

____

12. A warehouse shipped 68 bags of adult dog food and 45 bags of grain free dog food. How many more pounds of adult dog food did they ship?

____

Lesson Check

TEXAS Test Prep

Fill in the bubble completely to show your answer.

13. A farmer bought 19 bags of chicken feed. Each bag costs $57. How much does the farmer pay for the chicken feed?

Ⓐ $1,064

Ⓑ $1,074

Ⓒ $1,023

Ⓓ $1,083

14. Visitors at a petting zoo are given food to feed the ducks. A 50-pound bag of duck food costs $71. The zoo needs 44 bags of food for the summer months. How much does the duck food cost for the summer?

Ⓐ $3,550

Ⓑ $2,200

Ⓒ $3,124

Ⓓ $2,024

15. Large flower pots weigh 28 pounds each. One crate holds 35 pots. What is the weight of one crate of flower pots?

Ⓐ 780 pounds

Ⓑ 980 pounds

Ⓒ 940 pounds

Ⓓ 920 pounds

16. **Multi-Step** A store sells drinks in cartons of 6 each. Bonnie bought 2 cartons of lemonade and 2 cartons of fruit juice. Each bottle is 32 ounces. How many ounces did Bonnie buy?

Ⓐ 560 ounces

Ⓑ 42 ounces

Ⓒ 840 ounces

Ⓓ 768 ounces

17. **Multi-Step** Twelve adults and 63 students are going on a field trip to the aquarium. Tickets cost $18 for adults and $15 for students. What is the total cost of the tickets?

Ⓐ $1,350

Ⓑ $1,125

Ⓒ $1,161

Ⓓ $1,314

18. **Multi-Step** A bus company sold 39 one-way tickets and 20 round-trip tickets from West Elmwood to East Elmwood. One-way tickets cost $14. Round trip tickets cost $25. How much money did the bus company collect?

Ⓐ $1,046

Ⓑ $1,255

Ⓒ $916

Ⓓ $946

Name ______________________

TEKS Number and Operations—4.4.D
Also 4.4.G
MATHEMATICAL PROCESSES
4.1.C, 4.1.F

8.5 Multiply with Regrouping

Essential Question

How can you use regrouping to multiply 2-digit numbers?

Unlock the Problem

By 1914, Henry Ford had streamlined his assembly line to make a Model T Ford car in 93 minutes. How many minutes did it take to make 25 Model Ts?

▲ The first production Model T Ford was assembled on October 1, 1908.

Use place value and regrouping.

Multiply. 93 × 25 **Estimate.** 90 × 30 = ______

THINK	RECORD
STEP 1 • Think of 93 as 9 tens and 3 ones. • Multiply 25 by 3 ones.	1 25 × 93 ____ ← 3 × 25
STEP 2 • Multiply 25 by 9 tens.	4 ~~1~~ 25 × 93 75 ____ ← 90 × 25
STEP 3 • Add the partial products.	4 ~~1~~ 25 × 93 75 + 2,250 ____

So, 93 × 25 is 2,325. Since ______ is close to the estimate of ______, the answer is reasonable.

Math Talk

Mathematical Processes

Explain why you will get the same answer whether you multiply 93 × 25 or 25 × 93.

Different Ways to Multiply You can use different ways to multiply and still get the correct answer. Shawn and Patty both solved 67×40 correctly, but they used different ways.

Look at Shawn's paper.

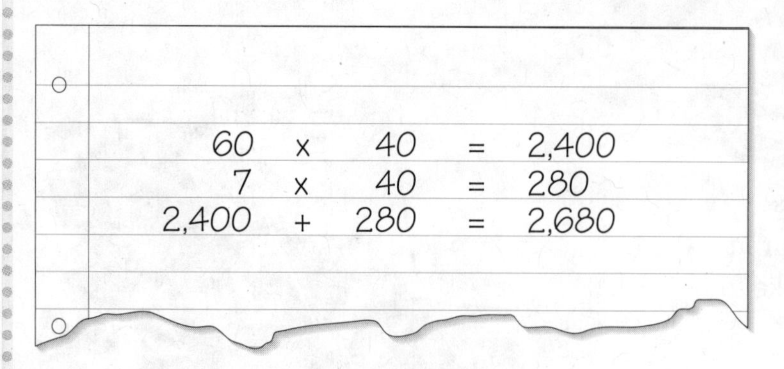

So, Shawn's answer is $67 \times 40 = 2,680$.

Look at Patty's paper.

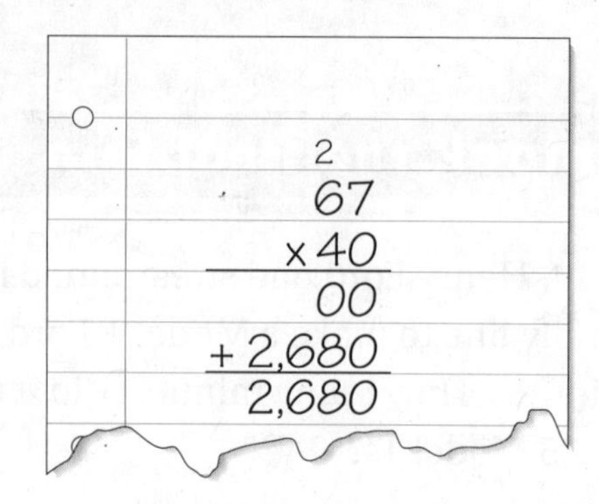

So, Patty also found $67 \times 40 = 2,680$.

1. What method did Shawn use to solve the problem?

____

2. What method did Patty use to solve the problem?

____

Share and Show

1. Look at the problem. Complete the sentences.

Multiply _____ and _____ to get 0.

Multiply _____ and _____ to get 1,620.

Add the partial products.

0 + 1,620 = _______

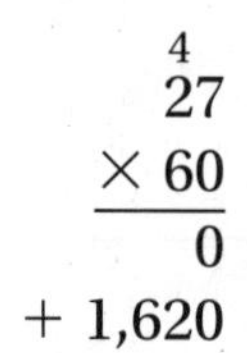

Math Talk

Mathematical Processes

Explain why you can omit zeros of the first partial product when you multiply 20×34.

Estimate. Then find the product.

2. Estimate: _______

$$\begin{array}{r} 68 \\ \times\ 53 \\ \hline \end{array}$$

3. Estimate: _______

$$\begin{array}{r} 61 \\ \times\ 54 \\ \hline \end{array}$$

4. Estimate: _______

$$\begin{array}{r} 90 \\ \times\ 27 \\ \hline \end{array}$$

Name ______________________________

Problem Solving

Practice: Copy and Solve **Estimate. Then find the product.**

5. 34×65 **6.** $42 \times \$13$ **7.** 60×17 **8.** 62×45 **9.** $57 \times \$98$

10. $92 \times \$54$ **11.** 75×20 **12.** 66×55 **13.** $73 \times \$68$ **14.** 72×40

Unlock the Problem

Real World

15. H.O.T. **Multi-Step Analyze** Machine A can label 11 bottles in 1 minute. Machine B can label 12 bottles in 1 minute. How many bottles can both machines label in 15 minutes?

Ⓐ 165 Ⓒ 245

Ⓑ 180 Ⓓ 345

a. What do you need to know? ______________________________

____

b. What numbers will you use? ______________________________

c. Tell why you might use more than one operation to solve the problem.

____

____

____

d. Solve the problem.

e. Fill in the bubble for the correct answer choice above.

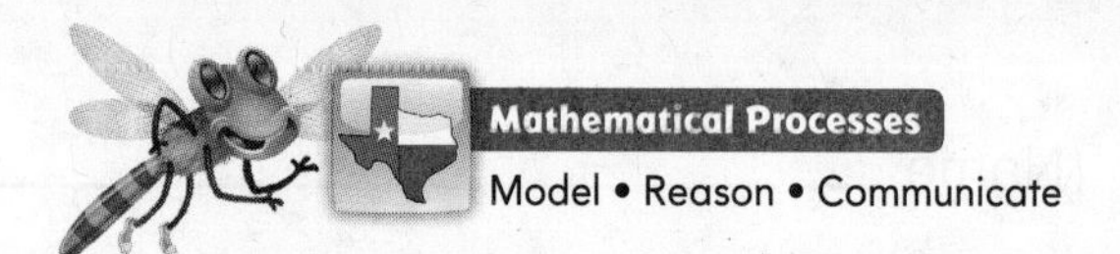

Daily Assessment Task

Fill in the bubble completely to show your answer.

16. A polo team is making 18 mallets from cane. Each mallet is 84 inches long. How many inches of cane do they use?

Ⓐ 1,512 inches

Ⓑ 756 inches

Ⓒ 1,482 inches

Ⓓ 1,412 inches

17. A principal purchases 68 *e*-readers for $79 each. How much does the principal pay for the *e*-readers?

Ⓐ $1,088

Ⓑ $4,802

Ⓒ $5,372

Ⓓ $4,372

18. H.O.T. **Multi-Step** There are 13 students in the sticker club. Each student puts 6 stickers on each of 34 pages in their scrapbook. How many stickers are in all of the scrapbooks?

Ⓐ 546 stickers

Ⓑ 2,652 stickers

Ⓒ 2,322 stickers

Ⓓ 2,312 stickers

TEXAS Test Prep

19. A toy company makes wooden blocks. A carton holds 85 blocks. How many blocks can 19 cartons hold?

Ⓐ 1,615

Ⓑ 1,575

Ⓒ 1,515

Ⓓ 850

Name ______________________

8.5 Multiply with Regrouping

Estimate. Then find the product.

1. Estimate ______

$$\begin{array}{r} 74 \\ \times\ 46 \\ \hline \end{array}$$

2. Estimate ______

$$\begin{array}{r} 28 \\ \times\ 13 \\ \hline \end{array}$$

3. Estimate ______

$$\begin{array}{r} 65 \\ \times\ 25 \\ \hline \end{array}$$

4. Estimate ______

$$\begin{array}{r} 19 \\ \times\ 32 \\ \hline \end{array}$$

5. Estimate ______

$$\begin{array}{r} 83 \\ \times\ 18 \\ \hline \end{array}$$

6. Estimate ______

$$\begin{array}{r} 40 \\ \times\ 72 \\ \hline \end{array}$$

Problem Solving Real World

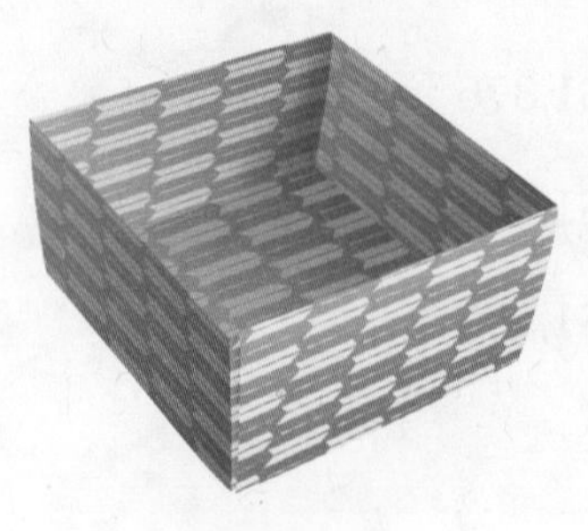

Jill can make 14 origami boxes in an hour. Nathan can make 17 origami boxes in an hour. How many boxes can both of them make in 12 hours?

7. What do you need to know?

____

____

8. What numbers will you use?

____

____

9. Tell why you might use more than one operation to solve the problem.

____

____

____

____

10. Solve the problem.

So, both people can make ______ boxes in 12 hours.

Lesson Check

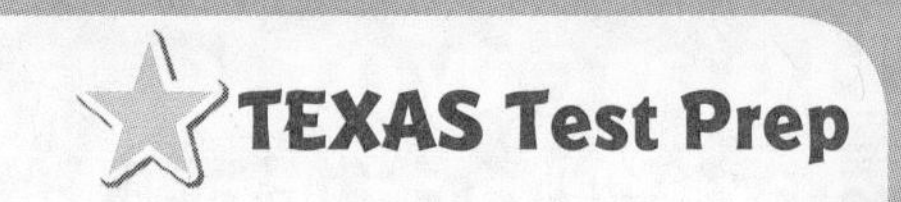

Fill in the bubble completely to show your answer.

11. Bags of lemons weigh 33 pounds each. What is the total weight of 46 bags of lemons?

Ⓐ 1,308 pounds
Ⓑ 1,518 pounds
Ⓒ 1,508 pounds
Ⓓ 1,418 pounds

12. Health club membership costs $65 a month. How much does a membership cost for 12 months?

Ⓐ $770
Ⓑ $690
Ⓒ $780
Ⓓ $775

13. There are 19 players on a baseball team. Uniforms cost $74 each. How much will uniforms for the team cost?

Ⓐ $1,406
Ⓑ $1,376
Ⓒ $1,216
Ⓓ $1,306

14. Jason bought 39 boards that are each 12 feet long. How many feet of lumber did he buy?

Ⓐ 458 feet
Ⓑ 358 feet
Ⓒ 368 feet
Ⓓ 468 feet

15. **Multi-Step** Owners of a summer camp are buying new cots for their cabins. There are 16 cabins. Each cabin needs 6 cots. Each cot costs $92. How much will the new cots cost?

Ⓐ $8,742
Ⓑ $9,022
Ⓒ $8,722
Ⓓ $8,832

16. **Multi-Step** A theater has 28 rows of 38 seats downstairs and 14 rows of 26 seats upstairs. How many seats does the theater have?

Ⓐ 1,428
Ⓑ 1,228
Ⓒ 1,408
Ⓓ 1,208

Name ______________________________

TEKS Number and Operations—4.4.D
Also 4.4.G
MATHEMATICAL PROCESSES
4.1.A, 4.1.C, 4.1.E

8.6 Choose a Multiplication Method

Essential Question How can you find and record products of two 2-digit numbers?

Unlock the Problem (Real World)

Did you know using math can help prevent you from getting a sunburn?

The time it takes to burn without sunscreen multiplied by the SPF, or sun protection factor, is the time you can stay in the sun safely with sunscreen.

If today's UV index is 8, Erin will burn in 15 minutes without sunscreen. If Erin puts on lotion with an SPF of 25, how long will she be protected?

- Underline the sentence that tells you how to find the answer.
- Circle the numbers you need to use. What operation will you use?

____

One Way Use partial products to find 15 × 25.

$$\begin{array}{r} 25 \\ \times\ 15 \\ \hline \end{array}$$

☐	← 10 × 2 tens = 20 tens
☐	← 10 × 5 ones = 50 ones
☐	← 5 × 2 tens = 10 tens
+ ☐	← 5 × 5 ones = 25 ones
☐	← Add.

Draw a picture to check your work.

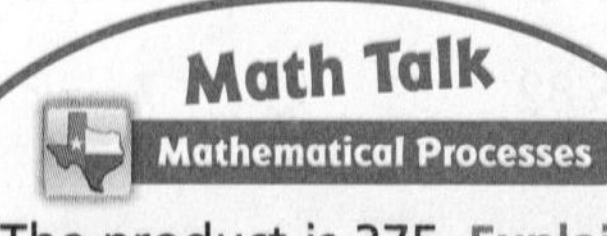

Math Talk Mathematical Processes

The product is 375. Explain what 375 means for Erin.

Another Way Use regrouping to find 15 × 25.

Estimate. 20 × 20 = ______

STEP 1

Think of 15 as 1 ten 5 ones. Multiply 25 by 5 ones, or 5.

$$\begin{array}{r} {}^{2}\\ 25 \\ \times\ 15 \\ \hline \square \end{array} \leftarrow 5 \times 25$$

STEP 2

Multiply 25 by 1 ten, or 10.

$$\begin{array}{r} {}^{2}\\ 25 \\ \times\ 15 \\ \hline 125 \\ \square \end{array} \leftarrow 10 \times 25$$

STEP 3

Add the partial products.

$$\begin{array}{r} {}^{2}\\ 25 \\ \times\ 15 \\ \hline 125 \\ +\ 250 \\ \hline \square \end{array}$$

Share and Show

1. Find the product.

			5	4	
	×		2	9	

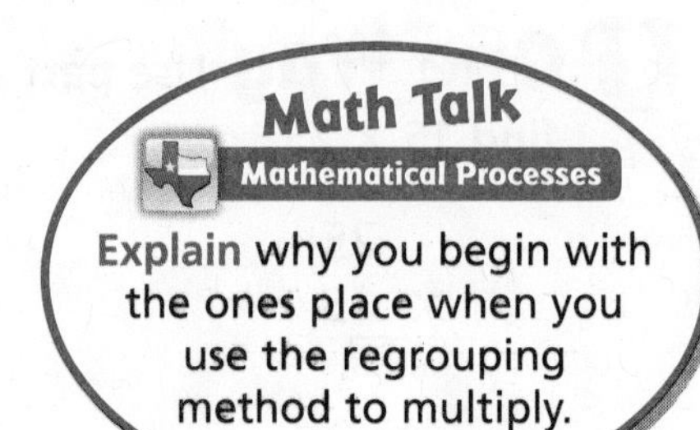

Estimate. Then choose a method to find the product.

2. Estimate: ______ $\begin{array}{r} 36 \\ \times\ 14 \\ \hline \end{array}$

3. Estimate: ______ $\begin{array}{r} 63 \\ \times\ 42 \\ \hline \end{array}$

4. Estimate: ______ $\begin{array}{r} 84 \\ \times\ 53 \\ \hline \end{array}$

5. Estimate: ______ $\begin{array}{r} 71 \\ \times\ 13 \\ \hline \end{array}$

Problem Solving

Practice: Copy and Solve **Estimate. Find the product.**

6. 29 × $ 82
7. 57 × 79
8. 80 × 27
9. 32 × $ 75

Algebra **Use mental math to find the number.**

10. 30 × 14 = 420, so 30 × 15 = ______.

11. 25 × 12 = 300, so 25 × ______ = 350.

Name ______________________

Unlock the Problem

12. H.O.T. **Multi-Step Apply** Martin collects stamps. He counted 48 pages in his collector's album. The first 20 pages each have 35 stamps in 5 rows. The rest of the pages each have 54 stamps. How many stamps does Martin have in his album?

a. What do you need to know? ______________________

b. How will you use multiplication to find the number of stamps?

____

c. Tell why you might use addition and subtraction to help solve the problem.

____

____

d. Show the steps to solve the problem.

e. Complete the sentences.

Martin has a total of ________ stamps on the first 20 pages.

There are ________ more pages after the first 20 pages in Martin's album.

There are ________ stamps on the rest of the pages.

There are ________ stamps in the album.

13. H.O.T. **Multi-Step** One group of 15 students read for 30 minutes. Another group of 25 students read for 45 minutes. How many minutes did the students spend reading? **Explain.**

____

____

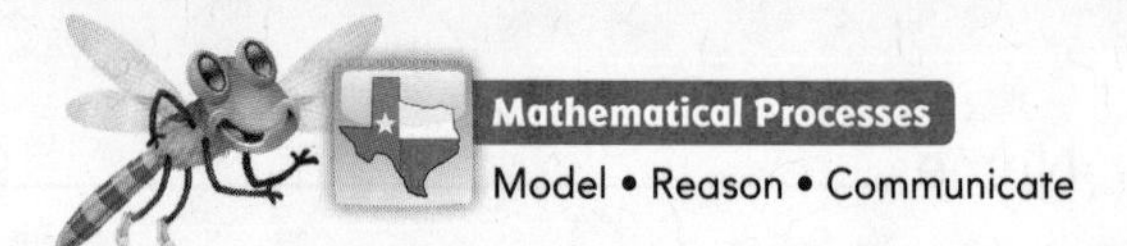

Daily Assessment Task

Fill in the bubble completely to show your answer.

14. When a cheetah runs, its stride is 22 feet long. What distance does the cheetah run in 45 strides?

Ⓐ 980 feet

Ⓑ 990 feet

Ⓒ 198 feet

Ⓓ 99 feet

15. Student tickets to a theme park cost $27. How much do 32 student tickets cost?

Ⓐ $810

Ⓑ $854

Ⓒ $864

Ⓓ $288

16. **Multi-Step** A theater has 52 rows of 26 seats. There are people sitting in 241 seats. How many seats are empty?

Ⓐ 175 seats

Ⓑ 111 seats

Ⓒ 1,101 seats

Ⓓ 1,111 seats

TEXAS Test Prep

17. Each row of peach trees has 37 trees. There are 16 rows. How many peach trees are there?

Ⓐ 53

Ⓑ 259

Ⓒ 592

Ⓓ 342

Name ______

8.6 Choose a Multiplication Method

Estimate. Then choose a method to find the product.

1. Estimate ______

$$\begin{array}{r} 34 \\ \times\ 16 \\ \hline \end{array}$$

2. Estimate ______

$$\begin{array}{r} 49 \\ \times\ 21 \\ \hline \end{array}$$

3. Estimate ______

$$\begin{array}{r} 62 \\ \times\ 55 \\ \hline \end{array}$$

Problem Solving Real World

A coach bought 56 items at the sports shop. He got 18 footballs for $32 each. The rest of the items were shoulder pads that cost $89 each. How much did the coach spend for the 56 items?

4. What do you need to know?

______

5. How will you use multiplication to find the total cost?

______

6. Tell why you might use addition and subtraction to solve the problem.

______

______

7. Show the steps to solve the problem.

8. Complete the sentences.

The coach spent ______ for footballs.

The coach bought ______ shoulder pads.

The coach spent ______ shoulder pads.

The coach spent a total of ______.

Lesson Check

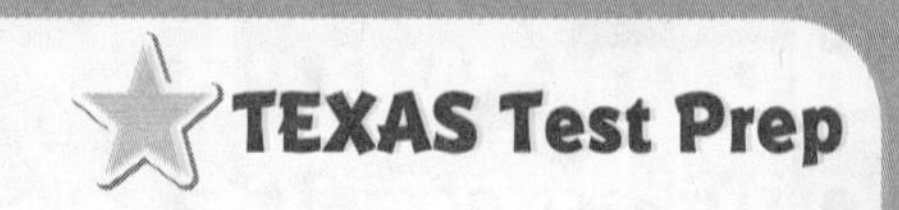

Fill in the bubble completely to show your answer.

9. A beach clean-up crew filled 34 garbage cans with litter. Each garbage can holds 55 gallons. How many gallons of garbage did the crew pick up?

   Ⓐ 1,770 gallons
   Ⓑ 1,670 gallons
   Ⓒ 1,650 gallons
   Ⓓ 1,870 gallons

10. Folding chairs cost $27 each. How much do 72 folding chairs cost?

   Ⓐ $1,844
   Ⓑ $1,944
   Ⓒ $1,954
   Ⓓ $1,934

11. There are 13 volunteers at the community garden. Each person works 15 hours a week. How many hours are spent working at the garden each week?

   Ⓐ 215 hours
   Ⓑ 185 hours
   Ⓒ 195 hours
   Ⓓ 205 hours

12. There are 25 paper plates in a package. Karen bought 20 packages. How many paper plates did Karen buy?

   Ⓐ 400
   Ⓑ 500
   Ⓒ 250
   Ⓓ 550

13. **Multi-Step** The town conservation manager bought 16 maple trees for $26 each. She paid with five $100 bills. How much change will the manager receive?

   Ⓐ $84
   Ⓑ $416
   Ⓒ $94
   Ⓓ $184

14. **Multi-Step** Section A of a stadium has 42 rows with 56 seats in each row. Section B has 64 rows with 54 seats in each row. If the stadium sells tickets for all the seats in both sections, how many tickets are sold?

   Ⓐ 5,498
   Ⓑ 5,808
   Ⓒ 5,608
   Ⓓ 5,698

Name ___________________________

8.7 PROBLEM SOLVING • Multiply 2-Digit Numbers

TEKS Number and Operations—4.4.D
Also 4.4.H

MATHEMATICAL PROCESSES
4.1.B, 4.1.F

Essential Question How can you use the strategy *draw a diagram* to solve multi-step multiplication problems?

Unlock the Problem

During the 2010 Great Backyard Bird Count, an average of 42 bald eagles were counted in each of 20 locations throughout Alaska. In 2009, an average of 32 bald eagles were counted in each of 26 locations throughout Alaska. Based on this data, how many more bald eagles were counted in 2010 than in 2009?

Use the graphic organizer to help you solve the problem.

Read

What do I need to find?

I need to find ______________ bald eagles were counted in 2010 than in 2009.

What information am I given?

In 2010, ______ locations counted an average of ______ bald eagles each.

In 2009 ______ locations counted an average of ______ bald eagles each.

Plan

What is my plan or strategy?

I can solve simpler problems.

Find the number of bald eagles counted in ______.

Find the number of bald eagles counted in ______.

Then draw a strip diagram to compare the ______ count to the ______ count.

Solve

- First, find the total number of bald eagles counted in 2010.

  ______ × ______

  = ______ bald eagles counted in 2010

- Next, find the total number of bald eagles counted in 2009.

  = ______ × ______

  = ______ bald eagles counted in 2009

- Last, draw a strip diagram. I need to subtract.

840 bald eagles in 2010
832 bald eagles in 2009 ?

840 − 832 = ______

So, there were ______ more bald eagles counted in 2010 than in 2009.

Try Another Problem

Prescott Valley, Arizona, reported a total of 29 mourning doves in the Great Backyard Bird Count. Mesa, Arizona, reported 20 times as many mourning doves as Prescott Valley. If Chandler reported a total of 760 mourning doves, how many more mourning doves were reported in Chandler than in Mesa?

Mourning dove ▲

Read	Solve
What do I need to find?	
What information am I given?	760 mourning doves in Chandler 580 mourning doves in Mesa ?
Plan **What is my plan or strategy?**	

- Is your answer reasonable? **Explain.** ______

Math Talk
Mathematical Processes
Describe another way you could solve this problem.

Name ___________________________________

Share and Show

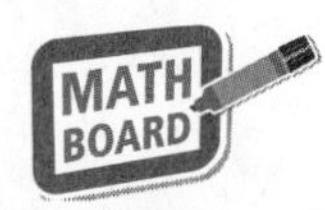

1. **Analyze** An average of 74 reports with bird counts were turned in each day in June. An average of 89 were turned in each day in July. How many reports were turned in for both months? (Hint: There are 30 days in June and 31 days in July.)

First, write the problem for June.

____

Next, write the problem for July.

____

Last, find and add the two products.

__________ reports were turned in for both months.

2. H.O.T. **Multi-Step** **What if** an average of 98 reports were turned in each day for the month of June? How many reports were turned in for June? **Describe** how your answer for June would be different.

____

____

____

Problem Solving Real World

3. H.O.T. **Multi-Step** On each of Maggie's bird-watching trips, she has seen at least 24 birds. If she has taken 4 of these trips each year over the past 16 years, at least how many birds has Maggie seen?

____

4. H.O.T. **Multi-Step** Each of 5 bird-watchers reported seeing 15 roseate spoonbills in a day. If they each reported seeing the same number of roseate spoonbills over 14 days, how many would be reported?

____

Unlock the Problem Tips

- ✓ Underline important facts.
- ✓ Choose a strategy.
- ✓ Use the Problem Solving MathBoard.

Write Math ▶ Show Your Work

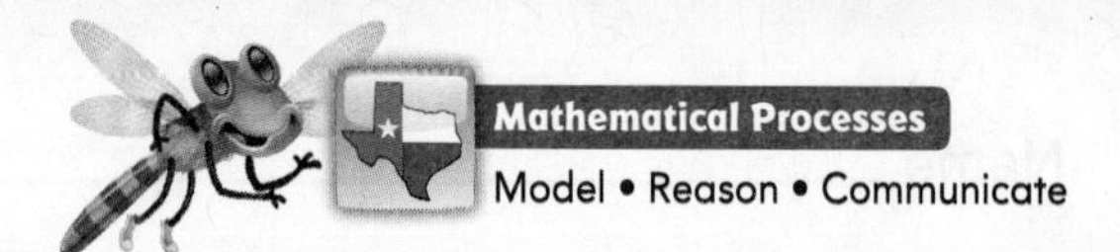

Daily Assessment Task

Fill in the bubble completely to show your answer.

5. Geoducks and tubeworms are two creatures that live a long time. Pam and Sierra use their ages to describe the ages of these sea creatures. Pam says "I'm 13. Geoducks live to be about 12 times my age." Sierra says "I'm 11. Tubeworms live to be about 15 times my age." How many years longer do tubeworms live than geoducks?

Ⓐ 27 years
Ⓑ 10 years
Ⓒ 9 years
Ⓓ 1 year

6. Multi-Step A restaurant buys 32 boxes of 21 packets of mustard each and 26 boxes of 35 packets of ketchup each. How many packets of mustard and ketchup does the restaurant buy?

Ⓐ 304 packets
Ⓑ 238 packets
Ⓒ 1,352 packets
Ⓓ 1,582 packets

7. Multi-Step There are 19 cases of 24 cans of vegetable soup each in the school cafeteria. There are 23 cases of 36 cans of chicken soup each in the cafeteria. How many cans of soup are in the school cafeteria?

Ⓐ 321 cans
Ⓑ 1,144 cans
Ⓒ 1,284 cans
Ⓓ 1,274 cans

TEXAS Test Prep

8. Carol is the treasurer of her bird-watching club. The club wants to order shirts for each of the 18 members. If each shirt costs $21, what is the cost for the members' shirts?

Ⓐ $39
Ⓑ $378
Ⓒ $380
Ⓓ $540

Name ____________________

8.7 PROBLEM SOLVING • Multiply 2-Digit Numbers

Problem Solving

1. One day, Sam's Sweats sold 83 pairs of sweat pants for $29 each and 75 sweat shirts for $24 each. How much did Sam collect on the two items?

   First write the problem for sweat pants.

   ____

   Next write the problem for sweat shirts.

   ____

   Last find the products and add.

   ____

2. Sam's Sweats sold 68 pairs of sweat pants and 70 sweat shirts the next day. How much did Sam collect on the two items that day? Describe the difference in the sales on the two days.

   ____

3. A factory got an order for 65 cases of shampoo. There are 15 bottles in each case. They have 1,000 bottles of shampoo in stock. Is there enough shampoo in stock to fill the order? If so, how many bottles will be left over? If not, how many more bottles are needed?

   ____

4. A store ordered 26 cartons of large dog beds and 22 cartons of small dog beds. There are 12 large dog beds in a carton and 16 small dog beds in a carton. Did the store order more large dog beds or more small dog beds? How many more?

   ____

Lesson Check

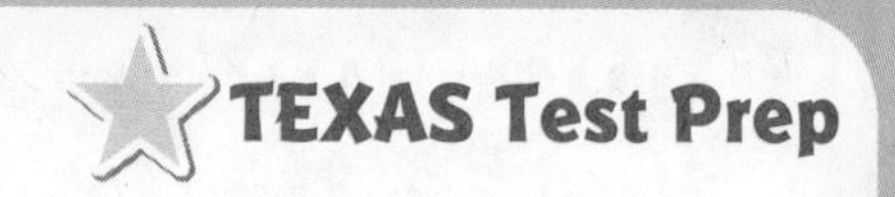

Fill in the bubble completely to show your answer.

5. **Multi-Step** Large postcards come in packages of 20. Small postcards come in packages of 25. A store buys 24 packages of large postcards and 18 packages of small postcards. Which statement is true?

   Ⓐ The store bought a total of 930 postcards.

   Ⓑ The store bought 30 more small postcards than large postcards.

   Ⓒ The store bought a total of 932 postcards.

   Ⓓ The store bought 68 more large postcards than small postcards.

6. **Multi-Step** Sarah can pack 16 books in a box. She has 14 boxes. She has 230 books to pack. Which statement is true?

   Ⓐ Sarah will have room for 1 more book in the last box she packs.

   Ⓑ Sarah has exactly the right number of boxes to pack all of the books.

   Ⓒ Sarah will have 1 box left over after she packs all of the books.

   Ⓓ Sarah needs 1 more box to pack all of the books.

7. **Multi-Step** Jeans cost $39 a pair. T-shirts cost $14 each. How much does it cost to buy 2 pairs of jeans and 3 T-shirts for each of the 6 members of the Walsh family?

   Ⓐ $720

   Ⓑ $1,908

   Ⓒ $870

   Ⓓ $626

8. **Multi-Step** There are 472 stuffed bears in stock at a factory. The factory has an order for 35 cartons of bears. There are 16 in a carton. How many more stuffed bears do they need to make to fill the order?

   Ⓐ 58

   Ⓑ 88

   Ⓒ 42

   Ⓓ 98

9. **Multi-Step** Glenn made 20 trays of 12 muffins each. Laurie made 15 trays of 18 muffins each. How many more muffins did Laurie make?

   Ⓐ 40

   Ⓑ 20

   Ⓒ 10

   Ⓓ 30

10. **Multi-Step** There are 48 crayons in a box. There are 12 boxes in a carton. Mr. Johnson ordered 6 cartons of crayons for the school. How many crayons did he get?

    Ⓐ 3,346

    Ⓑ 3,446

    Ⓒ 3,456

    Ⓓ 3,356

Name ____________________

Module 8 Assessment

Vocabulary

Vocabulary
counting numbers
compatible numbers
products

Choose the best term from the box to complete the sentence.

1. ____________ are numbers that are easy to compute mentally. (p. 273)

Concepts and Skills

2. Explain how to find 40 × 50 using mental math. TEKS 4.4.B

____

____

3. What is the first step in estimating 56 × 27? TEKS 4.4.G

____

Choose a method. Then find the product. TEKS 4.4.B, 4.4.D

4. 35 × 10 ________
5. 19 × 20 ________
6. 12 × 100 ________
7. 70 × 100 ________
8. 58 × 40 ________
9. 30 × 10 ________

Estimate the product. Choose a method. TEKS 4.4.G

10. 81 × 38 ________
11. 16 × $59 ________
12. 43 × 25 ________

Find the product. TEKS 4.4.C, 4.4.D

13. 13 × 13 ________

	10	3
10	100	30
3	30	9

14. 17 × 36 ________

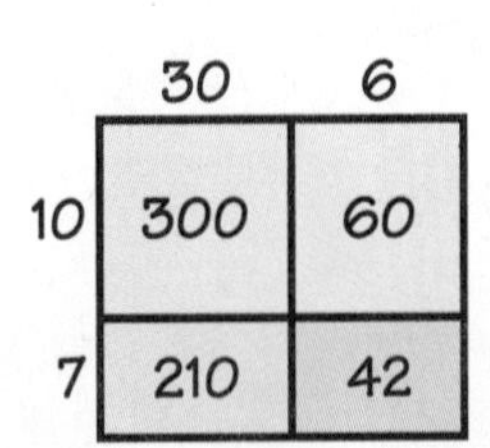

15. 24 × 14 ________

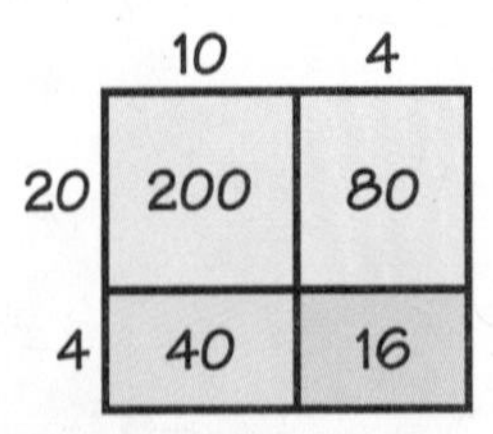

Fill in the bubble completely to show your answer.

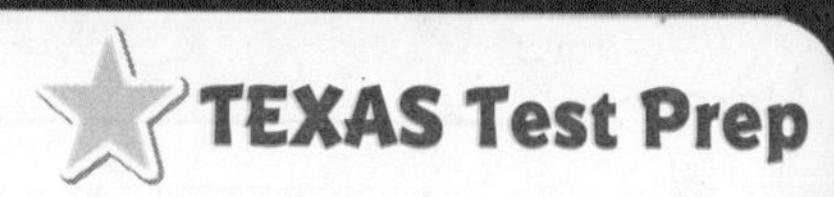

16. Ms. Traynor's class is taking a field trip to the zoo. The trip will cost $26 for each student. There are 22 students in her class. Which is the best estimate for the cost of the students' field trip? TEKS 4.4.G

Ⓐ $480
Ⓑ $600
Ⓒ $1,200
Ⓓ $6,000

17. Tatum wants to use partial products to find 15×32. Which shows a way to find 15×32? TEKS 4.4.D

Ⓐ $(10 \times 3) + (10 \times 2) + (30 \times 1) + (30 \times 50)$
Ⓑ $(10 \times 30) + (10 \times 2) + (50 \times 30) + (50 \times 2)$
Ⓒ $(10 + 30) + (10 + 2) + (30 + 10) + (30 + 5)$
Ⓓ $(10 \times 30) + (10 \times 2) + (5 \times 30) + (5 \times 2)$

18. Mike has 16 baseball cards. Niko has 17 times as many baseball cards as Mike does. How many baseball cards does Niko have? Use an array to help you solve. TEKS 4.4.C

Ⓐ 33
Ⓑ 274
Ⓒ 241
Ⓓ 272

19. Mary and her sister Emma are saving their money. Mary has saved 45 dimes and Emma has saved 20 times as many dimes as Mary. How many dimes has Emma saved? TEKS 4.4.B, 4.4.D

Ⓐ 850
Ⓑ 900
Ⓒ 870
Ⓓ 910

20. Mrs. Jones places 3 orders for school T-shirts. Each order has 16 boxes of shirts and each box holds 17 shirts. How many T-shirts does Mrs. Jones order? TEKS 4.4.D

Record your answer and fill in the bubbles on the grid. Be sure to use the correct place value.

			.		
0	0	0		0	0
1	1	1		1	1
2	2	2		2	2
3	3	3		3	3
4	4	4		4	4
5	5	5		5	5
6	6	6		6	6
7	7	7		7	7
8	8	8		8	8
9	9	9		9	9

Name ______________________________

9.1 Remainders

Essential Question How can you use arrays to divide whole numbers that do not divide evenly?

Investigate

Materials ■ square tiles

Erica and 2 friends are playing a game of dominoes. There are 19 dominoes in the set. Erica wants each player to receive the same number of dominoes. Can she divide them equally among the 3 players? Why or why not?

You can use an array to find the number of dominoes each player will receive.

A. Use 19 tiles to represent the 19 dominoes. Make an array to find how many rows of 3 are in 19 and if any are left over.

B. Make a row of 3 tiles.

C. Continue to make as many rows of 3 tiles as you can.

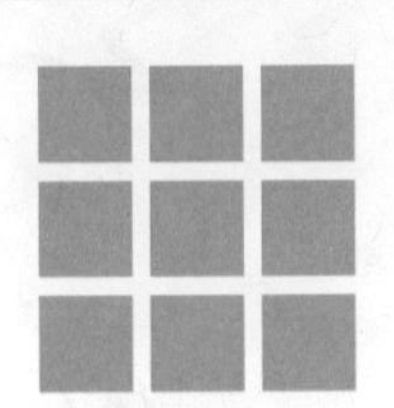

Leftover Tiles

D. Find the number of rows of three tiles and the number of tiles left over. Record your answer.

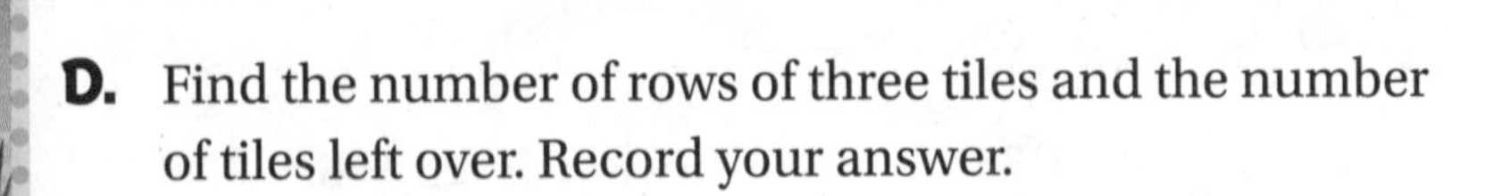

______ rows of 3 tiles

______ tile left over

So, each player gets ______ dominoes with ______ domino left over.

Math Talk

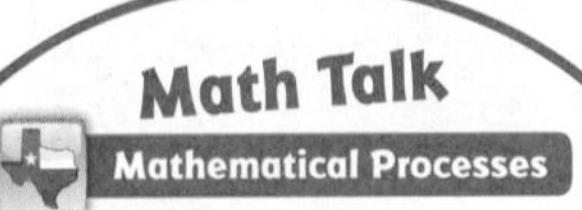

Explain how the model helped you find the number of dominoes each player receives. Why is 1 tile left over?

Make Connections

When a number cannot be divided evenly, the amount left over is called the **remainder**.

Use square tiles to find 29 ÷ 5.

- Use 29 tiles.
- Use the tiles to make rows of 5. The number of tiles left over is the remainder.

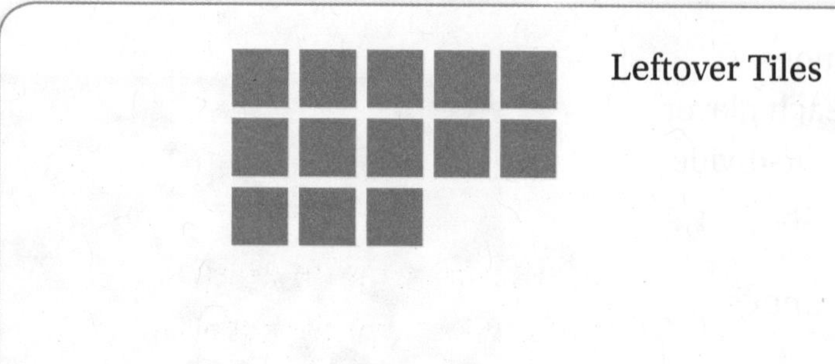

For 29 ÷ 5, the quotient is ______ and the remainder is ______, or 5 r4.

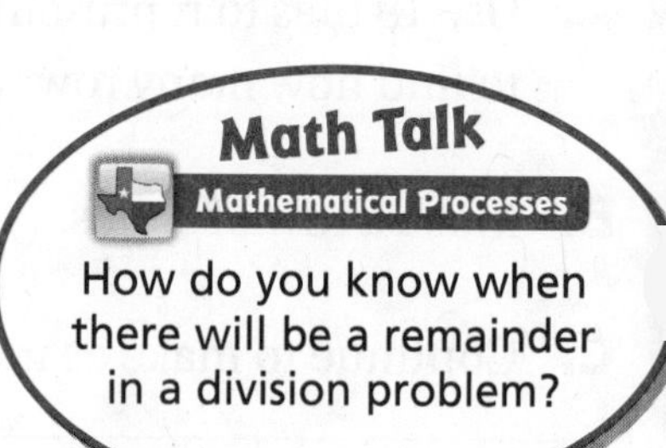

Share and Show

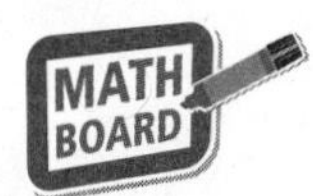

Use tiles or draw an array to find the quotient and remainder.

1. 29 ÷ 4 ______

2. 34 ÷ 5 ______

3. 25 ÷ 3 ______

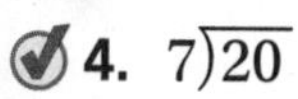

4. $7\overline{)20}$ ______

5. 19 ÷ 3 ______

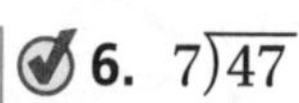

6. $7\overline{)47}$ ______

7. $4\overline{)35}$ ______

8. 23 ÷ 8 ______

Name ______________________________

Problem Solving

Multi-Step What's the Error?

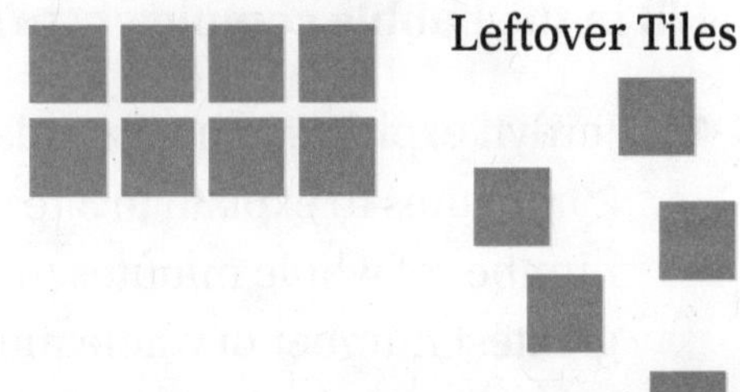

9. Macy, Kayley, Maddie, and Rachel collected 13 marbles. They want to share the marbles equally. How many marbles will each of the 4 girls get? How many marbles will be left over?

   Frank used an array to solve this problem. He says his array represents $4\overline{)13}$. What is his error?

Look at the way Frank solved this problem. Find and describe his error.

____

____

____

____

____

____

____

____

Use tiles or draw an array to model and solve the problem.

So, each of the 4 girls will get ______ marbles and ______ marble will be left over.

10. H.O.T. **Explain** how you use an array to find the quotient and remainder.

____

____

____

____

Mathematical Processes
Model • Reason • Communicate

Daily Assessment Task

Fill in the bubble completely to show your answer.

11. Jordyn explains to her friends how to play checkers. She has 29 minutes to explain to 3 teams. She wants to take the same number of whole minutes to explain to each team. What is the greatest number of whole minutes she can take to explain the rules to each team?

Ⓐ 8 minutes
Ⓑ 4 minutes
Ⓒ 9 minutes
Ⓓ 10 minutes

12. Use Tools Kenny wants to put 37 books on 5 shelves. He wants the same number of books on each shelf and he will put the remaining books in a box. How many books does Kenny put in the box? Use tiles or draw an array to help you find the number of books Kenny put in the box.

Ⓐ 6 books
Ⓑ 2 books
Ⓒ 7 books
Ⓓ 3 books

13. Multi-Step Barb puts 60 games into boxes to donate. Each box can hold 7 games. How many more games does Barb need so that all the boxes can have 7 games?

Ⓐ 3 games
Ⓑ 8 games
Ⓒ 2 games
Ⓓ 9 games

TEXAS Test Prep

14. Rena has 23 DVDs that she wants to sort into rows of 6 each. How many DVDs will Rena have left over?

Ⓐ 3
Ⓑ 5
Ⓒ 17
Ⓓ 4

Name ____________________

MATHEMATICAL PROCESSES
4.1.A, 4.1.G

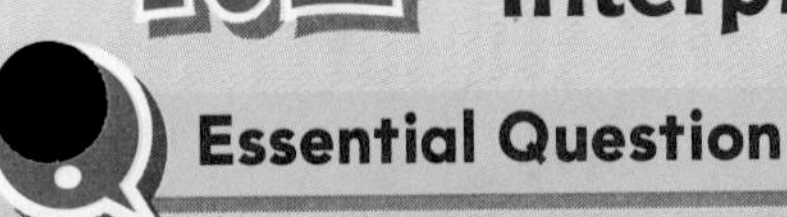

9.2 Interpret the Remainder

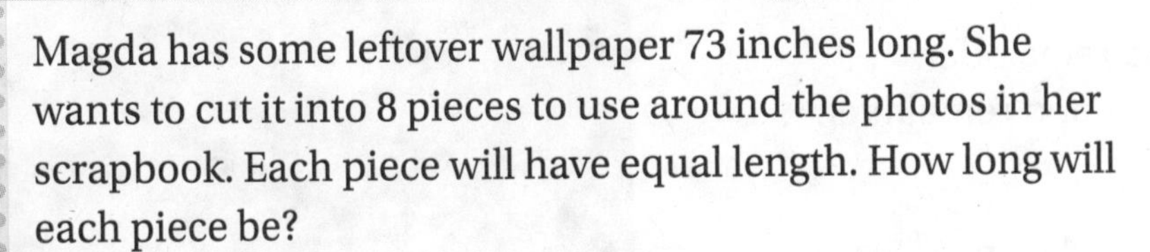

Unlock the Problem (Real World)

Magda has some leftover wallpaper 73 inches long. She wants to cut it into 8 pieces to use around the photos in her scrapbook. Each piece will have equal length. How long will each piece be?

When you solve a division problem with a remainder, the way you interpret the remainder depends on the situation and the question.

One Way Write the remainder as a fraction.

The divisor is ______ pieces.

The __________ is 73 inches.

Divide to find the quotient and remainder. $8\overline{)73}$ = 9 r1

The remainder represents 1 inch left over, which can also be divided into 8 equal parts and written as a fraction.

$\frac{\text{remainder}}{\text{divisor}} =$ ______

Remember

You can use multiples, counters, or draw a quick picture to divide.

Write the quotient with the remainder written as a fraction. ______

So, each piece will be ______ inches long.

Try This!

Jim made 32 ounces of soup for 3 adults and 2 children. If each person gets the same amount, how many ounces will each person get? Complete the division.

$\overline{)32}$

Each person gets ______ ounces.

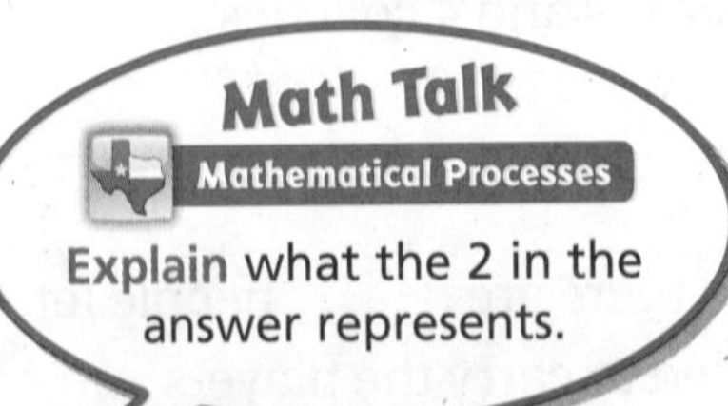

Other Ways

A Use only the quotient.

Ben is a tour guide at a glass-blowing studio. He can take no more than 7 people at a time on a tour. If 80 people want to see the glass-blowing demonstration, how many groups of 7 people will Ben show around?

First, divide to find the quotient and remainder.
Then, decide how to use the quotient and remainder.

The quotient is ______.

The remainder is ______.

$$\begin{array}{r} 11 \text{ r } \square \\ 7\overline{)80} \end{array}$$

Ben can give tours to 7 people at a time. The quotient is the number of tour groups of exactly 7 people he can show around.

So, Ben gives tours to ______ groups of 7 people.

B Add 1 to the quotient.

If Ben gives tours to all 80 people, how many tours will he give? A tour can have no more than 7 people. To show all 80 people around, Ben will have to give 1 more tour.

So, Ben will give ______ tours in all for 80 people.

C Use only the remainder.

Ben gives tours to all 80 people. After he completes the tours for groups of 7 people, how many people are in his last tour?

The remainder is 3.

So, Ben's last tour will have ______ people.

Try This!

Soccer players and their coaches are driven to soccer games in vans. Each van holds 9 people. How many vans are needed for 27 players and 4 coaches?

Divide. ______ ÷ 9 ______

Since there are ______ people left over, ______ vans are needed to carry the players and coaches.

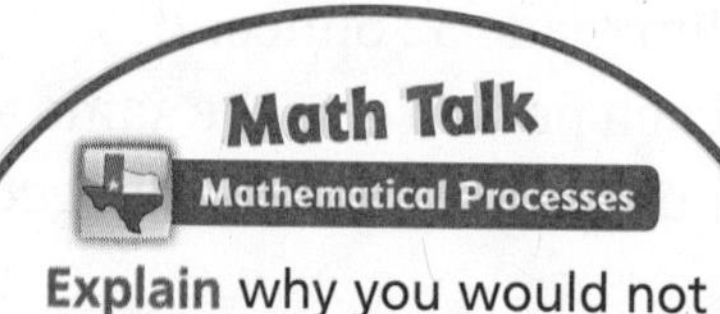

Name ______________________________

Share and Show

1. Olivia baked 53 mini-loaves of banana bread to be sliced for snacks at a craft fair. She will place an equal number of loaves in 6 different locations. How many loaves will be at each location?

   a. Divide to find the quotient and remainder. $6\overline{)53}$ ☐ r ☐

   b. Decide how to use the quotient and remainder to answer the question.

   ____

Interpret the remainder to solve.

2. **What if** Olivia wants to put only whole loaves at each location? How many loaves will be at each location?

   ____

3. Ed carves 22 small wooden animals to sell at the craft fair. He displays them in rows with 4 animals in a row. How many animals will not be in equal rows?

   ____

Problem Solving Real World

Interpret the remainder to solve.

4. Myra has a 17-foot roll of crepe paper to make 8 streamers to decorate for a party. How long will each streamer be if she cuts the roll into equal pieces?

   ____

5. **H.O.T.** **Multi-Step** Juan has a piano recital next month. Last week he practiced for 8 hours in the morning and 7 hours in the afternoon. A full practice session is 2 hours long. How many full practice sessions does Juan complete?

   ____

6. **H.O.T.** A total of 25 students sign up to be hosts on Parents' Night. Teams of 3 students greet parents. How many students cannot be on a team? How many more students must help so everyone is on a team? **Explain.**

   ____

   ____

Mathematical Processes
Model • Reason • Communicate

Daily Assessment Task

Fill in the bubble completely to show your answer.

7. **Apply** Jim has a puppet pattern that calls for 6 feet of fleece. He has 50 feet of fleece. If he makes the greatest number of puppets possible, how much fleece will he have left?

   Ⓐ 2 feet
   Ⓒ 4 feet
   Ⓑ 7 feet
   Ⓓ 8 feet

8. Deshawn wants to place 77 photos in an album. Each page of the album holds 9 photos. What is the least number of pages Deshawn will need to use so that all 77 of the photos are placed in the album?

   Ⓐ 5 pages
   Ⓒ 8 pages
   Ⓑ 9 pages
   Ⓓ 6 pages

9. **Multi-Step** Kathy has 10 tortillas that she will use to make mini pizzas. She has 43 pepperoni slices and will use 7 of them on each pizza. After she makes as many pepperoni pizzas as she can, she will make cheese pizzas. How many cheese pizzas will Kathy make?

   Ⓐ 3
   Ⓑ 6
   Ⓒ 5
   Ⓓ 4

TEXAS Test Prep

10. Mr. Alia gives a "Good Job" badge to each of the 74 students who help at a school event. There are 8 badges in a package. How many packages will he open?

   Ⓐ $9\frac{1}{4}$
   Ⓑ 9
   Ⓒ 2
   Ⓓ 10

Name ______________________

9.2 Interpret the Remainder

1. The principal at Oak School ordered 25 pizzas for the fourth grade classes to share. He will deliver an equal number of pizzas to each of 8 classes. How many pizzas will each class receive?

   a. Divide to find the quotient and remainder.

   $8\overline{)25}$ ___ r ___

   b. Decide how to use the quotient and remainder to answer the question.

   ____

2. What if the principal wants to deliver only whole pizzas to each class? How many pizzas will each class receive?

   ____

3. A total of 58 trophies will be given out at the swim meet. Each box holds 6 trophies. How many boxes are needed to carry the trophies?

   Divide 58 ÷ 6 ______________

   Since there are ______ trophies left over,

   ______ boxes are needed to carry 58 trophies.

Problem Solving Real World

4. Chandra has 15 feet of ribbon to make bows for 6 cheer team members. How much ribbon can she use for each bow if she cuts the ribbon into equal pieces?

   ____

5. A group of 34 students will go to the museum. Each van can hold 6 students. What is the least number of vans needed to transport the students?

   ____

Lesson Check

TEXAS Test Prep

Fill in the bubble completely to show your answer.

6. Rachel wants to place 50 cupcakes in boxes to sell at the school carnival. If each box holds 4 cupcakes, how many boxes can she fill with exactly 4 cupcakes?

Ⓐ 14
Ⓑ 16
Ⓒ 12
Ⓓ 13

7. At a wedding reception, there are 75 people seated at tables. Each table seats 8 people. How many full tables are there?

Ⓐ 9
Ⓑ 8
Ⓒ 10
Ⓓ 7

8. Blake guides nature trail walks for groups of no more than 6 people. If 46 people want to go on a walk, how many people will be in a group of less than 6?

Ⓐ 6
Ⓑ 2
Ⓒ 7
Ⓓ 4

9. Maria has 20 yards of fabric to make 8 tablecloths. How long will each tablecloth be if she cuts the fabric into equal pieces?

Ⓐ $2\frac{1}{2}$ yards
Ⓑ 3 yards
Ⓒ $\frac{1}{2}$ yard
Ⓓ 2 yards

10. Multi-Step A total of 56 students signed up to play in a flag football league. If each team has 10 students, how many more students will need to sign up so all of the students can be on a team?

Ⓐ 6
Ⓑ 4
Ⓒ 5
Ⓓ 2

11. Multi-Step Jerome and Scott are combining their money to buy raffle tickets. Jerome has $7 and Scott has $10. If each ticket costs $3, how many tickets can they buy?

Ⓐ 4
Ⓑ 3
Ⓒ 5
Ⓓ 2

Name ______________________________

9.3 Divide Tens, Hundreds, and Thousands

Essential Question How can you divide numbers through thousands by whole numbers through 10?

Unlock the Problem (Real World)

Dustin is packing apples in gift boxes. Each gift box holds 4 apples. How many boxes can Dustin pack with 120 apples?

You can divide using basic facts and place value.

Example 1 Divide. $120 \div 4$

STEP 1 Identify the basic fact. $12 \div 4$

STEP 2 Use place value. $120 =$ ______ tens

STEP 3 Divide. 12 tens $\div 4 =$ ______ tens ← Think: 4×3 tens $= 12$ tens

$=$ ______

$120 \div 4 = 30$

So, Dustin can pack ______ boxes.

Example 2 Divide. $1,200 \div 4$

STEP 1 Identify the basic fact. $12 \div 4$

STEP 2 Use place value. $1,200 =$ ______ hundreds

STEP 3 Divide. 12 hundreds $\div 4 =$ ______ hundreds ← Think: 4×3 hundreds $= 12$ hundreds

$=$ ______

$1,200 \div 4 = 300$

Math Talk Mathematical Processes

Describe the pattern in the place value of the dividends and quotients.

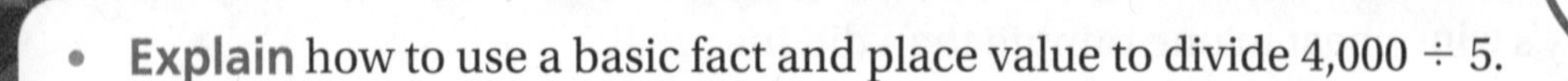

- **Explain** how to use a basic fact and place value to divide $4,000 \div 5$.

____

____

Share and Show

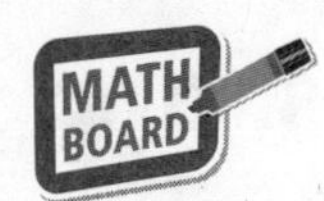

1. Divide. 2,800 ÷ 7

   What basic fact can you use? ___________

   2,800 = 28 ___________

   28 hundreds ÷ 7 = ___________

   2,800 ÷ 7 = ___________

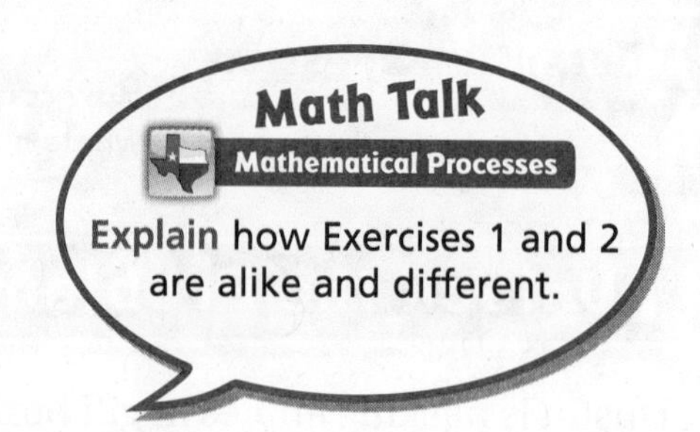

2. Divide. 280 ÷ 7

   What basic fact can you use? ___________

   280 = 28 ___________

   28 tens ÷ ___________ = 4 ___________

   280 ÷ 7 = ___________

Use basic facts and place value to find the quotient.

3. 360 ÷ 6 = ___________
4. 2,000 ÷ 5 = ___________
5. 4,500 ÷ 9 = ___________

Problem Solving

Algebra Find the unknown number.

6. 420 ÷ ■ = 60 ___________
7. ■ ÷ 4 = 30 ___________
8. 810 ÷ ■ = 90 ___________

9. H.O.T. Divide 400 ÷ 40. **Explain** how patterns and place value can help.

____

____

____

10. **Multi-Step** In 3 minutes, a damselfly's wings beat 2,700 times and a butterfly's wings beat 2,100 times. About how many more times did the damselfly's wings beat in one minute than did the butterfly's wings?

____

Name ___________________________

Problem Solving Real World

11. Jamal put 600 pennies into 6 equal rolls. How many pennies were in each roll?

____

12. Sela has 6 times as many coins now as she had 4 months ago. If Sela has 240 coins now, how many did she have 4 months ago?

____

13. **H.O.T.** **Multi-Step** Chip collected 2,090 dimes. Sue collected 1,910 dimes. They divided all their dimes into 8 equal stacks. How many dimes are in each stack?

____

____

14. **Communicate** Mr. Roberts sees a rare 1937 penny. The cost of the penny is $210. If he saves $3 a week, will Mr. Roberts have enough money to buy the penny in one year? **Explain.**

____

____

____

15. **H.O.T.** **Multi-Step** **Analyze** Mrs. Roberts sold each of 5 coins for the same dollar amount. She received a total of $300. Each coin cost her $32. How much money did she make on each coin? Explain how you got your answer.

____

____

____

Write Math ▶ **Show Your Work**

Daily Assessment Task

Fill in the bubble completely to show your answer.

16. Jeremy has a shelf that is 150 centimeters long. If each DVD case is 3 centimeters wide, how many DVD cases can fit on the shelf?

Ⓐ 50

Ⓑ 5

Ⓒ 45

Ⓓ 30

17. Aaron has 480 sports cards. He needs to place the same number of cards in each of 6 storage boxes. How many sports cards will be in each storage box?

Ⓐ 9

Ⓑ 80

Ⓒ 8

Ⓓ 72

18. Multi-Step Suri picks 125 tomatoes and Lynn picks 85 tomatoes. They pack the tomatoes into boxes so there are 7 in each box. How many boxes do they use?

Ⓐ 3

Ⓑ 70

Ⓒ 18

Ⓓ 30

TEXAS Test Prep

19. Which number sentence is NOT true?

Ⓐ $150 \div 5 = 30$

Ⓑ $400 \div 8 = 500$

Ⓒ $4,500 \div 9 = 500$

Ⓓ $5,600 \div 7 = 800$

Name ______________________________

9.3 Divide Tens, Hundreds, and Thousands

1. Divide. 3,600 ÷ 4

What basic fact can you use? ____________

3,600 = 36 ____________

36 hundreds ÷ 4 = ____________

3,600 ÷ 4 = ____________

2. Divide. 360 ÷ 4

What basic fact can you use? ____________

360 = 36 ____________

36 tens ÷ ________ = 9 ________

360 ÷ 4 = ____________

Use basic facts and place value to find the quotient.

3. 240 ÷ 6 = ________

4. 3,000 ÷ 6 = ________

5. 2,100 ÷ 7 = ________

6. 490 ÷ 7 = ________

7. 5,600 ÷ 8 = ________

8. 320 ÷ 4 = ________

Find the unknown number.

9. 480 ÷ ■ = 80 ________

10. ■ ÷ 9 = 50 ________

11. 640 ÷ ■ = 80 ________

Problem Solving

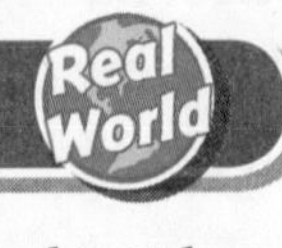

12. The sandwich shop delivered 240 box lunches for the high school band. An equal number of boxes will be placed on each of 6 tables. How many boxes will be on each table?

____

13. Roy bought a package of 500 index cards. He wants to divide the cards into 5 equal stacks. How many cards will be in each stack?

____

Lesson Check

TEXAS Test Prep

Fill in the bubble completely to show your answer.

14. Which number sentence is not true?

Ⓐ $540 \div 9 = 60$

Ⓑ $4,900 \div 7 = 70$

Ⓒ $3,000 \div 6 = 500$

Ⓓ $1,600 \div 8 = 200$

15. What number correctly completes the equation?

$$\blacksquare \div 9 = 800$$

Ⓐ 72

Ⓑ 720

Ⓒ 7,200

Ⓓ 72,000

16. The school office received a shipment of 250 pens. If the shipment was divided equally into 5 boxes, how many pens were in each box?

Ⓐ 250

Ⓑ 25

Ⓒ 5

Ⓓ 50

17. City workers counted how many large trucks passed over a bridge in one week. If 3,500 trucks passed over the bridge in one week, about how many trucks passed over the bridge each day?

Ⓐ 700

Ⓑ 70

Ⓒ 500

Ⓓ 50

18. **Multi-Step** Eileen collected 98 empty cans to recycle and Carl collected 82 cans. They packed an equal number of cans into three boxes to take to the recycling center. How many cans were in each box?

Ⓐ 60

Ⓑ 6

Ⓒ 40

Ⓓ 4

19. **Multi-Step** A baker sold 8 cakes for the same dollar amount. He received a total of $240. Each cake cost the baker $18 to make. How much money did he make on each cake?

Ⓐ $30

Ⓑ $12

Ⓒ $21

Ⓓ $13

Name ______________________________

9.4 Estimate Quotients Using Compatible Numbers

TEKS Number and Operations—4.4.G
MATHEMATICAL PROCESSES 4.1.C, 4.1.D, 4.1.G

Essential Question

How can you use compatible numbers to estimate quotients?

Unlock the Problem (Real World)

A horse's heart beats 132 times in 3 minutes. About how many times does it beat in 1 minute?

You can use compatible numbers to estimate quotients.

Compatible numbers are numbers that are easy to compute mentally.

- Will a horse's heart beat more or fewer than 132 times in 1 minute?

  ____

- What operation will you use to solve the problem?

  ____

Example 1 Estimate. 132 ÷ 3

STEP 1 Find a number close to 132 that divides easily by 3. Use basic facts.

12 ÷ 3 is a basic fact. 120 divides easily by 3.

15 ÷ 3 is a basic fact. 150 divides easily by 3.

Think: Choose 120 because it is closer to 132.

STEP 2 Use place value.

120 = ______ tens

12 ÷ 3 = ______

12 tens ÷ 3 = ______ tens

120 ÷ 3 = ______

So, a horse's heart beats about ______ times a minute.

Example 2 Use compatible numbers to find two estimates that the quotient is between. 1,382 ÷ 5

STEP 1 Find two numbers close to 1,382 that divide easily by 5.

______ ÷ 5 is a basic fact.
1,000 divides easily by 5.

______ ÷ 5 is a basic fact.
1,500 divides easily by 5.

1,382 is between ______ and ______.

STEP 2 Divide each number by 5. Use place value.

1,000 ÷ 5

______ hundreds ÷ 5 = ______ hundreds, or ______

1,500 ÷ 5

______ hundreds ÷ 5 = ______ hundreds, or ______

So, 1,382 ÷ 5 is between ______ and ______.

Math Talk

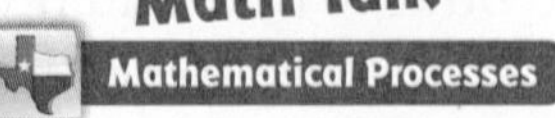

Mathematical Processes

Explain which estimate you think is more reasonable.

Share and Show

1. Estimate. 1,718 ÷ 4

Think: What number close to 1,718 is easy to divide by 4?

_____ is close to 1,718. What basic fact can you use? _____ ÷ 4

_____ is close to 1,718. What basic fact can you use? _____ ÷ 4

Choose 1,600 because ______________________________.

16 ÷ 4 = _____

1,600 ÷ _____ = _____

1,718 ÷ 4 is about _____

Math Talk

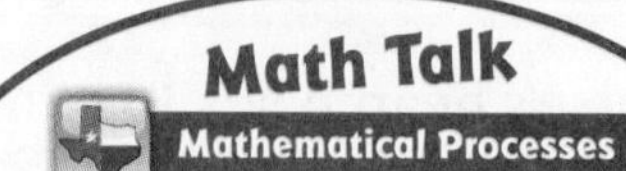

Explain how your estimate might change if the problem were 1,918 ÷ 4.

Use compatible numbers to estimate the quotient.

2. 455 ÷ 9 _____

3. 1,509 ÷ 3 _____

4. 176 ÷ 8 _____

5. 2,795 ÷ 7 _____

Problem Solving

Algebra **Estimate to compare. Write <, >, or =.**

6. 613 ÷ 3 ◯ 581 ÷ 2

_____ estimate _____ estimate

7. 364 ÷ 4 ◯ 117 ÷ 6

_____ estimate _____ estimate

8. 2,718 ÷ 8 ◯ 963 ÷ 2

_____ estimate _____ estimate

9. Mr. Morrison put 4,689 miles on his car the first 6 months he owned it. If he drove the same number of miles each month, about how many miles did he drive in one month? Use compatible numbers to find two estimates that the quotient is between.

____

10. **Multi-Step** Leigh wants to buy a bike for $429 and a helmet for $38. If she saves $8 a week, about how many weeks will it take her to save the money to buy the bike and helmet?

____

Name ______________________________

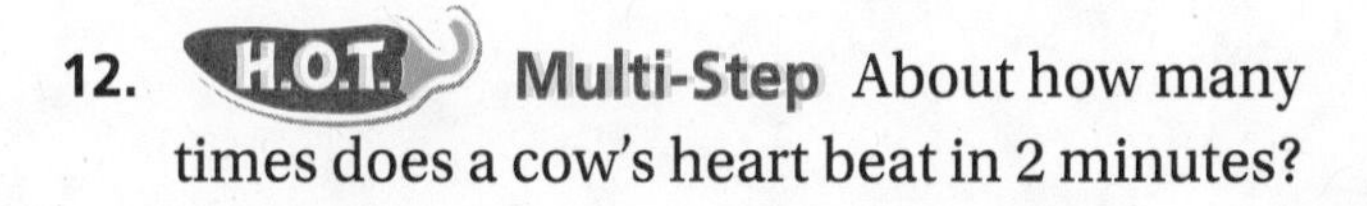

Use the table for 11–14.

Animal Heartbeats in 5 Minutes

Animal	Number of Heartbeats
Whale	31
Cow	325
Pig	430
Dog	520
Chicken	1,375

11. About how many times does a chicken's heart beat in 1 minute?

____

12. H.O.T. **Multi-Step** About how many times does a cow's heart beat in 2 minutes?

____

13. H.O.T. About how many times faster does a cow's heart beat than a whale's?

____

14. Write Math ▶ **What's the Question?** The answer is about 100 beats in 1 minute.

____

____

____

15. **Use Tools** Jamie and his two brothers divided a package of 126 toy cars equally. About how many cars did each of them receive?

____

16. H.O.T. **Multi-Step** Martha had 154 stamps and her sister had 248 stamps. They combined their collections and put the stamps in an album. If they put 8 stamps on each page, about how many pages would they need?

____

Write Math ▶ **Show Your Work**

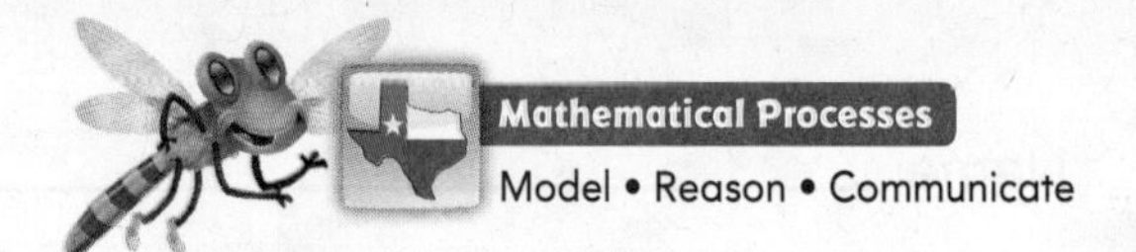

Daily Assessment Task

Fill in the bubble completely to show your answer.

17. **Reasoning** Dakota has 105 quills that she will use to make bracelets. She needs 4 quills for each. About how many bracelets can she make?

    Ⓐ about 20

    Ⓑ about 29

    Ⓒ about 16

    Ⓓ about 25

18. Nick and his three friends divided 252 cards equally. About how many cards did each of them receive?

    Ⓐ about 55

    Ⓑ about 20

    Ⓒ about 60

    Ⓓ about 380

19. **Multi-Step** A carpenter has 168 doorknobs in his workshop. Of those doorknobs, 96 are round and the rest are square. If he wants to place 7 square doorknobs in each bin, about how many bins would he need?

    Ⓐ about 7

    Ⓑ about 23

    Ⓒ about 10

    Ⓓ about 13

TEXAS Test Prep

20. A monkey's heart beats 1,152 times in 6 minutes. Which is the best estimate of the number of times the monkey's heart beats in 1 minute?

    Ⓐ about 1,000

    Ⓑ about 200

    Ⓒ about 100

    Ⓓ about 2,000

Homework and Practice

TEKS Number and Operations—4.4.G
MATHEMATICAL PROCESSES 4.1.C, 4.1.D, 4.1.G

Name ______________________

9.4 Estimate Quotients Using Compatible Numbers

Use compatible numbers to estimate the quotient.

1. 486 ÷ 6 ______

2. 2,239 ÷ 7 ______

3. 2,930 ÷ 4 ______

4. 5,216 ÷ 8 ______

5. 396 ÷ 7 ______

6. 1,739 ÷ 9 ______

Estimate to compare. Write <, >, or =.

7. 264 ÷ 9 ◯ 458 ÷ 5

______ estimate ______ estimate

8. 2,805 ÷ 4 ◯ 3,592 ÷ 6

______ estimate ______ estimate

9. 719 ÷ 8 ◯ 176 ÷ 2

______ estimate ______ estimate

10. 2,501 ÷ 4 ◯ 1,486 ÷ 3

______ estimate ______ estimate

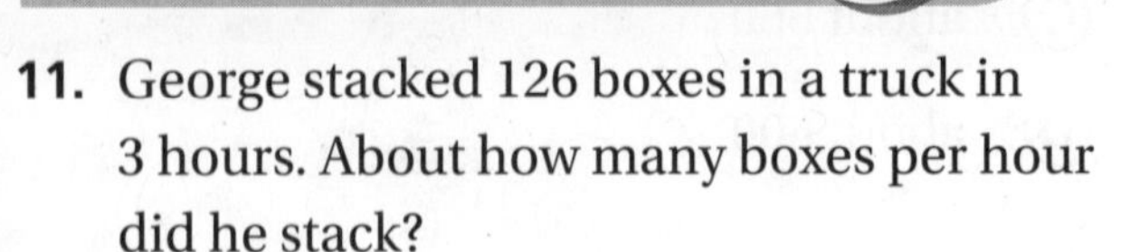

11. George stacked 126 boxes in a truck in 3 hours. About how many boxes per hour did he stack?

______

12. Casey stacked 441 books equally on 9 shelves. About how many books are on each shelf?

______

Lesson Check

Fill in the bubble completely to show your answer.

13. Marcie went to the golf course to practice putting. If she made 372 putts in 4 hours, about how many putts did she make each hour?

Ⓐ about 70

Ⓑ about 100

Ⓒ about 80

Ⓓ about 90

14. Wendy and 8 other members of her scout troop sold a total of 2,684 boxes of cookies. About how many boxes did each member sell if each scout sold about the same number of boxes?

Ⓐ about 500

Ⓑ about 300

Ⓒ about 400

Ⓓ about 200

15. Mr. Danielson drove 1,998 miles for his job last week. If he drove about the same number of miles each day, about how many miles did he drive each of the 7 days?

Ⓐ about 500 miles

Ⓑ about 300 miles

Ⓒ about 400 miles

Ⓓ about 200 miles

16. Sharon has 572 sheets of construction paper to make autograph books for the business fair. Each book will use 8 sheets of paper. About how many books can Sharon make?

Ⓐ about 70

Ⓑ about 60

Ⓒ about 80

Ⓓ about 50

17. **Multi-Step** A total of 8,644 people went to the football game. Of those people, 5,100 sat on the home side and the rest sat on the visitor's side. If they filled 8 equal-sized sections on the visitor's side, about how many people sat in each of these sections?

Ⓐ about 500

Ⓑ about 600

Ⓒ about 1,100

Ⓓ about 400

18. **Multi-Step** If Cade shoots 275 free throw baskets in 2 hours, about how many can he shoot in 5 hours?

Ⓐ about 700

Ⓑ about 140

Ⓒ about 660

Ⓓ about 600

Name ______________________________

4.5 Division and the Distributive Property

Essential Question

How can you use the Distributive Property to find quotients?

Investigate

Hands On

Materials ■ color pencils ■ grid paper

You can use the Distributive Property to break apart numbers to make them easier to divide.

The Distributive Property of division says that dividing a sum by a number is the same as dividing each addend by the number and then adding the quotients.

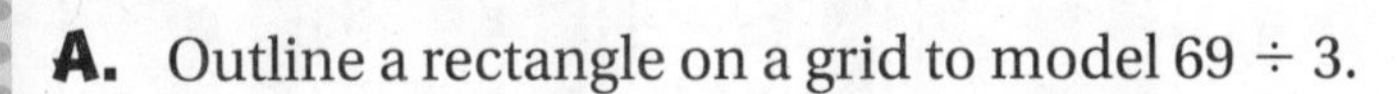

A. Outline a rectangle on a grid to model 69 ÷ 3.

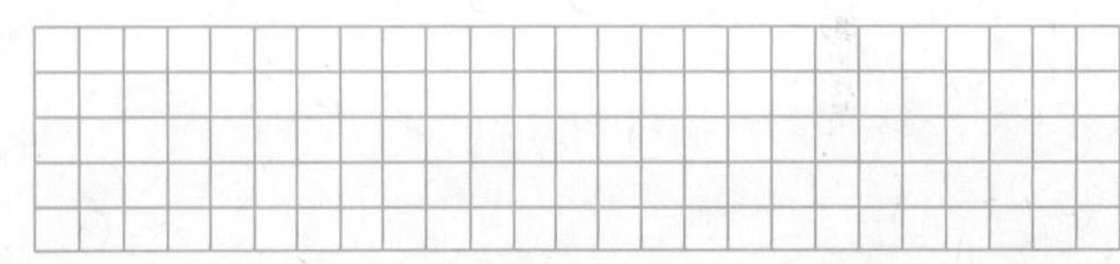

Shade columns of 3 until you have 69 squares.

How many groups of 3 can you make? ______

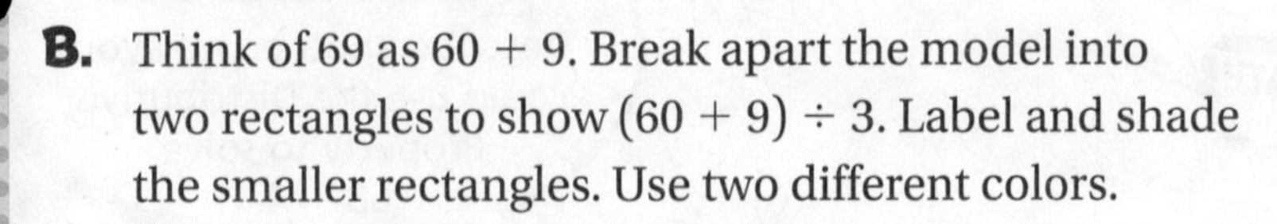

B. Think of 69 as 60 + 9. Break apart the model into two rectangles to show (60 + 9) ÷ 3. Label and shade the smaller rectangles. Use two different colors.

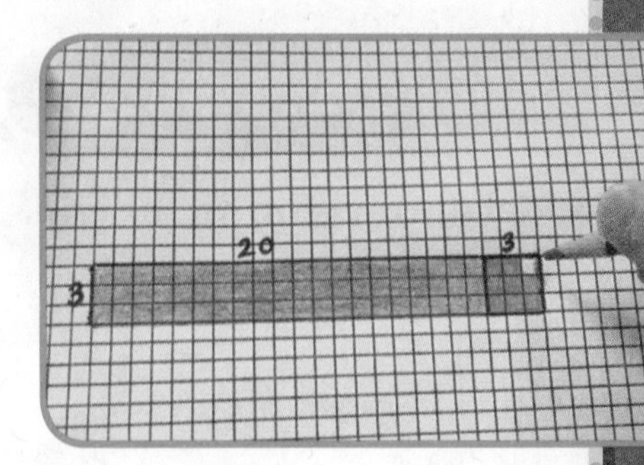

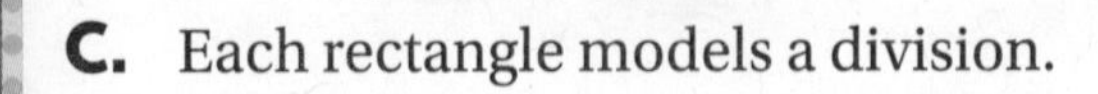

C. Each rectangle models a division.

69 ÷ 3 = (______ ÷ 3) + (______ ÷ 3)

= ______ + ______

= ______

D. Outline another model to show 68 ÷ 4.

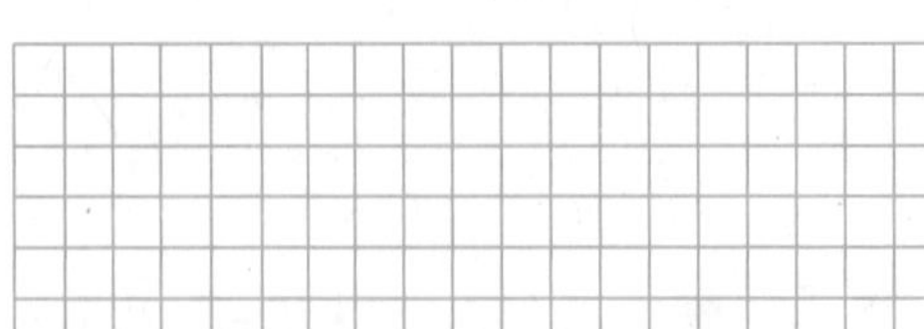

How many groups of 4 can you make? ______

E. Think of 68 as 40 + 28. Break apart the model, label, and shade to show two divisions.

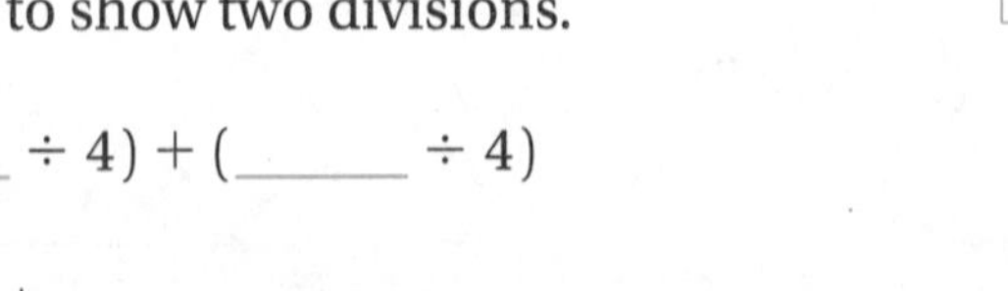

68 ÷ 4 = (______ ÷ 4) + (______ ÷ 4)

= ______ + ______ = ______

Make Connections

You can also model $68 \div 4$ using base-ten blocks.

STEP 1 Model 68.

$68 =$ _____ $+$ _____

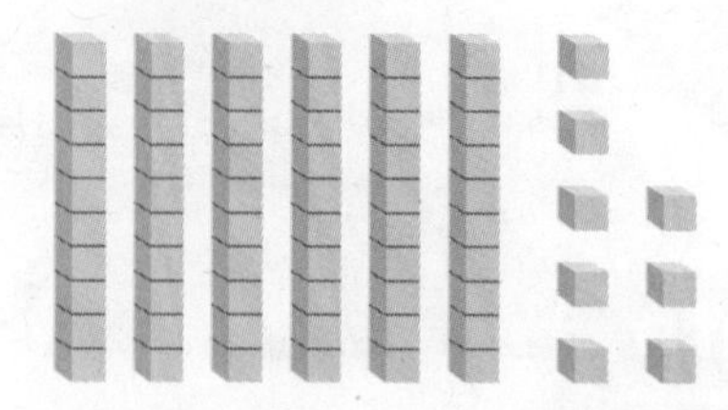

STEP 2 Divide the longs into 4 equal groups. 4 longs divide into 4 equal groups with 2 longs left. Regroup 2 longs as 20 small cubes. Divide them evenly among the 4 groups.

$60 \div 4 =$ _____

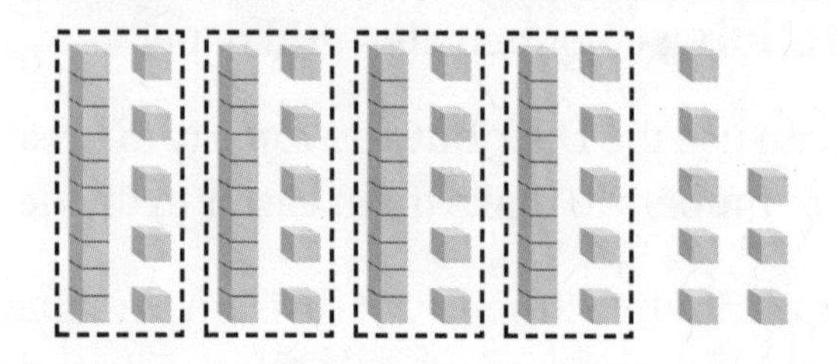

STEP 3 Divide the 8 small cubes into the 4 equal groups.

$8 \div 4 =$ _____

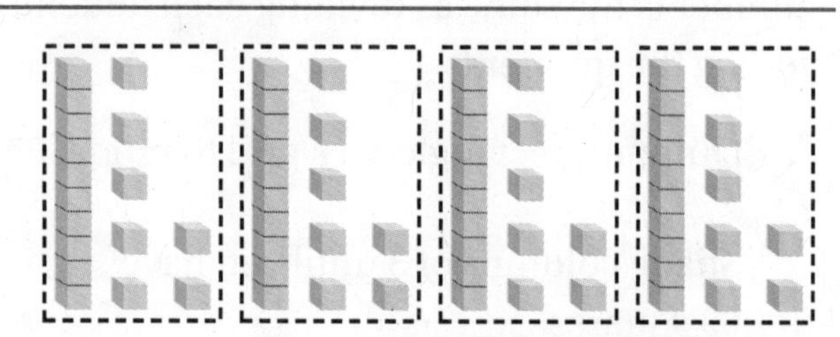

So, $68 \div 4 = (60 \div 4) + (8 \div 4) =$ _____ $+$ _____ $=$ _____

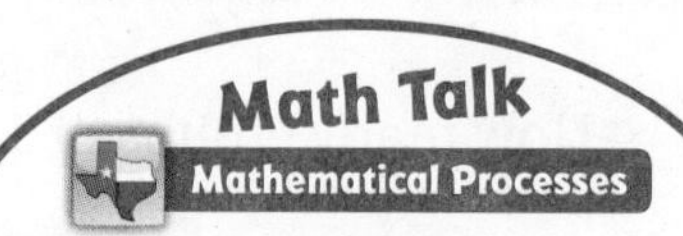

Describe another way you could use the Distributive Property to solve $68 \div 4$.

Share and Show

Model the division on the grid.

1. $26 \div 2 = ($ _____ $\div 2) + ($ _____ $\div 2)$

   $=$ _____ $+$ _____

   $=$ _____

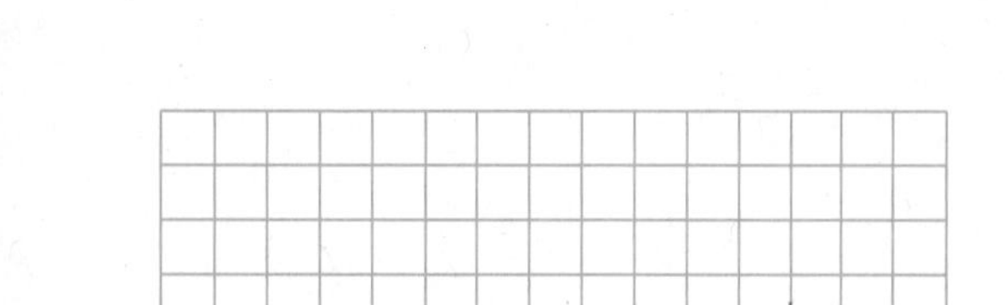

2. $45 \div 3 = ($ _____ $\div 3) + ($ _____ $\div 3)$

   $=$ _____ $+$ _____

   $=$ _____

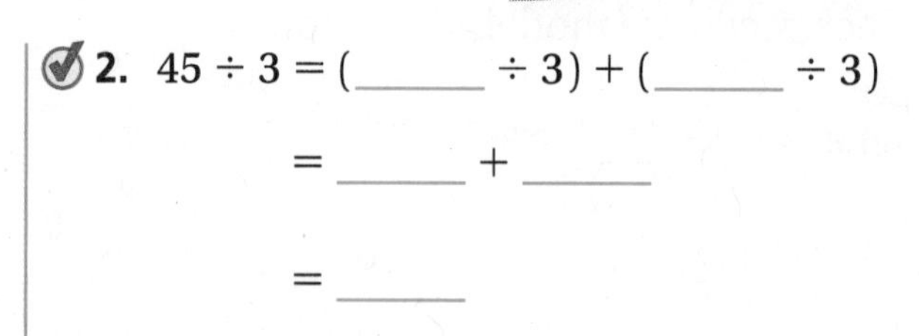

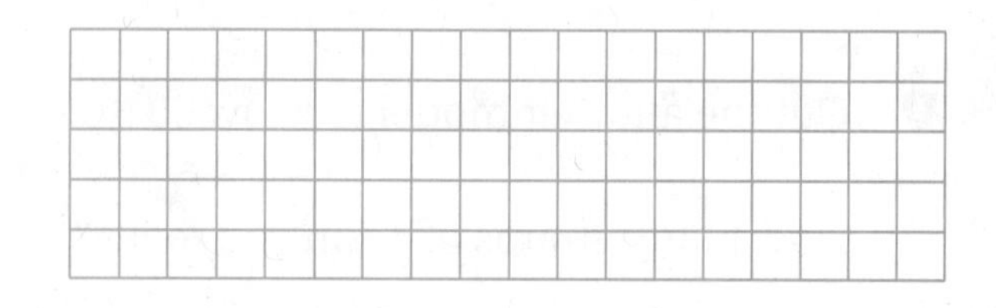

3. **H.O.T.** **Evaluate** To find the quotient $91 \div 7$, would you break up the dividend into $90 + 1$ or $70 + 21$? Explain.

____

____

Name ______________________________

Problem Solving (Real World)

Multi-Step Pose a Problem

4. Christelle went to a gift shop. The shop sells candles in a variety of sizes and colors. The picture shows a display of candles.

   Write a problem that can be solved using the picture.

Pose a problem.

Solve your problem.

5. H.O.T. **Describe** how you could change the problem by changing the number of rows of candles. Then solve the problem.

____

____

____

____

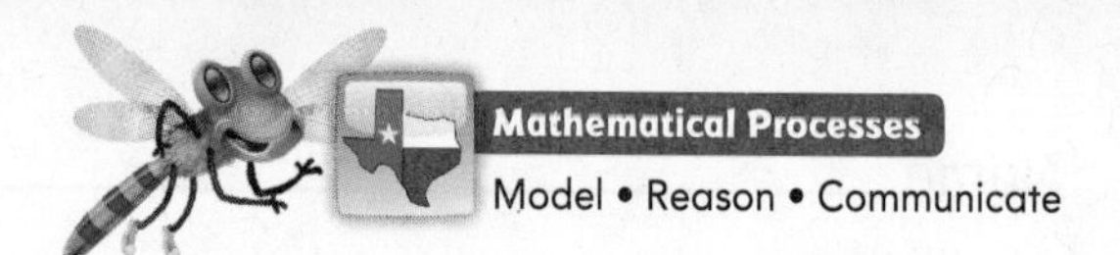

Daily Assessment Task

Fill in the bubble completely to show your answer.

6. **Apply** During the day on Mercury, the temperature can reach 816°F, which is 6 times warmer than the highest temperature found on Earth. What temperature is the highest found on Earth?

   Ⓐ 129°F

   Ⓑ 132°F

   Ⓒ 136°F

   Ⓓ 137°F

7. The chorus has 72 singers. The singers practice in 3 groups of equal size. Which expression is same as $72 \div 3$?

   Ⓐ $(42 \div 3) + (30 \div 3)$

   Ⓒ $(40 \div 3) + (30 \div 3)$

   Ⓑ $(45 \div 3) + (25 \div 3)$

   Ⓓ $(57 \div 3) + (18 \div 3)$

8. **Multi-Step Analyze** Terrance needs $150 to buy a bike. He has $36 saved. If he earns an equal amount over each of the next 3 weeks, how much must he earn each week to save enough for his bike?

   Ⓐ $50

   Ⓑ $40

   Ⓒ $38

   Ⓓ $62

TEXAS Test Prep

9. Max had 200 baseball cards. He gave 14 of them to his younger brother. Max wants to arrange his remaining cards in equal rows of 6 cards each. How many rows of cards will Max have?

   Ⓐ in 35 rows

   Ⓑ in 31 rows

   Ⓒ in 33 rows

   Ⓓ in 36 rows

Homework and Practice

TEKS Number and Operations—4.4.E *Also 4.4.F*
MATHEMATICAL PROCESSES 4.1.A, 4.1.D, 4.1.E, 4.1.F

Name ______________________

9.5 Division and the Distributive Property

Model the division on the grid.

1. $48 \div 4 = (\_\_\_\_ \div 4) + (\_\_\_\_ \div 4)$

$= \_\_\_\_ + \_\_\_\_$

$= \_\_\_\_$

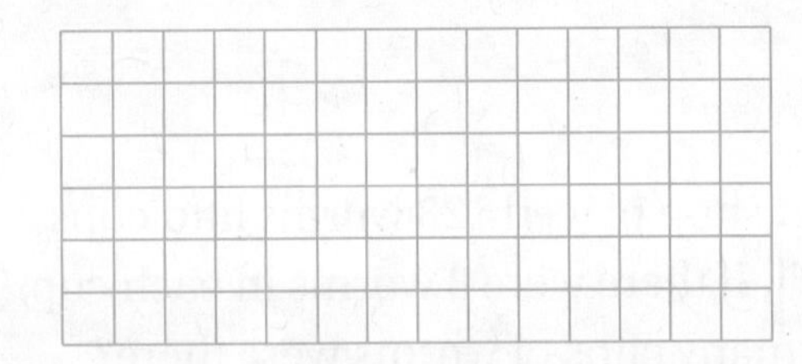

2. $36 \div 3 = (\_\_\_\_ \div 3) + (\_\_\_\_ \div 3)$

$= \_\_\_\_ + \_\_\_\_$

$= \_\_\_\_$

3. $28 \div 2 = (\_\_\_\_ \div 2) + (\_\_\_\_ \div 2)$

$= \_\_\_\_ + \_\_\_\_$

$= \_\_\_\_$

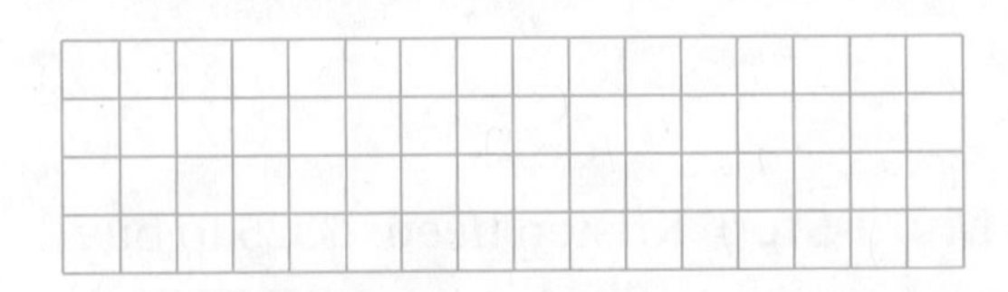

4. $48 \div 3 = (\_\_\_\_ \div 3) + (\_\_\_\_ \div 3)$

$= \_\_\_\_ + \_\_\_\_$

$= \_\_\_\_$

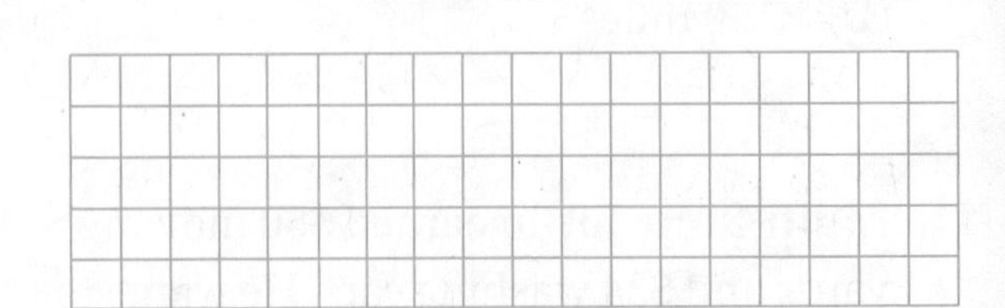

Problem Solving

5. There are 69 jobs for workers at the amusement park. There are 3 workers for each ride. How many rides are there?

____

6. The music club needs to sell 856 raffle tickets in order to buy new music stands. If each of the 8 members in the club wants to sell the same number of tickets, how many tickets does each member need to sell?

____

Lesson Check

Fill in the bubble completely to show your answer.

7. Mr. Dominguez divided 68 students into 4 groups of equal size. Which of the following correctly uses the Distributive Property to find the number of students in each group?

   Ⓐ $(30 \div 4) + (28 \div 4)$

   Ⓑ $(60 \div 4) + (10 \div 4)$

   Ⓒ $(30 \div 4) + (30 \div 4)$

   Ⓓ $(32 \div 4) + (36 \div 4)$

8. The store clerk divided 168 shirts equally onto 4 different display tables. How many shirts did the clerk place on each table?

   Ⓐ 32

   Ⓑ 44

   Ⓒ 42

   Ⓓ 31

9. On his vacation, Walter drove 780 miles. If he drove an equal number of miles each day for 6 days, how many miles did he drive each day?

   Ⓐ 130 miles

   Ⓑ 140 miles

   Ⓒ 120 miles

   Ⓓ 150 miles

10. A bait shop placed 128 worms into cups to sell. If there were 8 worms in each cup, how many cups of worms were there?

    Ⓐ 24

    Ⓑ 16

    Ⓒ 12

    Ⓓ 18

11. **Multi-Step** Justin earned $50 mowing yards and $34 washing cars. He wants to divide his money into 3 equal accounts. How much will he put in each account?

    Ⓐ $14

    Ⓑ $18

    Ⓒ $24

    Ⓓ $28

12. **Multi-Step** Kristen needs $325 to buy a plane ticket. She has saved $277. If she saves an equal amount each week over the next 4 weeks, how much must she save each week to have enough for the ticket?

    Ⓐ $48

    Ⓑ $12

    Ⓒ $44

    Ⓓ $14

Name ______________________________

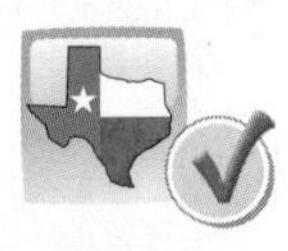

Module 9 Assessment

Vocabulary

Vocabulary
counting numbers
compatible numbers
remainder

Choose the best term from the box to complete the sentence.

1. Numbers that are easy to compute mentally are called

   ________________. (p. 329)

2. When a number cannot be divided evenly, the amount

   left over is called the ________________. (p. 312)

Concepts and Skills

Use an array to find the quotient and remainder. TEKS 4.4.E

3. $26 \div 6$ ______

4. $19 \div 4$ ______

Use basic facts and place value to find the quotient. TEKS 4.4.F

5. $810 \div 9 =$ ______

6. $210 \div 7 =$ ______

7. $3{,}000 \div 6 =$ ______

Use compatible numbers to estimate the quotient. TEKS 4.4.G

8. $635 \div 9$

   ______

9. $412 \div 5$

   ______

10. $490 \div 8$

    ______

Use grid paper or base-ten blocks to model the quotient. Then record the quotient. TEKS 4.4.E

11. $63 \div 3 =$ ______

12. $85 \div 5 =$ ______

13. $168 \div 8 =$ ______

Fill in the bubble completely to show your answer.

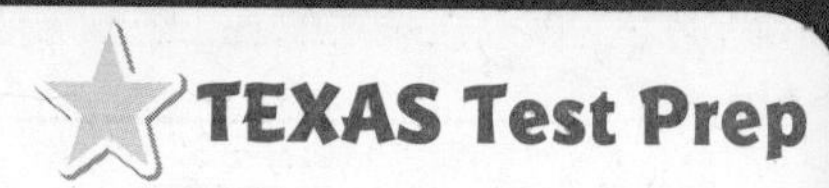

14. Ana has 296 coins in her coin collection. She put the same number of coins in each of 5 jars and 2 boxes. About how many coins are in each jar and box? TEKS 4.4.G

Ⓐ about 400 coins

Ⓑ about 40 coins

Ⓒ about 200 coins

Ⓓ about 20 coins

15. There are 4 students on a team for a relay race. How many teams can be made from 27 students? TEKS 4.4.H

Ⓐ 4

Ⓑ 3

Ⓒ 6

Ⓓ 7

16. A snack vendor had 400 bags of peanuts and 240 bags of popcorn. She sold the same number of bags of snacks at each of 8 baseball games. If she sold all her snacks, how many bags of snacks did she sell at each game? TEKS 4.4.F

Record your answer and fill in the bubbles on the grid. Be sure to use the correct place value.

			.		
⓪	⓪	⓪		⓪	⓪
①	①	①		①	①
②	②	②		②	②
③	③	③		③	③
④	④	④		④	④
⑤	⑤	⑤		⑤	⑤
⑥	⑥	⑥		⑥	⑥
⑦	⑦	⑦		⑦	⑦
⑧	⑧	⑧		⑧	⑧
⑨	⑨	⑨		⑨	⑨

Name ______________________________

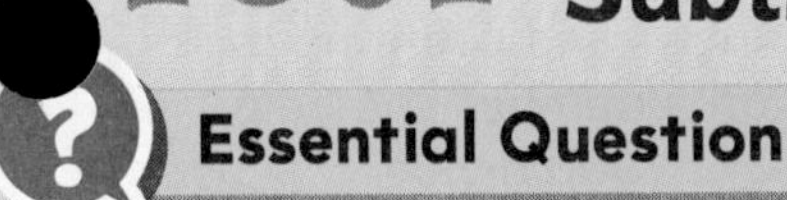

Divide Using Repeated Subtraction

Essential Question How can you use repeated subtraction and multiples to find quotients?

Investigate

Hands On

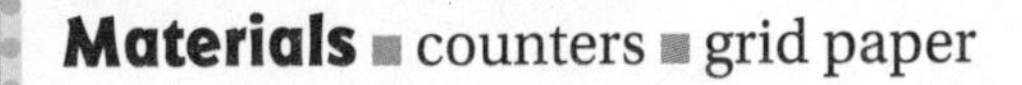

Materials ■ counters ■ grid paper

John is building a backyard pizza oven with an arch opening. He has 72 bricks. He will place 6 bricks at a time as he builds the oven. If he arranges the bricks in piles of 6, how many piles will he have?

You can use repeated subtraction to divide 72 ÷ 6.

A. Begin with 72 counters. Subtract 6 counters.

How many are left? ______

B. Record the subtraction on grid paper as shown. Record the number of counters left and the number of times you subtracted.

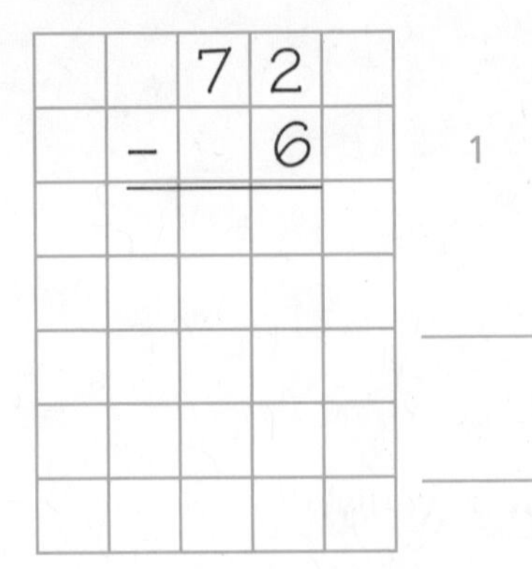

1 time

______ times

______ times

C. Can you reach zero evenly? Explain.

____

____

D. Count the number of times you subtracted 6 counters. ______

So, there are ______ piles of 6 bricks.

Make Connections

Another way to divide by repeated subtraction is to use a number line. Count back by 4s from 52 to find $52 \div 4$.

Math Talk
Mathematical Processes
Explain how subtracting counters and counting back on a number line help you divide.

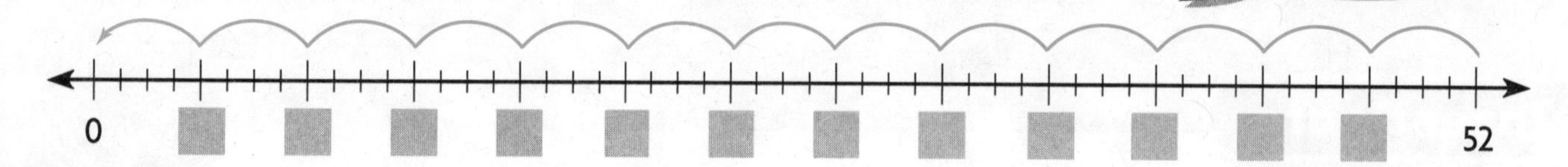

How many equal groups of 4 did you subtract? ______

So, $52 \div 4 =$ ______

Share and Show

MATH BOARD

Use repeated subtraction to divide.

1. $84 \div 7$ ____________

2. $60 \div 4$ ____________

3. $91 \div 8$ ____________

Draw a number line to divide.

4. $65 \div 5 =$ ______

5. $78 \div 6 =$ ______

6. H.O.T. Write Math ▶ Can you divide 32 by 3 evenly? Use the number line to explain your answer.

____

____

____

Name ____________________

Unlock the Problem Real World

7. H.O.T. **Multi-Step Communicate** A new playground will be 114 feet long. Builders need to allow 3 feet at each end of the playground and 9 feet of space for each piece of climbing equipment. They want to put as many climbers along the length of the playground as possible. How many climbers can they place?

a. What are you asked to find?

____

____

b. How can you use repeated subtraction to solve the problem?

____

____

c. How could you use multiples of the divisor to solve the problem in fewer steps?

____

____

d. Show steps to solve the problem.

e. Complete the sentences.

There are ______ equal parts of the playground, each ______ feet long.

So, ______ climbers can fit along the length of the playground.

8. **Multi-Step Analyze** There are 128 students in the fourth grade and 114 students in the fifth grade. Half of these students can use the playground at the same time. How many students is that?

____

9. H.O.T. **Multi-Step** There are 84 seats in one section of the auditorium. Half the seats are in rows of 6 seats and the other half are in rows of 7 seats. How many rows of seats are there in that section all together?

____

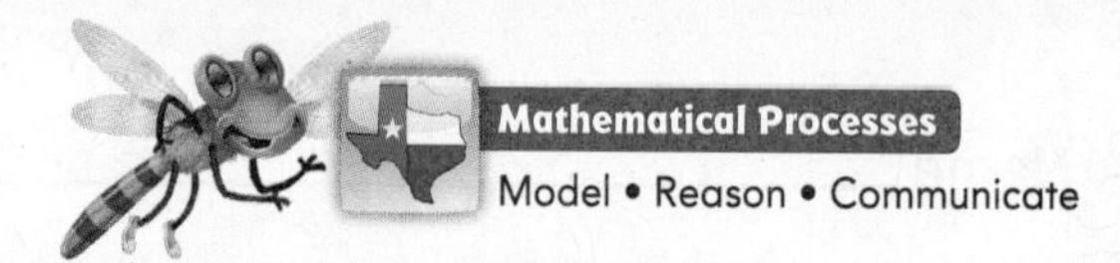

Daily Assessment Task

10. Donna watches her hamster and counts that he blinks 24 times in 3 minutes. If he blinks the same amount every minute, how many times does he blink in 1 minute?

Ⓐ 6 times

Ⓑ 8 times

Ⓒ 7 times

Ⓓ 5 times

11. Mrs. Morse makes gift bags for her students. She has 51 boxes of pencils to share equally among her 3 classes. How many boxes of pencils does each class receive?

Ⓐ 10

Ⓑ 16

Ⓒ 17

Ⓓ 14

12. **Multi-Step** Marcus will work for 30 minutes on his homework exercises. He plans to spend 2 minutes on each of his 5 math exercises. He will spend the rest of his time answering 4 history questions. How much time does he plan to spend on each history question?

Ⓐ 5 minutes

Ⓑ 7 minutes

Ⓒ 6 minutes

Ⓓ 4 minutes

TEXAS Test Prep

13. An architect designed the school auditorium. There are 84 seats in Section A. Each row has 6 seats. How many rows of seats are in Section A?

Ⓐ 24

Ⓑ 14

Ⓒ 4

Ⓓ 60

Homework and Practice

TEKS Number and Operations—4.4.F
MATHEMATICAL PROCESSES 4.1.C, 4.1.D

Name ______________________

10.1 Divide Using Repeated Subtraction

Use repeated subtraction to divide.

1. 65 ÷ 5 = ______

2. 98 ÷ 7 = ______

3. 79 ÷ 5 = ______

4. 37 ÷ 6 = ______

5. 48 ÷ 4 = ______

6. 59 ÷ 3 = ______

Draw a number line to divide.

7. 45 ÷ 5 = ______

8. 90 ÷ 6 = ______

9. 74 ÷ 8 = ______

Problem Solving Real World

10. Last Saturday, 72 students signed up to play basketball. If there are 6 equal-sized teams, how many players are on each team?

11. The pet store is open for 63 hours each week. If it is open 9 hours each day, how many days is it open each week?

Lesson Check

TEXAS Test Prep

Fill in the bubble completely to show your answer.

12. The china shop is packing dishes to move to a new location. There are 112 blue serving bowls to pack equally into 8 boxes. How many bowls will be in each box?

Ⓐ 13

Ⓑ 11

Ⓒ 12

Ⓓ 14

13. There are 60 seeds in a flower package. If Carol puts an equal number of seeds in each of her 5 flowerpots, how many seeds will be in each pot?

Ⓐ 20

Ⓑ 12

Ⓒ 8

Ⓓ 15

14. How many groups of 9 can you subtract from 117?

Ⓐ 13

Ⓑ 12

Ⓒ 14

Ⓓ 15

15. There are 48 students in a gym class. If the students line up in equal rows of 8, how many rows will there be?

Ⓐ 8

Ⓑ 6

Ⓒ 5

Ⓓ 7

16. **Multi-Step** Mrs. Jenkins opened 2 boxes of crayons. Each box contains 64 crayons. She wants to divide the crayons evenly between 8 groups. How many crayons will each group receive?

Ⓐ 18

Ⓑ 8

Ⓒ 16

Ⓓ 24

17. **Multi-Step** John has $40 to spend at the yard sale. He buys 6 books for $2 each. He would like to spend the rest of his money on model cars for his collection. If the cars cost $7 each, how many can he buy?

Ⓐ 7

Ⓑ 6

Ⓒ 5

Ⓓ 4

Name ____________________________

10.2 Divide Using Partial Quotients

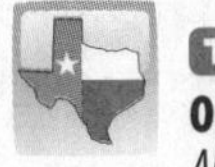

TEKS Number and Operations—4.4.F
Also 4.4.E
MATHEMATICAL PROCESSES
4.1.A, 4.1.C, 4.1.E

Essential Question

How can you use partial quotients to divide by 1-digit divisors?

Unlock the Problem — Real World

At camp, there are 5 players on each lacrosse team. If there are 125 people on lacrosse teams, how many teams are there?

- Underline what you are asked to find.
- Circle what you need to use.
- What operation can you use to find the number of teams?

____

One Way Use partial quotients.

In the **partial quotient** method of dividing, multiples of the divisor are subtracted from the dividend and then the partial quotients are added together.

Divide. 125 ÷ 5 **Write.** $5\overline{)125}$

STEP 1

Start by subtracting a greater multiple, such as 10 times the divisor. For example, you know that you can make at least 10 teams of 5 players.

Continue subtracting until the remaining number is less than the multiple, 50.

STEP 2

Subtract smaller multiples, such as 5, 2, or 1 times the divisor until the remaining number is less than the divisor. In other words, keep going until you no longer have enough players to make a team.

Then add the partial quotients to find the quotient.

$5\overline{)125}$		Partial Quotients
− ____	10 × ____	10
____		
− ____	10 × ____	10
____		
− ____	5 × ____	+5
____		

Math Talk

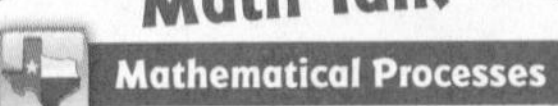

Explain how you found the total number of teams after finding the partial quotients.

So, there are ______ lacrosse teams.

Another Way Use area models to record the partial quotients.

Jarod and Mi also found the number of teams using partial quotients. They recorded the partial quotients using area models. They each still had 25 as the quotient.

Jarod

5 | 125

10
5 | 50 | 75 — 125 − ___ = 75

10 10
5 | 50 | 50 | 25 — 75 − ___ = 25

10 10 5
5 | 50 | 50 | 25 — 25 − ___ = 0

10 + 10 + 5 = ______

Mi

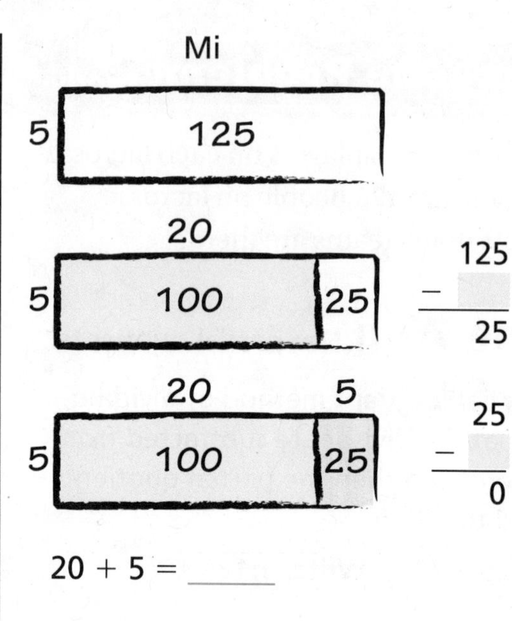

20 + 5 = ______

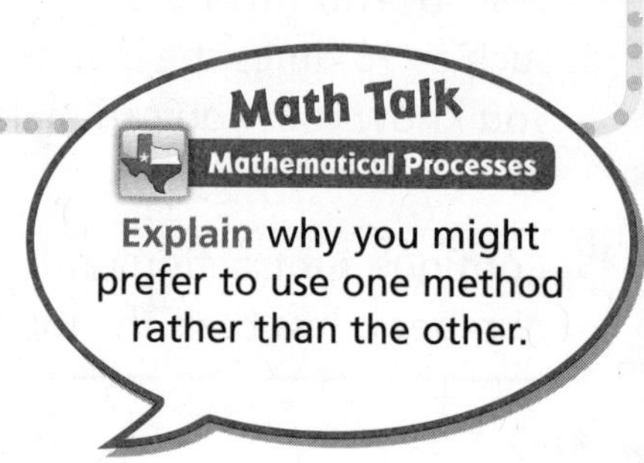

Share and Show

1. Lacrosse is played on a field 330 ft long. How many yards long is a lacrosse field? (3 feet = 1 yard)

Divide. Use partial quotients.

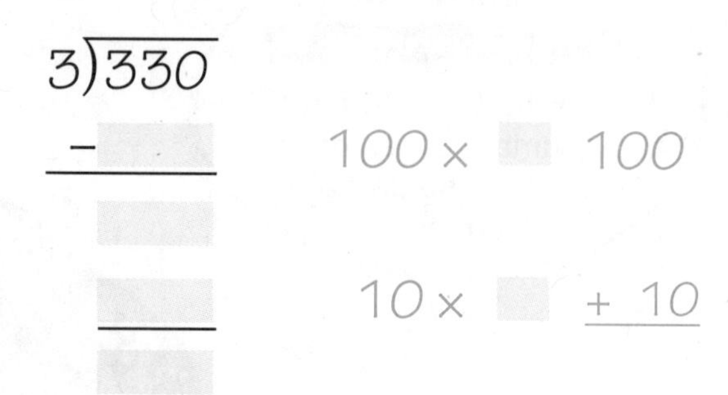

So, the lacrosse field is ______ yards long.

Name ____________________

Divide. Use partial quotients.

2. $3\overline{)225}$

Divide. Use area models to record the partial quotients.

3. $428 \div 4 =$ ______

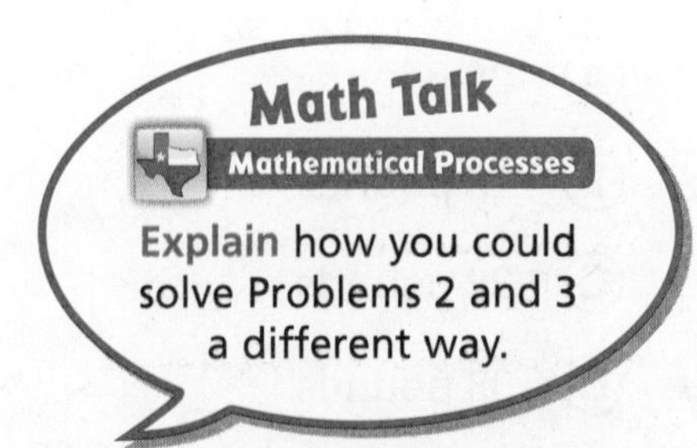

Problem Solving Real World

Use the table for 4–5.

4. **Multi-Step** Rob filled 9 plastic boxes with basketball cards and hockey cards. There were the same number of cards in each box. How many cards did he put in each box?

____

5. **H.O.T. Multi-Step** Rob filled 3 fewer plastic boxes with football cards than the nine boxes he filled with basketball cards and hockey cards. How many boxes did he fill? How many football cards were in each box?

____

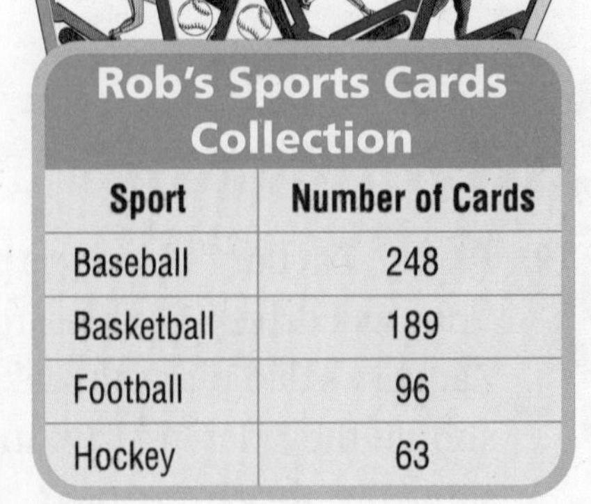

Rob's Sports Cards Collection

Sport	Number of Cards
Baseball	248
Basketball	189
Football	96
Hockey	63

6. **H.O.T. Communicate** What is the least number you can divide by 5 to get a three-digit quotient? Explain how you found your answer.

____

____

____

____

____

____

Write Math ▸ Show Your Work

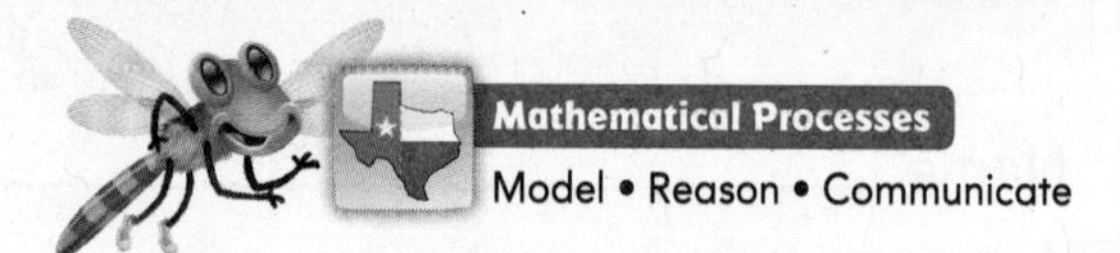

Daily Assessment Task

7. On the American frontier, salt was 4 times as expensive as beef. Suppose a family on the frontier buys 112 pounds of beef. How much salt could they purchase with the same amount of money?

Ⓐ 28 pounds

Ⓑ 13 pounds

Ⓒ 22 pounds

Ⓓ 33 pounds

8. Multi-Step A family that owns an orchard collects 153 pounds of apples in one day and 126 pounds the next day. If the harvest is divided equally among 9 containers, how many pounds of apples are in each container?

Ⓐ 19 pounds

Ⓑ 37 pounds

Ⓒ 31 pounds

Ⓓ 27 pounds

9. Apply Zachary's family is planning a trip to Washington D.C. They will drive 837 miles from their home in St. Louis, Missouri. Zachary's dad plans to make the trip in 3 days. How many miles should they plan to drive in each day if they want to drive the same distance every day?

Ⓐ 314 miles

Ⓑ 239 miles

Ⓒ 409 miles

Ⓓ 279 miles

TEXAS Test Prep

10. There are 80 fourth grade students and 46 fifth grade students who signed up to learn how to play lacrosse. If there are 6 students in each group, how many groups are there?

Ⓐ 120

Ⓑ 20

Ⓒ 21

Ⓓ 12

Name ______________________________

10.3 Model Division with Regrouping

Essential Question How can you use base-ten blocks or an algorithm to model division with regrouping?

Investigate

Materials ■ base-ten blocks

The librarian wants to share 54 books equally among 3 classes. How many books will she give to each class?

A. Draw 3 circles to represent the classes. Then use base-ten blocks to model 54. Show 54 as 5 tens and 4 ones.

B. Share the tens equally among the 3 groups.

C. If there are any tens left, regroup them as ones. Share the ones equally among the 3 groups.

D. There are ______ ten(s) and ______ one(s) in each group.

So, the librarian will give ______ books to each class.

Make Connections

Divide. $76 \div 3$

$3\overline{)76}$

Record each step.

STEP 1

Share the 7 tens equally among 3 groups.

There are ______ tens in each group.

______ tens were used. There is ______ ten left over.

$3\overline{)76}$ with labels: tens in each group; − tens used; ten left over

STEP 2

One ten cannot be shared among 3 groups without regrouping.
Regroup 1 ten.

There are now ______ ones to share.

$$\begin{array}{r} 2 \\ 3\overline{)76} \\ -6 \\ \hline \square \end{array}$$

← ones to share

STEP 3

Share the ones equally among 3 groups.

There are ______ ones in each group.

______ ones were shared. There is ______ one left over.

ones in each group

$$\begin{array}{r} 2\square \\ 3\overline{)76} \\ -6 \\ \hline 16 \\ -\square \\ \hline \square \end{array}$$

← ones used

← one left over

Use a quick picture to check your work.

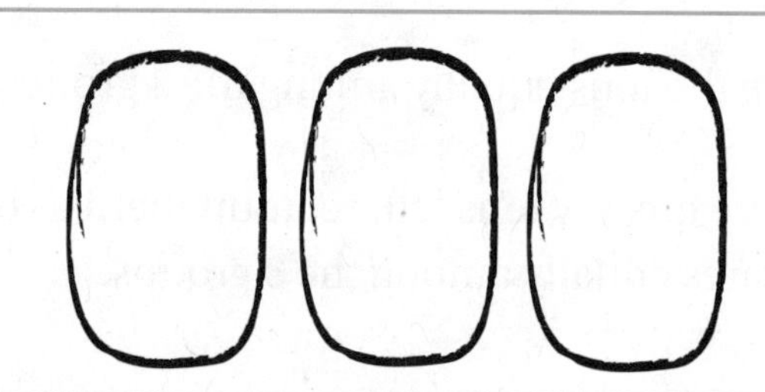

So, there are 3 groups of ______ and ______ left over.

Share and Show

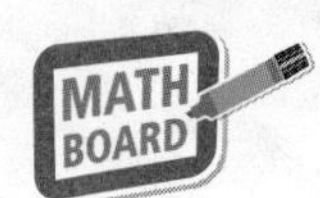

Divide. Use base-ten blocks.

1. 48 ÷ 3 ______
2. 84 ÷ 4 ______
3. 72 ÷ 5 ______

Divide. Record the steps. Draw quick pictures to check your work.

4. 59 ÷ 2 ______

tens in each group

ones in each group

$$\begin{array}{r} \square\square \\ 2\overline{)59} \\ -\square \\ \hline \square \\ -\square \\ \hline \square \end{array}$$

← tens used

← ones to share

← ones used

← one left over

Name ______________________________

Problem Solving (Real World)

Sense or Nonsense?

5. **H.O.T.** **Multi-Step Use Diagrams** Angela and Zach drew quick pictures to find 68 ÷ 4. Whose quick picture makes sense? Whose quick picture is nonsense? **Explain** your reasoning.

I drew 1 ten and 2 ones in each group.

I drew 1 ten a
7 ones in each group.

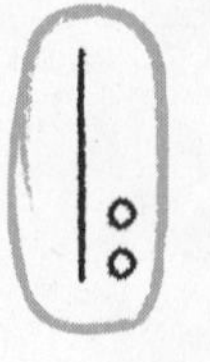
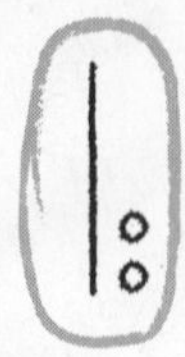

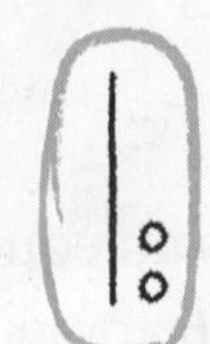

____
____
____
____
____
____
____

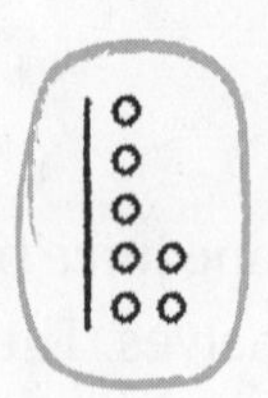

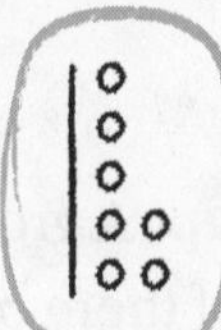

____
____
____
____
____
____
____

6. **H.O.T.** **Analyze** What did Angela forget to do after she shared the tens equally among the 4 groups?

____

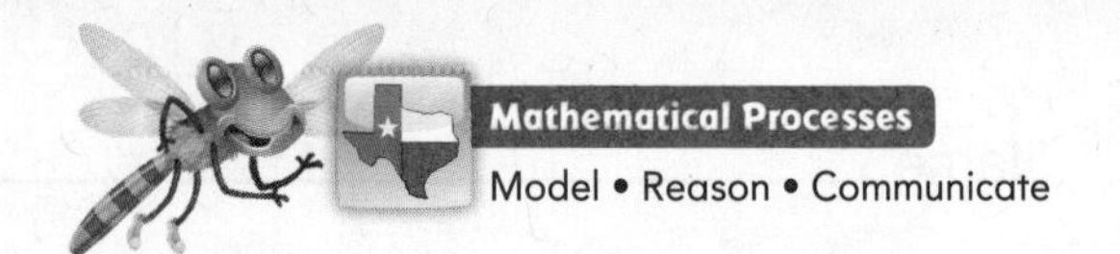

Daily Assessment Task

Fill in the bubble completely to show your answer.

7. **Use Tools** Lisa has 51 small toys. She puts an equal number of toys in each of 3 bottles. How many toys does Lisa put in each bottle? Use base-ten blocks or a quick picture to solve.

   Ⓐ 10

   Ⓑ 14

   Ⓒ 17

   Ⓓ 18

8. Jay shares 84 baseball cards equally among 6 friends. How many baseball cards does he give each friend?

   Ⓐ 13

   Ⓑ 20

   Ⓒ 10

   Ⓓ 14

9. **Multi-Step** A grocer has 78 grape juice boxes. He puts an equal number of them on each of 3 shelves. The grocer has 96 apple juice boxes. He puts an equal number of them on each of 4 shelves. How many more grape juice boxes than apple juice boxes are on each shelf?

   Ⓐ 4 Ⓒ 6

   Ⓑ 2 Ⓓ 1

TEXAS Test Prep

10. Parker rode his bike a total of 85 miles over five weeks. He rode the same number of miles each week. How far did he ride each week?

   Ⓐ 80 miles

   Ⓑ 11 miles

   Ⓒ 16 miles and 5 miles left over

   Ⓓ 17 miles

Name ______________________

10.3 Model Division with Regrouping

Divide. Use base-ten blocks.

1. $68 \div 4$ ______
2. $39 \div 3$ ______
3. $75 \div 6$ ______
4. $84 \div 4$ ______
5. $96 \div 9$ ______
6. $60 \div 4$ ______

Divide. Record the steps. Draw quick pictures to check your work.

7. $63 \div 2$ ______

$2\overline{)63}$

8. $74 \div 3$ ______

$3\overline{)74}$

Problem Solving Real World

9. There are 48 students ready to run relay races on field day. How many teams of 4 can be formed?

____

10. A total of 78 students will go on the Saturday field trip to the museum. Each van can carry 6 students. What is the least number of vans needed?

____

Lesson Check

TEXAS Test Prep

Fill in the bubble completely to show your answer.

11. Laura picked 90 flowers and divided them equally into 6 vases. How many flowers are in each vase?

Ⓐ 18

Ⓑ 9

Ⓒ 12

Ⓓ 15

12. A jewelry store clerk has 72 rings to display. The clerk arranges the rings in 6 equal rows. How many rings are in each row?

Ⓐ 12

Ⓑ 14

Ⓒ 10

Ⓓ 13

13. Chris has collected 96 leaves for his nature book. If he places 6 leaves on each page, how many pages will he use?

Ⓐ 16

Ⓑ 11

Ⓒ 15

Ⓓ 12

14. At the plant store, there are 64 flowerpots divided equally onto 4 shelves. How many flowerpots are on each shelf?

Ⓐ 12

Ⓑ 14

Ⓒ 16

Ⓓ 21

15. **Multi-Step** Mindy is preparing cookie boxes for gifts. She divides 36 chocolate chip cookies evenly into 6 boxes. Then she divided 54 sugar cookies evenly into the same 6 boxes. How many cookies are in each of Mindy's boxes?

Ⓐ 12

Ⓑ 15

Ⓒ 8

Ⓓ 16

16. **Multi-Step** A gardener has 52 red rose bushes and 40 yellow rose bushes. He plants an equal number of each color in 4 gardens. How many more red rose bushes than yellow rose bushes are in each garden?

Ⓐ 4

Ⓑ 13

Ⓒ 10

Ⓓ 3

Name ______________________________

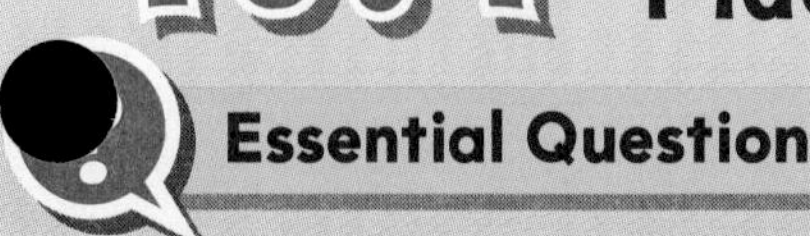

10.4 Place the First Digit

Essential Question How can you use place value to know where to place the first digit in the quotient?

Unlock the Problem (Real World)

Jaime took 144 photos on a digital camera. The photos are to be placed equally in 6 photo albums. How many photos will be in each album?

- Underline what you are asked to find.
- Circle what you need to use.

Example Divide. 144 ÷ 6

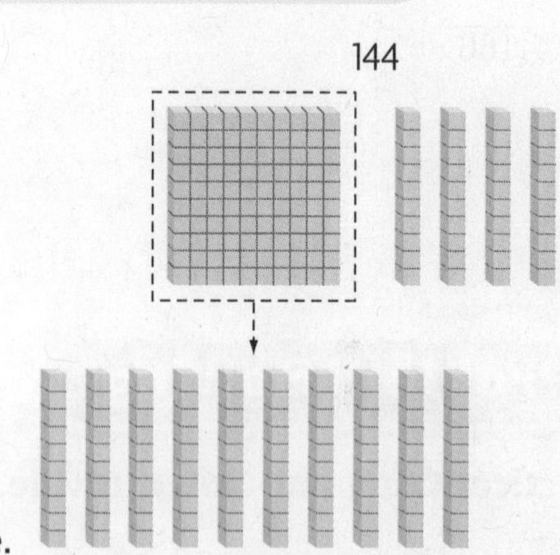

STEP 1 Use place value to place the first digit.
Look at the hundreds in 144.
1 hundred cannot be shared among 6 groups without regrouping.
Regroup 1 hundred as 10 tens.

Now there are ______ tens to share among 6 groups.

The first digit of the quotient will be in the ______ place.

STEP 2 Divide the tens.

$$6\overline{)144}$$ quotient: 2

Divide. 14 tens ÷ 6

Multiply. 6 × 2 tens

Subtract. 14 tens − 12 tens
Check. 2 tens cannot be shared among 6 groups without regrouping.

STEP 3 Divide the ones.
Regroup 2 tens as 20 ones.

Now there are ______ ones to share among 6 groups.

$$\begin{array}{r} 24 \\ 6\overline{)144} \\ -12\downarrow \\ \hline 24 \\ - \quad \\ \hline \end{array}$$

Divide. ______ ones ÷ ______

Multiply. ______ × ______ ones

Subtract. ______ ones − ______ ones
Check. 0 ones cannot be shared among 6 groups.

So, there will be ______ photos in each album.

Math Idea
After you divide each place, the remainder should be less than the divisor.

Math Talk

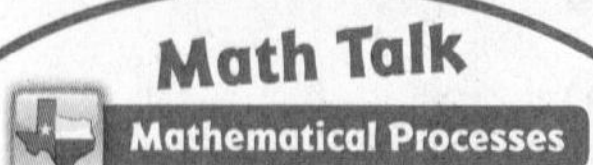

Explain how the answer would change if Jaime had 146 photos.

Share and Show

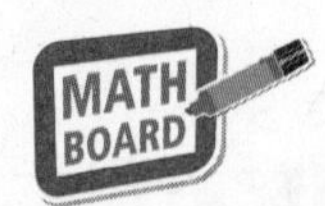

1. There are 452 pictures of dogs in 4 equal groups. How many pictures are in each group? **Explain** how you can use place value to place the first digit in the quotient.

$4\overline{)452}$

Divide.

2. $4\overline{)166}$

3. $5\overline{)775}$

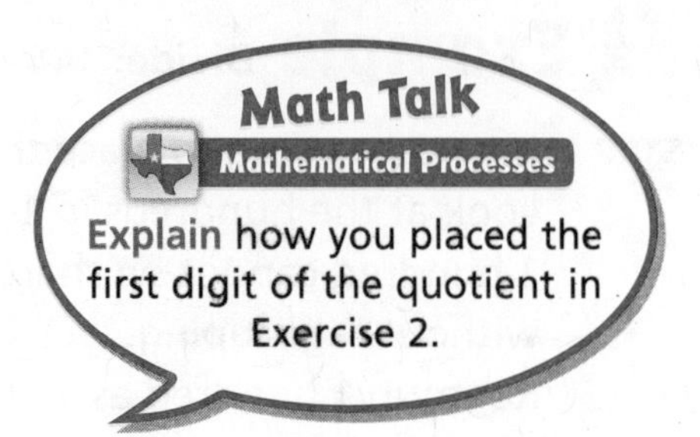

Problem Solving

Practice: Copy and Solve **Divide.**

4. 516 ÷ 2

5. 516 ÷ 3

6. 516 ÷ 4

7. 516 ÷ 5

8. H.O.T. Look back at your answers to Exercises 4–7. What happens to the quotient when the divisor increases? **Explain.**

9. **Multi-Step** Reggie has 192 pictures of animals. He wants to keep half and then divide the rest equally among three friends. How many pictures will each friend get?

   (A) 96
   (B) 32
   (C) 48
   (D) 64

10. H.O.T. **Multi-Step** There are 146 students, 5 teachers, and 8 chaperones going to the theater. To reserve their seats, they need to reserve entire rows. Each row has 8 seats. How many rows must they reserve?

   (A) 20
   (B) 18
   (C) 19
   (D) 158

Name ______________________________

Unlock the Problem

11. H.O.T. **Multi-Step** Nan wants to put 234 pictures in an album with a blue cover. How many full pages will she have in her album?

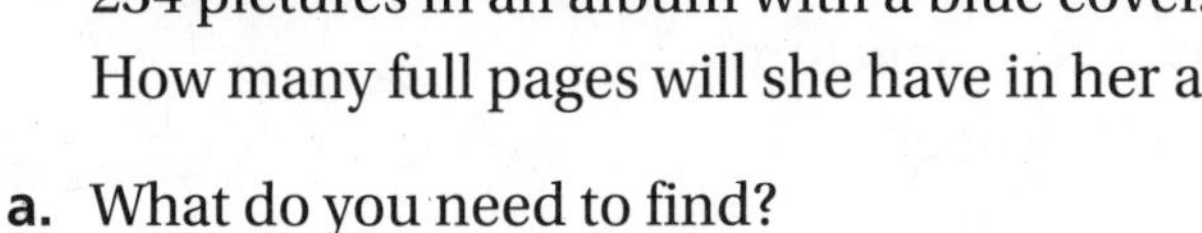

Photo Albums

Color of cover	Pictures per page
Blue	4
Green	6
Red	9

a. What do you need to find?

____

b. Communicate How will you use division to find the number of full pages?

____

____

____

c. Show the steps you will use to solve the problem.

d. Complete the following sentences.

Nan has _____ pictures.

She wants to put the pictures in an album with pages that each hold _____ pictures.

She will have an album with _____ full pages and _____ pictures on another page.

12. Apply Juan wants to put his 672 pictures in an album with a green cover. How many full pages will he have in his album?

____

13. H.O.T. **Multi-Step** Talia has 162 pictures to put in a photo album. If she wants only full pages, which color albums could she use?

____

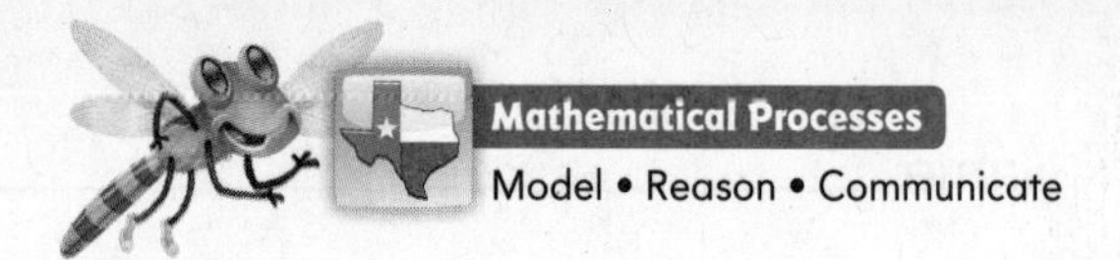

Daily Assessment Task

Fill in the bubble completely to show your answer.

14. Danny makes a website to showcase images of unusual manhole covers. He takes 264 pictures for the site. Danny places 8 pictures on each page of the site. How many pages of pictures does Danny's site have?

Ⓐ 33 pages

Ⓑ 330 pages

Ⓒ 3 pages

Ⓓ 30 pages

15. Debi celebrates her birthday with friends at an arcade. Debi's parents want to share 300 tokens equally among the 9 friends. Debi uses division to find how many tokens each person gets. In which place is the first digit of the quotient?

Ⓐ thousands

Ⓑ hundreds

Ⓒ tens

Ⓓ ones

16. **Multi-Step** Debi's parents want to share 300 tokens equally among the 9 friends. After Debi's parents give each person the same number of tokens, how many tokens are left over?

Ⓐ 0 tokens

Ⓑ 2 tokens

Ⓒ 1 token

Ⓓ 3 tokens

TEXAS Test Prep

17. Kat wants to put 485 pictures in an album with a red cover. There are 9 pictures per page. She uses division to find out how many full pages she will have. In which place is the first digit of the quotient?

Ⓐ thousands

Ⓑ hundreds

Ⓒ tens

Ⓓ ones

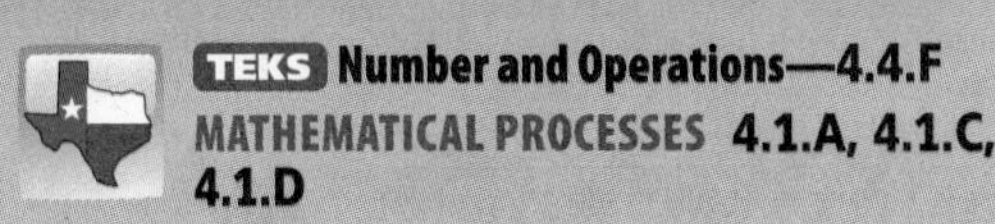

Homework and Practice

Name ____________________

10.4 Place the First Digit

Divide.

1. $8\overline{)720}$

2. $4\overline{)173}$

3. $7\overline{)511}$

4. $3\overline{)139}$

5. $5\overline{)324}$

6. $9\overline{)414}$

7. $6\overline{)228}$

8. $8\overline{)159}$

9. $428 \div 2$ ________

10. $428 \div 3$ ________

11. $428 \div 4$ ________

12. $428 \div 5$ ________

Problem Solving

13. Camp Mesquite will provide 4 buses for 212 campers. If each bus carries the same number of campers, how many campers will ride in each bus?

____

14. The garden center received a shipment of 132 daisies. If each table displays the same number of daisies, how many daisies will be placed on each of 3 tables?

____

Lesson Check

TEXAS Test Prep

Fill in the bubble completely to show your answer.

15. Lauren collected 532 pennies in a donation box. She wants to divide the pennies equally into 4 containers. Lauren uses division to find how many pennies to put into each container. In which place is the first digit of the quotient?

Ⓐ thousands
Ⓑ hundreds
Ⓒ tens
Ⓓ ones

16. Mark opens a box of 500 cups for the football concession stand. Mark uses division to divide the cups equally among 6 windows. In which place is the first digit of the quotient?

Ⓐ ones
Ⓑ tens
Ⓒ hundreds
Ⓓ thousands

17. Mrs. Samson bought 294 craft sticks for a class project. She divides her class into 7 groups and gives each group an equal number of sticks. If she uses all of the sticks, how many will each group receive?

Ⓐ 40
Ⓑ 43
Ⓒ 41
Ⓓ 42

18. Cassie read 483 pages of her book in one week. If she read the same number of pages each day, how many pages did she read in 1 day?

Ⓐ 78
Ⓑ 79
Ⓒ 69
Ⓓ 68

19. **Multi-Step** Mr. Parsons bought 293 apples to make pies for his shop. Six apples are needed for each pie. If Mr. Parsons makes the most apple pies possible, how many apples will be left over?

Ⓐ 5
Ⓑ 1
Ⓒ 3
Ⓓ 6

20. **Multi-Step** At an art school, 112 students are in 4 equal-sized drawing classes. There are 120 students in 5 equal-sized painting classes. How many more students are in one drawing class than are in one painting class?

Ⓐ 28
Ⓑ 5
Ⓒ 25
Ⓓ 4

Name ____________________

10.5 Divide by 1-Digit Numbers

Essential Question How can you divide multi-digit numbers?

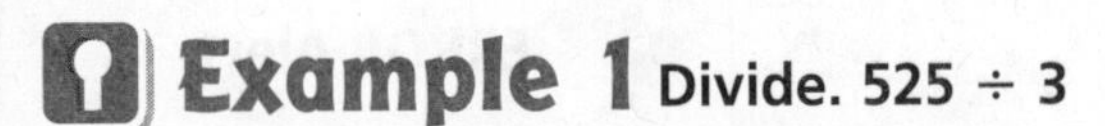

Students in the third, fourth, and fifth grades made 525 origami animals to display in the library. Each grade made the same number of animals. How many animals did each grade make?

Example 1 Divide. 525 ÷ 3

STEP 1 Use place value to place the first digit. Look at the hundreds in 525. Five hundreds can be shared among 3 groups without first regrouping. The first digit of the quotient will be in the ____________ place.

STEP 2 Divide the hundreds.

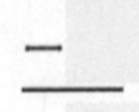

$$\begin{array}{r} 1 \\ 3\overline{)525} \\ -\square \\ \hline \square \end{array}$$

Divide. Share ______ hundreds equally among ______ groups.

Multiply. ______ × ______

Subtract. ______ − ______

Check. ______ hundreds cannot be shared among 3 groups without regrouping.

Math Talk Mathematical Processes

At the checking step, what would you do if the number is greater than the divisor?

STEP 3 Divide the tens.

$$\begin{array}{r} 17 \\ 3\overline{)525} \\ -3\downarrow \\ \hline 22 \\ -\square \\ \hline \square \end{array}$$

Divide. Share ____________ equally among ______ groups.

Multiply. ____________________

Subtract. ______ − ______

Check. ____________________

____

____________________.

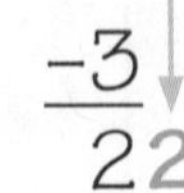

STEP 4 Divide the ones.

$$\begin{array}{r} 175 \\ 3\overline{)525} \\ -3\downarrow \\ \hline 22 \\ -21\downarrow \\ \hline 15 \\ -\square \\ \hline \square \end{array}$$

Divide. Share ____________ equally among ______ groups.

Multiply. ____________________

Subtract. ______ − ______

Check. ____________ are left.

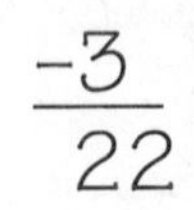

So, each class made ____________ origami animals.

There are 8,523 sheets of origami paper to be divided equally among 8 schools. How many sheets of origami paper will each school get?

Example 2 Divide. 8,523 ÷ 8

STEP 1 Use place value to place the first digit.

Look at the thousands in 8,523.
8 thousands can be shared among 8 groups without regrouping.

The first digit of the quotient will be

in the __________ place.

STEP 2 Divide the thousands.

STEP 3 Divide the hundreds.

STEP 4 Divide the tens.

STEP 5 Divide the ones.

So, each school will get ______ sheets of origami paper.

There will be ______ sheets left.

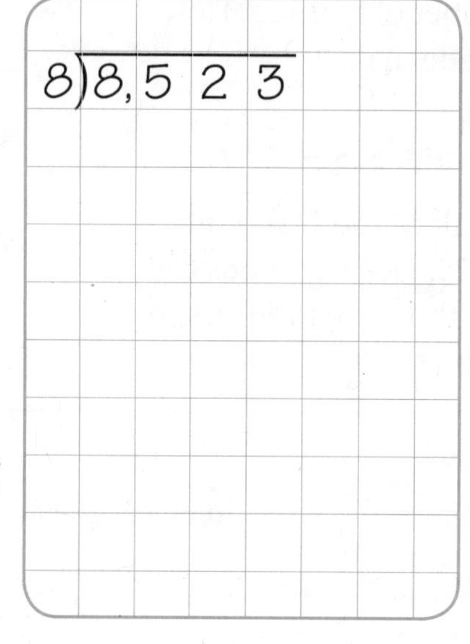

ERROR Alert

Place a zero in the quotient when a place in the dividend cannot be divided by the divisor.

Share and Show

1. Ollie used 852 beads to make 4 bracelets. He put the same number of beads on each bracelet. How many beads does each bracelet have?

So, each bracelet has ______ beads.

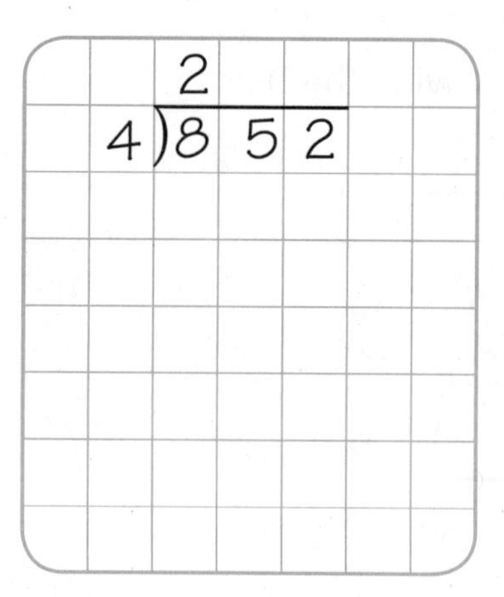

Divide.

2. $2\overline{)394}$

3. $2\overline{)803}$

4. $4\overline{)3,448}$

Name ______________________________

Problem Solving (Real World)

Use the table for 5–7.

The Craft Store	
Item	**Price**
Origami Book	$24 each
Origami Paper	$6 per pack
Origami Kit	$8 each

5. **H.O.T.** **Multi-Step** Four teachers bought 10 origami books and 100 packs of origami paper for their classrooms. They will share the cost of the items equally. How much should each teacher pay?

____

6. **H.O.T.** **Communicate** Six students shared equally the cost of 18 of one of the items in the chart. Each student paid $24. What item did they buy? **Explain** how to use division to find your answer.

____

____

____

____

____

7. **Apply** Ms. Alvarez has $1,482 to spend on origami paper. How many packs can she buy?

____

8. **Multi-Step** Evan made origami cranes with red, blue, and yellow paper. The number of cranes in each color is the same. If there are 342 cranes, how many of them are either blue or yellow?

____

9. **H.O.T.** **Multi-Step** In 4 months, Mr. Nash wants to buy a car for $3,458. He already has saved $1,226. How much must he save each month to have the total amount he needs if he saves the same amount each month?

____

Write Math ▶ **Show Your Work**

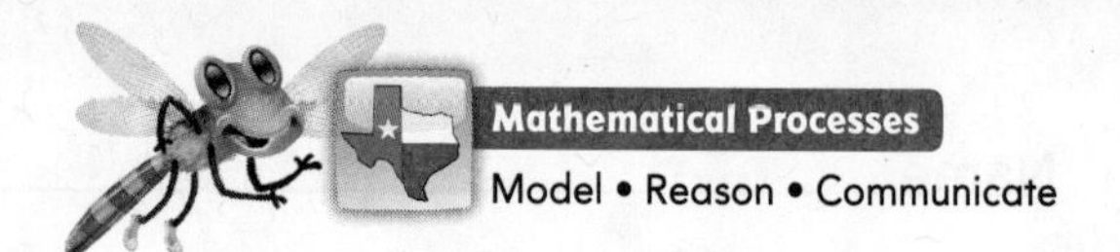

Daily Assessment Task

Fill in the bubble completely to show your answer.

10. **Apply** A company made 1,215 yards of copper wire. They want to wrap the same amount of wire on each of three spools. How many yards of wire will be on each spool?

Ⓐ 45 yards

Ⓑ 405 yards

Ⓒ 414 yards

Ⓓ 43 yards

11. Pam's school is opening a new school library. She is packing books to help move. She can fit 8 books in each box. The school has 1,088 books. How many boxes does she need?

Ⓐ 136 boxes

Ⓑ 111 boxes

Ⓒ 211 boxes

Ⓓ 174 boxes

12. **Multi-Step** Mrs. Paul is buying supplies for art class. She can buy small bottles of paint for $2 each and each canvas costs $1. She has $40 to spend. If she buys 14 canvases, how many bottles of paint can she buy?

Ⓐ 26 bottles

Ⓑ 13 bottles

Ⓒ 52 bottles

Ⓓ 39 bottles

TEXAS Test Prep

13. An artist made 515 origami animals in 5 days. She made the same number of animals each day. How many origami animals did she make each day?

Ⓐ 510

Ⓑ 103

Ⓒ 13

Ⓓ 2,060

Homework and Practice

TEKS Number and Operations—4.4.F
MATHEMATICAL PROCESSES 4.1.A, 4.1.C, 4.1.D, 4.1.E

Name ____________________

10.5 Divide by 1-Digit Numbers

Divide.

1.

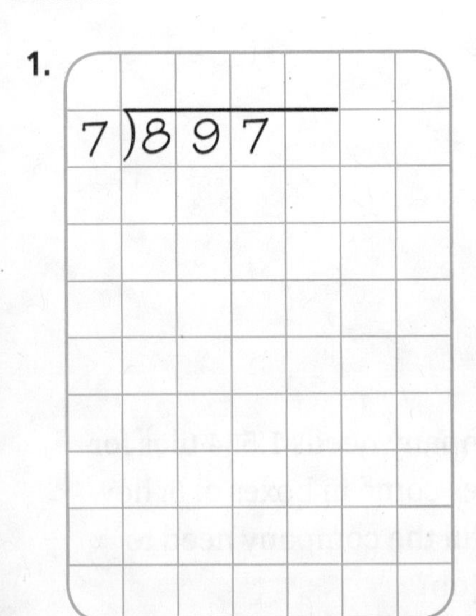

2. 3)6, 2 4 6

3.

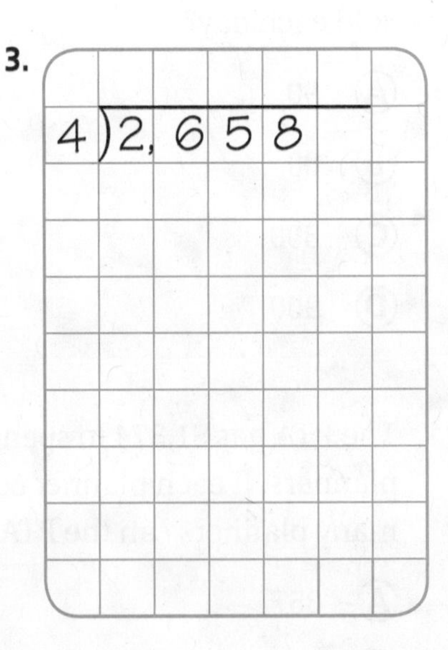

4. 3)1106

5. 5)2078

6. 6)7,380

Problem Solving Real World

7. A busy coffee shop sold 1,160 cups of coffee in five days. If the same amount of cups were sold each day, how many cups were sold in 1 day?

____

8. The coffee shop sold 340 slices of pie in five days. If the same number of slices were sold each day, how many slices of pie were sold in 1 day?

____

Lesson Check

Fill in the bubble completely to show your answer.

9. The computer club is selling 4,500 raffle tickets to win a new laptop computer. If they want to divide the tickets evenly to sell over 5 days, how many tickets can be sold each day?

Ⓐ 90

Ⓑ 80

Ⓒ 800

Ⓓ 900

10. The football booster club sold 456 slices of pizza at the game. If each pizza was sliced into 8 pieces, how many pizzas did the booster club sell?

Ⓐ 56

Ⓑ 60

Ⓒ 57

Ⓓ 55

11. The PTA has $1,374 to spend on student planners. If each planner costs $3, how many planners can the PTA purchase?

Ⓐ 357

Ⓑ 428

Ⓒ 358

Ⓓ 458

12. A flooring company needs 1,554 tiles for a job. If the tiles come in boxes of 6, how many boxes will the company need to complete the job?

Ⓐ 259

Ⓑ 268

Ⓒ 279

Ⓓ 369

13. **Multi-Step** Jessica wants to read 1,500 pages over her summer break. So far, she has read 412 pages. If she reads the same number of pages each week for the next 8 weeks, how many pages will she have to read each week to achieve her goal?

Ⓐ 272

Ⓑ 136

Ⓒ 125

Ⓓ 187

14. **Multi-Step** The flower shop received a shipment of 248 pink roses and 256 red roses. The shop owner uses 6 roses to make an arrangement. How many arrangements can the shop owner make if he uses all the roses?

Ⓐ 86

Ⓑ 74

Ⓒ 84

Ⓓ 75

Name ____________________

Module 10 Assessment

Vocabulary

Vocabulary
compatible numbers
partial quotient

Choose the best term from the box to complete the sentence.

1. You use the ________________ method of dividing when multiples of the divisor are subtracted from the dividend and then the quotients are added together. (p. 349)

Concepts and Skills

Use repeated subtraction to divide. TEKS 4.4.F

2. $78 \div 6 =$ _____

3. $57 \div 3 =$ _____

4. $98 \div 7 =$ _____

Divide. Use partial quotients. TEKS 4.4.F

5. $184 \div 8 =$ _____

6. $276 \div 6 =$ _____

7. $742 \div 7 =$ _____

8. $552 \div 4 =$ _____

Divide. TEKS 4.4.F

9. $3\overline{)987}$

10. $7\overline{)501}$

11. $5\overline{)153}$

12. $4\overline{)808}$

13. $9\overline{)9,742}$

14. $2\overline{)4,113}$

Fill in the bubble completely to show your answer.

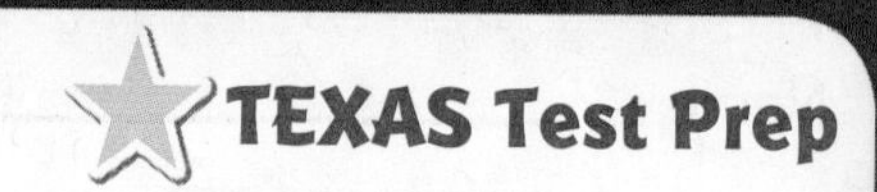

15. Mrs. Valdez bought 6 boxes of roses. Each box had 24 roses. She divided all the roses into 9 equal-sized bunches. How many roses were in each bunch? TEKS 4.4.F

Ⓐ 54

Ⓑ 16

Ⓒ 2 r6

Ⓓ 18

16. There are 152 students playing instruments in the marching band and 24 students carry flags. All of the students are arranged in equal rows of 8 students for a parade. How many rows of students are there? TEKS 4.4.F

Ⓐ 22 rows

Ⓑ 220 rows

Ⓒ 21 rows

Ⓓ 120 rows

17. A trucking company used 8 trucks to ship an order of 820 boxes and another order of 428 boxes. The 8 trucks were each loaded with an equal number of boxes. How many boxes were loaded onto each truck? TEKS 4.4.F

Record your answer and fill in the bubbles on the grid. Be sure to use the correct place value.

			.		
⓪	⓪	⓪		⓪	⓪
①	①	①		①	①
②	②	②		②	②
③	③	③		③	③
④	④	④		④	④
⑤	⑤	⑤		⑤	⑤
⑥	⑥	⑥		⑥	⑥
⑦	⑦	⑦		⑦	⑦
⑧	⑧	⑧		⑧	⑧
⑨	⑨	⑨		⑨	⑨

Name ______________________________

Unit 2 Assessment

Vocabulary

Vocabulary
compatible numbers
Distributive Property
partial product
partial quotient
remainder

1. When a number cannot be divided evenly, the amount left over is called the ______________. (p. 308)

2. In the ______________ method of dividing, multiples of the divisor are subtracted from the dividend and then the quotients are added together. (p. 345)

Concepts and Skills

Estimate. Then find the sum or difference. TEKS 4.4.A, 4.4.G

3. Estimate: __________

$$\begin{array}{r} 4.08 \\ -\ 1.74 \\ \hline \end{array}$$

4. Estimate: __________

$$\begin{array}{r} 19.2 \\ +\ 12.68 \\ \hline \end{array}$$

5. Estimate: __________

$$\begin{array}{r} 21.4 \\ -\ 16.97 \\ \hline \end{array}$$

Estimate. Then find the product. TEKS 4.4.D, 4.4.G

6. Estimate: __________

$$\begin{array}{r} 306 \\ \times\ \ 8 \\ \hline \end{array}$$

7. Estimate: __________

$$\begin{array}{r} \$924 \\ \times\ \ 5 \\ \hline \end{array}$$

8. Estimate: __________

$$\begin{array}{r} 8{,}798 \\ \times\ \ 6 \\ \hline \end{array}$$

9. Estimate: __________

$$\begin{array}{r} 59 \\ \times\ 29 \\ \hline \end{array}$$

10. Estimate: __________

$$\begin{array}{r} 85 \\ \times\ 46 \\ \hline \end{array}$$

11. Estimate: __________

$$\begin{array}{r} 76 \\ \times\ 38 \\ \hline \end{array}$$

Find the quotient. TEKS 4.4.E, 4.4.F

12. $3\overline{)987}$

13. $6\overline{)8{,}348}$

14. $8\overline{)4{,}897}$

Fill in the bubble completely to show your answer.

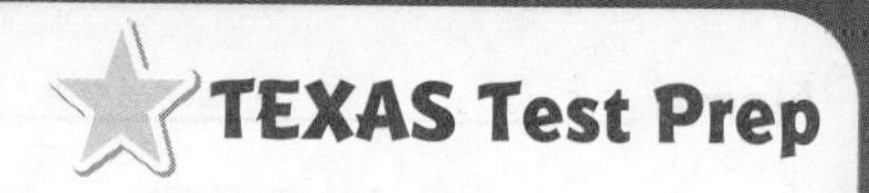

15. During September and October of 2008, the Grand Canyon National Park recorded a total of 792,426 visitors. If there were 359,396 visitors in October, how many people visited the park in September? TEKS 4.4.A

Ⓐ 1,151,822

Ⓑ 447,170

Ⓒ 433,030

Ⓓ 433,130

16. Mary has 2 bags of apples. One bag weighs 4.56 pounds and the other bag weighs 3.85 pounds. If she gave her sister 1.25 pounds of apples, how many pounds of apples would Mary have? TEKS 4.4.A

Ⓐ 3.31 pounds

Ⓑ 7.16 pounds

Ⓒ 2.6 pounds

Ⓓ 6.16 pounds

17. At Reptile World, there are 7 times as many alligators as crocodiles. If there are 117 crocodiles in the west enclosure and 183 crocodiles in the east enclosure, how many alligators are there? TEKS 4.4.D

Ⓐ 1,281

Ⓑ 307

Ⓒ 2,100

Ⓓ 819

18. Gardeners at The Seed Stop are planting vegetable seeds in trays. In each tray, there are 12 rows with 8 sections in each row. If they plant one seed in each section, how many plants will there be in 53 trays if all of the seeds germinate? TEKS 4.4.D

Ⓐ 1,060

Ⓑ 5,088

Ⓒ 636

Ⓓ 3,010

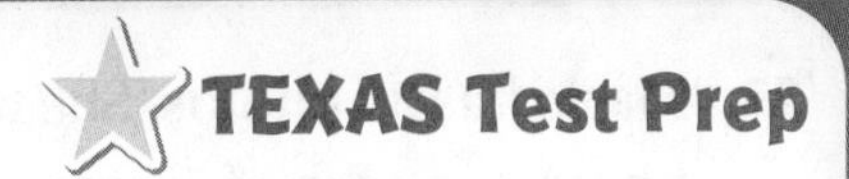

Fill in the bubble completely to show your answer.

19. The correct answer to a homework problem is 2,000. Which equation could have been the homework problem? TEKS 4.4.B, 4.4.C

Ⓐ $5 \times 4{,}000 =$

Ⓑ $50 \times 400 =$

Ⓒ $50 \times 40 =$

Ⓓ $50 \times 4{,}000 =$

20. Jill sold 35 adult tickets for a fundraiser. An adult ticket costs $18. How much did Jill collect for the tickets? Use an area model to help you solve. TEKS 4.4.C, 4.4.D, 4.4.H

Ⓐ $615

Ⓑ $630

Ⓒ $740

Ⓓ $515

1. A baby animal at the zoo eats about 30 pounds of food each day. If each baby animal eats the same amount each day, how many pounds of food do 12 baby animals eat in 5 days? TEKS 4.4.B, 4.4.D

Ⓐ 3,605 pounds

Ⓑ 1,800 pounds

Ⓒ 720 pounds

Ⓓ 3,595 pounds

22. A tour of the island includes 106 tourists and 8 guides. Each tour van can only hold 7 people. What is the least number of vans needed so that all of the tourists and guides go on the tour? TEKS 4.4.H

Ⓐ 17

Ⓑ 15

Ⓒ 16

Ⓓ 18

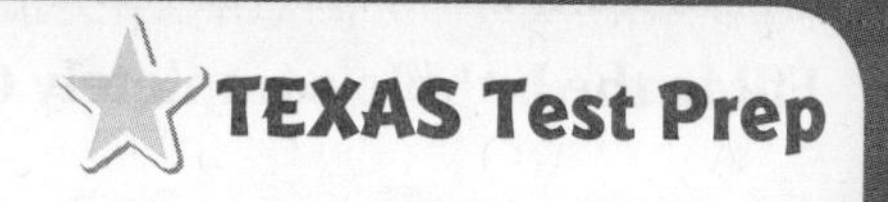

23. Maria has 39 photos. She wants to put the same number of photos on each of 7 pages. Which of the following describes an array that would help Maria know how many photos can be on each page? TEKS 4.4.E

Ⓐ an array with 5 rows of 8 squares

Ⓑ an array with 6 rows of 7 squares

Ⓒ an array with 4 rows of 7 squares with 11 left over squares

Ⓓ an array with 5 rows of 7 squares with 4 leftover squares

24. Mr. Bigham has 8 months to save $456 to buy a bike. He wants to save an equal amount each month. How much must he save each month to have enough to buy the bike? Use an area model to help you solve. TEKS 4.4.E

Ⓐ $57

Ⓑ $47

Ⓒ $3,648

Ⓓ $67

25. There are 156 math students in the 4th grade. There are 6 math classes of equal size. How many math students are in each class? TEKS 4.4.E

Ⓐ 200

Ⓑ 45

Ⓒ 26

Ⓓ 52

26. Allison's Bakery will donate $1,200 worth of baked goods to a school event. The school wants to order 12 loaves of holiday bread, 18 dozen biscuits, 12 dozen bagels, and 14 dozen multigrain rolls. Is the cost of the baked goods under the $1,200 donation limit? Explain how you found your answer. If yes, what could the school add to the order? If no, what could the school remove from the order? TEKS 4.4.D

Price List

Bakes Goods	Price
Holiday Bread	$20
Biscuits	$12/dozen
Bagels	$28/dozen
Multigrain Rolls	$22/dozen

Glossary

Pronunciation Key

a	add, map	f	fit, half	n	nice, tin	p	pit, stop	yo͞o	fuse, few
ā	ace, rate	g	go, log	ng	ring, song	r	run, poor	v	vain, eve
â(r)	care, air	h	hope, hate	o	odd, hot	s	see, pass	w	win, away
ä	palm, father	i	it, give	ō	open, so	sh	sure, rush	y	yet, yearn
b	bat, rub	ī	ice, write	ô	order, jaw	t	talk, sit	z	zest, muse
ch	check, catch	j	joy, ledge	oi	oil, boy	th	thin, both	zh	vision, pleasure
d	dog, rod	k	cool, take	ou	pout, now	t͟h	this, bathe		
e	end, pet	l	look, rule	o͝o	took, full	u	up, done		
ē	equal, tree	m	move, seem	o͞o	pool, food	û(r)	burn, term		

ə the schwa, an unstressed vowel representing the sound spelled a in above, e in sicken, i in possible, o in melon, u in circus

Other symbols:
- • separates words into syllables
- ′ indicates stress on a syllable

acute angle [ə•kyo͞ot′ ang′gəl] **ángulo agudo** An angle that measures greater than 0° and less than 90° (p. 450)
Example:

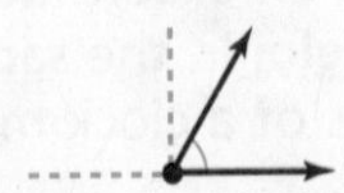

acute triangle [ə•kyo͞ot′ trī′ang•gəl] **triángulo acutángulo** A triangle with three acute angles (p. 456)
Example:

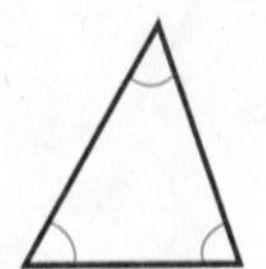

addend [a′dend] **sumando** A number that is added to another in an addition problem
Example: 2 + 4 = 6;
2 and 4 are addends.

addition [ə•di′shən] **suma** The process of finding the total number of items when two or more groups of items are joined; the opposite operation of subtraction

A.M. [ā•em′] **a. m.** The times after midnight and before noon

analog clock [anəl• ôg kläk] **reloj analógico** A tool for measuring time, in which hands move around a circle to show hours, minutes, and sometimes seconds
Example:

angle [ang′gəl] **ángulo** A shape formed by two line segments or rays that share the same endpoint (p. 450)
Example:

area [âr′ē•ə] **área** The number of unit squares needed to cover a flat surface (p. 427)
Example:

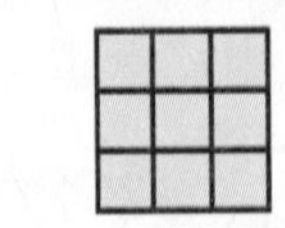

area = 9 square units

array [ə•rā′] **matriz** An arrangement of objects in rows and columns
Example:

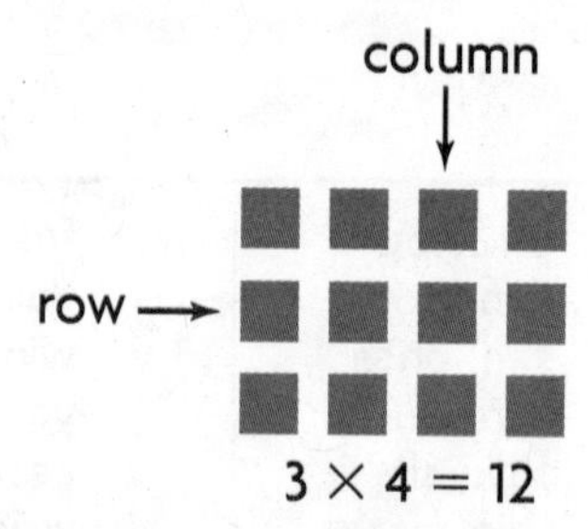

Associative Property of Addition [ə•sō′shē•āt•iv präp′ər•tē əv ə•dish′ən] **propiedad asociativa de la suma** The property that states that you can group addends in different ways and still get the same sum
Example: $3 + (8 + 5) = (3 + 8) + 5$

Associative Property of Multiplication [ə•sō′shē•ə•tiv präp′ər•tē əv mul•tə•pli•kā′shən] **propiedad asociativa de la multiplicación** The property that states that you can group factors in different ways and still get the same product
Example: $3 \times (4 \times 2) = (3 \times 4) \times 2$

bar graph [bär graf] **gráfica de barras** A graph that uses bars to show data
Example:

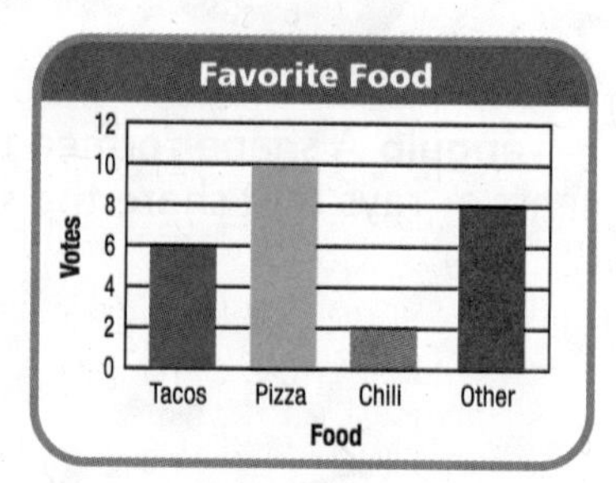

base [bās] **base** A polygon's side or a two-dimensional shape, usually a polygon or circle, by which a three-dimensional shape is measured or named
Examples:

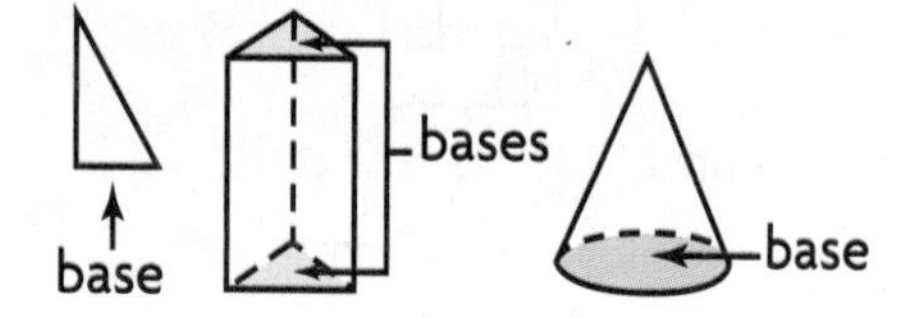

benchmark [bench′märk] **punto de referencia** A known size or amount that helps you understand a different size or amount (p. 113)

budget [bŭj′ĭt] **presupuesto** An organized plan for spending and saving money (p. 659)

calendar [kal′ən•dər] **calendario** A table that shows the days, weeks, and months of a year

capacity [kə•pas′i•tē] **capacidad** The amount a container can hold when filled

Celsius (°C) [sel′sē•əs] **Celsius** A metric scale for measuring temperature

centimeter (cm) [sen′tə•mēt•ər] **centímetro (cm)** A metric unit for measuring length or distance
1 meter = 100 centimeters
Example:

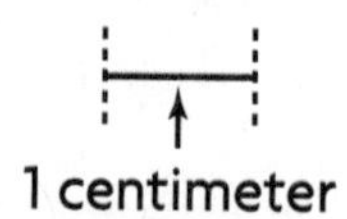

cent sign (¢) [sent sīn] **símbolo de centavo (¢)** A symbol that stands for *cent* or *cents*
Example: 53¢

clockwise [kläk′wīz] **en el sentido de las manecillas del reloj** In the same direction in which the hands of a clock move (p. 488)

closed shape [klōzd shāp] **figura cerrada** A two-dimensional shape that begins and ends at the same point
Examples:

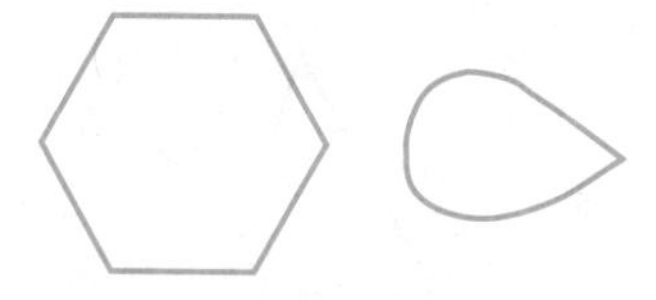

common denominator [käm′ən dē•näm′ə•nāt•ər] **denominador común** A common multiple of two or more denominators
Example: Some common denominators for $\frac{1}{4}$ and $\frac{5}{6}$ are 12, 24, and 36.

common factor [käm′ən fak′tər] **factor común** A number that is a factor of two or more numbers

common multiple [käm′ən mul′tə•pəl] **múltiplo común** A number that is a multiple of two or more numbers

Commutative Property of Addition [kə•myo͞ot'ə•tiv präp'ər•tē əv ə•dish'ən] **propiedad conmutativa de la suma** The property that states that when the order of two addends is changed, the sum is the same
Example: 4 + 5 = 5 + 4

Commutative Property of Multiplication [kə•myo͞ot'ə•tiv präp'ər•tē əv mul•tə•pli•kā'shən] **propiedad conmutativa de la multiplicación** The property that states that when the order of two factors is changed, the product is the same
Example: 4 × 5 = 5 × 4

compare [kəm•pâr'] **comparar** To describe whether numbers are equal to, less than, or greater than each other

compatible numbers [kəm•pat'ə•bəl num'bərz] **números compatibles** Numbers that are easy to compute mentally (p. 273)

composite number [kəm•päz'it num'bər] **número compuesto** A number having more than two factors
Example: 6 is a composite number, since its factors are 1, 2, 3, and 6.

corner [kôr'nər] **vértice** See *vertex*.

counterclockwise [kount•er•kläk'wīz] **en el sentido contrario de las manecillas del reloj** In the opposite direction in which the hands of a clock move (p. 487)

counting number [kount'ing num'bər] **número positivo** A whole number that can be used to count a set of objects (1, 2, 3, 4, . . .)

cube [kyo͞ob] **cubo** A three-dimensional shape with six square faces of the same size
Example:

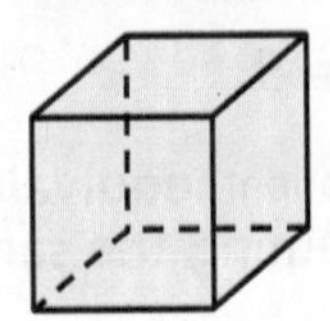

cup (c) [kup] **taza (tz)** A customary unit used to measure capacity and liquid volume (p. 537)
1 cup = 8 ounces

data [dāt'ə] **datos** Information collected about people or things

decagon [dek'ə•gän] **decágono** A polygon with ten sides and ten angles

decimal [des'ə•məl] **número decimal** A number with one or more digits to the right of the decimal point (p. 31)

decimal point [des'ə•məl point] **punto decimal** A symbol used to separate dollars from cents in money amounts, and to separate the ones and the tenths places in a decimal (p. 31)
Example: 6.4
↑ decimal point

decimeter (dm) [des'i•mēt•ər] **decímetro (dm)** A metric unit for measuring length or distance (p. 549)
1 meter = 10 decimeters

degree (°) [di•grē'] **grado (°)** The unit used for measuring angles and temperatures (p. 493)

denominator [dē•näm'ə•nāt•ər] **denominador** The number below the bar in a fraction that tells how many equal parts are in the whole or in the group
Example: $\frac{3}{4}$ ← denominator

diagonal [dī•ag'ə•nəl] **diagonal** A line segment that connects two vertices of a polygon that are not next to each other
Example:

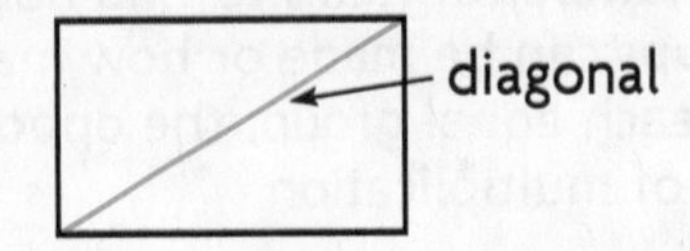

difference [dif'ər•əns] **diferencia** The answer to a subtraction problem

digit [dij'it] **dígito** Any one of the ten symbols 0, 1, 2, 3, 4, 5, 6, 7, 8, or 9 used to write numbers

digital clock [dij'i•təl kläk] **reloj digital** A clock that shows time to the minute, using digits
Example:

dime [dīm] **moneda de 10¢** A coin worth 10 cents and with a value equal to that of 10 pennies; 10¢
Example:

dimension [də•men′shən] **dimensión** A measure in one direction

Distributive Property [di•strib′yo͞o•tiv präp′ər•tē] **propiedad distributiva** The property that states that multiplying a sum by a number is the same as multiplying each addend by the number and then adding the products (p. 229)
Example: $5 \times (10 + 6) = (5 \times 10) + (5 \times 6)$

divide [də•vīd′] **dividir** To separate into equal groups; the opposite operation of multiplication

dividend [dəv′ə•dend] **dividendo** The number that is to be divided in a division problem
Example: $36 \div 6$; $6\overline{)36}$; the dividend is 36.

divisible [də•viz′ə•bəl] **divisible** A number is divisible by another number if the quotient is a counting number and the remainder is zero
Example: 18 is divisible by 3.

division [də•vi′zhən] **división** The process of sharing a number of items to find how many equal groups can be made or how many items will be in each equal group; the opposite operation of multiplication

divisor [də•vī′zər] **divisor** The number that divides the dividend
Example: $15 \div 3$; $3\overline{)15}$; the divisor is 3.

dollar [däl′ər] **dólar** Paper money worth 100 cents and equal to 100 pennies; $1.00
Example:

dot plot [dät plöt] **diagrama de puntos** A graph that records each piece of data on a number line (p. 609)
Example:

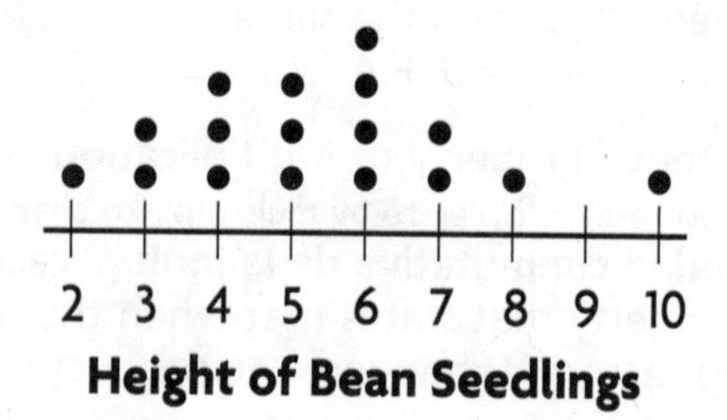

elapsed time [ē•lapst′ tīm] **tiempo transcurrido** The time that passes from the start of an activity to the end of that activity

endpoint [end′point] **extremo** The point at either end of a line segment or the starting point of a ray

equal groups [ē′kwəl gro͞opz] **grupos iguales** Groups that have the same number of objects

equal parts [ē′kwəl pärts] **partes iguales** Parts that are exactly the same size

equal sign (=) [ē′kwəl sīn] **signo de igualdad (=)** A symbol used to show that two numbers have the same value
Example: $384 = 384$

equal to [ē′kwəl to͞o] **igual a** Having the same value
Example: $4 + 4$ is equal to $3 + 5$.

equation [ē•kwā′zhən] **ecuación** A number sentence which shows that two quantities are equal
Example: $4 + 5 = 9$

equivalent [ē•kwiv′ə•lənt] **equivalente** Having the same value or naming the same amount

equivalent decimals [ē•kwiv′ə•lənt des′ə•məlz] **decimales equivalentes** Two or more decimals that name the same amount

equivalent fractions [ē•kwiv'ə•lənt frak'shənz] **fracciones equivalentes** Two or more fractions that name the same amount (p. 75)
Example: $\frac{3}{4}$ and $\frac{6}{8}$ name the same amount.

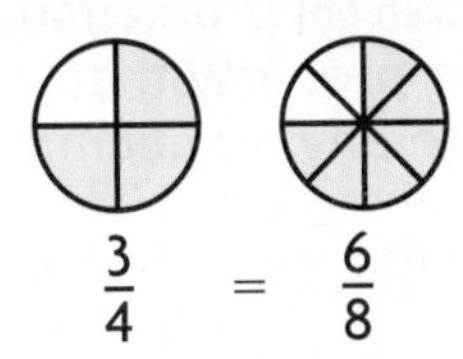

$$\frac{3}{4} = \frac{6}{8}$$

estimate [es'tə•māt] *verb* **estimar** To find an answer that is close to the exact amount

estimate [es'tə•mit] *noun* **estimación** A number that is close to the exact amount (p. 23)

even [ē'vən] **par** A whole number that has a 0, 2, 4, 6, or 8 in the ones place

expanded form [ek•span'did fôrm] **forma desarrollada** A way to write numbers by showing the value of each digit (p. 11)
Example: 253 = 200 + 50 + 3

expression [ek•spresh'ən] **expresión** A part of a number sentence that has numbers and operation signs but does not have an equal sign

fact family [fakt fam'ə•lē] **familia de operaciones** A set of related multiplication and division equations, or addition and subtraction equations
Example: 7 × 8 = 56 8 × 7 = 56
56 ÷ 7 = 8 56 ÷ 8 = 7

factor [fak'tər] **factor** A number that is multiplied by another number to find a product

Fahrenheit (°F) [fâr'ən•hīt] **Fahrenheit (°F)** A customary scale for measuring temperature

financial institution [fə•năn'shəl ĭn•stĭ•tōō'shən] **institución financiera** A business, like a bank, that collects money, keeps it safe, and provides money for people and businesses to borrow (p. 665)

fixed expense [fĭkst ĭk•spĕns'] **gastos regulares** Expenses that occur regularly and the amount does not change (p. 641)

fluid ounce (fl oz) [flōō'id ouns] **onza fluida (oz fl)** A customary unit used to measure liquid capacity and liquid volume (p. 537)
1 cup = 8 fluid ounces

foot (ft) [fŏŏt] **pie (ft)** A customary unit used for measuring length or distance
1 foot = 12 inches

formula [fôr'myōō•lə] **fórmula** A set of symbols that expresses a mathematical rule (p. 422)
Example: Area = length × width, or $A = l \times w$

fraction [frak'shən] **fracción** A number that names a part of a whole or part of a group
Example:

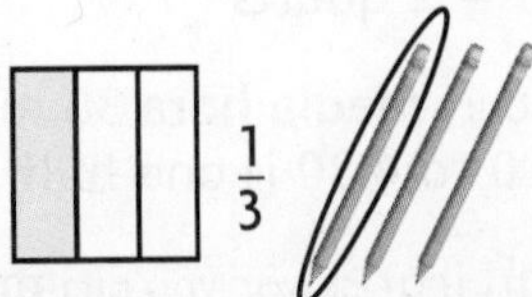

fraction greater than 1 [frak'shən grāt'ər <u>th</u>an wun] **fracción mayor que 1** A number which has a numerator that is greater than its denominator

frequency [frē'kwən•sē] **frecuencia** The number of times the data occurs. (p. 597)

frequency table [frē'kwən•sē tā'bəl] **tabla de frecuencia** A table that uses numbers to record data about how often something happens (p. 597)
Example:

Favorite Color

Color	Frequency
Blue	10
Red	7
Green	5
Other	3

gallon (gal) [gal'ən] **galón (gal)** A customary unit for measuring capacity and liquid volume (p. 537)
1 gallon = 4 quarts

gram (g) [gram] **gramo (g)** A metric unit for measuring mass
1 kilogram = 1,000 grams

greater than sign (>) [grāt′ər t͟hən sīn] **signo de mayor que (>)** A symbol used to compare two quantities, with the greater quantity given first
Example: $6 > 4$

grid [grid] **cuadrícula** Evenly divided and equally spaced squares on a shape or flat surface

half gallon [haf gal′ən] **medio galón** A customary unit for measuring capacity and liquid volume (p. 537)
1 half gallon = 2 quarts

half hour [haf our] **media hora** 30 minutes
Example: 4:00 to 4:30 is one half hour.

half-square unit [haf skwâr yo͞o′nit] **media unidad cuadrada** Half of a unit of area with dimensions of 1 unit × 1 unit

height [hīt] **altura** The measure of a perpendicular from the base to the top of a two-dimensional shape

hexagon [hek′sə•gän] **hexágono** A polygon with six sides and six angles
Examples:

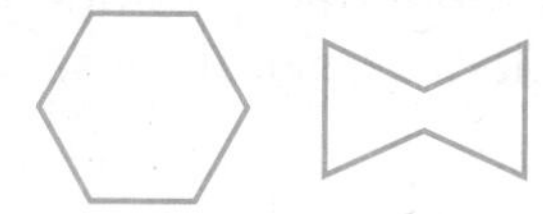

horizontal [hôr•i•zänt′l] **horizontal** In the direction from left to right

hour (hr) [our] **hora (h)** A unit used to measure time
1 hour = 60 minutes

hundredth [hun′drədth] **centésimo** One of one hundred equal parts (p. 31)
Example:

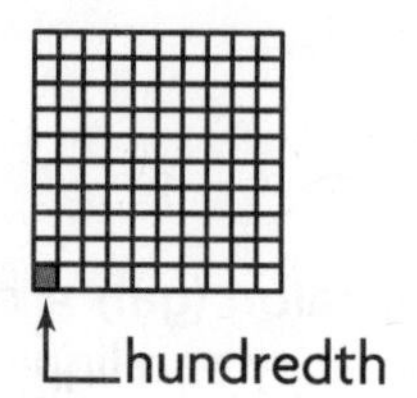

Identity Property of Addition [ī•den′tə•tē präp′ər•tē əv ə•dish′ən] **propiedad de identidad de la suma** The property that states that when you add zero to any number, the sum is that number
Example: 16 + 0 = 16

Identity Property of Multiplication [ī•den′tə•tē präp′ər•tē əv mul•tə•pli•kā′shən] **propiedad de identidad de la multiplicación** The property that states that the product of any number and 1 is that number
Example: 9 × 1 = 9

inch (in.) [inch] **pulgada (pulg)** A customary unit used for measuring length or distance
Example:

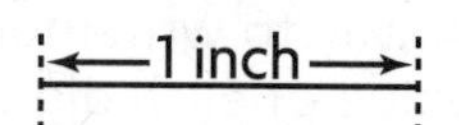

input/output table [ĭn′po͝ot/out′po͝ot tā′bəl] **tabla de entrada y salida** A table that matches each input value with an output value, where the output values are determined by the pattern, or function (p. 415)

interest [ĭn′trĭst] **interés** The additional money paid by a borrower to a lender in exchange for the use of the lender's money. For example, you earn interest from a bank if you have a savings account. (p. 653)

intersecting lines [in•tər•sekt′ing līnz] **líneas intersecantes** Lines that cross each other at exactly one point (p. 461)
Example:

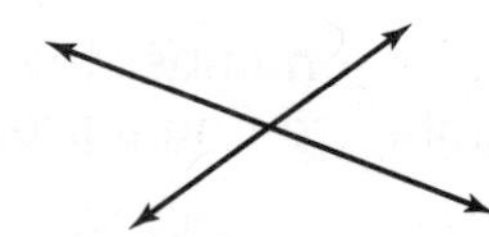

inverse operations [in′vûrs äp•ə•rā′shənz] **operaciones inversas** Operations that undo each other, such as addition and subtraction or multiplication and division
Example: 6 × 8 = 48 and 48 ÷ 6 = 8

key [kē] **clave** The part of a map or graph that explains the symbols

kilogram (kg) [kil′ō•gram] **kilogramo (kg)** A metric unit for measuring mass
1 kilogram = 1,000 grams

kilometer (km) [kə•läm′ət•ər] **kilómetro (km)** A metric unit for measuring length or distance (p. 520)
1 kilometer = 1,000 meters

length [lengkth] **longitud** The measurement of the distance between two points

less than sign (<) [les than sīn] **signo de menor que (<)** A symbol used to compare two quantities, with the lesser quantity given first
Example: 3 < 7

line [līn] **línea** A straight path of points in a plane that continues without end in both directions with no endpoints (p. 449)
Example:

line graph [līn graf] **gráfica lineal** A graph that uses line segments to show how data change over time

line of symmetry [līn əv sim′ə•trē] **eje de simetría** An imaginary line on a shape about which the shape can be folded so that its two parts match exactly (p. 473)
Example:

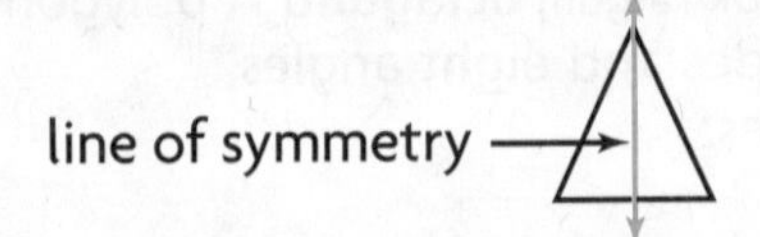

line segment [līn seg′mənt] **segmento** A part of a line that includes two points called endpoints and all the points between them (p. 449)
Example:

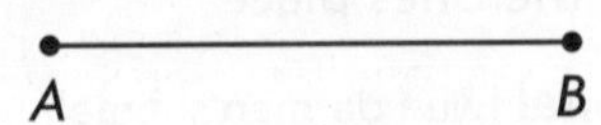

line symmetry [līn sim′ə•trē] **simetría axial** What a shape has if it can be folded about a line so that its two parts match exactly (p. 473)

linear units [lin′ē•ər yōō′nits] **unidades lineales** Units that measure length, width, height, or distance

liquid volume [lik′wid väl′yōōm] **volumen de un líquido** The measure of the space a liquid occupies (p. 537)

liter (L) [lēt′ər] **litro (L)** A metric unit for measuring capacity and liquid volume
1 liter = 1,000 milliliters

loan [lōn] **préstamo** The money that is lent by a bank or other financial institution (p. 665)

mass [mas] **masa** The amount of matter in an object

meter (m) [mēt′ər] **metro (m)** A metric unit for measuring length or distance
1 meter = 100 centimeters

midnight [mid′nīt] **medianoche** 12:00 at night

mile (mi) [mīl] **milla (mi)** A customary unit for measuring length or distance (p. 519)
1 mile = 5,280 feet

milliliter (mL) [mil′i•lēt•ər] **mililitro (ml)** A metric unit for measuring capacity and liquid volume (p. 555)
1 liter = 1,000 milliliters

millimeter (mm) [mil′i•mēt•ər] **milímetro (mm)** A metric unit for measuring length or distance (p. 549)
1 centimeter = 10 millimeters

million [mil′yən] **millón** The counting number after 999,999; 1,000 thousands; written as 1,000,000

millions [mil′yənz] **millones** The period after thousands

minute (min) [min′it] **minuto (min)** A unit used to measure short amounts of time
1 minute = 60 seconds

mixed number [mikst num′bər] **número mixto** An amount given as a whole number and a fraction (p.105)

multiple [mul′tə•pəl] **múltiplo** The product of a number and a counting number is called a multiple of the number
Example:

3	3	3	3	
× 1	× 2	× 3	× 4	← counting numbers
3	6	9	12	← multiples of 3

multiplication [mul•tə•pli•kā′shən] **multiplicación** A process to find the total number of items in equal-sized groups, or to find the total number of items in a given number of groups when each group contains the same number of items; multiplication is the inverse of division

multiply [mul′tə•plī] **multiplicar** To combine equal groups to find how many in all; the opposite operation of division

nickel [nik′əl] **moneda de 5¢** A coin worth 5 cents and with a value equal to that of 5 pennies; 5¢
Example:

noon [no͞on] **mediodía** 12:00 in the day

not equal to sign (≠) [not ē′kwəl to͞o sīn] **signo de no igual a** A symbol that indicates one quantity is not equal to another
Example: $12 \times 3 \neq 38$

number line [num′bər līn] **recta numérica** A line on which numbers can be located
Example:

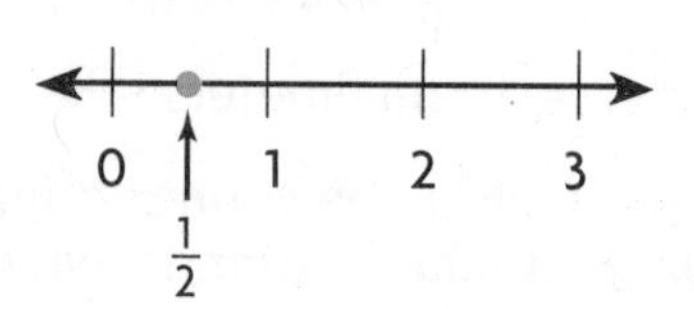

number sentence [num′bər sent′ns] **oración numérica** A sentence that includes numbers, operation symbols, and a greater than or less than symbol or an equal sign
Example: $5 + 3 = 8$

numerator [no͞o′mər•āt•ər] **numerador** The number above the bar in a fraction that tells how many parts of the whole or group are being considered

Example: $\frac{2}{3}$ ← numerator

obtuse angle [äb•to͞os′ ang′gəl] **ángulo obtuso** An angle that measures greater than 90° and less than 180° (p. 450)
Example:

Word History

The Latin prefix ***ob-*** means "against." When combined with ***-tusus***, meaning "beaten," the Latin word ***obtusus***, from which we get ***obtuse***, means "beaten against." This makes sense when you look at an obtuse angle, because the angle is not sharp or acute. The angle looks as if it has been beaten against and become blunt and rounded.

obtuse triangle [äb•to͞os′ trī′ang•gəl] **triángulo obtusángulo** A triangle with one obtuse angle (p. 456)
Example:

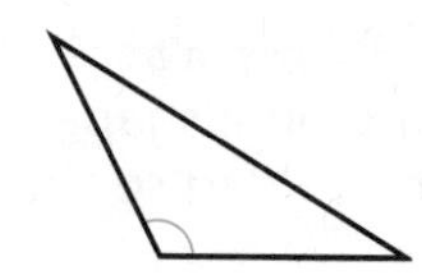

octagon [äk′tə•gän] **octágono** A polygon with eight sides and eight angles
Examples:

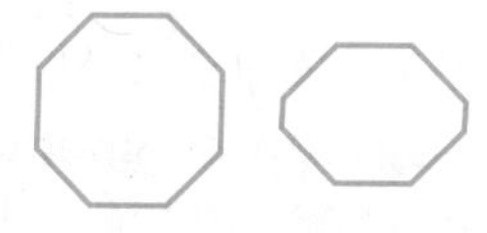

odd [od] **impar** A whole number that has a 1, 3, 5, 7, or 9 in the ones place

one-dimensional [wun də•men′shə•nəl] **unidimensional** Measured in only one direction, such as length
Examples:

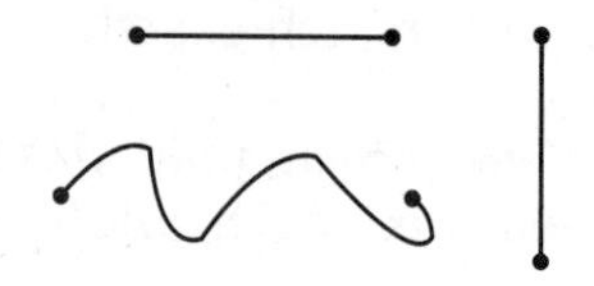

open shape [ō′pən shāp] **figura abierta** A shape that does not begin and end at the same point
Examples:

order [ôr′dər] **orden** A particular arrangement or placement of things one after the other

order of operations [ôr′dər əv äp•ə•rā′shənz] **orden de las operaciones** A special set of rules which gives the order in which calculations are done

ounce (oz) [ouns] **onza (oz)** A customary unit for measuring weight (p. 531)
1 pound = 16 ounces

parallel lines [pâr′ə•lel līnz] **líneas paralelas** Lines in the same plane that never intersect and are always the same distance apart (p. 461)
Example:

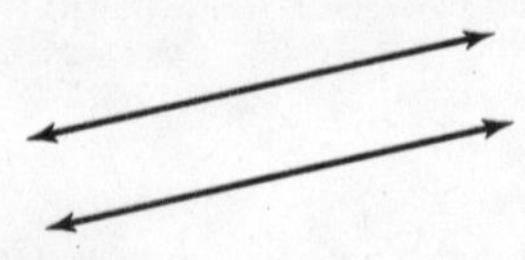

Word History

Euclid, an early Greek mathematician, was one of the first to explore the idea of parallel lines. The prefix ***para-*** means "beside or alongside." This prefix helps you understand the meaning of the word ***parallel***.

parallelogram [pâr•ə•lel′ə•gram] **paralelogramo** A quadrilateral whose opposite sides are parallel and of equal length (p. 467)
Example:

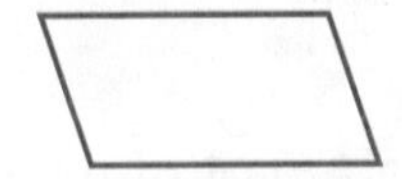

parentheses [pə•ren′thə•sēz] **paréntesis** The symbols used to show which operation or operations in an expression should be done first

partial product [pär′shəl präd′əkt] **producto parcial** A method of multiplying in which the ones, tens, hundreds, and so on are multiplied separately and then the products are added together (p. 230)

partial quotient [pär′shəl kwō′shənt] **cociente parcial** A method of dividing in which multiples of the divisor are subtracted from the dividend and then the quotients are added together (p. 349)

pattern [pat′ərn] **patrón** An ordered set of numbers or objects; the order helps you predict what will come next (p. 409)
Examples: 2, 4, 6, 8, 10

pattern unit [pat′ərn yo͞o′nit] **unidad de patrón** The part of a pattern that repeats
Example:

pentagon [pen′tə•gän] **pentágono** A polygon with five sides and five angles
Examples:

perimeter [pə•rim′ə•tər] **perímetro** The distance around a figure (p. 421)

period [pir′ē•əd] **período** Each group of three digits in a multi-digit number; periods are usually separated by commas or spaces. (p. 11)
Example: 85,643,900 has three periods.

perpendicular lines [pər•pən•dik′yo͞o•lər līnz] **líneas perpendiculares** Two lines that intersect to form four right angles (p. 461)
Example:

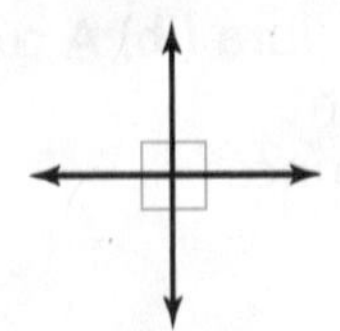

pictograph [pĭk'tə·grăf'] **pictografía** A graph that uses symbols to show and compare information
Example:

How We Get To School	
Walk	✱✱✱
Ride a Bike	✱✱✱✱
Ride a Bus	✱✱✱✱✱✱
Ride in a Car	✱✱

Key: Each ✱ = 10 students.

pint (pt) [pīnt] **pinta (pt)** A customary unit for measuring capacity and liquid volume (p. 537)
1 pint = 2 cups

place value [plās val'yōō] **valor posicional** The value of a digit in a number, based on the location of the digit

plane [plān] **plano** A flat surface that extends without end in all directions
Example:

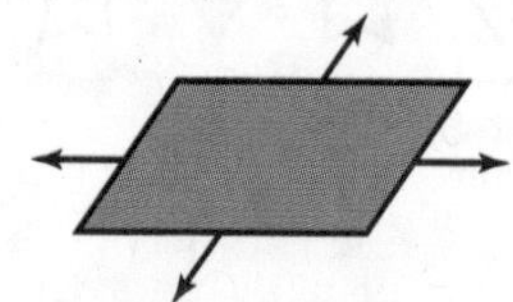

plane shape [plān shāp] **figura plana** See *two-dimensional shape*.

P.M. [pē•em] **p. m.** The times after noon and before midnight

point [point] **punto** An exact location in space (p. 449)

polygon [päl'i•gän] **polígono** A closed two-dimensional shape formed by three or more straight sides that are line segments
Examples:

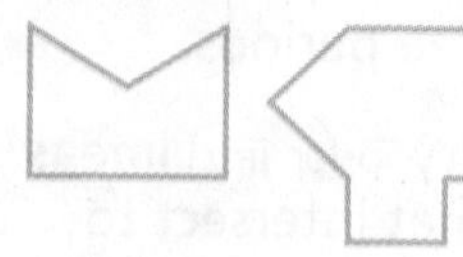

Polygons

Not Polygons

pound (lb) [pound] **libra (lb)** A customary unit for measuring weight (p. 531)
1 pound = 16 ounces

prime number [prīm num'bər] **número primo** A number that has exactly two factors: 1 and itself
Examples: 2, 3, 5, 7, 11, 13, 17, and 19 are prime numbers. 1 is not a prime number.

prism [priz'əm] **prisma** A solid figure that has two same size, same polygon-shaped bases, and other faces that are all rectangles
Examples:

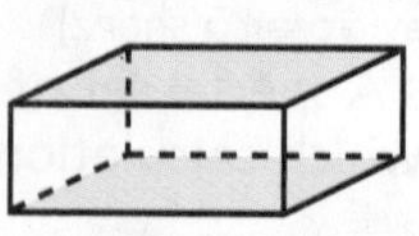

rectangular prism

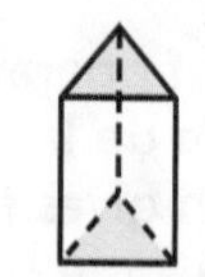

triangular prism

product [präd'əkt] **producto** The answer to a multiplication problem

profit [prŏf'ĭt] **ganancia** The amount left after all the expenses are subtracted from the amount of money received from selling an item or service (p. 647)

protractor [prō'trak•tər] **transportador** A tool for measuring the size of an angle (p. 499)

quadrilateral [kwä•dri•lat'ər•əl] **cuadrilátero** A polygon with four sides and four angles

quart (qt) [kwôrt] **cuarto (ct)** A customary unit for measuring capacity and liquid volume (p. 537)
1 quart = 2 pints

quarter hour [kwôrt'ər our] **cuarto de hora** 15 minutes
Example: 4:00 to 4:15 is one quarter hour

quotient [kwō'shənt] **cociente** The number, not including the remainder, that results from dividing
Example: 8 ÷ 4 = 2; 2 is the quotient.

ray [rā] **semirrecta** A part of a line; it has one endpoint and continues without end in one direction (p. 449)
Example:

rectangle [rek′tang•gəl] **rectángulo** A quadrilateral with two pairs of parallel sides, two pairs of sides of equal length, and four right angles (p. 467)
Example:

rectangular prism [rek•tang′gyə•lər priz′əm] **prisma rectangular** A three-dimensional shape in which all six faces are rectangles
Example:

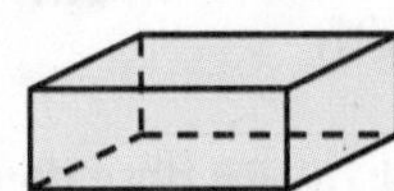

regroup [rē•gro͞op′] **reagrupar** To exchange amounts of equal value to rename a number
Example: 5 + 8 = 13 ones or 1 ten 3 ones

regular polygon [reg′yə•lər päl′i•gän] **polígono regular** A polygon that has all sides that are equal in length and all angles equal in measure
Examples:

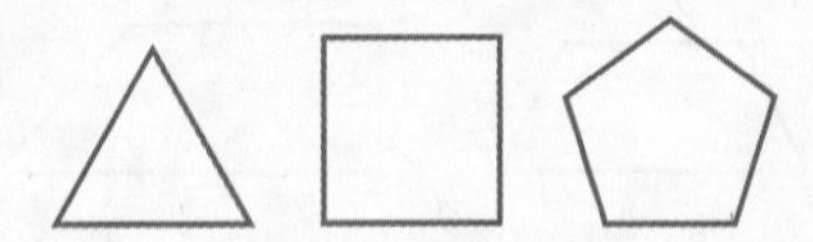

related facts [ri•lāt′id fakts] **operaciones relacionadas** A set of related addition and subtraction, or multiplication and division, number sentences
Examples: 4 × 7 = 28   28 ÷ 4 = 7
7 × 4 = 28   28 ÷ 7 = 4

remainder [ri•mān′dər] **residuo** The amount left over when a number cannot be divided equally (p. 312)

rhombus [räm′bəs] **rombo** A quadrilateral with two pairs of parallel sides and four sides of equal length (p. 467)
Example:

right angle [rīt ang′gəl] **ángulo recto** An angle that forms a square corner (p. 450)
Example:

right triangle [rīt trī′ang•gəl] **triángulo rectángulo** A triangle with one right angle (p. 456)
Example:

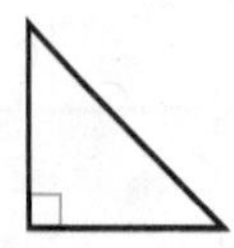

round [round] **redondear** To replace a number with another number that tells about how many or how much (p. 23)

rule [ro͞ol] **regla** A procedure (usually involving arithmetic operations) to determine an output value from an input value

scale [skāl] **escala** A series of numbers placed at fixed distances on a graph to help label the graph

second (sec) [sek′ənd] **segundo (s)** A small unit of time (p. 563)
1 minute = 60 seconds

simplest form [sim′pləst fôrm] **mínima expresión** A fraction is in simplest form when the numerator and denominator have only 1 as a common factor (p. 88)

solid shape [sä′lid shāp] **cuerpo geométrico** See *three-dimensional figure.*

square [skwâr] **cuadrado** A quadrilateral with two pairs of parallel sides, four sides of equal length, and four right angles (p. 467)
Example:

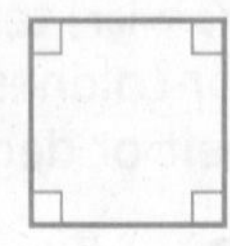

square unit [skwâr yo͞o′nit] **unidad cuadrada** A unit used to measure area such as square foot, square meter, and so on (p. 427)

standard form [stan′dərd fôrm] **forma normal** A way to write numbers by using the digits 0–9, with each digit having a place value (p. 11)
Example: 3,540 ← standard form

stem-and-leaf plot [stĕm ənd lēf plŏt] **diagrama de tallo y hojas** A graph that shows groups of data arranged by place value (p. 621)

straight angle [strāt ang′gəl] **ángulo llano** An angle whose measure is 180° (p. 450)
Example:

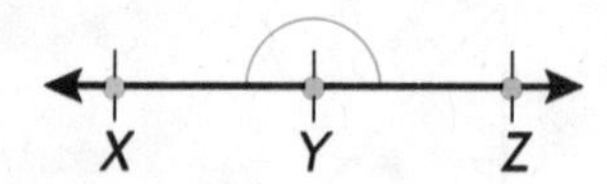

subtraction [səb•trak′shən] **resta** The process of finding how many are left when a number of items are taken away from a group of items; the process of finding the difference when two groups are compared; the opposite operation of addition

sum [sum] **suma o total** The answer to an addition problem

survey [sûr′vā] **encuesta** A method of gathering information

tally table [tal′ē tā′bəl] **tabla de conteo** A table that uses tally marks to record data

Word History

Some people keep score in card games by making marks on paper (IIII). These marks are known as tally marks. The word ***tally*** is related to ***tailor***, from the Latin ***talea***, meaning "twig." In early times, a method of keeping count was by cutting marks into a piece of wood or bone.

temperature [tem′pər•ə•chər] **temperatura** The degree of hotness or coldness usually measured in degrees Fahrenheit or degrees Celsius

tenth [tenth] **décimo** One of ten equal parts (p. 31)
Example:

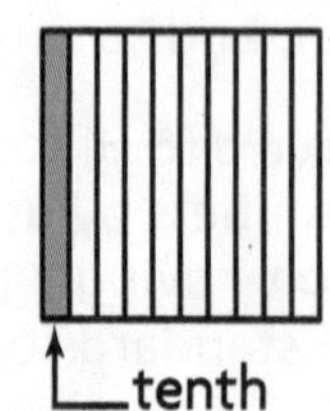

term [tûrm] **término** A number or object in a pattern (p. 409)

thousands [thou′zəndz] **millares** The period after the ones period in the base-ten number system

three-dimensional [thrē də•men′shə•nəl] **tres dimensiones** Measured in three directions, such as length, width, and height
Example:

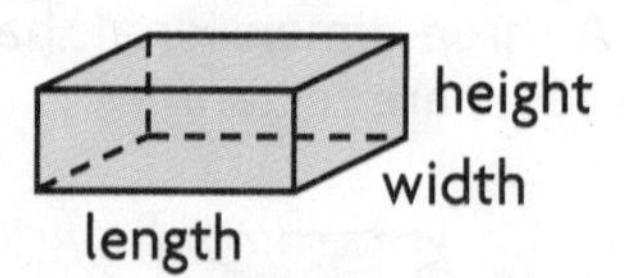

three-dimensional figure [thrē də•men′shə•nəl fig′yər] **figura de tres dimensiones** A figure having length, width, and height

ton (T) [tun] **tonelada (t)** A customary unit used to measure weight (p. 532)
1 ton = 2,000 pounds

trapezoid [trap′i•zoid] **trapecio** A quadrilateral with exactly one pair of parallel sides (p. 467)
Examples:

triangle [trī′ang•gəl] **triángulo** A polygon with three sides and three angles
Examples:

two-dimensional [to͞o də•men′shə•nəl] **dos dimensiones** Measured in two directions, such as length and width
Example:

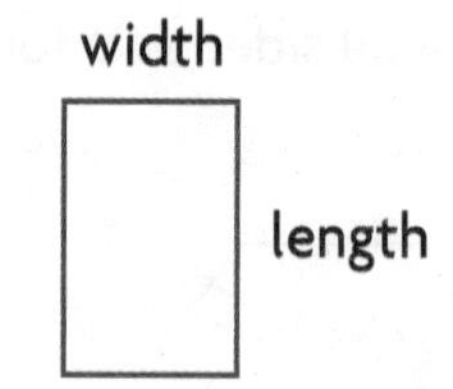

two-dimensional figure [to͞o də•men′shə•nəl fig′yər] **figura de dos dimensiones** A figure that lies in a plane; a shape having length and width

unit fraction [yoo͞′nit frak′shən] **fracción unitaria** A fraction that has a numerator of one (p. 99)

unit square [yoo͞′nit skwâr] **cuadrado de una unidad** a square that is 1 unit long and 1 unit wide (p. 427)

variable [vâr′ē•ə•bəl] **variable** A letter or symbol that stands for a number or numbers

variable expense [vâr'ē•ə•bəl ĭk•spĕns'] **gastos variables** Expenses in which the amount does change based on need or choice (p. 641)

Venn diagram [ven dī′ə•gram] **diagrama de Venn** A diagram that shows relationships among sets of things
Example:

2-Digit Numbers | **Even Numbers**

35, 17, 29 | 12, 10 | 8, 6, 4

vertex [vûr′teks] **vértice** The point at which two rays of an angle meet or two (or more) line segments meet in a two-dimensional shape
Examples:

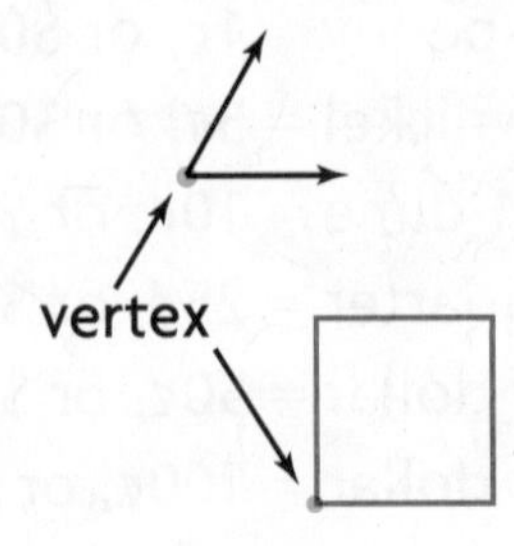

vertical [vûr′ti•kəl] **vertical** In the direction from top to bottom

weight [wāt] **peso** How heavy an object is

whole [hōl] **entero** All of the parts of a shape or group

word form [wûrd fôrm] **en palabras** A way to write numbers by using words
Example: Four hundred fifty-three thousand, two hundred twelve

yard (yd) [yärd] **yarda (yd)** A customary unit for measuring length or distance
1 yard = 3 feet

Zero Property of Multiplication [zē′rō präp′ər•tē əv mul•tə•pli•kā′shən] **propiedad del cero de la multiplicación** The property that states that the product of 0 and any number is 0
Example: $0 \times 8 = 0$

Table of Measures

METRIC	CUSTOMARY
Length	
1 centimeter (cm) = 10 millimeters (mm)	1 foot (ft) = 12 inches (in.)
1 meter (m) = 1,000 millimeters	1 yard (yd) = 3 feet, or 36 inches
1 meter = 100 centimeters	1 mile (mi) = 1,760 yards, or 5,280 feet
1 meter = 10 decimeters (dm)	
1 kilometer (km) = 1,000 meters	
Capacity and Liquid Volume	
1 liter (L) = 1,000 milliliters (mL)	1 cup (c) = 8 fluid ounces (fl oz)
	1 pint (pt) = 2 cups
	1 quart (qt) = 2 pints, or 4 cups
	1 half gallon = 2 quarts
	1 gallon (gal) = 2 half gallons, or 4 quarts
Mass/Weight	
1 kilogram (kg) = 1,000 grams (g)	1 pound (lb) = 16 ounces (oz)
	1 ton (T) = 2,000 pounds

TIME
1 minute (min) = 60 seconds (sec)
1 half hour = 30 minutes
1 hour (hr) = 60 minutes
1 day (d) = 24 hours
1 week (wk) = 7 days
1 year (yr) = 12 months (mo), or about 52 weeks
1 year = 365 days
1 leap year = 366 days
1 decade = 10 years
1 century = 100 years

MONEY
1 penny = 1¢, or $0.01
1 nickel = 5¢, or $0.05
1 dime = 10¢, or $0.10
1 quarter = 25¢, or $0.25
1 half dollar = 50¢, or $0.50
1 dollar = 100¢, or $1.00

Table of Measures

SYMBOLS			
$<$	is less than	$\perp$	is perpendicular to
$>$	is greater than	$\parallel$	is parallel to
$=$	is equal to	$\overleftrightarrow{AB}$	line AB
$\neq$	is not equal to	$\overrightarrow{AB}$	ray AB
¢	cent or cents	$\overline{AB}$	line segment AB
$	dollar or dollars	$\angle ABC$	angle ABC or angle B
°	degree or degrees	$\triangle ABC$	triangle ABC

FORMULAS			
Perimeter		**Area**	
Polygon	$P =$ sum of the lengths of sides	Rectangle	$A = l \times w$
Rectangle	$P = (2 \times l) + (2 \times w)$ or $P = 2 \times (l + w)$		
Square	$P = 4 \times s$